DATE DUE

MY 16 '99			
MY 27 99			
JE 18 00			

DEMCO 38-296

CyberLaw

Springer

New York
Berlin
Heidelberg
Barcelona
Budapest
Hong Kong
London
Milan
Paris
Santa Clara
Singapore
Tokyo

Jonathan Rosenoer

CyberLaw
■
The Law of
the Internet

Springer

Spear Street Tower, Suite 3300
One Market
San Francisco, CA 94105
USA

Library of Congress Cataloging-in-Publication Data
Rosenoer, Jonathan.
    CyberLaw : the law of the Internet / Jonathan Rosenoer.
        p.   cm.
    Includes bibliographical references and index.
    ISBN 0-387-94832-5 (hardcover)
        1. Computer networks—Law and legislation—United States.
    2. Internet (Computer network)   I. Title.
    KF390.5.C6R668   1996
343.73099′9—dc20
[347.303999]   96-25479

Printed on acid-free paper.

Production managed by Lesley Poliner; manufacturing supervised by Jacqui Ashri.
Typeset by G & S Typesetters, Austin, Tx.
Printed and bound by R.R. Donnelley and Sons, Harrisonburg, VA.
Printed in the United States of America.

9 8 7 6 5 4 3 2

ISBN 0-387-94832-5 Springer-Verlag New York Berlin Heidelberg   SPIN 10631366

To
my muse, Shery,
and
my amuselets,
Michal, Nicholas, and Sophie

Preface

In 1990, I joined Stanford University's Macintosh Users' Group. Already working as an attorney, I volunteered to write a monthly column on computer law. The response was very encouraging, and developed into CyberLaw™ & CyberLex™—free educational services on computer law for computer users. Both have been published for a number of years by major computer users groups, including the Boston Computer Society, BMUG (based in northern California), and the MacValley Users' Group (based in southern California), as well as commercial online services, such as America Online and the WELL.

Over the years, I've received encouraging e-mail messages from across the United States and all points of the globe. Many correspondents were working in small businesses and found the articles useful, as they could not afford access to specialized legal services and publications to keep up-to-date. I remember one gentleman from the South, who wrote to thank me for an article on copyright law. He wanted to write about hunting dogs for an Internet publication, but was concerned about losing his copyright. Something I wrote gave him sufficient comfort to have the article published, and he was very relieved. He seemed very happy to be published in the new online medium.

In 1993, online services and the Internet were just beginning their rush into popular culture. Very few people had been focusing on legal issues relating to the online world. (Lance Rose, Mike Godwin, and Lee Tien are people I recall from very early on.) Business people and corporate counsel were having great difficulty locating knowledgeable attorneys who had any experience with computers, let alone the online world. An in-house lawyer for a Silicon Valley computer company told me that his company had received a threatening letter from a person who had been "flamed" in an Internet newsgroup by a company employee who sent his posting via the company's e-mail system. The "victim" of the flame was seeking to hold the company responsible. The lawyer called one of the best-respected law firms in Silicon Valley, but was dismayed when told that they had no attorneys who knew anything about this. A little while later, attorneys working for two of the largest commercial online services complained to me that they simply could not find attorneys to call about online issues who could answer their questions without embarking on forty-hour research projects at their expense.

Similar comments led to this book. It is written for business men and women seeking an introduction to the various areas of law applicable to the online world. Included are descriptions of the different substantive topics, from copyright to tax law. Accompanying these descriptions are articles on court decisions and legal developments that appeared in CyberLaw, supplying an in-depth discussion of the key issues. To provide context and a feel for how the law has developed, there is also a section devoted to important legal news reported over the past five years. In this latter section, you can see trends develop—such as the crackdown on hackers, the government's push to expand police powers over the online world, and the clash between free-speech advocates and publishing interests—as well as many issues that were resolved short of final court decision. And you'll find hundreds of footnotes.

One reason for the footnotes is to allow further access to key legal decisions governing the online world. Other court decisions are noted to assist the reader in navigating uncharted territory. Also referenced are legal arguments and rulings made in a number of controversies that were settled. Although these arguments and rulings may have no value as precedent, much time and money was spent in their preparation and they provide good insight into the state of the law and where it might be headed.

In sum, this book is for business people—and perhaps a number of lawyers. It is intended to provide a picture of the legal landscape as it now exists, along with sufficient additional information to enable the reader more fully to evaluate new developments and what their impact may be.

Jonathan Rosenoer
Greenbrae, California
May 1996

Acknowledgments

A number of people and organizations have helped me produce CyberLaw™ and CyberLex™ as free educational services and should be recognized. Principal among them are David Hayes of Fenwick & West, in Palo Alto, California; BMUG; Boston Computer Society; MacValley Users Group; America Online; The WELL; Best Internet Communications; Portal Information Network; InterNex; the former Stanford University Macintosh Users Group. Other key people were Bill Fenwick of Fenwick & West, who encouraged me to switch to my first Macintosh computer; John Perry Barlow, who made me think; Mike Godwin and Lance Rose, lawyers who helped the people who really built the online world; Steve Brill, Barbara Johnson, David Johnson, and Peter Scheer, who gave me the opportunity to work in the online world with Counsel Connect; Dr. Martin Gilchrist and Springer-Verlag, who gave me the opportunity to write this book; Alan Morelli and Geoff Berkin at Manatt, Phelps & Phillips, in Los Angeles, who have provided much sound advice and assistance; and Chuck Marson, who painstakingly read this book in draft and offered many helpful comments.

Many thanks to my friends, particularly those on the Counsel Connect system, who have discussed issues with me in a very helpful way. Also to Itzik, Michal, Rananah, Shachar, Eyal, and my mom and dad:-)

Contents

1

Copyright

A. Exclusive Rights

In general terms, copyright provides an author with a tool to protect a work from being taken, used, and exploited by others without permission.[1] The owner of a copyrighted work has the exclusive right to reproduce it, prepare derivative works based upon it, distribute copies by sale or other transfer of ownership, to perform and display it publicly, and to authorize others to do so.[2]

For a company that depends upon intellectual property for its livelihood, such as a software company or an Internet-based publisher, copyright law provides a framework that ensures that the company can compete in the marketplace. The importance of copyright is illustrated by comparing what happens to an appliance company when a refrigerator is stolen with what happens to a software company when its source code is stolen. The refrigerator company will simply have one less item of merchandise to sell and a loss reflected by the refrigerator's price. The software company, however, will suddenly be faced with the prospect of a market flooded with exact copies of its product—sold or given away by another. Without the ability to prevent unauthorized copying, sale, and distribution of its product, the software company will not be able to survive.

---

[1] 17 U.S.C. § 106.
[2] There are, of course, some important exceptions and limitations. "Fair use" is one important limitation. Another provides that copyright protection is not available for any work of the U.S. government. 17 U.S.C. § 105.

1

B. Subject Matter of Copyright

Copyright law protects "original works of authorship." Sheer hard work alone will not suffice[3]—a modicum of creativity is required.[4] The work does not have to be the first of its kind, or novel—it just has to be the independent product of the author, not copied from another source.[5] Copyright, in fact, does not protect against independent creation of similar or identical works.

Certain items are excluded from copyright protection. Section 102(b) of the Copyright Act states,

In no case does copyright protection for an original work of authorship extend to any idea, procedure, process, system, method of operation, concept, principle, or discovery, regardless of the form in which it is described, explained, illustrated, or embodied in such work.[6]

A number of important court decisions explain how these limitations relate to computer software, interfaces, and the "look and feel" of a program. (Software elements that cannot be copyrighted may, in fact, be eligible for patent protection.)

Copyright is held by an author upon a work's creation and "fixation" in tangible form, so that it can be perceived directly or with the aid of a machine or other device.[7]

If a group creates a work, the copyright may be held jointly. An independent contractor may hold the copyright in a work made for someone else if there is no express agreement to the contrary. But an employer will be the "owner" of a work created by an employee within the scope of employment. Persons seeking to build Internet sites with the help of others should be sure to acquire the

---

[3] See *Feist Publications, Inc. v. Rural Telephone Service Co.*, 499 U.S. 340, 359–60, 111 S.Ct. 1282, 113 L.Ed.2d 358 (1991) (rejecting argument that effort expended on creating a publication, in this case a directory, can translate into copyright protection).

[4] See *West Publ. Co. v. Mead Data Central, Inc.*, 799 F.2d 1219, 1226–27 (8th Cir. 1986), *cert. denied*, 479 U.S. 1070, 107 S.Ct. 962 (1987) (West's arrangement of legal decisions entails enough intellectual labor and originality to receive copyright protection)

[5] See *Grand Upright Music, Ltd. v. Warner Bros. Records, Inc.*, 780 F.Supp. 182 (S.D.N.Y. 1991) (use of digitized sample in song may infringe copyright).

[6] Importantly, there is also no copyright in government works. 17 U.S.C. § 105.

[7] Notably, the U.S. Court of Appeals for the Ninth Circuit, has decided that a copy of a computer program loaded into RAM is "fixed" for purposes of copyright protection. *MAI Sys. Corp. v. Peak Computer*, 991 F.2d 511, 518–19 (9th Cir. 1993), *cert. denied*, 114 S.Ct. 671 (1994); see also, *Advanced Computer Servs. v. MAI Sys. Corp.*, 845 F.Supp. 356, 362–64 (E.D. Va. 1994).

rights to the materials that are the basis for the site, or they will face difficult issues down the road.[8]

C. Formalities

Previously, persons seeking to protect works under copyright law had to take certain steps to avoid having them fall into the public domain, where they are freely available to all comers. The primary step was to include a copyright notice (e.g., "© 1995 Jonathan Rosenoer"). But since the United States joined the Berne Convention, it is no longer strictly necessary to so do. Virtually everyone, however, continues to use the notice, and a recent ruling by a federal court states that a simple copyright notice may be sufficient to support a demand that an Internet provider or bulletin board service (BBS) operator remove an infringing copy from its system and prevent its transmission to the Internet.[9] As many seem to hold the mistaken belief that information placed on the Internet is free for the taking, perhaps the continued use of such notices is the wiser course—if only for educational value. In certain countries, the notice "All rights reserved" is required.

Registering a work with the Copyright Office is a critical step to be taken in protecting a work under copyright law. While time and money costs are involved, significant benefits are gained by completing the registration process in a timely manner. These benefits include statutory damages (between $500 and $20,000 for each work infringed, and up to $100,000 if the infringement was willful) as well as attorneys' fees.[10] A registration certificate also provides prima facie evidence of copyright ownership and validity,[11] and is required to enforce copyrights in works of U.S. origin, among others.

To protect a work from the date of first publication, it must be registered within 3 months of that time.[12] The work may be registered by the owner or an exclusive licensee. There is a "mandatory" deposit requirement, but it is not a condition of copyright protection.[13]

---

[8] See *Tasini v. New York Times Co.*, 93 Civ. 8678 (S.D.N.Y. filed Dec. 16, 1993) (suit by freelance writers over reproduction of articles on online services without consent).
[9] See *Religious Technology Center v. Netcom On-Line Communication Serv.*, 907 F.Supp. 1361 (N.D. Cal. 1995) ("Where works contain copyright notices within them, it is hard to argue that a defendant did not know the works were copyrighted.")
[10] 17 U.S.C. § 504(c).
[11] Ibid. § 410(c).
[12] Ibid. § 412(2).
[13] Ibid. § 407(a).

D. Infringement

1. Direct Infringement

A copyright is infringed when one of the exclusive rights of the copyright holder is violated.[14] These include the right to reproduce a copyrighted work, prepare derivative works based upon it, distribute copies by sale or other transfer of ownership, to perform and display it publicly, and to authorize others to do so.[15]

In an infringement action, a plaintiff is required to "prove ownership of the copyright and 'copying' by the defendant."[16] Proof of a defendant's intent to infringe is not an element of the plaintiff's case.[17] A defendant, for example, cannot escape liability on the grounds of unconscious copying or of basing a work on that of third person who has, in fact, unlawfully copied from another. And, similarly, a publisher cannot escape liability simply by publishing infringing material provided by a third party.

In a decision over the unauthorized posting of copyrighted *Playboy* photographs on a BBS, the court ruled that

Intent to infringe is not needed to find copyright infringement. Intent or knowledge is not an element of infringement, and thus even an innocent infringer is liable for infringement; rather, innocence is significant to a trial court when it fixes statutory damages, which is a remedy equitable in nature.[18]

But a federal court in California distinguishes that decision over *Playboy* photographs by finding it to be over liability for violating the plaintiff's "right to publicly *distribute and display* copies of its work," as distinct from a case in which an Internet service provider is claimed to be "liable because its computers in fact made copies" of a copyrighted work.[19] This latter case, involving published and unpublished

---

[14] Ibid. § 501(a).

[15] Ibid. § 106.

[16] *Sid & Marty Krofft Television Prods. v. McDonald's Corp.*, 562 F.2d 1157, 1162 (9th Cir. 1977).

[17] See *Costello Publ. Co. v. Rotelle*, 670 F.2d 1035, 1044 (D.C. Cir. 1981).

[18] *Playboy Enters. v. Frena*, 839 F.Supp. 1552, 1559 (M.D. Fla. 1993) (there are indications in the trademark part of the opinion, however, that the system operator was not an innocent third party without a hand in what was going on); see also, *D.C. Comics Inc. v. Mini Gift Shop*, 912 F.2d 29, 35 (2d Cir. 1990) ("[A] finding of innocent infringement does not absolve the defendant of liability under the Copyright Act. . . . The reduction of statutory damages for innocent infringement requires an inquiry into the defendant's state of mind to determine whether he or she 'was not aware and had no reason to believe that his or her acts constituted an infringement'").

[19] *Religious Technology Center v. Netcom On-Line Communication Serv.*, 907 F.Supp. 1361 (N.D. Cal. 1995).

works of L. Ron Hubbard (the late founder of the Church of Scientology), may relieve Internet providers from harsh potential liability.[20] In the Scientology case, the court held that Internet providers cannot be held liable for "incidental copies automatically made on their computers using their software as a part of a process initiated by a third party." Where the actions of a provider are automatic and indiscriminate, said the court, "[o]nly the subscriber should be liable for causing the distribution of plaintiff's work. . . ."

In cases of direct copyright infringement, it does not matter whether a direct profit is derived from the infringing works.[21] In a lawsuit involving unauthorized copies of Sega video games,[22] the BBS owner claimed he did not profit from distribution of infringing copies that were uploaded to his board by subscribers and then downloaded by other subscribers. According to the court, which counted the commercial purpose and character of the unauthorized copying against a claimed defense of fair use, the defendant profited from the operation of the BBS through direct payment or barter. In addition, he profited indirectly by the existence of this "distribution network" for Sega games that increased the prestige of his BBS, and also by the increased market for video game copiers and other goods or services sold by him.

2. Contributory Infringement

Liability for copyright infringement may be imposed on persons who have not themselves engaged in the infringing activity, but where it may be seen as "just to hold one individual accountable for the actions of another."[23] Contributory infringement occurs, for example, where a person "with knowledge of the infringing activity, induces, causes or materially contributes to the infringing conduct of another."[24] "Substantial" or "pervasive" involvement is required.[25]

In the California Scientology case, the court held that even if an

---

[20] Ibid.
[21] Though this is relevant to a criminal copyright infringement prosecution. See 17 U.S.C. § 506(a); *United States v. LaMacchia*, 871 F.Supp. 535, 541–42 (D. Mass. 1994).
[22] *Sega Enters. v. MAPHIA*, 857 F.Supp. 679 (N.D. Cal. 1994).
[23] See *Sony Corp. v. Universal City Studios*, 464 U.S. 417, 435, 78 L.Ed.2d 574, 104 S.Ct. 774 (1984)
[24] See *Gershwin Publishing Corp. v. Columbia Artists Management, Inc.*, 443 F.2d 1159, 1162 (2d Cir. 1971).
[25] See *Apple Computer, Inc. v. Microsoft Corp.*, 821 F.Supp. 616, 625 (N.D. Cal. 1993), *aff'd in part and rev'd in part*, 35 F.3d 1435 (9th Cir. 1994), *cert. denied*, 130 L.Ed.2d 1129, 115 S.Ct. 1176 (1995); *Demetriades v. Kaufmann*, 690 F.Supp. 289, 294 (S.D.N.Y. 1988).

Internet provider may not be found liable for direct copyright infringement where "incidental copies [are] automatically made on [its] computers using [its] software as a part of a process initiated by a third party," the provider may still be held liable as a contributory infringer.[26] An Internet provider may be liable for contributory infringement, says the court, if it knows or should have known of the infringement and fails to do anything about it. The provider will have a defense, however, where it "cannot reasonably verify a claim of infringement, either because of a fair use defense, the lack of copyright notices on the copies, or the copyright holder's failure to provide the necessary documentation to show that there is a likely infringement. . . ."

3. Vicarious Liability

Neither knowledge nor participation is required in cases of vicarious liability. The rule is that a defendant may be held liable for the actions of the primary infringer where the defendant has the right and ability to control the infringer's acts and receives a direct financial benefit from the infringement.[27]

In the California Scientology case,[28] the court ruled that there was a genuine issue of fact over whether an Internet provider's terms and conditions of service in combination with an alleged ability to screen messages before they are posted gave it the right and ability to supervise the conduct of its subscribers. But the court dismissed a claim of vicarious liability against the provider on account of subscriber postings because the plaintiffs could not provide any evidence of direct financial benefit the provider received from the infringing postings at issue. The provider charged a fixed fee and there was no evidence that the infringing postings enhanced the value of its services to subscribers or attracted new subscribers.[29]

The result in the Scientology case should not change if the Inter-

---

[26] *Religious Technology Center v. Netcom On-Line Communication Serv.*, 907 F.Supp. 1361 (N.D. Cal. 1995).

[27] *Shapiro, Bernstein & Co. v. H.L. Green Co.*, 316 F.2d 304, 306 (2d Cir. 1963) (copyright infringement action against owner of department store chain where concessionaire was selling counterfeit phonograph records); *Religious Technology Center v. Netcom On-Line Communication Serv.*, 907 F.Supp. 1361 (N.D. Cal. 1995).

[28] *Religious Technology Center v. Netcom On-Line Communication Serv.*, 907 F.Supp. 1361 (N.D. Cal. 1995).

[29] Cf., *Fonovisa, Inc. v. Cherry Auction, Inc.*, No. 94-15717 (9th Cir. Jan. 25, 1996) (sufficient allegation of direct financial benefit found where alleged facts reflect "defendants reap substantial financial benefits from admission fees, concession stand sales and parking fees, all of which flow directly from customers who want to buy the counterfeit recordings at bargain basement prices").

net provider was, instead, the operator of a dial-up BBS that either charged a fixed fee or no fee at all. A different case may be presented, however, by an Internet provider or BBS that charged a fixed fee for a period of time and more for extra time, or that profited from sale of products and services related to the infringing activity.[30]

E. Sources of Risk

Online systems are vulnerable to infringement liability from at least four different sources. The person creating the system may incorporate unauthorized copies of other peoples' works. Similarly, those operating and maintaining the system may add unauthorized copies. Subscribers may also upload infringing copies of works to a system. And infringing copies may be transmitted through the system.[31]

The first three sources of risk may be minimized by contract and license restrictions, as well as education. For example, a contractor may be asked to warrant that no infringing works, or parts thereof, are incorporated into the new system. The contractor may also be asked to indemnify and hold harmless the online system from any claim or liability related thereto.

Similarly, subscribers should be presented with terms and conditions of service that clearly prohibit the uploading of infringing works and confirm subscribers' agreement to hold the online system harmless for acts or omissions that result in claims and liability for copyright infringement.[32] System operators should also be trained on what acts may result in liability under copyright law.

The issue of whether online systems may be liable for infringing materials that pass across them is a matter of grave controversy, as its resolution will affect the development of the Internet. In *Religious Technology Center v. Netcom On-Line Communication Services*,[33] the plaintiffs urge that a BBS as well as an Internet provider should be liable for infringing material posted to an Internet newsgroup by a BBS subscriber. In this case, the BBS subscriber created a message containing infringing material that was transmitted to the BBS. The BBS, which briefly stores the message, forwards it to the Internet provider,

---

[30] See *Sega Enters. v. MAPHIA*, 857 F.Supp. 679 (N.D. Cal. 1994).

[31] See *Frank Music Corp. v. CompuServe, Inc.*, 93 Civ. 8153 (JFK) (S.D.N.Y. filed Nov. 29, 1993) (later settled, the case was based on allegations that a CompuServe music forum allowed users to post and copy copyrighted songs).

[32] It is not clear, however, that shrinkwrap license agreements are enforceable.

[33] No. C-95-20091 RMW (N.D. Cal. filed Feb. 8, 1995).

which, in turn, makes it available to Internet newsgroup servers world-wide. These servers maintain a copy of the message for a short period of time (eleven days on Netcom's server and three days on the BBS in this case) for the particular newsgroup's subscribers to review.

In reply to plaintiffs' charges, the Internet provider (Netcom) argues it "is 'ill-equipped' to do the 'policing' [plaintiffs] demand, and requiring [it to do so] would adversely affect the public's low-cost access to the information marketplace." If held accountable for the tortious acts of others, argues Netcom, it will face the type of problems that a federal court recently noted with respect to a local television network affiliate in holding that the affiliate had no editorial control over a network broadcast, serving only as a conduit not responsible for republishing defamatory content of a "60 Minutes" segment. In *Auvil v. CBS "60 Minutes,"* the court noted that

[The asserted liability] would force the creation of full time editorial boards at local stations throughout the country which possess sufficient knowledge, legal acumen and access to experts to continually monitor incoming transmissions and exercise on-the-spot discretionary calls or face $75 million dollar lawsuits at every turn. That is not realistic.[34]

As this case points out, there is tension between the Copyright Act and the First Amendment.[35] As noted by one court, however, "except perhaps in an extraordinary case, the fair use doctrine encompasses all claims of first amendment in the copyright field. . . ."[36]

F. World Wide Web Sites

A number of important issues arise regarding the creation and maintenance of World Wide Web sites. At the outset, it should be recognized that many Web authors learned their craft by reviewing, and in many cases copying, the way other sites were constructed. This is particularly easy to do with Mosaic-type Internet browsers (including the Netscape Navigator), which from the beginning have included a menu selection named "View" and a subheading named "Source." After studying the way a site has been constructed, viewers may then copy code they like into their own sites to capture the desired effect.

This whole process is arguably an infringement.[37] Downloading

---

[34] 800 F.Supp. 928, 931 (E.D. Wash. 1992).
[35] See Chapter I, part M. FIRST AMENDMENT, *infra.*
[36] *Twin Peak Prods. v. Publications Intern'l,* 996 F.2d 1366, 1378 (2d Cir. 1993).
[37] Despite the fact that custom, practice, and common sense reject the claim, there is support for the argument that the mere viewing of the source file is an infringingact. In *MAI Sys. Corp. v. Peak Computer,* 991 F.2d 511, 519 (9th Cir. 1993), *cert. dis-*

a file from an Internet site onto a viewer's hard disk without permission, express or implied, constitutes the making of an unauthorized copy in violation of the exclusive rights of the copyright owner. Such files are protected by copyright law if they contain a modicum of originality, as noted above. Companies have claimed, and courts enforce, copyright in the nonliteral elements (e.g., structure, sequence, and organization) of computer software.[38] Even if the viewer alters the code so that it is unrecognizable, it still may be argued that an infringement has occurred—particularly regarding the intermediate copy of the source code.[39]

Notwithstanding technical copyright arguments to the contrary, it must been recognized that the culture of the Web and its development have encouraged access to and borrowing of the html (hypertext markup language) coding that forms the basis for Web sites. Custom and practice on the Web serve as strong arguments that an implied license exists allowing the viewing, copying, and usage of html code found on sites across the Web.

G. Hypertext Links

The strength of the Web derives from the hypertext links that enable viewers to jump from one Internet site to another. Some have claimed that a person constructing an Internet site needs to obtain permission

---

missed , 126 L.Ed.2d 640, 114 S.Ct. 671 (1994), the U.S. Court of Appeals for the Ninth Circuit held that the mere loading of computer software into random access memory ("RAM") may violate copyright law. See also, *Advanced Computer Servs. v. MAI Sys. Corp.*, 845 F.Supp. 356, 364 n.9 (E.D. Va. 1994) (collecting cases); but see *Religious Technology Center v. Netcom On-Line Communication Services*, 907 F.Supp. 1361 (N.D. Cal. 1995) ("In any event, users should hardly worry about a finding of direct infringement; it seems highly unlikely from a practical matter that a copyright owner could prove such infringement or would want to sue such an individual").

[38] But see *Lotus Dev. Corp. v. Borland Int'l*, 49 F.3d 807, 815 (1st Cir. 1995), *aff'd*, ___ U.S. ___ (1996) (Lotus 1-2-3 menu command hierarchy is an unprotectable "method of operation"); *Computer Assocs. Intern'l v. Altai, Inc.*, 982 F.2d 693 (2d Cir. 1992).

[39] See *West Publ. Co. v. On Point Solutions, Inc.*, Civ No 1:93-CV-2071-MHS, 1994 U.S. Dist. Lexis 20040 (N.D. Ga. 1994) (permanent injunction based, among other things, on intermediate copying of West cases scanned by On Point, with West headnotes and syllabi temporarily stored on On Point's computers and then deleted prior to creation of On Point disks); *Sega Enters. v. Accolade, Inc.*, 977 F.2d 1510, 1519 (9th Cir. 1992) (intermediate copying of Sega's code would constitute copyright infringement unless Accolade could show that it was entitled to claim the benefit of an exception in the circumstances of the case); *Atari Games Corp. v. Nintendo of America, Inc.*, 975 F.2d 832, 843 (Fed. Cir. 1992) (fair use intermediate copying of protectable expression "must not exceed what is necessary to understand the unprotected elements of a work").

to include a link to another's home page or site. Such an argument might be based on cases such as *MAI Systems Corp. v. Peak Computer*, which holds that a copy of a work in RAM is a "copy" for copyright purposes.[40] But because the World Wide Web is, in essence, a protocol that exists only to link sites to each other, it is hard to see how anyone could claim the right to restrict site access only to those receiving specific permission to do so.

The act of implementing and maintaining a public-access Web site (i.e., one that is not protected by password or other security device) implies a license to enter and explore. In the case of real property, a license is permission to do some act or series of acts on the property of the licensor (e.g., cutting wood) without having any permanent interest in the property.[41] The World Wide Web's history, custom, and practice, as well as the reasonable expectations of the public—particularly now that there exist Web sites that require a password and user ID to enter[42]—all support the existence of such an implied license for Web site visitors. The fact that Web sites are composed of intellectual property, not real property, does not bar a license from being implied.[43]

And there is no copyrightable expression in a hypertext link, which merely contains the address of a document on the Web. The link really is nothing more than an unprotectable "method of operation."[44]

This is not to say that one cannot get into trouble by copying hypertext links. A number of Web sites contain collections of links to other sites as well as indexes to information on the Internet, with imbedded links. There may be copyrightable expression in the struc-

---

[40] 991 F.2d 511 (9th Cir. 1993), *cert. dismissed*, 126 L.Ed.2d 640, 114 S.Ct. 671 (1994); see also, *Advanced Computer Servs. v. MAI Sys. Corp.*, 845 F.Supp. 356, 364 n.9 (E.D. Va. 1994) (collecting cases).

[41] See *McCastle v. Scanlon*, 337 Mich. 122, 59 N.W.2d 114 (1953); 25 Am. Jur. 2d *Easements & Licenses* § 137.

[42] See *A.C.L.U. v. Reno*, No. 96-1458, Slip Opinion (3rd Cir. June 11, 1996), in which the court states that

"43. Web publishers have the choice to make their Web sites open to the general pool of all Internet users, or close them, thus making the information accessible only to those with advance authorization. Many publishers choose to keep their sites open to all in order to give their information the widest possible audience."

[43] See *Effects Assoc., Inc. v. Cohen*, 908 F.2d 555, 558–59 (9th Cir. 1990), *cert. denied*, 498 U.S. 1103, 112 L.Ed.2d 1086 (1991) (granting nonexclusive license to incorporate special effects footage into movie); *Gracen v. Bradford Exchange*, 698 F.2d 300, 303 (7th Cir. 1983) (issue of fact existed on scope of implied license to make a derivative work—a painting of Dorothy based on the film "The Wizard of Oz").

[44] See *Lotus Dev. Corp. v. Borland Int'l*, 49 F.3d 807, 815 (1st Cir. 1995), *aff'd*, __ U.S. __ (1996) (Lotus menu command hierarchy held an uncopyrightable "method of operation").

ture, sequence, and organization of those links. A person copying those links into another Web site could well be liable for copyright infringement.

H. Graphical Elements

Graphical elements are the primary reason for the popularity of the World Wide Web. While it is quite easy to copy graphics from sites around the Web and copy them into a new page, it is also clear that in most cases such copying constitutes copyright infringement. For example, the unauthorized copying of a Mickey Mouse graphic from a Walt Disney Internet site onto a personal Web page would clearly constitute copyright infringement.

In *Apple Computer, Inc. v. Microsoft Corp.*,[45] the court held that icons may be protectable under copyright law. The Apple case also explains that the original selection and arrangement of features in an interface may be protected by copyright law, albeit in certain cases only from virtually identical copying.[46]

I. E-Mail

E-mail is a tremendously popular feature of private online systems and the Internet. Because it is transmitted in digital form, e-mail is easily copied and retransmitted. There is no reason to suspect, however, that e-mail is free from coverage under copyright law.[47] Unless a message contains an unequivocal commitment to donate the content to the public domain, it should be treated as covered by copyright law even if a copyright notice is not included.

Sending unauthorized copies of copyrighted works via e-mail

---

[45] 821 F.Supp. 616, 622 (N.D. Cal. 1993), *aff'd*, 35 F.3d 1435 (9th Cir. 1994), *cert. denied*, 130 L.Ed.2d 1129, 115 S.Ct. 1176 (1995).
[46] *Apple Computer, Inc. v. Microsoft Corp.*, 35 F.3d 1435, 1442 (9th Cir. 1994), *cert. denied*, 130 L.Ed.2d 1129, 115 S.Ct. 1176 (1995).
[47] See *Salinger v. Random House, Inc.*, 811 F.2d 90, 94–95 (2d Cir.), *cert. denied*, 484 U.S. 890, 98 L.Ed.2d 177, 108 S.Ct. 213 (1987) ("The author of letters is entitled to a copyright in the letters, as with any other work of literary authorship. . . . The copyright owner owns the literary property rights, including the right to complain of infringing copying, while the recipient of the letter retains ownership of 'the tangible physical property of the letter itself.'"); *Meeropol v. Nizer*, 560 F.2d 1061, 1070–71 (2d Cir. 1977), *cert. denied*, 434 U.S. 1013, 54 L.Ed.2d 756 (1978) (unauthorized incorporation into book of substantial portions of copyrighted letters written by Ethel and Julius Rosenberg).

may result in liability to both the sender and the recipient, as well as the online system on which the e-mail is stored.[48]

It should be noted that federal law generally prohibits providers of online systems from reviewing the content of message traffic across their systems.[49] But there is an exception that allows an employee of a provider to intercept and disclose electronic communications in the normal course of employment if done to protect the rights or property of the provider.[50] Whether a provider could successfully utilize this exception to monitor all e-mail traffic across its system (assuming it is even possible to do so) will probably depend on whether the provider can be found liable for direct copyright infringement owing to automatic copies of messages made incident to its function as an e-mail provider, or whether it can only be held liable for contributory infringement if it has reason to know or actual knowledge of the infringing activity. If the latter is the case, as indicated in a California ruling involving a major Internet provider,[51] the provider would not be able to utilize this exception to routinely scan messaging for indicia of copyright infringement because it would have no interest to protect— until it had knowledge or reason to know of a particular infringing activity. If this were not the case, the exception would swallow the rule and open all e-mail to systematic interception and review.

J. Postings

An interesting issue is raised by postings of messages to private online services and Internet (Usenet) newsgroups. To the extent such postings exhibit the modicum of originality sufficient to trigger copyright protection, one must assume they are covered by copyright law.

Online services may, of course, provide for a different conclusion by use of contractual agreements with subscribers. For example, subscribers may agree to provide other subscribers with a license to copy

---

[48] See *Macromedia, Inc. v. VRHacker, et al.*, Case No. C95-1261 (N.D. Cal. filed April 13, 1995) (suit against individual America Online subscribers, alleging they infringed Macromedia copyrights by copying and distributing its works through use of America Online's e-mail system).

[49] See 18 U.S.C. § 2511.

[50] 18 U.S.C. § 2511 (2)(a)(i); see *United States v. Beckley*, 259 F.Supp. 567, 571 (N.D. Ga. 1965) ("Where, as here alleged, a corrupt employee allows long distance calls to be made without charge and in a manner which bypasses the regular bookkeeping procedures of the company the only reasonable means of protection is the monitoring of such calls.")

[51] See *Religious Technology Center v. Netcom On-Line Communication Services*, 907 F.Supp. 1361 (N.D. Cal. 1995).

postings and use them for noncommercial purposes. If an online service seeks an assignment of copyright in subscriber postings, it will face a hurdle found in the Copyright Act, which provides that a transfer of copyright ownership is not valid unless it is in writing, signed by the "owner of the rights conveyed."[52]

Some online services claim a compilation copyright in the materials posted by their subscribers. The Copyright Act defines a "compilation" as

a work formed by the collection and assembling of preexisting materials or of data that are selected, coordinated, or arranged in such a way that the resulting work as a whole constitutes an original work of authorship.[53]

It remains to be seen whether an online service may be able to show sufficient selection, coordination, or arrangement to support the claimed copyright. In many cases, subscriber postings are simply responses to postings by other subscribers, with no participation by the online service whatsoever.

Posting a message to an Internet newsgroup causes it to be copied and stored on computers across the world for their subscribers to review. Similarly, posting a message on an online service causes a copy to be made on the service's computers. In making such postings, is content donated to the public?

At the outset, it should be noted that if the person making the posting does not own its content[54] (including all the parts thereof) and is not otherwise authorized to post it, then the posting itself may be a copyright infringement. The act of posting does not immunize others who make a copy. To the contrary, the owner of each computer to which a copy is made is arguably also guilty of copyright infringement.[55] Although there may be support in the Copyright Act for such a claim extending to all computers on which a copy may be found, placed there through the automatic processes that enable the Internet to function, the result is absurd—threatening thousands, if not millions, of persons with liability for the act of an individual over whom they have no control or connection, other than an Internet link.[56]

---

[52] 17 U.S.C. § 204(a).

[53] Ibid. § 101.

[54] E.g., the work was created in the course and scope of employment such that the employer is the "author" and owner of the copyright.

[55] This argument is made by the plaintiffs in *Religious Technology Center v. Netcom On-Line Communication Services*, No. C-95-20091 RMW (N.D. Cal. filed Feb. 8, 1995).

[56] See *Religious Technology Center v. Netcom On-Line Communication Services*, 907 F.Supp. 1361 (N.D. Cal. 1995).

What are the rights of persons who come across material online? The answer depends on the facts of the particular case. There are three common circumstances: (1) the copyright owner states that he or she is donating the work to the public domain; (2) the owner gives written permission for others to use the work for noncommercial purposes only; and (3) the owner says nothing.

In the first case, an issue to consider is, How does an owner donate a work to the public domain via the Internet? Although there is no court decision yet on this point, it may be fair to conclude that a donation to the public domain needs to be in writing and signed. What then of postings to Internet newsgroups that are archived and searchable? The answer may be that the author has simply donated a copy to the Internet community but has retained the copyright.[57]

If the owner's writing reveals any intent to exert any control over the work in the future, there has probably not been a donation to the public domain. For example, if the owner states that a work can be copied by all comers, but not modified, it is arguable that only a license was intended. A donation to the public domain should at the very least be accompanied by words expressing the intent irrevocably to relinquish all right, title, and interest in and to the worldwide copyrights of a work. Since it is virtually impossible to compensate someone for donation of a work to the public domain, there may be a risk that a third party (such as an heir or a creditor) could void the donation.

As for the "signature," may a typed name in an electronic message constitutes a signature? There is support for the position that it is sufficient for a person to type his or her name, intending it to be a signature.

The second case involves permission to use a work for noncommercial purposes only. There is here the same issue of whether the permission, a license, is sufficiently supported by a signed writing. Can a license be made for noncommercial purposes only? Yes. And use in excess of a license may give rise to a suit for both breach of the license as well as copyright infringement.

In the third case, the author says nothing and there is no expressed intent to relinquish copyright protection. An online system may anticipate these questions by providing some answers in its terms and conditions of usage, to which all subscribers agree.

---

[57] See *Salinger v. Random House, Inc.*, 811 F.2d 90, 94–95 (2d Cir. 1987) ("The author of letters is entitled to a copyright in the letters, as with any other work of literary authorship. . . . The copyright owner owns the literary property rights, including the right to complain of infringing copying, while the recipient of the letter retains ownership of 'the tangible physical property of the letter itself' ").

In absence of some type of permission, it is technically arguable that even the simple act of making of a copy of a work in RAM to view the work online constitutes copyright infringement.[58] A very popular graphical Internet browser—the Netscape Navigator—automatically downloads inline images and text onto the viewer's own hard disk. In so doing, the Netscape Navigator facilitates use of the Internet at tolerable speed, using regular phone lines and standard modems.[59] In this case, one might argue that this action is covered by an implied license, but the better view may be that such copying is a fair use.[60] And if it's a fair use to cache in this way, then it's also a fair use simply to browse material on the Internet.

K. Criminal Liability

It is a federal criminal offense to infringe copyright "willfully and for purposes of commercial advantage or private financial gain."[61] Upon conviction, courts are authorized to order the "forfeiture and destruction or other disposition of all infringing copies . . . and all implements, devices, or equipment used in the manufacture of such infringing copies. . . ."[62] Use as well as distribution of an article with a fraudulent copyright notice is a criminal offense, as is fraudulent removal of a copyright notice.[63] It is also a crime to make a false representation in a copyright registration statement, or in a statement connected to the registration.[64]

Felony sanctions for copyright infringement were first authorized in 1982, and extended to include computer software. A five-year sentence and a fine[65] may apply to a person who reproduces or distributes, within any 180-day period, at least ten copies of one or more

---

[58] See *MAI Sys. Corp. v. Peak Computer*, 991 F.2d 511, 519 (9th Cir. 1993), *cert. dismissed*, 126 L.Ed.2d 640, 114 S.Ct. 671 (1994); *Advanced Computer Servs. v. MAI Sys. Corp.*, 845 F.Supp. 356, 364 n.9 (E.D. Va. 1994); *Religious Technology Center v. Netcom On-Line Communication Services*, 907 F.Supp. 1361 (N.D. Cal. 1995).

[59] By storing text and images in a cache, the Netscape Navigator allows a user to return to a previously viewed site without having to reload its data.

[60] But as technology changes, such use may no longer be seen as fair. See *American Geophysical Union v. Texaco Inc.*, 37 F.3d 881, 892 (2d Cir. 1994) (quoting the District Court, the Second Circuit stated, "To the extent the copying practice was 'reasonable' in 1973 . . . it has ceased to be 'reasonable' as the reasons that justified it before [photocopying licensing] have ceased to exist").

[61] 17 U.S.C. § 506(a).

[62] Ibid. § 506(b).

[63] Ibid. §§ 506(c), (d).

[64] Ibid. § 506(e).

[65] See 18 U.S.C. § 3571, which provides for a fine of up to $250,000 for an individual, and up to $500,000 for an organization found guilty of an offense.

copyrighted works, with a retail value of more than $2,500.[66] For a second or subsequent copyright offense, a ten-year prison term is authorized.

The development of criminal copyright laws is traced in a court decision on the prosecution of David LaMacchia, a student at the Massachusetts Institute of Technology.[67] He established a computer bulletin board and encouraged others to upload computer software applications and games. Uploaded programs were transferred to a second board, where persons with passwords could download the programs. In early 1994, LaMacchia was indicted by a federal grand jury on one count of conspiring "with persons unknown" to violate the wire fraud statute.[68] The indictment did not allege that LaMacchia sought or derived any personal benefit, but that he

devised a scheme to defraud that had as its object the facilitation "on an international scale" of the "illegal copying and distribution of copyrighted software" without payment of license fees and royalties to software manufacturers and vendors.[69]

Proceeding under the wire fraud statute was useful to the prosecution, observed the district court, because "the mail and wire fraud statutes do not require that a defendant be shown to have sought to personally profit from the scheme to defraud."[70] But the court ruled that illegal conduct alone cannot satisfy the fraud element of the wire fraud statute. The court went on to dismiss the case against La-Macchia, holding that copyright prosecutions should be limited to Section 506 of the Copyright Act and other incidental statutes that refer explicitly to copyright and copyrighted works.

L. Fair Use

As described by the U.S. Supreme Court, "[f]air use was traditionally defined as 'a privilege in others than the owner of the copyright to use the copyrighted material in a reasonable manner without his consent.'"[71] The fair use privilege is now codified at Section 107 of the Copyright Act:

Notwithstanding the provisions of section 106 and 106A, the fair use of a copyrighted work, including such use by reproduction in copies or phonorecords or by any

---

[66] 18 U.S.C. §§ 2319(b)(1), (b) (2).

[67] *United States v. LaMacchia*, 871 F.Supp. 535 (D. Mass. 1994).

[68] 18 U.S.C. § 1343.

[69] *United States v. LaMacchia*, 871 F.Supp. 535, 536 (D. Mass. 1994).

[70] Ibid., 871 F. Supp. 535, 541–42 (D. Mass. 1994).

[71] *Harper & Row, Publishers, Inc. v. Nation Enterprises*, 471 U.S. 539, 549, 85 L.Ed.2d 588, 105 S.Ct. 2218 (1985).

other means specified by that section, for purposes such as criticism, comment, news reporting, teaching (including multiple copies for classroom use), scholarship, or research, is not an infringement of copyright. In determining whether the use made of a work in any particular case is a fair use the factors to be considered shall include—

(1) the purpose and character of the use, including whether such use is of a commercial nature or for nonprofit educational purposes;
(2) the nature of the copyrighted work;
(3) the amount and substantiality of the portion used in relation to the copyrighted work as a whole; and
(4) the effect of the use upon the potential market for or value of the copyrighted work.[72]

Importantly, review of this nonexclusive list makes clear that simply copying a small portion of a work and acknowledging the source is not necessarily a "fair use."

To invoke the fair use defense, a person must have an authorized copy of the work.[73] A fair use claim may be denied where an original work has been copied but then transformed so that it no longer resembles the original. In certain instances, however, such "intermediate" copying may be allowed to provide access to unprotected ideas and processes.[74]

In a case concerning the Internet posting of copies of published and unpublished works of the Church of Scientology by Dennis Erlich, a former church member, his claimed purpose was to "evoke discussion regarding various Scientology philosophies." The court accepted this claim, as there was "insufficient evidence to support plaintiffs' claim that Erlich's copying was made out of spite or for other destructive reasons. . . ."[75] But the court noted that despite his critical purpose, Erlich did little other than copy the Church's work.[76] And

---

[72] 17 U.S.C. § 107.

[73] See *Atari Games Corp. v. Nintendo of America, Inc.*, 975 F.2d 832, 843 (Fed. Cir. 1992); *Sega Enters. v. MAPHIA*, 857 F.Supp. 679, 687 (N.D. Cal. 1994).

[74] See *Sega Enters. v. Accolade, Inc.*, 977 F.2d 1510, 1527–28 (9th Cir. 1992) (intermediate copying allowed to understand unprotected ideas and processes); but see *West Publ. Co. v. On Point Solutions, Inc.*, Civ. No. 1:93-CV-2071-MHS, 1994 U.S. Dist. Lexis 20040 (N.D. Ga. 1994) (permanent injunction based, among other things, on intermediate copying of West cases scanned by On Point, with West headnotes and syllabi temporarily stored on On Point's computers and then deleted prior to creation of On Point disks).

[75] *Religious Technology Center v. Netcom On-Line Communication Services*, No. C-95-20091 RMW, Order Granting in Part and Denying in Part Plaintiffs' Application for a Preliminary Injunction and Defendant Erlich's Motion to Dissolve the TRO. . . . (N.D. Cal. filed Sept. 22, 1995).

[76] According to the Supreme Court, it is important to note whether the new work "adds something new, with a further purpose or different character, altering the first with new expression, meaning, or message. . . ." *Campbell v. Acuff-Rose Music, Inc.*, 114 S.Ct. 1164, 1171, 127 L.Ed.2d 500 (1994).

there was no evidence that Erlich personally profited, financially or professionally, as a result of the postings. The court commented, "[i]f mere recognition by one's peers constituted 'personal profit' to defeat a finding of a noncommercial use, courts would seldom find any criticism fair use and much valuable criticism would be discouraged."[77] The fact Erlich may have obtained his copies of the church's works in an unauthorized manner did not bar his fair use defense, but was considered with the other factors.

The church works copied by Erlich were both published and unpublished, so a portion of the second factor worked in favor of the plaintiffs as well as in favor of Erlich. The same result obtained due to the fact that parts of the works were creative, fictional, or highly original (due broad protection), and other portions were factual, informational, or functional (due lesser protection).

On the amount and substantiality of the portion used, Erlich claimed that as to some documents he copied only a small part of a larger collection. But the court found that "[i]t appears that Erlich copied all or almost all of many of the works, which were predominantly short documents of less than three pages, and mostly with no comments or with very brief comments at the beginning or end."[78] The Court ruled that "this factor weighs heavily in plaintiffs' favor, especially as to the unpublished works, where the amount of acceptable copying is even lower."[79]

Regarding the effect of Erlich's postings on the potential market for the works, the court was "not convinced that postings like Erlich's postings could be effectively used by rival Scientology-like religious groups." The court also found it "unlikely that Erlich's noncommercial use, or widespread conduct like Erlich's by others, would diminish or prejudice the potential sale of plaintiffs' works, interfere with their marketability, or fulfill the demand for the works."[80]

Balancing all the factors, the court ruled against Erlich on the fair use defense. According to the court,

Although criticism is a favored use, where that "criticism" consists of copying large portions of plaintiffs' works—and sometimes all of those works—with often no more than one line of criticism, the fair use defense is inappropriate. Erlich has not adequately justified his copying verbatim large portions of plaintiffs' works. . . .

-----

[77] *Religious Technology Center v. Netcom On-Line Communication Services*, No. C-95-20091 RMW, Order Granting in Part and Denying in Part Plaintiffs' Application for a Preliminary Injunction and Defendant Erlich's Motion to Dissolve the TRO. . . . (N.D. Cal. filed Sept. 22, 1995).
[78] Ibid.
[79] Ibid.
[80] Ibid.

While use of a large percentage or the "heart" of the copyrighted work does not rule out fair use *per se*, other factors are not sufficiently in Erlich's favor to overcome this third factor.[81]

Interestingly, when later considering a fair use defense raised by Netcom, the Internet access provider on whose computers Erlich's postings were automatically copied, the court held that Netcom's total copying of Erlich's postings would not otherwise defeat an otherwise valid fair use defense. The court observed that

Netcom ... made available to the Usenet exactly what was posted by Erlich.... [T]he mere fact that all of a work is copied is not determinative of the fair use question, where such total copying is essential given the purpose of the copying. ... Netcom had no practical alternative way to carry out its socially useful purpose; a Usenet server must copy all files, since the prescreening of postings for potential copyright infringement is not feasible.[82]

M. First Amendment

The First Amendment provides that "Congress shall make no law ... abridging the freedom of speech, or of the press. ..."

It has been argued that the protections of the First Amendment are broader than the fair use defense under the Copyright Act. But, as noted by the U.S. Court of Appeals for the Second Circuit, "except perhaps in an extraordinary case, 'the fair use doctrine encompasses all claims of the first amendment in the copyright field.'"[83]

In a case over the unauthorized publication of excerpts from the memoirs of former president Gerald R. Ford covering his pardon of President Nixon, it was argued that the substantial public import of the material excused a use 'that would ordinarily not pass muster as a fair use." But the U.S. Supreme Court affirmed that "copyright's idea/ expression dichotomy 'strike[s] a definitional balance between the First Amendment and the Copyright Act by permitting free communication of facts while still protecting an author's expressions.'"[84] Ideas and facts that are narrated, for example, cannot be copyrighted. But copyright does protect the original expression contained in the narrative. A ruling to the contrary, adopting the defendant's argument, "would expand fair use to effectively destroy any expectation of copyright protection in the work of a public figure."[85]

---

[81] Ibid.
[82] Ibid.
[83] *Twin Peak Prods. v. Publications Intern'l*, 996 F.2d 1366, 1378 (2d Cir. 1993).
[84] *Harper & Row, Publishers, Inc. v. Nation Enterprises*, 471 U.S. 539, 556, 85 L.Ed.2d 588, 105 S.Ct. 2218 (1985).
[85] Ibid.

N. Software Rental

Businesses interested in the Internet as a computer software distribution channel should take note of the Computer Software Rental Amendment Act of 1990.[86] This act precludes commercial rental or loan of computer software without authorization of the copyright owner (as distinguished from the owner of a particular copy of a computer program).

The Computer Software Rental Amendment Act is an exception to the general rule that the purchaser or subsequent owner of a work may sell, rent, and otherwise dispose of it.[87] Under the Act, the copyright owner has the right to authorize, for purposes of direct or indirect commercial advantage, the disposition of a computer program "by rental, lease, or lending, or by any other act or practice in the nature of rental, lease, or lending."[88]

O. Proposals for Change

The government has examined the intellectual property implications of what they term the "national information infrastructure,"[89] and legislation has been proposed to implement some of the conclusions.[90] The entire process has been characterized by critics as a wholesale giveaway to copyright industry lobbyists at the expense of the public.[91]

The government's analysis and proposed legislation fails to recognize and address key issues related to Internet and online technology, and thereby threatens the continued development of the medium it purportedly seeks to enhance. For example, the unauthorized electronic transmission of copyrighted material is deemed a distribution of copies to the public. It is not clear how this will affect Internet service providers. All documents or images sent over the Internet are broken into very small packets at the point of connection to the Internet and are then sent to their destination. In the process, individual

---

[86] 17 U.S.C. § 109.

[87] This rule is also known as the "first sale" doctrine.

[88] 17 U.S.C. § 109(b)(1)(A); see also *Central Point Software v. Global Software & Accessories*, 880 F.Supp. 957. 964 (E.D.N.Y. 1995) ("Congress intended to proscribe not only transactions that are called rentals, but also practices that are in substance rentals").

[89] Information Infrastructure Task Force, Working Group on Intellectual Property Rights, *Intellectual Property and the National Information Infrastructure: The Report of the Working Group on Intellectual Property Rights* (Sept. 1995).

[90] See "NII Copyright Protection Act of 1995," 104 S. 1284, 104 H.R. 2441.

[91] See P. Samuelson, "The Copyright Grab," *Wired* 4, no. 1 (Jan. 1996): 134.

packets may take different routes. At the destination, they are reassembled. Will service and access providers find themselves responsible for screening every packet that moves onto and across the Internet to determine whether it might be an unauthorized transmission of copyrighted material? What information might put them on notice that they may be required to take steps to prevent further transmission, if it is indeed possible to do anything? And if possible, how much might have to be spent?

The government proposals anticipate the development of copyright management information that publishers may include in digital copies of their works. It would be illegal to remove or alter this information. Will this information be used to force service and access providers to develop screening tools? And if publishers are able to track digital copies, what are the privacy implications for consumers?

Insofar as copyright owners may use technology, such as encryption, to protect their "rights," the Government proposes to prohibit persons from manufacturing or developing technologies or services that might circumvent such efforts. In addition to the "chill" such a prohibition would place on the development of useful products and services that might be put to an unintended but infringing purpose, the prohibition itself appears to greatly expand the monopoly rights of copyright owners. For example, a copyrighted work may contain substantial elements that are not protected or protectable by copyright law. The copyright owner should not be able to prevent a person from copying and using those elements.[92] But by using advanced technology buttressed by the proposed legislation, such usage may be effectively prevented. In addition, in using such technology, a copyright owner may be able to effectively prevent a fair use of the work.

All things considered, government proposals and the proposed legislation they have generated seek substantive changes only in favor of the copyright industry. The public has been presented by the government with an unbalanced analysis based on discrete court decisions, presented as gospel, disregarding cogent authority and criticism to the contrary. Online service providers and end users are left to work out their issues in court, while the copyright industry is provided congressional relief.

---

[92] See *Sega Enters. v. Accolade, Inc.*, 977 F.2d 1510, 1527–28 (9th Cir. 1992); cf. *ProCD, Inc. v. Zeidenberg*, 95-C-0671-C, 1996 U.S. Dist. Lexis 167 (W.D. Wisc. 1996) *rev'd*, No. 96–1139, Slip Opinion (7th Cir. June 20, 1996).

APPENDIX

[CyberLaw™ 5/93]

REPAIR DEEMED UNLAWFUL

According to a recent decision by the Ninth Circuit, an independent service company may violate copyright law where in the course of repairing a customer's computer and diagnosing a problem or confirming that a repair has been successful, the company's technician turns on the computer and views an error message displayed by the computer's operating system. (*MAI Systems Corp. v. Peak Computer, Inc., et al.*, Nos. 92–55363, 93–55106 (9th Cir. April 7, 1993).) This decision shocked independent service providers, who believe the Ninth Circuit's decision may well destroy the market for third-party service of high-technology equipment. It is also notable because it holds that the mere loading of computer software into random access memory (RAM) may violate copyright law, and indicates that a software company may severely restrict the use of its product by a purchaser. The legal action itself well illustrates the growing pressure on copyright law exerted by high-technology companies seeking new ways to protect their enterprises.

MAI Systems Corp. is a former manufacturer of microcomputers and designer of software to run its computers; MAI is now in the business of servicing its computers and software. In 1990, Peak Computer, Inc. began to maintain and repair MAI computer systems owned by more than one hundred customers in southern California. Peak's maintenance and repair service necessarily involves turning on customer computers, which causes the automatic loading of MAI operating system software into RAM.

In March 1992, MAI filed suit in federal court against Peak, alleging copyright infringement, among other things. This led to the issuance of a permanent injunction against Peak and its employees, which includes the following language:

Peak [and certain others] are permanently enjoined from copying . . . or otherwise infringing MAI's copyrighted works. . . . The "copying" enjoined herein specifically *includes the acts of loading, or causing to be loaded, directly or indirectly, any MAI software from any magnetic storage or read only memory device into the electronic random access memory of the central processing unit of a computer system.* As used herein, "computer system" means an MAI central processing unit in combination with either a video display, printer, disk drives, and/or keyboard. (Emphasis added.)

Peak appealed, and a three-judge panel of the Ninth Circuit Court of Appeals reviewed the claim, among others, that Peak violated MAI's copyright by running MAI software licensed to MAI's customers. To prevail, stated the Ninth Circuit, MAI had to prove " 'copying' of protectable expression" beyond the scope allowed MAI customers.

The Ninth Circuit observed that MAI customers were licensed to use MAI software for their own internal information processing. (MAI software licenses allegedly state that "Customer may use the Software . . . solely to fulfill Customer's own internal information processing needs on the particular items of Equipment . . . for which the Software is configured and furnished by [MAI].") The loading of software by MAI customers into RAM was allowed under the license. However, the licenses given by MAI do not, according to the Ninth Circuit, allow third parties to use or copy the licensed software. "Any 'copying' done by Peak," the Ninth Circuit held, "is 'beyond the scope' of the license."

Under the Copyright Act, one of the exclusive rights of a copyright owner is to reproduce copyrighted works in copies and to authorize others to do so. (17 U.S.C. Section 106.) "Copies" are defined by the act as "material objects . . . in which a work is *fixed* . . . and from which the work can be perceived, reproduced, or otherwise communicated, either directly or with the aid of a machine or device." (17 U.S.C. Section 101; emphasis added.) "A work is 'fixed' in a tangible medium of expression," explains the act, "when its embodiment in a copy . . . by or under the authority of the author, is sufficiently permanent or stable to permit it to be perceived, reproduced, or otherwise communicated for a period of more than transitory duration." (17 U.S.C. Section 101.)

The Ninth Circuit noted that the district court's judgment for MAI reflected that court's "conclusion that a 'copying' for purposes of copyright law occurs when a computer program is transferred from a permanent storage device to a computer's RAM." The Ninth Circuit found this conclusion to be supported by the record in this case and by the law.

The Ninth Circuit observed that

As part of diagnosing a computer problem at the customer site, the Peak technician runs the computer's operating system software [which is automatically loaded into RAM when an MAI computer is turned on], allowing the technician to view the system error log, which is part of the operating system, thereby enabling the technician to diagnose the problem.

In the opinion of the Ninth Circuit, the ability of the Peak technician to view the system error log adequately demonstrates that the "representation created in the RAM is 'sufficiently permanent or stable to permit it to be perceived, reproduced, or otherwise communicated for a period of more than transitory duration.'"

On this issue of fixation, the Ninth Circuit also looked to a 1984 decision holding that "the copying of copyrighted software onto silicon chips and subsequent sale of those chips is not protected by Section 117 of the Copyright Act." (Under Section 117, "the 'owner' of a copy of a computer program [is allowed] to make or authorize the making of another copy . . . [provided that it] is an essential step in the utilization of the computer program, or . . . that such new copy is for archival purposes only. . . .") As stated by the court in that case,

RAM can be simply defined as a computer component in which data and computer programs can be temporarily recorded. Thus, the purchaser of [software] desiring to utilize all of the programs on the diskette could arrange to copy [the software] into RAM. This would only be a temporary fixation. It is a property of RAM that when the computer is turned off, the copy of the program recorded in RAM is lost.

While recognizing this language not to be dispositive, the Ninth Circuit found it to support the proposition that a "copy made in RAM is 'fixed' and qualifies as a copy under the Copyright Act."

Although no court decision specifically holds that the loading of software into RAM creates a "copy" under the Copyright Act, the Ninth Circuit stated that it is "generally accepted that the loading of software into a computer constitutes the creation of a copy under the Copyright Act." The Ninth Circuit acknowledged, however, that its authority for such general acceptance is *"troubling* since they do not specify that a copy is created regardless of whether the software is loaded into the RAM, the hard disk or the read only memory ('ROM')." (Emphasis added.)

In light of the above, the Ninth Circuit held that Peak violated MAI's copyright by running MAI software belonging to Peak's customers. Two weeks later, on April 21, 1993, Peak filed a petition requesting that the case be reheard by the Ninth Circuit as a whole.

In its petition, Peak alleges that important public policy considerations have been neglected. Peak asserts that if the decision in this case were to be allowed to stand, it

would fundamentally change the nature of the [entire industry of independent third-party computer maintenance and repair services] and would essentially create a monopoly in favor of the computer manufacturers, who would now be able to garner the computer repair and service market by simply obtaining a copyright on their software. . . . In the wake of the Court's decision, nothing would prevent manufacturers from licensing the software in products that are commonly 'owned' by the buyer, such as cameras, cars or computers.

Peak also urges that, among other things, the fair use doctrine applies to protect its activities.

Independent Service Network International (ISNI), an organization of over two hundred independent service organizations in the business of servicing equipment manufactured by others, also filed a petition for rehearing as a "friend of the court." Echoing Peak, ISNI warns that "[i]f [independent service organizations] cannot turn on a customer's computer and load its operating system into RAM, they cannot test the operation and functioning of the computer; only very limited servicing of the computer, if any, can be performed." The ultimate impact would be,

the destruction of a large part of the independent service industry for high-technology equipment, forcing owners and users of computer systems and other high-technology equipment with operating systems to use only manufacturer-provided service, even if it is more costly and less efficient.

Such a result, argues ISNI, is contrary to the public policies underlying the Copyright Act, a consideration ignored and not well served by the Ninth Circuit three-judge panel that considered this case. According to ISNI, four factors related to public policy support the need for rehearing. First, "the effect of the decision may very well be to destroy aftermarkets of service of high technology equipment," the importance of which was recently recognized by the U.S. Supreme Court. Second, "the Copyright Act was never intended to confer a patent-like monopoly over a copyrighted product, let alone confer monopoly power with respect to a product that is not copyrighted such as a computer." Third, Section 117 of the Copyright Act should be recognized to allow the *"rightful possessor* of computer programs to use them if such use is 'essential' to the operation of the computer system." (Emphasis added; in this case the Ninth Circuit held that Peak customers do not "qualify as 'owners' under Section 117 because MAI only licensed its software.) Fourth, "turning on a [computer] and loading the operating system into . . . RAM in order to use and maintain the computer—the very function for which the operating system was created—constitutes fair use under the Copyright Act."

Although the underlying intent of the Copyright Act is to encourage the creation of works of authorship by ensuring that authors are fairly compensated, ISNI claims that this goal is "served so long as additional copies of software are not proliferated, such as in this instance, where only a temporary copy is made in order to use and maintain the associated computer system." Citing the U.S. Supreme Court, ISNI notes that "the 'reward' to the author is a 'secondary consideration' to the primary objective—that of the benefits derived by the public from those works of authorship."

On May 26, 1993, a number of computer maintenance companies filed suit in Virginia against MAI, alleging violations of antitrust laws. The plaintiffs allege, among other things, that MAI threatens to drive them out of the market.

[CyberLaw™ 10/93]

FREE SPEECH & TOASTERS

The chief purpose of the First Amendment guarantee of freedom of speech and of the press is to facilitate the flow of information. The Copyright Clause is also a part of the Constitution and was intended, in major part, to promote free speech by providing access to copyrighted materials. (See L. R. Patterson & S. W. Lindberg, *The Nature of Copyright* (1991)). Little attention has been paid to the relationship between the First Amendment and the Copyright Clause, however, and a recent legal decision illustrates the extent to which free speech values have been eroded when confronted by business interests in copyright litigation. In that case, the court compelled a publisher to remove a parody from a computer program without the benefit of a full trial, having found against the publisher, in substantial part, through the use of a fiction—that commercial use of copyrighted materials by someone other than the copyright holder raises a presumption of unfair exploitation of the material.

In 1989, Berkeley Systems, Inc. introduced a computer program designed to prevent images from burning into the screen of computer monitors. This "screen saver" utility program—named "After Dark"—became very popular, due in large part to its graphics displays. After Dark includes a number of graphics modules, including one that depicts 1950s, rounded, two-bread-slice toasters with angel wings, flying from right to left across the computer monitor screen accompanied by slices of toast. According to Berkeley's attorneys, Berkeley holds valid copyright and trademark registrations in the Flying Toaster.

Delrina Corporation publishes a new computer screen saver program called "Opus 'n Bill." The program features the comic-strip characters Opus (a penguin) and Bill the Cat, created by Berkeley Breathed. As described by Delrina's counsel,

[I]rreverent satire, caricature, and parody are at the heart of Breathed's unique and well-known brand of humor, and they are present throughout the various screen sequences or 'modules' in Opus 'n Bill. The timely and prominent objects of this unique humor include the country's hottest corporation (Microsoft), richest citizen (Bill Gates), most popular movie (Jurassic Park), latest fad (bungee jumping), and most popular animal (the Clintons' 'first cat' Socks), and even the fad of screen saver programs themselves.

In an Opus 'n Bill module named "Death Toasters," the character Opus fires a shotgun at flying toasters. The toasters fly in formation and launch an attack of their own against Opus, by firing toast or diving from above to knock him down. According to Delrina, the parody is clearly aimed at Berkeley, "the established and self-proclaimed leader in the screen saver software field." Berkeley is not amused.

At the end of September 1993, Berkeley (having filed an action for copyright and trademark infringement and unfair competition) requested a court order enjoining Delrina's marketing and sale of products incorporating the flying toaster design. Berkeley claimed that Delrina is engaging in "a blatant attempt to confuse consumers and to improperly trade on the enormous good will [Berkeley] has developed through its creative genius and intensive marketing efforts." Berkeley noted that a syndicated article had appeared in major metropolitan newspapers showing Delrina's Death Toasters, and Berkeley had been contacted by confused industry members. A preliminary injunction would, according to Berkeley, "protect the legitimate and valuable rights it has acquired in the FLYING TOASTER design and to preserve the reputation it has developed for making the FLYING TOASTER design available only under the Berkeley label."

In opposition, Delrina notes that its flying toasters are different from Berkeley's toasters. Delrina's toasters are four-legged, with stubby wings, and they fly in formation; Berkeley's toasters are " '50's-style,' legless toasters with large angel wings flying lazily across the screen in a seemingly random and endless pattern. . . ." Further, each Delrina product contains the following disclaimer:

THIS PRODUCT CONTAINS A PARODY OF BERKELEY SYSTEMS, INC.'S FLYING TOASTER DESIGN. DELRINA'S PRODUCT IS NOT PRODUCED, SPONSORED OR APPROVED BY BERKELEY SYSTEMS, INC. WE POKE FUN AT, BUT ARE NOT ATTEMPTING TO INSULT EITHER THAT COMPANY OR ITS PRODUCTS.

On the matter of alleged trademark infringement, Delrina claims there is no likelihood of consumers being deceived because

[Berkeley's] allegations of consumer deception in this case are belied by: (1) the clear nature of the parody itself; (2) the explicit disclaimers accompanying the product that identify the 'Death Toasters' sequence as a parody, disassociate Delrina from Berkeley, and explain Breathed's humorous intent; and (3) the media coverage of the release of Delrina's screen saver, which point out the parody.

Since there is no intent to confuse the public, claims Delrina, there is no actionable trademark infringement. Delrina also urges that the "very strength of [Berkeley's] mark weighs against a likelihood of confusion. . . ." In addition, since Delrina's Opus 'n Bill screen saver is an obvious parody, it is a form of expression protected under the First Amendment.

On the issue of copyright infringement, Delrina observes that the flying toaster design is not Berkeley's creation; "[t]hese toasters have been around at least since 1973, when the rock group Jefferson Airplane used them on the cover of its album *30 Seconds Over Winterland*." Delrina argues that Berkeley is not the creator of the flying toaster design and has no right, therefore, to bring a copyright action based on its reproduction. (The *San Jose Mercury News* reports that a record album designer named Bruce Steinberg is the creator of the flying toasters. According to Steinberg, singer Grace Slick was poking fun at Jefferson Airplane's road crew, called "quippies." Slick twisted a well-known joke by asking, "Why did the quippie throw the toaster out of the window? Because he wanted to see time fly." The joke fell flat but served as the inspiration for an album cover featuring flying toasters.)

Delrina also argues that there are only a limited number of ways to depict a flying toaster and that its toasters are not sufficiently similar to Berkeley's to support a finding of copyright infringement. And in any event, Delrina's use of parody is protected by the First Amendment and its use of part of Berkeley's product to make that parody is protected as a fair use.

Conceding that it may have used a small part of Berkeley's work in its parody, Delrina further maintains that:

[Berkeley's] copyrighted work itself is the entire screen saver program, which [Berkeley] concedes contains numerous different 'modules,' of which 'flying toasters' is only one. *Opus 'n Bill* overlaps with [Berkeley's] screen saver program in only one aspect (of many aspects) of one display (of many displays) contained in the entire program.

Additionally, Delrina asserts that it only used enough of the program to conjure up Berkeley's product to make the parody.

In reply, Berkeley argues that its "FLYING TOASTERS screen saver is an original work that was independently and spontaneously created without access to any earlier artwork." Its work, therefore, commands the full range of copyright protection. Berkeley also claims that as Delrina admits copying the flying toasters to make its parody, Berkeley has presented a *prima facie* case of infringement and that the sole question to be addressed is "fair use." According to Berkeley, parody is not a presumptively "fair use," and that defense can only be established by meeting four statutory factors—which Delrina has not done.

Following a hearing, the United States District Court for the Northern District of California found that Berkeley had shown a reasonable likelihood of success on its copyright infringement claim and enjoined Delrina from using the flying toasters in its Opus 'n Bill screen saver. The court did not reach the trademark issue, due to its finding of probable success on the copyright claim.

The court held Berkeley had established ownership of a valid copyright, despite Delrina's showing that the flying toaster icon had been used previously on a record album jacket. Berkeley's copyright registration certificates, observed the court, "are prima facie evidence of the validity of the copyright." And, as stated by the court, the copyright statute only requires that a copyrighted work be an independent creation, not that it be novel.

Berkeley had also shown copying by Delrina, albeit indirectly. Delrina had access to Berkeley's flying toasters, and there is substantial similarity between Berkeley's flying toasters and Delrina's Death Toasters. To the extent that there exist differences in expression between Delrina's toasters and Berkeley's (smaller wings, beating with greater rapidity, flying in different formation), the court noted that the test for substantial similarity of expression is based upon a side-by-side comparison of the two works—not an element-by-element dissection. Here, an ordinary reasonable person would find that Delrina captured the total concept and feel of Berkeley's toasters despite the distinctions, and that is all that is required.

The court also did not accept the claim there is only a limited number of ways to depict a flying toaster, and that therefore Berkeley's toasters should be protected only against exact copying:

[Delrina] could differentiate their winged toaster from [Berkeley's] and still express the idea of a flying toaster: the toaster could be a four slice toaster, or . . . a toaster oven, of an obviously different size, with very large wings or a different type of wing altogether, such as an airline wing.

Although differentiating Delrina's toasters could result in a less effective parody, the court noted that "at times the copyright law may require that parodists sacrifice the best parody to the interest of the copyright owner in his or her original expression."

Finding Berkeley has "demonstrated probable success on the merits by making out a prima facie case of copyright infringement," the court went on to consider Delrina's defense of parody, which, observed the court, "is not a presumptively fair use." According to the court, "parody as a defense to copyright infringement is considered within the framework of the fair use defense" and is based on consideration of four factors:

(1) the purpose and character of the use, including whether such use is of a commercial nature or is for nonprofit educational purposes;
(2) the nature of the copyrighted work;
(3) the amount and substantiality of the portion used in relation to the copyrighted work as a whole; and
(4) the effect of the use upon the potential market for or value of the copyrighted work.

On the first factor, the court held that Delrina's commercial use "raises a presumption of unfair exploitation of the copyrighted material." This presumption may be rebutted, however, by "*convincing* the court that the parody does not *unfairly* diminish the economic value of the original."

On this latter point, the court found that "the two modules, DEATH TOASTERS and FLYING TOASTERS, are whimsical, humorous displays and could appeal to the same consumers, thus risking commercial substitution." There was no evidence that "consumers who wish to buy [Berkeley's] FLYING TOASTERS would not begin to buy [Delrina's] DEATH TOASTERS out of a desire to purchase any screen saver with flying winged toasters, with or without the addition of Opus shooting them down." Delrina had not shown that any commercial substitution would be because consumers thought the parody of the winged toasters was more humorous. There was, in fact, no evidence either way. The court held that Delrina had not, therefore, rebutted the presumption of unfair use created by Delrina's commercial use of the toasters.

On Delrina's claim it had "taken no more than necessary to conjure up the image of [Berkeley's] screen saver in order to parody it," the court acknowledged that three factors have been considered in determining whether a parody has "taken excessively from the original in the circumstances—the degree of public recognition of the original work, the ease of conjuring up the original in the chosen medium, and the focus of the parody." But in this case, the court did not feel it necessary fully to address the issue, "given the presumption of unfair use that occurs once the commercial nature of the use is established." Despite the fact that flying toasters appear in only one of more than thirty modules in Berkeley's "After Dark," the court was impressed by the fact that the flying toaster is Berkeley's registered trademark and that the company and its screen saver are "strongly identified with the winged, two-bread slice, 1950's style toaster." (The court also noted that Delrina's parody appears in an identical medium, a computer screen, and that "[t]hose who would grasp the humor of the Death Toasters mode would recognize the parody if the toasters were substantially less similar.)

In light of the above, the court entered a preliminary injunction prohibiting Delrina from using the flying toasters in its Death Toasters module, in its packaging, or in connection with the advertising, distribution, or sale of the Opus 'n Bill screen saver. (Further information concerning the court's ruling can be found in the following opinion: *Berkeley Systems, Inc. v. Delrina (U.S.) Corp., et al.,* No. C93-3545-EFL (N.D. Cal. Oct. 8, 1993).) A Delrina manager later commented that the company will lose hundreds of thousands of dollars as a result of the ruling because it will have to change its packaging and promotional materials and destroy forty to fifty thousand boxes imprinted with the offending toasters.

The case of the Death Toasters highlights the fact that the subject matter of both the First Amendment and the Copyright Clause is the same, i.e., information. The fact the information is communicated by parody does not disqualify it from free speech protection. To the contrary, parody is one of the forces that led to the establishment of the free speech protections we enjoy today. The court's decision here illustrates that copyright law is being driven with great regard to private, commercial interests. The reason why free speech rights receive short shrift in cases such as this is aptly analyzed in *The Nature of Copyright*:

Logically, political rights[, such as free speech rights,] must be regarded as more important than [an individual's rights to control the products of his or her effort for profit], since the latter ultimately have to be both recognized and enforced by the government that is sustained by political rights. Proprietary rights tend to be concrete, however, whereas political rights are typically abstract, and in a one-to-one combat of ideas the concrete usually has the advantage over the abstract. In copyright litigation, for example, an accusation that a defendant has stolen the plaintiff's property is much more powerful than the claim that a defendant is exercising a free-speech right. The larger truth as to the importance of political rights is often lost in the legal melee.

In this case, it is deeply troubling not only that free speech values received such little attention but that the Death Toasters were effectively banned without a jury's consideration. If the First Amendment's guarantee of free speech and intent to prohibit the government from acting as censor is to have substantive content in copyright cases, at the very least there should be more deference to allowing juries to determine factual questions and less reliance on presumptions that prejudice the outcome in favor of private, commercial interests.

[CyberLaw™ 11/93]

THE END OF FAIR USE

A few weeks ago, the United States Supreme Court heard arguments in a case concerning a 1989 rap parody of the classic song "Oh, Pretty Woman," coauthored in 1964 by Roy Orbison and William Dees. The song is "about a lonely man's romantic longing for a pretty woman he sees walking down the street." The parody, named "Pretty Woman" and created by the rap group 2 Live Crew, "taunt[s] a succession of unappealing women, including a 'big hairy woman,' a 'bald headed women' and a 'two timin' woman.'" According to 2 Live Crew, the parody was "intended for a specific audience, young urban blacks," and its purpose "was to mock the banality of white centered rock-n-roll music by attacking one of its time honored ballads." In 1990, 2 Live Crew was sued for, among other things, copyright infringement by Acuff-Rose Music, Inc., assignee of the copyright to "Oh, Pretty Woman." 2 Live Crew defended on the grounds that its parody is a protected "fair use" of the original song, and this argument was accepted by the trial court but rejected by the Sixth Circuit Court of Appeals. At the Supreme Court, 2 Live Crew argues, among other things, that the Sixth Circuit erred in giving undue weight to the fact that its parody was published as part of a commercial endeavor. This case is important to computer software publishers and hardware manufacturers, because at its heart the case is a call for a balancing of an author's right to compensation for his work and the public's interest in the widest possible dissemination of ideas and information. This issue has been emerging with increased frequency in computer litigation, particularly with respect to user interfaces and interoperable software and hardware.

For years, authors and publishers have argued that they are entitled to vigorous enforcement of copyright law to protect monopoly rights regarding use of their products. They claim that copyright law supplies authors with the incentive to create and disseminate ideas and argue that as a matter of fairness and justice, ownership of works created should be exclusive and absolute. In the 2 Live Crew case, these concepts are expressed by a number of interested third parties as follows:

"Congress has given broad protection and a bundle of exclusive rights to the owners of copyrights in musical works intending that, through exploitation of their rights, they will be rewarded for their creativity and motivated to compose and publish additional musical works."

But these views are not universally accepted. In *The Nature of Copyright*, a recent book written by a professor of law, L. Ray Patterson, and a professor of English, Stanley W. Lindberg, (both at the University of Georgia) the authors sharply dispute fundamental propositions forwarded on behalf of authors and publishers. For example, according to Patterson and Lindberg,

"A common presumption seems to be that, without copyright, authors would not create and publishers would not disseminate works— a presumption whose logic fails in the face of reality. Thousands of books consisting of public-domain works [(i.e., those not protected by copyright law)]—including works by Chaucer, Shakespeare, Milton, Pope, Swift, Austin, . . . and so forth—are published now without copyright protection. And both radio and television were born, prospered, and passed through their golden years without the benefit of copyright protection for live broadcasts."

Significantly, Patterson and Lindberg observe that "the nature and purpose of copyright law has dimmed" and its "fundamentals are now largely obscured" in a process "vigorously cultivated by copyright owners in promoting an industry-oriented view as to the rights copyright entails." They suggest that the rights of the public "are far more important than most of us have been led to believe." And they bolster this view by recounting the origin of copyright law not as an author's right, but as a statute to protect the public from publishers.

As set forth in *The Nature of Copyright*, copyright began in England as a publisher's right. To establish the right to print and publish a book, the title of a manuscript (the "copy") had to be registered with the Stationers' Company (a group of bookbinders, printers, and booksellers granted a charter by the sovereign). The right so perfected was an exclusive right to publish in perpetuity. The foundation of the right, however, was only an agreement between the members of the company.

The stationers, being good businessmen, worked for many years for a public law that would forbid anyone to print a book in violation of the stationers' copyright. This desire neatly coincided with the sovereign's desire to control the press through licensing. Beginning in 1557, most printing was allowed only by the members of the Stationers' Company.

In 1710, more than fifteen years after the end of legally sanctioned censorship in England, Parliament enacted a law (the Statute of Anne) to protect copyright. But it was titled "An act for the encouragement of learning, by vesting the copies of printed books in the authors or purchasers of such copies during the times therein mentioned." Evidently, Parliament's motivation in passing the statute did not coincide with the interests of the booksellers. According to Patterson and Lindberg,

[The Statute of Anne] transformed the stationers' copyright—which had been used as a device of monopoly and an instrument of censorship—into a trade-regulation concept to promote learning and to curtail the monopoly of publishers. . . .

The features of the Statute of Anne that justify the epithet of trade regulation included the limited term of copyright, the availability of copyright to anyone, and price-control provisions. Copyright, rather than being perpetual, was now limited to a term of fourteen years, with a like renewal term being available only to the author (and only if the author were living at the end of the first term).

The Statute of Anne also created a public domain for literature. "Under the old system, all literature belonged to some booksellers forever, and only literature that met the censorship standards as administered by the booksellers could ever appear in print."

Passage of the Statute of Anne led to a long campaign by the booksellers to secure from the courts a perpetual copyright for authors—which could be assigned to publishers. According to Patterson and Livingston, with time obscuring the design of Parliament in enacting the Statute of Anne, copyright came to be viewed as a natural-law right of the author as well as the statutory grant of a limited monopoly. The result ever since has been confusion as to the nature of copyright: one theory holding that copyright's origin occurs at the creation of a work, the other that its origin exists only through the copyright statute.

Over time, publishers were able to use the authors' rights argument to gain enlargement of the rights of copyright. But as noted by Patterson and Lindberg, the notion of copyright as an author's right was and remains a fiction—authors assign their entire rights to publishers, who then gain the whole benefit of copyright law.

The public interest factor was not, however, written out of American law. To the contrary, the U.S. Constitution expressly states that the purpose of Copyright laws is "[t]o *Promote the Progress of Science and useful Arts. . . .*" And a significant limitation on the rights of copyright holders is found in the "fair use" doctrine, set out at Section 107 of the Copyright Act as follows:

[T]he fair use of a copyrighted work, including such use by reproduction in copies or phonorecords or by any other means specified . . . for purposes such as criticism, comment, news reporting, teaching (including multiple copies for classroom use), scholarship, or research, is not an infringement of copyright. In determining whether the use made of a work in any particular case is a fair use the factors to be considered shall include:

(1) the purpose and character of the use, including whether such use is of a commercial nature or is for nonprofit educational purposes;
(2) the nature of the copyrighted work;
(3) the amount and substantiality of the portion used in relation to the copyrighted work as a whole; and
(4) the effect of the use upon the potential market for or value of the copyrighted work.

Interestingly, Patterson and Lindberg also note the relationship between copyright law and the free-speech rights guaranteed by the First Amendment. As described above, copyright formerly served as a tool of censors in England. The authors posit that Parliament, in creating a statutory copyright, "was concerned with rendering copyright ineffective not only as an instrument of monopoly but also as a device of censorship." They state,

Whether or not the drafters of the U.S. Constitution fully comprehended the free-speech values in the provisions of the Statute of Anne we cannot know, but we do know that they made direct use of the wording of the statute's title, and it is clear that those words incorporate free-speech values. The three policies that the copyright clause [of the U.S. Constitution] mandates—the promotion of learning, the preservation of the public domain, and the protection of the author—are consistent with and essential to free-speech rights.

The relationship of the First Amendment to copyright law has also been argued in the 2 Live Crew case respecting the "fair use" doctrine.

In the 2 Live Crew case, Acuff-Rose Music argues that "there is no need for a separate First Amendment analysis [in this case] because First Amendment protections are "already embodied in the Copyright Act's distinction between copyrightable expression and uncopyrightable facts and ideas, and the latitude for scholarship and comment traditionally afforded by fair use." One must not forget, Acuff-Rose Music urges, that copyright owners are protected by First Amendment values—"protections afforded the copyright owner are themselves an 'engine of free expression,' supplying authors with 'the economic incentive to create and disseminate ideas.'"

These views are shared by Michael Jackson, Mac Davis, Dolly Parton, and a number of songwriter associations, who filed a "friend of the court" brief. In a separate "friend of the court" brief filed on behalf of the estates and trusts of Ira and George Gershwin, Alan Jay Lerner, Frederick Loewe, and Cole Porter, among others, there is asserted the view that exclusive rights of copyright are not antithetical to First Amendment values.

These views are disputed, however, in papers filed on behalf of a number of other "friends of the court": Home Box Office, Comedy Partners (doing business as Comedy Central, a cable television service), Fox Inc. (producer, through a subsidiary, of among other things, "In Living Color" and "The Simpsons"), *Mad* magazine, and National Broadcasting Company, Inc. HBO and the others state that in certain cases, "monopoly rights in expression are at odds with the freedom of expression guaranteed by the First Amendment." They add that mechanical application of the "fair use" analysis may eviscerate First Amendment rights. To protect First Amendment rights, "copyright law should be tailored to accomplish its intended purpose, i.e., promoting creative achievement. . . ."; the focus of the fair use test should be to assess the legitimacy of a new work, "not merely to recite the statutory factors." Congress itself did not intend that the four statutory fair use factors be the exclusive means of assessing fair use in all circumstances.

These points are echoed in papers submitted by another "friend of the court," the American Civil Liberties Union (ACLU). According to the ACLU,

To be sure, fair use "creates tensions between the Copyright Act's goal of protecting an author's works and first amendment principles of ensuring the unimpeded flow of information. . . ." The doctrine therefore calls for a careful balancing of the "interests of authors and inventors in the control and exploitation of their writings and discoveries on the one hand, and society's competing interest in the free flow of ideas, information, and commerce on the other. . . ." (Citations omitted.)

The ACLU also notes that the U.S. Supreme Court has observed that a case-by-case determination of fair use claims is required and that the inquiry need not be limited to consideration of the four statutory fair-use factors.

With regard to "fair use" itself, Acuff-Rose Music takes the position that there are no presumptively fair uses of a copyrighted work. Acuff-Rose Music claims that the first step in the fair use analysis (the purpose and character of the use) should be taken in light of a presumption that *every commercial use of copyrighted material is unfair.* The presumption does not apply because the alleged infringer may make a profit, but, according to Acuff-Rose Music, only "where the user is capitalizing primarily on the commercial appeal of the copyrighted material itself. . . ."

2 Live Crew notes, however, that this limitation is a recent construction by Acuff-Rose Music—the Sixth Circuit had announced simply "that the admittedly commercial nature of the derivative work . . . requires the conclusion that the first factor weighs against a finding of fair use." Whether the alleged infringing use is of a commercial nature is just the beginning, says 2 Live Crew. The court should then proceed to whether there has been a productive and creative use of the original that is the source of the commercial appeal of the new work, rather than the previous success of the existing work.

The Harvard Lampoon, Inc., which also filed a brief as a "friend of the court," observes,

In performing the fair use analysis, courts have historically favored 'productive' uses, where the copier adds an original contribution to the copied work, over 'non-productive' uses, where the copier appropriates the original without adding a socially valuable creative element.

This view is apparently shared by a number of songwriters and composers, who argue in this case that a copier is to be credited if the new work "serves a transformative purpose, i.e., uses and transforms a limited portion of a prior copyrighted work in the course of creating a new work for a socially desirable purpose. . . ."

In the 2 Live Crew case, the debate over the second and third steps in the analysis (concerning the nature and amount used of the copyrighted work) centered upon whether a creative work should be subject to a greater degree of copyright protection than a factual work, and whether 2 Live Crew had taken more from the original than reasonably necessary.

On the fourth step in the analysis (the effect of the use upon the market or value of the copyrighted work), Acuff-Rose Music emphasizes that a "copyright holder *need not have suffered actual competitive injury*. Rather, as the statute itself provides, there must be only 'potential' for such injury." (Emphasis added.) And where "the intended use [by the alleged infringer] is for commercial gain," Acuff-Rose Music maintains, "the *likelihood [of future harm] may be presumed*." (Emphasis added; in reality, this means that the proponent of the fair use must prove a negative—"that the use does not reduce the market for plaintiff's work.")

2 Live Crew acknowledges that courts have placed much importance on the fourth fair use factor and observes that a presumption of harm is reasonable where the alleged infringing user is exploiting the commercial appeal of the original. In this case, however, 2 Live Crew claims that the appeals court erred by examining whether there has been an impairment of the copyright owner's ability to license the copyrighted work for future works of the *same type as the alleged infringing one* (in this case, a rap parody of "Oh, Pretty Woman"). The court should have focused, instead, on the market for the original copyrighted product and whether the new use adversely affected the existing and/or potential market for the original.

As noted in *The Nature of Copyright*, one of the problems in the 2 Live Crew case really is that the four statutory fair use factors have no substantive content:

> The first, for example, implies that a nonprofit educational use is more likely than a commercial use to qualify as a fair use, although the wording in no way excludes commercial fair use. The second factor—the nature of the work—does not even imply what kind of work is relevant for fair-use purposes, and the third and fourth factors appear to be similarly devoid of any guidance for their application.

Clearly, the Supreme Court has a great opportunity to clarify the law and restore the public interest as a respected end in copyright analysis. And the decision in this case will have an immediate effect on computer hardware and software manufacturers, many of whom have been struggling to bring innovative and useful products to market in the face of unyielding opposition from entrenched companies who have expended vast sums to persuade Congress and courts of a view of copyright law that protects their monopolies. The importance of this case should not be underestimated—if 2 Live Crew is not allowed to "mock the banality of white centered rock-n-roll music," we may be condemned to live with mundane software and hardware standards marketed by companies that have little incentive to develop new and useful products.

(The lower court citations for the 2 Live Crew case are *Campbell*, *et al. v. Acuff-Rose Music, Inc.*, 754 F.Supp. 1150 (M.D. Tenn. 1991), 972 F.2d 1429 (6th Cir. 1992). The Supreme Court case number is 92–1292.)

[CyberLaw™ 4/94]

PIRATES

With increased use of computer bulletin boards and greater access to the Internet, there has been a corresponding rise in concern about the rights and obligations of those who join the online community. Although U.S. laws were recently strengthened to protect copyright holders, computer users increasingly voice opinions indicating that they are unaware of the scope of intellectual property laws, copyright law in particular. Some users apparently do not know that activities they encourage or in which they participate are subject to criminal prosecution. (Congress recently passed a law making it a felony to make a relatively few unauthorized copies of a copyrighted computer program.)

In fact, virtually all material published on the Internet and computer bulletin boards is subject to copyright protection, whether or not it is accompanied by a formal copyright notice. In two recent court decisions, involving *Playboy* photographs and Sega video games, operators of computer bulletin board services were held liable in connection with the illicit copying of copyrighted materials on their services, among other things. These two decisions provide notice to the online community and bulletin board providers that copyright holders are becoming more aggressive in protecting their material and are increasingly focusing their attention on the online world. And in the *Playboy* case, the court ruled that a bulletin board provider might be found liable for copyright infringement on his board whether or not the provider was aware of it.

The target of the *Playboy* case was George Frena, who operated a subscription computer bulletin board service named Tech Warehouse BBS. Subscribers to the Tech Warehouse BBS were able to browse different areas of the BBS and download high-quality copies of *Playboy* photographs to their own computers. One hundred and seventy images available on the BBS were copyrighted by *Playboy*. Frena admits that he did not obtain *Playboy*'s authorization or consent for its images to appear on his BBS. He claims, however, that BBS subscribers uploaded the images.

Playboy sued Frena for copyright and trademark infringement as well as unfair competition. Upon receipt of notice of the suit, Frena removed the photographs from the BBS and monitored it to prevent further *Playboy* photographs from being uploaded.

Upon *Playboy*'s motion for partial summary judgment, a U.S. district court in Florida noted that the Copyright Act of 1976 provides that

the owner of a copyright . . . has the exclusive rights to do and to authorize any of the following: (1) to reproduce the copyrighted work in copies . . . ; (2) to prepare derivative works based upon the copyrighted work; (3) to distribute copies . . . of the copyrighted work to the public . . . and (5) in the case of . . . pictorial . . . works . . . to display the copyrighted work publicly.

The court ruled that Frena had violated *Playboy*'s statutory and exclusive right to distribute copies of its photographs to the public:

Frena supplied a product containing unauthorized copies of a copyrighted work. It does not matter that Defendant Frena claims he did not make the copies himself.

The court also ruled that Frena had infringed *Playboy*'s display right— its exclusive right to show a copy of its work publicly, i.e., "at a place open to the public or . . . where a substantial number of persons outside of a normal circle of family and its social acquaintances is gathered."

In his defense, Frena argued that his conduct was protected by the "fair use" privilege under copyright law. But this defense was rejected. Frena's use was commercial (he provided his BBS to those who paid $25 per month or purchased products from him) and, according to the court, a presumptively unfair exploitation of *Playboy*'s rights. As the photographs in question may be characterized as fantasy and entertainment, continued the court, they are less susceptible to a fair use defense than factual works. The court also ruled, among other things, that "by pirating the photographs for which [*Playboy*] had become famous, Defendant Frena has taken a very important part of [*Playboy*'s] copyrighted publications." (In an aside, the court noted that it "is not implying that people do not read the articles in [*Playboy*'s] magazine.")

In a ruling that may startle the providers of online services, the court held Frena liable for copyright infringement despite the fact he may have been unaware of it. As stated by the court,

Intent to infringe is not needed to find copyright infringement. Intent or knowledge is not an element of infringement, and thus even an innocent infringer is liable for infringement; rather, innocence is significant to a trial court when it fixes statutory damages, which is a remedy equitable in nature.

Frena was also found guilty of trademark infringement. *Playboy*'s registered trademarks were used in the file descriptors for 170 images found on the BBS. Frena argued that he had never placed the words *Playboy* or *Playmate* onto the BBS. Instead, these words had been uploaded into the BBS index by subscribers to accompany material uploaded by them onto the BBS. Frena had, he claims, "innocently and without malice, allowed subscribers to upload whatever they wanted onto the BBS." But the court ruled that intent or bad faith is unnecessary for a violation of the Trademark Act (also known as the Lanham Act).

In a trademark case, the court observed, the central inquiry concerns "likelihood of confusion." "[L]ack of intent to deceive does nothing to alleviate confusion precipitated by similarity of trademarks." Here, the court found, "It is likely that customers of Defendant Frena would believe that [*Playboy*] was the source of Defendant Frena's images and that [*Playboy*] either sponsored, endorsed, or approved Defendant Frena's use of [*Playboy*] images."

In addition, Frena was held liable for unfair competition, which is broader than trademark infringement. Frena falsely inferred and described the origin of *Playboy*'s photographs. According to the court, Frena made it appear that *Playboy* had authorized Frena's product. He was also guilty of "reverse passing off," for removing *Playboy* trademarks from photographs. As stated by the court, Frena deleted *Playboy*'s text from *Playboy*'s photographs, to which he added his own text including his name, Techs Warehouse BBS, and telephone number.

The *Playboy* case was later settled by the parties. It was dismissed on January 31, 1994. (For further information on this case, see *Playboy Enterprises, Inc. v. Frena, et al.*, 839 F.Supp. 1552 (M.D. Fla. 1993).

Copyright and trademark infringement as well as unfair competition were also claims brought by Sega Enterprises Ltd. and Sega of America, Inc. against a computer bulletin board service (MAPHIA) and one of its system operators (Chad Scherman), who ran MAPHIA from his home, as well as several other individuals operating online computer bulletin boards and the boards themselves.

Sega is a manufacturer and distributor of computer video systems and games. Sega video games are stored in a cartridge on a read only memory (ROM) chip. While Sega games cannot be copied using the game console on which they run, they can be copied. PARSEC TRADING CO., affiliated with a network of BBS systems including MAPHIA, sells video game copiers called "Super Magic Drive" and

"Multi Game Hunter" that are capable of copying Sega games. Scherman admits that these copiers are used for making unauthorized copies of Sega games and in some instances to avoid purchasing Sega's game cartridges.

Scherman claims that the video game copiers could be used for game development and to make backup copies. The court, however, ruled that these "incidental capabilities have not been shown to be the primary use of such copiers" and, further, that there is no need to make backups as "the ROM cartridge format is not susceptible to breakdown and because defective cartridges are replaced by Sega."

On Sega's request for a preliminary injunction against Scherman and MAPHIA, the court found that MAPHIA BBS users uploaded unauthorized copies of Sega video games onto the BBS, that Scherman and the MAPHIA BBS knew of the uploading and downloading of unauthorized copies of Sega games (including "prerelease" versions), and that they specifically solicited and encouraged this activity. In fact, the court found evidence that a direct fee or barter was charged by MAPHIA or an affiliate for downloading privileges. A posting on the MAPHIA BBS included the following:

Thank you for purchasing a Console Back Up Unit (copier) from PARSEC TRADING. As a free bonus for ordering from Dark Age, you receive a COMPLEMENTARY Free Download Ratio on our Customer Support BBS. This is if you cannot get hold of SuperNintendo or Sega Genesis games. You can download up to 10 megabytes, which is equal to approximately 20 normal-sized SuperNintendo or Genesis games.

Scherman claimed that he did not profit from distribution of Sega's products. But, according to the court, Scherman profited from the operation of the BBS through direct payment and/or barter. In addition, ruled the court, Scherman profited indirectly by the existence of this "distribution network" for Sega games that increases the prestige of the MAPHIA BBS and also by the increased market for video game copiers and other goods or services sold by him. The court further noted that use of the BBS gave rise to increased telephone communications, which led to an increase in demand for telephone calling card numbers sold by Scherman.

On the issue of copyright infringement, the court held that Sega had established that unauthorized copies of its games were placed on the MAPHIA BBS by unknown users, with the knowledge of Scherman. Sega also established that unauthorized copies of its games were downloaded by users of the BBS, which copying was facilitated and encouraged by the MAPHIA BBS. Such activities, ruled the court, amount to contributory copyright infringement. Sega was also able to establish likelihood of success on its claims of direct copyright infringement based on Scherman's operation of the MAPHIA BBS.

Scherman raised a "fair use" defense to the copyright infringement claims, which was rejected by the court. To invoke a fair use defense, observed the court, "an individual must possess an authorized copy of a literary work." But Scherman admitted that he did not own any Sega games. The court also noted, among other things, that

Because users of the MAPHIA bulletin board are likely and encouraged to download Sega games therefrom to avoid having to buy video game cartridges from Sega, by which avoidance such users and Defendants both profit, the commercial purpose and character of the unauthorized copying weighs against a finding of fair use. . . .

Based on Defendants' own statement that 45,000 bulletin boards like MAPHIA operate in this country, it is obvious that should the unauthorized copying of Sega's video games by Defendants and others become widespread, there would be a substantial and immeasurable adverse effect on the market for Sega's copyrighted video game programs.

The court also found Sega likely to establish that Defendant's use of Sega's trademark in its file sections and file descriptors, as well as on programs made available and encouraged for downloading on the MAPHIA BBS, constitute trademark infringement. Sega was similarly likely to prevail on its claims of unfair competition and false designation of origin. On the trademark claim, the court noted,

[Sega] need not prove that any person actually has been mistaken because of Defendant's use [of Sega's trademark]. . . . Once a product is put into commerce, confusion, mistake, or deception occurring at some future time is sufficient to establish liability for trademark infringement.

Interestingly, in Sega's case a defense was raised under the Electronic Communications and Transactional Records Act (18 U.S.C. Section 2701(a)), which prohibits a person from "intentionally access[ing] without authorization a facility through which an electronic communication service is provided." Sega had collected evidence of the defendants' activities by having one of its employees access the MAPHIA BBS through use of a pseudonym, using information supplied by an authorized user who was an informant.

The court ruled that as the MAPHIA BBS was open to the public and normally accessed by the use of an alias or pseudonym, access by the Sega employee under a pseudonym was authorized. Further, the Electronic Communications and Transactional Records Act itself, observed the court, allows for access authorized by a user of an electronic service with respect to communications for that user. The court further ruled that failure to identify oneself in the course of an investigation does not provide a defense when such identification could have defeated the investigation.

In light of the above, the court confirmed the seizure of Scherman's computer and memory devices, among other things. (The memory had been copied and returned to Scherman with the Sega games deleted.) The court also issued a preliminary injunction against the defendants, requiring Sega to post a $50,000 bond as security for the injunction. (For further information on this case, see *Sega Enterprises Ltd., et al. v. MAPHIA, et al.*, No. C 93–4262 CW (N.D. Cal. 1994).

The *Playboy* and Sega video game cases should be read by operators of computer bulletin boards as indicators of the risks they run in operating those boards. In a 1991 case in New York concerning allegedly defamatory remarks published in a forum on CompuServe, on facts peculiar to that case the court found CompuServe to be a distributor to be judged under a standard of whether it knew or should have known of the allegedly defamatory remarks. But arguably the *Playboy* case sets a harsher standard of liability in copyright and trademark cases, i.e., that intent or knowledge are not necessary for liability. And in the Sega case, the court clears the way for surveillance of bulletin board systems.

The *Playboy* and Sega decisions will undoubtedly pressure bulletin board providers to monitor all that flows onto their boards. In the CompuServe case, the court recognized that imposing such a burden on the operator of an online service would place an impermissible burden on the First Amendment. (See *Cubby, Inc. v. CompuServe, Inc., et al.*, 776 F.Supp. 135 (S.D.N.Y. 1991).) This argument does not appear to have been raised in either the *Playboy* or Sega case, and it may offer an avenue of relief for providers. In the meantime, however, they have to beware and realize that their operations may lead to costly litigation and liability (civil and criminal).

[CyberLaw™ 7/94]

INFORMATION & INFRASTRUCTURE

As the pace of information technology quickens and increasing attention is paid to the national information infrastructure (NII), a working group chaired by the commissioner of patents and trademarks, Bruce Lehman, is examining the intellectual property implications of the NII. Lehman's Working Group on Intellectual Property Rights has issued a preliminary draft report, in which the Working Group reviews the state of the law and recommends certain changes in the Copyright Act, among other things. According to the Group, the nation's intellectual property laws are beginning to fit like a tight coat under the weight of technological innovation. "There is no need for a new [coat]," says the Group, "but the old one needs a few alterations."

The Working Group observes that under the Copyright Act, one fundamental test for copyright protection is fixation "in any tangible medium of expression, now known or later developed, from which [an original work of authorship] can be perceived, reproduced, or otherwise communicated, either directly or with the aid of a machine or device." Digital formats, such as floppy disks, CD-ROMs and other digital storage devices, have been found sufficiently stable so that works in such formats meet the fixation requirement. "Works are not sufficiently fixed if they are 'purely evanescent or transient' in nature," observes the Working Group. It questions, however, whether a work transmitted "live" via the NII, where no copy has been made prior to or simultaneous with transmission, meets the fixation requirement.

"Publication" was a key requirement for protection under the Copyright Act. Publication under the act is

the distribution of copies or phonorecords of a work to the public by sale or other transfer of ownership, or by rental, lease, or lending. The offering to distribute copies or phonorecords to a group of persons for purposes of further distribution, public performance or public display constitutes publication. A public performance, or display of a work does not of itself constitute publication.

This definition, notes the Working Group, was intended to make clear that there is no "publication" if a work does not change hands. If a sufficient number of copies of a work were offered to an online service (such as a bulletin board system) operator or others for upload onto the NII, the Group states that publication may occur.

Respecting "multimedia" works, the Working Group notes the terms "multimedia" and "mixed media" are misnomers. "In these works, it is the *types* or *categories* of works included that are "multiple" or "mixed"—not the *media*." Multimedia works are not categorized under the Copyright Act, but the Working Group is confident that they would be considered audiovisual works. Categorization of works, says the Working Group, "holds a great deal of significance under the Copyright Act." For example,

The public performance right is limited to 'literary, musical, dramatic, and choreographic works, pantomimes, and motion pictures and other audiovisual works. The public display right is limited to literary, musical, dramatic, and choreographic works, pantomimes, and pictorial, graphic, or sculptural works, including the individual images of a motion picture or other audiovisual work.

According to the Working Group, "increasing 'cross-breeding' of types of works demonstrates that categorization may no longer be useful. Its necessity is also questionable, except, perhaps, in the case of sound recordings, which are not granted the full panoply of rights."

The Copyright Act grants owners certain exclusive rights, including the right to reproduce a work. According to the Working Group, in the absence of a defense the reproduction right is infringed whenever a work is "uploaded" from a user's computer to a bulletin board system or other server, downloaded from such a system or server, or transferred from one computer network user to another. The Working Group also states that an infringing copy is made

When a work is placed into a computer, whether on a disk, diskette, ROM, or other storage device or in RAM for more than a very brief period. . . .

When a printed work is 'scanned' into a digital file. . . .

When other works—including photographs, motion pictures, or sound recordings—are digitized. . . .

Under current technology, when a user's computer is being used as a 'dumb' terminal to 'look at' a file resident on another computer (such as a BBS or Internet host). . . .

Modification of the content of a downloaded file, states the Group, is also an infringement of a copyright owner's right to prepare derivative works.

The right to distribute copies is another important right held by the copyright owner. But this right is qualified by the "first sale" doctrine, which allows the owner of a particular copy of a work to sell or otherwise dispose of possession of that copy. (Notably, the owner of a copy of a computer program may not rent, lease, or rent that copy for commercial advantage.) Concerned that an owner could retain a work and simply provide another person with a copy, the Group suggests that the first sale doctrine is not appropriate to transactions involving digitized works.

With the exception of sound recordings, the right to perform a work publicly is another of the exclusive rights granted by the Copyright Act. States the Working Group,

When any NII user visually 'browses' through copies of works in any medium (but not through a list of titles or other 'menus' that are not copies of the works), a public display occurs. A display is 'public' on the same terms as a 'performance'; therefore, virtually all NII uses would appear to fall within the law's current comprehension of 'public display.'

On the matter of "fair use" (which the Working Group believes to be a limitation on the rights of copyright owners, not a right of users), the Working Group acknowledges an argument that "the Copyright

Act would be unconstitutional if such limitations did not exist, as they provide some alleviation of First Amendment and other concerns." Given recent court decisions, the Group anticipates litigation in the gray area between commercial uses that involve no "transformative" use by users which "will likely always be infringing" and "nonprofit educational transformative uses [which] will likely often be fair." The Group foresees that "technological means of tracking transactions and licensing will lead to reduced application and scope of fair use."

A person who infringes on the exclusive rights of a copyright holder is an infringer of copyright. As held in a recent court decision, "innocent" infringement is infringement all the same. In cases where there is no direct evidence of copying, the original work may be compared with the alleged infringing work to determine whether the two are sufficiently similar to infer copying and, therefore, infringement. In cases where the end product is not substantially similar to a copyrighted work, the Working Group notes that a finding of infringement may be based on the initial input of a copyrighted work into a user's computer.

"Direct participation in infringing activity," notes the Working Group, "is not a prerequisite for infringement liability . . ." Infringement actions may be based on vicarious liability (e.g., a supervisor being held liable for the acts of an employee) or contributory infringement (e.g., a BBS operator who has knowledge of the uploading and downloading of unauthorized copies of a copyrighted video game, and who also solicited the copying).

On liability of operators of online systems for infringing material posted onto and downloaded from their systems, the Group notes that in one case an operator was held directly liable for the display and distribution of unauthorized copies of a copyrighted work, and in the other the operator was held liable for contributory infringement. (See *Playboy Enterprises Inc. v. Frena*, 839 F.Supp. 1552 (M.D. Fla. 1993), *Sega Enterprises Ltd. v. MAPHIA*, No. C 93-4262 CW, 1994 U.S.Dist. LEXIS 5266 (N.D. Cal. Mar. 28, 1994).) Two recent libel cases may also provide guidance in this area. In those cases (one involving a television network and the other involving CompuServe), liability was not imposed for transmission of alleged defamatory material where it could not be shown that the defendant did not know or have reason to know of the defamatory content of the material at issue. (See *Auvil v. CBS "60 Minutes"*, 800 F.Supp. 928 (E.D. Wash. 1992), *Cubby, Inc. v. CompuServe, Inc.*, 776 F.Supp. 135 (S.D.N.Y. 1991).)

Other subjects reviewed by the Working Group include conflict of laws issues, international copyright treaties (with a focus on the principle of national treatment), copyright harmonization, private copying royalty systems, moral rights, patent and trademark law (the first case on the relationship between trademarks and Internet site names is pending).

Technology may, of course, be used to restrict unauthorized access to copyrighted works. The Working Group discusses encryption as a method for controlling access at the file level, and notes that there is an ongoing review of government policy concerning export of computer and networking technologies. (The Group notes that the Audio Home Recording Act requires recording and interface devices to control serial copying.) "Software-based systems for tracking and monitoring uses of copyrighted works," says the Group, "are contemplated in the development of the NII." Electronic licenses, "analogous to the 'shrink-wrapped' licenses used for prepackaged software," may also be used in connection with works offered through the NII.

The Working Group also recommends that amendments to the Copyright Act, as it finds the pace of technological advance has outstripped intellectual property law. First, the Group recommends that the Copyright Act be amended to make clear that copies of a work can be distributed to the public by transmission, and that this is within the exclusive distribution right of the copyright owner. The Group also suggests that the term "publication" include the concept of distribution by transmission, and that import prohibitions be amended to reflect that copies of copyrighted works can be imported by transmission.

Second, the Group would limit the first sale doctrine so that it does not apply where the owner of a copy transmits a copy of it to another. The reason for this is the owner has not relinquished possession of the particular copy owned.

Third, the Group would prohibit the "importation, manufacture and distribution of devices, as well as the provision of services, that defeat anti-copying systems." Interestingly, the Group includes a gaping loophole in its proposed legislation, allowing that such actions may be taken "with the authority of the copyright owner or the law."

Fourth, the Group seeks to prohibit the fraudulent inclusion, removal, or alteration of copyright management information. Such information might include the name of the copyright owner and terms and conditions for use of the work, among other things.

Fifth, a public performance right for sound recordings is suggested.

There are a number of other issues discussed by the Working Group. It will be sponsoring a conference to develop guidelines for fair uses of copyrighted works by schools and public libraries. Another conference will be held on intellectual property education.

[CyberLaw™ 9/94]

APPLE LOSES

I. A Compromise Agreement

In John Sculley's book *Odyssey*, he describes a conflict that arose between Microsoft Corp. and Apple Computer, Inc. in November 1985. Sculley recounts that Microsoft was developing a program called "Windows" which would give IBM computers Macintosh-like graphic features. Microsoft's Bill Gates called Sculley and said he was upset to hear that Apple was about to sue Microsoft. If this were true Gates wanted to hear it from Sculley. According to Sculley, Gates continued: "[I]f we are on a collision course, I want to know it because we'll stop all development on Mac products. I hope we can find a way to settle this thing." Sculley recognized that Apple could not sue its most important software supplier—"the only company developing successful software for the Macintosh in a turbulent time." So they "hammered out a compromise license agreement, which," says Sculley, "was satisfactory to Microsoft yet protected the integrity of our Macintosh technology for Apple." Almost ten years later, that agreement insulated Microsoft from liability on copyright claims over the graphical user interface (GUI) in Apple's Lisa and Macintosh computers.

II. Licensing Visual Displays

In *Apple Computer, Inc. v. Microsoft Corp., Hewlett-Packard Co.*, No. 93–16833 (9th Cir. Sept. 19, 1994), the Ninth Circuit Court of Appeal reviewed Apple's appeal of judgments entered in favor of Microsoft and Hewlett-Packard by a district court, and paid particular attention to the 1985 agreement. In the agreement, Microsoft acknowledged "that the visual displays in Windows 1.0 are derivative works of the visual displays generated by Apple's Lisa and Macintosh graphical user interface programs." Apple, for its part, granted Microsoft "a non-exclusive, royalty-free, nontransferable license 'to use these derivative works in present and future software programs and to license them' to third parties for use in new software programs."

On appeal, Apple claimed that the agreement does not permit later Windows products to look more like the Macintosh than Windows 1.0 looked. The Ninth Circuit noted that the agreement licenses use of "derivative works," which refer to the visual displays generated by Apple's Lisa and Macintosh GUI programs. Dismissing Apple's claim, the Ninth Circuit quoted the lower court:

> Had it been the parties' intent to limit the license to the Windows 1.0 interface, they would have known how to say so. Instead, the 'derivative works' covered by the license are identified as the 'visual displays' in the Windows 1.0 interface, not the interface itself.

The Ninth Circuit also observed that Apple had tried to limit Microsoft's license to Windows 1.0. But Microsoft rejected Apple's first draft of the agreement incorporating such a limitation.

Apple further argued that the lower court's interpretation of the agreement is wrong because "it would be unreasonable to suppose that Apple knowingly gave away its most valuable technological asset. . . ." But, says the Ninth Circuit, Apple did receive value sufficient legally to support the agreement, including Microsoft's agreement to release an improved version of Microsoft Word for the Macintosh and to delay release of an IBM-compatible version of Excel.

III. Authorized Copying

On whether the "total concept and feel" (i.e., the selection and arrangement of related images and their animation) of the Macintosh GUI had been unlawfully copied by Microsoft and Hewlett-Packard, the Ninth Circuit observed that it does "not start at ground zero." The outcome of Apple's infringement claims is "fundamentally affect[ed]" by the fact that Apple "*licensed* the right to copy almost all of its visual displays." As noted by the Ninth Circuit,

> Authorized copying accounts for more than 90% of the allegedly infringing features in Windows 2.03 and 3.0, and two-thirds of the features in New Wave. More than that, the 1985 Agreement and the negotiations leading up to Microsoft's license left Apple no right to complain that selection and arrangement of *licensed* elements make the interface as a whole look more 'Mac-like' than Windows 1.0.

IV. An Infringement Test

For Apple to prevail on its copyright infringement claims, it had to prove ownership of a valid copyright and that Microsoft and Hewlett-Packard had copied unlicensed, protected elements of its copyrighted work. Such copying might be shown by direct or indirect evidence.

In cases where copying is sought to be proved by indirect evidence, the Ninth Circuit utilizes a two-part test with "extrinsic" and "intrinsic" components:

> [T]he extrinsic test . . . objectively considers whether there are substantial similarities in both ideas and expression, whereas the intrinsic test . . . measure[s] expression

subjectively. Because only those elements of a work that are protectable and used without the author's permission can be compared when it comes to the ultimate question of illicit copying, we use analytic dissection to determine the scope of copyright protection before works are considered 'as a whole.' (Citations omitted.)

Implementing this test, the Ninth Circuit requires a plaintiff to identify the source of the alleged similarity between its work and the alleged infringing work. The court then determines whether any of the allegedly similar features are protected by copyright. If, as in Apple's case, a license is involved, the court determines which features a defendant is entitled to copy. After separating the protectable from the unprotectable features, the court applies certain limiting doctrines. Next, the court determines the degree of protection to be afforded the plaintiff's work (e.g., "broad" or "thin") and the standard "for a subjective comparison of the works to determine whether, as a whole, they are sufficiently similar to support a finding of illicit copying."

V. Unprotectable Features

The ideas of a graphical user interface and a desktop metaphor are embodied in the Macintosh GUI. Neither are protectable, as confirmed by the Ninth Circuit. Ideas embodied in the desktop metaphor also are not protectable, including use of windows to display multiple display images, iconic representation of familiar objects from the office environment, manipulation of icons to convey instructions and to control operation of the computer, use of menus, and opening and closing objects as a means of retrieving, transferring, and storing information. Apple's use of animation, overlapping windows, and well-designed icons were licensed to Microsoft and therefore also found not protectable.

The limiting principles implicated in this case, as found by the Ninth Circuit, are "merger," "*scenes a faire*," and "originality." Under the merger doctrine, "when an idea and its expression are indistinguishable, or 'merged,' the expression will only be protected against nearly identical copying." Similarly, under the doctrine of *scenes a faire*,

when similar features in a videogame [—a work viewed as closely analogous to a GUI—] are '"as a practical matter indispensable, or at least standard, in the treatment of a given [idea],'" they are treated like ideas and are therefore not protected by copyright. Furthermore, . . . "the mere *indispensable* expression of these ideas, based on the technical requirements of the videogame medium, may be protected only against virtually identical copying." (Citations omitted.)

Here, the Ninth Circuit observed that "use of overlapping windows inheres in the idea of windows." Protected similarity could not be based on the use of overlapping windows, but "Apple's *particular expression* may be protected." The Ninth Circuit also noted that GUIs are partly artistic and functional, stating:

To the extent that GUIs are artistic, there is no dispute that creativity . . . is constrained by power and speed of computers. . . . Design alternatives are further limited by the GUI's purpose of making interaction between the user and the computer more "user friendly." These, and similar environmental and ergonomic factors which limit the range of possible expression in GUIs, properly inform the scope of copyright protection.

On originality, the Ninth Circuit recognized that "protection extends only to those components of a work that are original to the author, although original selection and arrangement of otherwise uncopyrightable components may be protectable." For example, the Ninth Circuit upheld the denial of protection to certain GUI items because of Apple's admitted heavy borrowing from iconic treatments in the Xerox Star and an IBM Pictureworld research report. The Ninth Circuit also found that even if certain folder and page icon designs were original to Apple, they "added so little to the mix of protectable material that the outcome could not reasonably be affected."

In its appeal, Apple complained that the lower court had twisted its arm to provide a list of features in its work that were similar to features in Windows 2.03, 3.0, and New Wave (a product of Hewlett-Packard). According to Apple, the court was only to consider the works as a whole. But the Ninth Circuit found Apple's complaint misplaced—the lower court was justified in requesting a list of similarities for use in meeting its obligation to identify similarities, determine their source, and decide which elements of the GUI are protectable. Moreover, the lower court had numerous demonstrations of the GUI as a whole.

VI. Virtual Identity & Attorneys' Fees

In light of the above, the Ninth Circuit held that any claim of infringement Apple may have against Microsoft "must rest on the copying of Apple's *unique selection and arrangement*" of the protectable and unlicensed features Apples claimed were copied. Further, ruled the Ninth Circuit, the Macintosh GUI only qualifies for "thin" protection, i.e., against virtually identical copying.

Apple contested this virtual identity standard, but the Ninth Circuit rejected the claim because Apple had failed to do so before the lower court at the appropriate time. The Ninth Circuit similarly dismissed Apple's claim that a jury should have evaluated the works side-by-side, as Apple had elected not to have a jury do so.

The suit between the parties was not fully resolved by the Ninth Circuit. It was sent back to the lower court for reconsideration in accordance with a recent decision by the U.S. Supreme Court on the award of attorneys' fees to prevailing defendants.

VII. Looking to Lotus

Many in the computer industry will be disappointed by the Apple decision because it was considerably influenced by the license given to Microsoft by Apple. The Ninth Circuit did not resolve a number of open questions about the scope of copyright protection that may be afforded nonliteral aspects of computer software, i.e., the "total concept and feel" as opposed to the actual code of the software. More definitive answers will be provided by the decision on the appeal currently pending between Lotus Development Corp. and Borland International, Inc. over alleged infringement of Lotus 1-2-3.

[CyberLaw™ 12/94]

PHOTOCOPYING UNLAWFUL

I. Employer Found Liable

Has a court decision "ended fair-use photocopying with respect to a large population of journals?" Will it "require that an intellectual property lawyer be posted at each copy machine?" In a recent case over photocopying articles from a scholarly journal, the U.S. Court of Appeals for the Second Circuit held a researcher's employer liable for copyright infringement. (*American Geophysical Union v. Texaco Inc.*, No. 92–9341 (2d Cir. Oct. 28, 1994).) The Second Circuit recommended that the employer either purchase more subscriptions to the journal or obtain a license to produce photocopies of the articles. This decision is important as it rules unlawful a widespread activity long considered reasonable and customary, and makes clear that technological advances are leading courts and industries to rethink matters previously thought settled.

II. Researcher Copies Articles

American Geophysical Union and eighty-two other publishers of scientific and technical journals filed a class action copyright infringement suit against Texaco, claiming that the company had engaged in unauthorized copying of articles from their journals. Texaco, in response, claimed that its copying was a fair use, and the parties agreed to an initial trial on this defense. To promote efficiency, the parties agreed that the trial would exclusively focus on the photocopying of particular journal articles by one Texaco researcher.

Texaco employs between 400 and 500 researchers nationwide. One of them is Dr. Donald H. Chickering II, a scientist at a Texaco research center in Beacon, New York. His files contain copies of eight articles appearing in the *Journal of Catalysis*, a monthly publication produced by a major publisher of scholarly journals named Academic Press, Inc. Since 1988, Texaco has purchased three subscriptions to the journal for its Beacon facility.

Chickering himself, or other Texaco employees at his behest, copied eight journal articles in their entirety. The Second Circuit observed that Chickering "apparently believed . . . these articles would facilitate his current or future research." Chickering did not, however, generally use the journal articles immediately, "but placed the photocopied articles in his files to have them available for later reference as needed." Chickering did not use five of the eight copied articles.

III. Photocopying & Fair Use

Following the initial trial, the district court held that Texaco's photocopying of the articles for Chickering did not constitute a fair use. Texaco appealed.

Upon appeal, the Second Circuit identified the issue to be decided to be whether copying of the eight articles was properly determined not to be a fair use. Broad issues not expressly addressed by the Second Circuit include, "whether photocopying of scientific articles is fair use, or at least the only more slightly limited issue of whether photocopying of such articles is fair use when undertaken by a research scientist employed at a for-profit corporation."

The fair use doctrine is codified in 17 U.S.C. Section 107:

[T]he fair use of a copyrighted work, including such use by reproduction in copies . . . for purposes such as criticism, comment, news reporting, teaching (including multiple copies for classroom use), scholarship, or research, is not an infringement of copyright. In determining whether the use made of a work in any particular case is a fair use the factors to be considered shall include—

(1) the purpose and character of the use, including whether such use is of a commercial nature or is for nonprofit educational purposes;
(2) the nature of the copyrighted work;
(3) the amount and substantiality of the portion used in relation to the copyrighted work as a whole; and
(4) the effect of the use upon the potential market for or value of the copyrighted work.

The fact that a work is unpublished shall not itself bar a finding of fair use if such finding is made upon consideration of all the above factors.

The doctrine of fair use, explains the Second Circuit, is "[t]raditionally conceived as based on authors' implied consent to reasonable uses of their work . . . or on an exception to authors' monopoly privileges needed in order to fulfill copyright's purpose to promote the arts and sciences." (Citations omitted.) The Second Circuit warns, however, that

the invention and widespread availability of photocopying technology threatens to disrupt the delicate balances established by the Copyright Act. . . . Indeed, if the issue were open, we would seriously question whether the fair use analysis that has developed with respect to works of authorship alleged to use portions of copyrighted material is precisely applicable to copies produced by mechanical means. . . . Mechanical 'copying' of an entire document . . . is obviously an activity entirely different from creating a work of authorship.

IV. Archival Photocopying

Analyzing the case under the four factors in Section 107, the Second Circuit looked first to "the purpose and character of the use." Here, Chickering had six of the eight articles photocopied after seeing them in the original copy of the journal containing each of them. He did so, "at least initially, for the same basic purpose that one would normally seek to obtain the original—to have it available on his shelf for ready reference if and when he needed to look at it." (Five of the articles were never used at all.)

Chickering's copying served other purposes, including avoiding damage to the original and freeing him from having to cart around the entire issue. The Second Circuit allowed that it may have been a fair use if Chickering had bought a copy of the journal, placed it on his shelf, noticed he wanted a chart, formula, or other material to take into the lab, asked the library to make a photocopy to use in the lab, and then used it in the lab "(especially if he did not retain it and build up a mini-library of photocopied articles.)" Here, however, Chickering's photocopying was "archival," leading the Second Circuit to rule against Texaco on the first factor.

Texaco raised a number of significant arguments on the first factor that were rejected. Texaco claimed that the purpose of the copying was for research, but the Second Circuit dismissed this on the grounds that

Chickering has not used portions of articles from *Catalysis* in his own published piece of research, nor has he had to duplicate some portion of copyrighted material directly in the course of conducting an experiment or investigation. Rather, entire articles were copied as an intermediate step that might abet Chickering's research.

Similarly, the Second Circuit rejected Texaco's objection that the district court had placed undue reliance on the fact that Texaco is a for-profit corporation conducting research primarily for commercial gain. While Texaco was not gaining direct or indirect commercial gain through the photocopying, the Second Circuit recognized that the copying "could be regarded simply as another 'factor of production' utilized in Texaco's efforts to develop profitable products."

V. Not a Reasonable Practice

Texaco also made the important point that Chickering's photocopying "constitutes a use that has historically been considered 'reasonable and customary.'" But the Second Circuit held this argument today to be "insubstantial." Quoting the district court,

> To the extent the copying practice was 'reasonable' in 1973 . . . it has ceased to be 'reasonable' as the reasons that justified it before [photocopying licensing] have ceased to exist.

VI. Factual Works

Having lost on the first statutory factor, Texaco did win the second concerning the nature of the copyrighted work. The scope of fair use is greater for factual rather than nonfactual works. The journal articles at issue were predominantly factual and, noted the Second Circuit, "the evidence suggests that Chickering was interested exclusively in the facts, ideas, concepts, or principles contained within the articles."

VII. Entire Works Copied

The Second Circuit did find against Texaco on the third factor, the amount and substantiality of the portion used in relation to the copyrighted work as a whole. Rejecting the claim that what was copied only constitutes a small portion of the total compendium of works encompassed by the journal, the Second Circuit observed that each article is an original work of authorship entitled to copyright protection. The Second Circuit concluded, accordingly, that Texaco copied entire "works."

VIII. Lost Licensing Revenue

The "single most important element of fair use," says the Second Circuit, is the fourth factor, "the effect of the use upon the potential market for or value of the copyrighted work." This factor is "concerned with the category of a defendant's conduct, not merely specific instances of copying."

Here, the Second Circuit recognized, there is "no traditional market for, nor a clearly defined value of, individual journal articles." Writers of academic and scientific articles are not paid anything other than "the reward of being published, publication being a key to professional advancement and prestige for the author." Publishers have traditionally published these articles only in journal format. Reprints are "usually available from publishers only in bulk quantities and with some delay." On "the effect of Texaco's photocopying upon the potential market for or value of these individual articles," the Second Circuit found that in the absence of photocopying Texaco would not purchase back issues or enormously enlarge the number or its subscriptions to the journal.

The publishers were able to prevail on the fourth factor, however, primarily because of lost licensing revenue:

Though the publishers still have not established a conventional market for the direct sale and distribution of individual articles, they have created, primarily through the [Copyright Clearance Center Inc.], a workable market for institutional users to obtain licenses for the right to produce their own copies of individual articles via photocopying. The District Court found that many major corporations now subscribe to the CCC system for photocopying licenses. Since the Copyright Act explicitly provides that copyright holders have the 'exclusive rights' to 'reproduce' and 'distribute copies' of their works, see 17 U.S.C. Sections 106(1) & (3), and since there currently exists a viable market for licensing these rights for individual journal articles, it is appropriate that potential licensing revenues for photocopying be considered in a fair use analysis. (Citation omitted.)

IX. Music Companies Do It

In light of the above, the Second Circuit ruled that Texaco's copying did not constitute a fair use. In the face of criticism that its ruling "has ended fair-use photocopying with respect to a large population of journals" or "would seem to require that an intellectual property lawyer be posted at each copy machine," the Second Circuit noted the "ease with which music royalties have been collected and distributed for performances at thousands of cabarets, without the attendance of intellectual property lawyers in any capacity other than as customers." The Second Circuit recommended that Texaco use the existing licensing scheme if it wishes to continue this copying, or purchase one more subscription for each researcher who wants to keep journal issues on the office shelf. The Second Circuit also suggested that if the parties could not settle this case, it might explore the possibility of a court-imposed compulsory license.

[CyberLaw™ 3/95]

METHODS OF OPERATION

I. The Opposition Awakes

After a district court in Massachusetts held Borland International Inc. liable for infringing Lotus 1-2-3, several third-party briefs were filed in opposition to the decision in conjunction with Borland's appeal. A number of computer scientists advised the U.S. Court of Appeals for the First Circuit that if upheld, the district court's rulings "will have a catastrophic impact on the computer software industry." This group included Marvin Minsky (an MIT professor and one of the founders of artificial intelligence), John McCarthy (a Stanford University professor and developer of the Lisp programming language as well as the concept of time-sharing computer systems), and Chris Hofstader of the League for Programming Freedom, among others. Other briefs in opposition to the district court were filed by the American Committee for Interoperable Systems (ACIS), an informal organization of companies that develop computer software and hardware products that interoperate with computer systems developed by other companies; copyright law professors from around the nation; the Software Entrepreneurs' Forum, a non-profit group (based in Silicon Valley) of more than one thousand independent software developers, consultants, and software providers; and eighteen computer user groups. It is not possible to measure the extent to which these arguments influenced the First Circuit, but they make clear that a wide range of persons are concerned about the direction taken by courts in their application of intellectual property laws to the computer industry. Notably, many of their arguments were endorsed in the First Circuit's recent decision reversing the district court and finding that Borland had not infringed Lotus's copyright.

II. Compatibility Attacked

After three years of development, in 1987 Borland released its first Quattro program, a spreadsheet program that, according to Borland, "included enormous innovations over competing spreadsheet products." In Quattro and Quattro Pro Version 1.0, Borland placed a virtually identical copy of the entire 1-2-3 menu tree, including the words and structure of 1-2-3's menu command hierarchy. Borland, however, did not copy any of Lotus 1-2-3's underlying code. The 1-2-3 menu command hierarchy was used in Borland's products so that users familiar with 1-2-3 would be able to switch to Borland's programs without having to learn new commands or rewrite their 1-2-3 macros.

In Quattro and Quattro Pro Version 1.0, users were offered a "Lotus Emulation Interface" to allow them to interact with the Borland programs as though they were using 1-2-3, "albeit with a slightly different-looking screen and with many Borland options not available on Lotus 1-2-3." According to the First Circuit,

> In effect, Borland allowed users to choose how they wanted to communicate with Borland's spreadsheet programs: either by using menu commands designed by Borland, or by using the commands and command structure used in Lotus 1-2-3 augmented by Borland-added commands.

In July 1990, Lotus Development Corp. sued Borland. The suit came four days after a district court had held that 1-2-3's "menu structure, taken as a whole—including the choice of menu command terms [and] the structure and order of those terms," was protected expression covered by Lotus's copyrights. *Lotus Dev. Corp. v. Paperback Software Int'l*, 740 F.Supp. 37, 68, 70 (D. Mass. 1990). In July 1992, the district court ruled that Lotus's menu command hierarchy is copyrightable expression because "[a] very satisfactory spreadsheet menu tree can be constructed using different commands and a different command structure from those of Lotus 1-2-3." The district court also held that Borland had infringed Lotus's copyright and concluded that a jury trial was needed to determine the extent of copying by Borland.

Following these rulings, Borland removed the Lotus Emulation Interface from its products. Borland's products retained partial compatibility with Lotus 1-2-3 through use of Quattro Pro's "Key Reader," which allowed Borland's programs to understand and perform some 1-2-3 macros. This meant, however, that users could no longer debug or modify macros or run most interactive macros. In response, Lotus filed a supplemental complaint alleging that Key Reader infringed its copyright. And Borland was allowed to amend its answer to raise a defense of "fair use."

The district court later held that Borland failed to show that its use of the Lotus 1-2-3 menu command hierarchy in the Emulation Interface was a fair use. The district court also held that Key Reader infringed Lotus's copyright and rejected Borland's defenses, including fair use.

III. Operation & Copyright

Borland appealed to the First Circuit, arguing that among other things, "the Lotus menu command hierarchy is not copyrightable because it is a system, method of operation, process, or procedure foreclosed from protection by 17 U.S.C. [Section] 102(b)." According to Borland, the outcome here was decided by the United States Supreme Court over one hundred years ago, in a case over a textbook explaining a new way to do accounting. In that case, the Supreme Court held that the copyright over the textbook did not grant a monopoly on the use of the accounting system. *Baker v. Selden*, 101 U.S. 99 (1879).

But the First Circuit did not agree that *Baker v. Selden* is as analogous as Borland urges. Here, Lotus does not claim a copyright over its accounting system. The subject of this appeal, observed the First Circuit, is "Lotus's monopoly over the commands it uses to operate the computer." And the first question to be considered is "whether the menu command hierarchy as a whole can be copyrighted."

Section 102(b) of the Copyright Act provides that

In no case does copyright protection for an original work of authorship extend to any idea, procedure, process, system, method of operation, concept, principle, or discovery, regardless of the form in which it is described, explained, illustrated, or embodied in such work.

According to the First Circuit, the Lotus 1-2-3 menu command hierarchy is an unprotectable "method of operation." The First Circuit explains that the Lotus command hierarchy provides the means by which users control and operate Lotus 1-2-3. It "does not merely explain and present Lotus 1-2-3's functional capabilities to the user; it also serves as the method by which the program is operated and controlled."

The district court had reasoned that the Lotus menu command hierarchy constitutes an "expression" of the "idea" of operating a computer program with commands arranged hierarchically into menus and submenus. Lotus made specific choices and an arrangement of command terms. Although competitors were free also to use commands employed in a hierarchy to operate their programs, the district court held that they are not free to use the specific command terms and arrangement that Lotus had used.

Although there may be some expressive choices in "choosing and arranging the Lotus command terms," the First Circuit holds that such expression is not copyrightable because it is part of Lotus 1-2-3's "method of operation":

If specific words are essential to operating something, then they are part of a "method of operation" and, as such, are unprotectable. This is so whether they must be highlighted, typed in, or even spoken, as computer programs no doubt will soon be controlled by spoken words.

Whether the Lotus command menu could have been designed differently is "immaterial," says the First Circuit, "to the question of whether it is a 'method of operation.'" Expressive choices "do not magically change the uncopyrightable menu command hierarchy into copyrightable subject matter."

IV. VCR's, Users, & Macros

According to the First Circuit, the Lotus command terms are not even equivalent to the labels on the buttons of a video cassette recorder (VCR). They are, instead, "equivalent to the buttons themselves." One cannot operate a VCR without buttons and one cannot operate Lotus 1-2-3 without its menu command hierarchy.

Importantly, the First Circuit explained its position with the computer user in mind:

Under Lotus's theory, if a user uses several different programs, he or she must learn how to perform the same operation in a different way for each program used. For example, if the user wanted the computer to print material, then the user would have to learn not just one method of operating the computer such that it prints, but many different methods. We find this absurd. The fact that there may be many different ways to operate a computer program, or even many different ways to operate a computer program using a set of hierarchically arranged command terms, does not make the actual method of operation chosen copyrightable; it still functions as a method for operating the computer and as such is uncopyrightable. . . .

Under the district court's holding, if the user wrote a macro to shorten the time needed to perform a certain operation in Lotus 1-2-3, the user would be unable to use that macro to shorten the time needed to perform that same operation in another program. Rather, the user would have to rewrite his or her macro using that other program's menu command hierarchy. This is despite the fact that the macro is clearly the user's own work product. We think that forcing the user to cause the computer to perform the same operation in a different way ignores Congress's direction in [Section] 102(b) that "methods of operation" are not copyrightable. That programs can offer users the ability to write macros in many different ways does not change the fact that, once written, the macro allows the user to perform an operation automatically.

V. On Keying Procedures

In reversing the district court and finding that Borland did not infringe the Lotus copyright by copying the 1-2-3 menu command hierarchy, the First Circuit noted that its decision is at odds with a decision by the Tenth Circuit in *Autoskill, Inc. v. National Educ. Support Sys., Inc.*, 994 F.2d 1476 (10th Cir.), *cert. denied*, 114 S.Ct. 307 (1993). In *Autoskill*, the court there rejected the argument that a keying procedure requiring students to respond to program inquiries by pressing the 1, 2, or 3 keys is uncopyrightable. The First Circuit remarks, "we fail to see how 'a student selecting a response by pressing the 1, 2, or 3 keys,' can be anything but an unprotectable method of operation."

[CyberLaw™ 4/95]

INTERNET INFRINGEMENT

I. To Silence a Critic

Will a new copyright infringement suit "prompt the dismantlement of the Internet [by establishing] a precedent whereby every user faces the potential of committing copyright infringement simply by the act of accessing the Internet." In this case, the Church of Scientology has pursued a critic over the Internet and into his home, demanding the seizure of literary works belonging to the church. The church also claims that his use of the works, including postings to an Internet newsgroup, constitutes copyright infringement and theft of trade secrets. To ensure that this critic is effectively silenced and deprived of access to a "press," the church has sued his Internet providers, alleging that they are guilty of the same offenses. At first, a federal court issued a restraining order against all defendants. The order against the access providers was later dissolved. But the church has renewed its efforts against them—threatening extension of copyright infringement liability, says one of the defendants, that "would impact, and possibly create liability for, each of the estimated thirty-six million users of the Internet."

II. Scientology Sues

Religious Technology Center and Bridge Publications Inc., California non-profit corporations (collectively, "Scientology"), are owners of rights to published and unpublished works of L. Ron Hubbard, founder of the Scientology religion. On February 8, 1995, Scientology sued a vocal critic of the church (Dennis Erlich), an Internet provider based in San Jose, California (Netcom On-Line Communication Services, Inc.), and the operator of an electronic bulletin board service (Tom Klemesrud) that links to the Internet through a connection provided by Netcom.

Scientology explains that Erlich is a former Scientologist who served the Churches of Scientology in various capacities between 1968 and 1982. While with the churches, Erlich received ministerial training and was provided access to a wide variety of written materials about the religion and its services. Erlich also allegedly agreed that he would "protect and maintain confidential" all information contained in certain unpublished Scientology works disclosed to him. In 1982, Erlich left the religion and, according to Scientology, engaged in activities "hostile to the Religion."

Scientology complains that Erlich engaged in unauthorized copying of published and unpublished literary works of L. Ron Hubbard, and that he published them on the Internet. Scientology further alleges that no one has access to the unpublished works without permission. Erlich "could only have obtained copies of these materials," says Scientology, "through his own theft, or by having received stolen property from another." Scientology claims that 154 pages of L. Ron Hubbard's literary works were copied unlawfully.

Netcom and Tom Klemesrud find themselves in this case because Scientology alleges that Erlich used their computer facilities to publish unauthorized copies of Hubbard's works in an Internet newsgroup named "alt.religion.scientology." In so doing, Scientology alleges that Netcom and Klemesrud have themselves infringed Scientology's copyrights. Scientology also alleges that Erlich, Netcom, and Klemesrud have engaged in trade secret misappropriation.

Scientology demanded that Erlich cease and desist in his reproduction and publication of Scientology documents, but according to Scientology,

Erlich . . . has made defiant responses to [Scientology] claiming the right to violate [Scientology's] rights. He has said that no local government or court in the U.S. has the power to tell him otherwise.

Scientology asked the U.S. district court in San Jose, California, to issue a temporary restraining order against Erlich, Netcom, and Klemesrud. (Notably, Scientology requested that this order be issued, in the first instance, without giving the defendants an opportunity to present their arguments to the contrary at a noticed hearing.) Citing the defendants' alleged refusal to stop their activities despite multiple requests, Scientology requested an order requiring them to refrain from violating Scientology copyrights and violating California trade secrets laws by making unauthorized reproductions of L. Ron Hubbard's works on the Internet or other databases. Among other things, Scientology requested impoundment of all unauthorized copies of Hubbard's works in the possession of Erlich, Netcom, and Klemesrud.

In support of its application for a temporary restraining order, Scientology asserts that "the difficulty of measuring the extent of injury to plaintiffs through Internet publication is justification itself for granting a temporary restraining order, since any remedy at law would be inadequate" (i.e., could not be compensated with a grant of money damages). Scientology adds,

[T]he unauthorized publication of the works is over an international network of computer networks which potentially exposes the infringements to 25 million users, with the attendant risk that the works could be copied and recopied virtually without limit. Plaintiffs have no control over the copying by the defendants and others, and that lack of control constitutes irreparable injury [also] sufficient to support the issuance of a preliminary injunction.

On February 10, 1995, the U.S. District Court issued the requested restraining order. *Religious Technology Center, et al. v. Netcom On-Line Communication Services, Inc., et al.*, Case No. C-95 20091 RMW (N.D. Cal. 2/10/95). Pending a hearing on whether a preliminary injunction should issue, the court restrained Erlich, Netcom, and Klemesrud, as well as persons working for or in concert with them, from unauthorized copying and publication of L. Ron Hubbard's copyrighted works, and from disclosing, displaying, or reproducing the unpublished confidential works of L. Ron Hubbard, among other things. In addition, the court issued a seizure order against Erlich and required Scientology to post a $25,000 bond.

III. Defending the Internet

A week later, Netcom filed its opposition to Scientology's request for injunctive relief. Describing itself as a company that "simply markets a computer program and maintains a computer switch which allows its subscribers to access the Internet themselves," Netcom states that it "does not maintain any database, bulletin board or any content-based service for its subscribers, except as a means of communicating to them or facilitating communications among them about the NETCOM service." Along with "tens of thousands of others," Netcom "is a link for USENET News, a world-wide distribution chain for local postings on a BBS."

Netcom notes that Klemesrud is a Netcom subscriber. Members of Klemesrud's service access the Internet via a connection he maintains with Netcom. There are five hundred members of Klemesrud's bulletin board service, with access to about nine hundred Usenet newsgroups via Netcom.

Netcom explains that Erlich, apparently a subscriber to Klemesrud's service, is able to dial into Klemesrud's computer and cause that computer to generate messages that are, in turn, posted to any number of newsgroup categories on the Usenet. One of the newsgroups is dedicated to discussing Scientology, and this is the newsgroup to which Erlich allegedly posted Scientology materials.

Netcom notes that "[a]ny material posted to a USENET newsgroup will eventually end up being transmitted to everyone on the USENET system, no matter where the message is posted from." "Any material loaded onto the Internet from any source connected to USENET," observes Netcom, "will eventually end up on the NETCOM system, whether or not it is generated by a NETCOM subscriber and whether or not the subscriber is 'cut off' by NETCOM."

According to Netcom,

[Scientology is] seeking to obtain an order from this Court that has never previously been granted by a court, or to defendant NETCOM's knowledge, ever even requested of a court. [Scientology demands] an unprecedented extension of [copyright] infringement liability that, if recognized by this Court, would impact each of the estimated 36 million users of the Internet.

If granted, says Netcom, the requested relief "will fundamentally alter the functioning of the world's largest electronic public library and potentially expose each of its millions of users to unlimited tort liability."

The temporary restraining order against it is unnecessary, claims Netcom, because the alleged offending material has already been seized from Erlich. There is no imminent threat that Erlich will continue his allegedly infringing practices. If the court were to find a basis for issuing an order against Erlich, says Netcom, that order would entirely address Scientology's claims.

Netcom contends that it cannot, in fact, terminate Erlich's access to the Internet. Erlich is not a Netcom subscriber and has no direct relationship with it. Scientology's demand, if granted by the court, would require Netcom to terminate services to Klemesrud—a step that would defeat Erlich's Internet access through that BBS and simultaneously cut off Klemesrud's five hundred active subscribers. The law, says Netcom, does not countenance such collective responsibility of individuals against whom Scientology alleges no wrongful act.

IV. Passive Transmitters

Scientology's attempt to assert liability over Netcom for copyright infringement simply cannot be supported, argues Netcom. It is a passive transmitter with no knowledge or control over the content of communications that pass over its access lines. The requested extension of "liability for copyright infringement to Internet access providers over whose transmission lines Internet users may convey infringing material, is," observes Netcom, "akin to seeking redress against the telephone company for torts committed by telephone." The extension of such liability, predicts Netcom, would have a dire result:

> In reality, a finding of liability on NETCOM's part under the facts of this case would inevitably prompt the dismantlement of the Internet because it would establish a precedent whereby every user faces the potential of committing copyright infringement simply by the act of accessing the Internet. Because everyone who accesses the USENET system automatically receives a complete copy of the postings transmitted by others, all USENET members could be subject to liability for direct infringement if any posting contains unauthorized, copyrighted materials.

Looking back to the Sony Betamax case, Netcom recalls that the U.S. Supreme Court reversed the court of appeal's decision holding Sony chargeable with knowledge of infringing activity because the reproduction of copyrighted material was a major use of the Betamax video cassette recorder. *Sony Corp. v. Universal City Studios, Inc.*, 464 U.S. 417 (1984). According to the Supreme Court, there was no precedent for the imposition of vicarious liability. The court found that because the Betamax was, in fact, capable of substantial noninfringing use (e.g., "time shifting," which was held to come within the "fair use" defense), Sony could not be held liable for contributory infringement.

In this case, Netcom points out that "the Internet and the Netcom access station are used for millions of legitimate communications." As in *Sony*, there is no support in the Copyright Act for imposition of liability against Netcom for a third party act. And the court here should be attentive to the Supreme Court's stated reluctance in *Sony* to expand copyright protection without explicit legislative guidance.

Netcom observes that there are only two prior instances where federal courts have found a BBS liable for direct copyright infringement. These cases involve storage of copyrighted material on a BBS database and subscribers who download and copy such material without permission of the copyright owner. Neither case involved an access provider linking the BBS to the Internet.

Extending infringement liability to companies that passively transmit protected materials over the Internet, says Netcom, is not even contemplated in the July 1994 Report of the Working Group on Intellectual Property Rights, which is "charged with recommending changes to the Copyright Act to accommodate the realities of the information superhighway." A leading commentator agrees that a BBS operator should be held liable as a contributory copyright infringer if he or she solicits or encourages infringing practices, but concludes that such liability is not appropriate where "the information service is less directly involved in the enterprise of creating unauthorized copies."

In *Sony*, the U.S. Supreme Court recognized that contributory infringers have traditionally been persons "in a position to control the use of copyrighted works by others and had authorized the use without permission from the copyright owner." Here, Netcom has no control over the use of copyrighted works by subscribers who post to Usenet and has in no way authorized the use of copyrighted works without permission of the copyrighted owner. About 150 megabytes of information, or 150 million keystrokes of information, pass over Netcom's transmission lines each day, making it impossible for Netcom to exercise editorial control.

Netcom also notes that the court here must consider the application of the fair use defense, giving the parties an opportunity to brief the issue. Netcom points out that although it had limited time to research the merits of Scientology's trade secret claims, Netcom was able to uncover a federal appellate court decision holding that Scientology's religious materials do not constitute trade secrets under California law. *Religious Technology Center v. Wollersheim*, 739 F.2d 1076 (9th Cir. 1986), *cert. denied*, 479 U.S. 1103 (1987).

V. Injunction Dissolved

On February 21, 1995, following a hearing, the court dissolved the temporary restraining order against Netcom and Klemesrud, and denied Scientology's request for a preliminary injunction against them. The court ruled that Scientology had not established a sufficient continuing threat of irreparable harm or a probability of success on the merits sufficient to support the requested relief. The court also found that "the threat of harm to those defendants and the public outweighs any further threat of harm to [Scientology], particularly in light of the seizure order and the continuing [temporary restraining order] against defendant Erlich."

Regarding Erlich, the court gave him until March 3, 1995, to respond to Scientology's request for a preliminary injunction. The court also made clear that nothing in the restraining order against Erlich shall be construed to prohibit fair use of the works of L. Ron Hubbard, which

includes use of the copyrighted work for the purpose of criticism, news reporting, teaching, scholarship, and research but does not include: (1) use of the material for a commercial purpose where the user stands to profit from exploitation of the copyrighted material without paying the customary price or giving the usual consideration or use that would have a significant effect on the potential market value of the copyrighted work; (2) use which fulfills the demand for the original work; or (3) use of the heart of the work—no more of a work may be taken than is necessary to make any accompanying comment understandable.

VI. Request Renewed

In March 1995, Scientology renewed its request for a preliminary injunction against Netcom and Klemesrud. Scientology claims that

Additional facts and evidence now available demonstrate that arguments raised earlier by those defendants should not insulate them from the injunctive remedy to which [Scientology is] entitled as to *all* defendants. Indeed, their principal defense—purported inability to deal with the subject infringements—is simply not true at all.

[CyberLaw™ 6/95]

RESTRAINING ACCESS

I. A Renewed Request

The Church of Scientology is pursuing a vocal critic named Dennis Erlich over the Internet and into court, along with an Internet provider (Netcom On-Line Communication Services, Inc.) and the operator of an electronic bulletin board service (Tom Klemesrud) that links to the Internet through a connection provided by Netcom. The case is brought by Religious Technology Center and Bridge Publications Inc. (collectively, "Scientology"), owners of rights to published and unpublished works of L. Ron Hubbard, founder of the Scientology religion. At the heart of the complaint is the allegation that Erlich used Netcom's and Klemesrud's computer facilities to publish unauthorized copies of Hubbard's works in an Internet newsgroup named "alt.religion.scientology." Scientology claims that Erlich has stolen trade secrets and that his postings constitute copyright infringement. It also alleges that his access providers are guilty of the same offenses. At first, a federal court issued a restraining order against all defendants. The order was later dissolved against the access providers, but the church has now renewed its efforts to obtain an injunction against them. At this point, one key issue is whether Netcom can again avoid liability for alleged copyright infringement by arguing that it is merely a passive conduit of Internet postings, particularly in the face of Scientology's allegation that Netcom has suspended and terminated customers' accounts for abuse of its "Terms and Conditions and Netiquette," as well as for copyright infringement? Another issue is whether Netcom has a better defense based on fundamental rights of freedom of speech and expression, as exercised by Erlich in posting to an Internet newsgroup dedicated to discussion of the Scientology religion? Scientology's renewed request now awaits decision by a federal court in California.

II. Additional Facts & Evidence

Scientology claims the exclusive right to reproduce and publish published and unpublished literary works of L. Ron Hubbard. It also claims that in 1993, a federal court decided that certain of these works are trade secrets under California law, as Scientology proved that there was economic advantage in keeping the materials secret, among other required factors.

Scientology alleges over two hundred instances of copyright infringement by Erlich. Ninety of those were allegedly through Klemesrud's and Netcom's systems, with materials stored in those systems for up to three days and several weeks respectively. Scientology claims that on February 26, 1995, Erlich violated the temporary restraining order (TRO) issued against him by making an eight-page posting through the defendants' systems.

In its renewed application for a preliminary injunction, Scientology argues that additional facts and evidence now demonstrate that Scientology is entitled to such relief against Netcom and Klemesrud. Indeed, says Scientology, "their principal defense—purported inability to deal with the subject infringements—is simply not true."

III. Refusal to Act

Defendants' systems are not mere conduits for Erlich's postings, claims Scientology—"defendants' equipment is itself generating and storing the unauthorized, infringing copies to service their paying customers. . . ." Both Netcom and Klemesrud were able, continues Scientology, to warn of violations of usage conditions and to cancel service. But, says Scientology,

They refused to take any action, being unwilling even to issue warnings not to engage in the infringing postings. By their refusal, coupled with their actual copying of Erlich's infringements onto their own disks to make them available for paying subscriber access over extended periods, they have embroiled themselves in this matter, and should be preliminarily enjoined from continuing their activities.

Erlich's February 26, 1995, eight-page posting in violation of the TRO demonstrates that he did not give up all copies of Scientology's works. The question of exerting control over Erlich's postings "was not mooted by the seizure and TRO, as Netcom contended in its opposition to the original injunction application."

In posting to Usenet newsgroups such as alt.religion.scientology, Erlich used Klemesrud's system to transfer Erlich's posting to Netcom's computer. Klemesrud's action in so doing, claims Scientology, "is analogous to that of the bulletin board operator enjoined in *Sega Enterprises Ltd. v. MAPHIA*, 857 F.Supp. 679, 683–684 (N.D. Cal. 1994), who stored unauthorized copies of Sega games on his BBS, which were uploaded and downloaded to his users."

In response to the argument of Klemesrud and Netcom that the requested relief would cripple their ability to function, Scientology remarks that the injunction sought "is narrowly tailored and deals with the situation at hand and any other *known* situations of which defendants are warned." Klemesrud, notes Scientology, is able to delete individuals form his system, has excluded hate groups and other objectionable groups from his system, has asked posters of "offensive, distasteful, and inappropriate" remarks "to take their accounts elsewhere," and would delete Erlich's postings if they are "wholesale copying" of religious texts in order to deprive the Church of Scientology of income.

According to Scientology, Klemesrud could limit Erlich's access so that he could not access newsgroups—"[a]s a matter of Internet 'Netiquette,' it is entirely appropriate for Klemesrud, as the systems operator (sysop) of a BBS, to take action against a copyright infringer on his system." According to Scientology,

> Where a user engages in unlawful postings, his immediate service provider is obligated by Netiquette to deal with his violations, first by warnings and ultimately by denial of access, if nothing else works. Furthermore, where the immediate provider will not deal with the problem, then the next provider up the line takes on the obligation of doing so. Thus, if Klemesrud refuses, Netcom should take the action itself.

Netcom could do so, alleges Scientology, by running a program to check the messages passing through its system, blocking those from Erlich "altogether, as properly warranted by his threats to ignore any court orders, and his subsequent February 26 posting in clear violation of the original and amended TRO." In addition, Scientology observes that the rules of Klemesrud's system, the Los Angeles Valley College BBS, allow removal of Erlich for "violating the BBS' rules and causing it to violate the rules of its access providers, thereby jeopardizing Los Angeles Valley College BBS, Netcom and the entire BBS community."

IV. Balancing Harm & Injury

Netcom responds by first explaining that Erlich made the February 26, 1995, posting before receiving a copy of the court's amended TRO and becoming aware that the fair use exception did not extend to the confidential materials identified in plaintiff's complaint. Upon receipt of the amended TROs, Erlich immediately wrote to the court and apologized if he had erred. Erlich, now represented by counsel, has not made an objectionable posting since that time. Scientology cannot, therefore, demonstrate a threat of irreparable harm to support its request for injunctive relief.

The purpose of an injunction is to preserve the status quo pending a determination of the action on the merits. Netcom argues that here, "rather than preserving the status quo, the injunctive relief [Scientology] request[s] would fundamentally alter the functioning of the Internet."

If an injunction should issue, Netcom says that it would have to disconnect Klemesrud and his approximately five hundred subscribers "or undertake, at great expense and with no guarantee of success, to attempt to modify its operating software to permanently block Erlich's access to the Internet. Thus, the harm the injunction would cause NETCOM greatly outweighs [Scientology's] threatened injury. . . ."

Netcom also claims that

it is inappropriate for [Scientology] to premise a request for injunctive relief against NETCOM on the alleged past and predicted future noncompliance of Mr. Erlich with the Court's amended TRO. The proper remedy for any violation of the TRO by Mr. Erlich is further action against Mr. Erlich, not NETCOM.

V. Infringement Liability

Regarding claimed copyright infringement, Netcom argues that it is neither liable for direct or contributory infringement, nor is it vicariously liable for Erlich's actions. Netcom's role here was as a temporary host of messages posted to newsgroups to which it provides access. This role, urges Netcom,

is qualitatively no different from the role of the thousands of other Usenet server sites who host the alt.religion.scientology newsgroup on their servers. . . . [I]f NETCOM were considered to be a direct infringer because of the computer dissemination of Usenet messages on the Internet, such a theory of liability would apply to the over 10,000 Usenet sites, and, possibly, the millions of Usenet participants.

To be held liable for contributory infringement, Netcom must have knowledge of the infringing conduct and materially participate in it. Netcom argues that it does not have the "certain, unequivocal, and advance knowledge courts require before holding a party contributorily liable for the acts of another." Also, its role in Erlich's alleged infringement does not constitute the "pervasive participation" courts require:

Rather than directing, authorizing or actively participating in Erlich's allegedly infringing activities, NETCOM simply serves as a passive transmitter of his and millions of other messages throughout the Internet. . . . NETCOM leases use of its computer facilities to its subscribers. The fact that NETCOM is just one of dozens of access providers and just one of thousands of Usenet server sites throughout the country illustrates the immateriality of its contribution to Erlich's conduct.

Regarding vicarious liability, Netcom states that such a claim depends upon a showing that a third party had "the right and ability to control the infringer and received a direct financial benefit from the infringement." Here, both elements are lacking. Netcom says that it "does not and cannot supervise Erlich's messages before they are posted." It also is unable, as a passive access provider, to exercise editorial control over the content of individual messages given the speed and volume of the message traffic transmitted via the Usenet. Netcom has never pre-screened postings, does not have software to do so, and, contrary to the assertions of Scientology's "consultants," does not believe that a software change could block Erlich's postings until it could review them. "It would be necessary," argues Netcom, "to entirely change the functioning of the USENET system in order to monitor information that is posted to it."

Netcom acknowledges that is has the contractual right to take certain remedial actions once a violation of its terms and conditions of service has been established. But its terms and conditions, adds Netcom, "do not say, nor could they given the technological realities, that NETCOM will **screen** for violations in advance of posting."

And Netcom's terms and conditions cannot be used by Scientology to establish that Netcom has the ability to control users within the meaning of the vicarious liability doctrine. A federal court has recently rejected the argument that the power to refuse to deal with an infringer is equivalent to the power to control him.

Netcom also argues that it does not benefit financially from content that passes through its system. The fixed-fee rentals Netcom receives from subscribers are not, it says, "deemed financially derivative of the alleged act of infringement because the fee remains the same regardless of the nature, extent, or lack thereof, or the use of the premises."

Netcom acknowledges and disputes Scientology's assertion that Netcom can be liable for copyright infringement because it hosts Erlich's postings on its Usenet server for several days. Assuming for the sake of argument that "its nonvolitional transmission of messages through a lease arrangement" could be construed as an act of copying, Netcom argues that it is protected by the "fair use doctrine which allows a person to use copyrighted material in a reasonable manner without the copyright holder's consent." Netcom also notes serious questions about whether Erlich has infringed Scientology's rights, including

(1) whether [Scientology] may properly maintain copyrights in the materials at issue);
(2) if so, whether [Scientology's] copyrights in the material remain enforceable; and
(3) whether Erlich's alleged use of his materials constitutes 'fair use" and, consequently, is nonactionable given his apparent reliance on them to facilitate commentary on the Church of Scientology and its practices.

VI. Speech, Religion, & Fair Use

On the First Amendment, Netcom argues that Internet users and Netcom subscribers, in particular, are guaranteed fundamental rights of freedom of speech and expression, association, and to engage in the distribution of information. Scientology's construction of copyright law, urges Netcom, would impair the First Amendment rights of millions of Internet users. It would also "curtail the exchange of information that is crucial to the development of art, science, industry, and indeed religion," contravening the Copyright Act and the First Amendment. Netcom adds that an injunction requiring Netcom permanently to bar Erlich from the Internet "would constitute an impermissible prior restraint."

If Scientology's position were accepted, Netcom claims that it will be faced with "an insoluble dilemma." On the one hand, it will face debilitating infringement liability if it does not eliminate access. On the other hand, if it were to eliminate access without a prior judicial determination, it will face liability under California law to Klemesrud's approximately five hundred noninfringing users for cutting off access to a public forum.

Netcom argues that it "is 'ill-equipped' to do the 'policing' [Scientology] demand[s], and requiring NETCOM would adversely affect the public's low-cost access to the information marketplace." If held accountable for the tortious acts of others, argues Netcom, it will face the type of problems that a federal court recently noted with respect to a local television network affiliate in holding that the affiliate had no editorial control over a network broadcast, serving only as a conduit not responsible for republishing defamatory content of a "60 Minutes" segment. In *Auvil v. CBS "60 Minutes,"* 800 F.Supp. 928 (E.D. Wash. 1992), the court noted that liability would force the creation of full time editorial boards at local stations throughout the country which possess sufficient knowledge, legal acumen and access to experts to continually monitor incoming transmissions and exercise on-the-spot discretionary calls or face $75 million dollar lawsuits at every turn. That is not realistic.

VII. Scientology's Reply

In response, Scientology observes, among other things, that Netcom's claims are belied by the deposition testimony of its own witnesses:

Per Netcom's admissions, Netcom is not the passive transmitter it has led the Court to believe. Netcom regularly exercises controls over its customers' postings. It has: (1) suspended over 1,180 customers' accounts for abuse of its Terms and Conditions and Netiquette; (2) suspended accounts of copyright infringers without court order or legal opinion; and (3) terminated a bulletin board account without regard to whether others would be affected by the termination.

Similarly, Scientology notes that where Netcom earlier stated that it was impossible to deal with Erlich's postings other than to terminate Klemesrud's account, Netcom now admits that it merely does not currently have the software to do so. Accordingly, says Scientology,

Netcom can, and does, control abuses on its system, and preliminarily enjoining it from permitting abuse of plaintiff's rights will not require it to do anything it has not done as a routine part of its business many times before.

Scientology also alleges that Netcom does, in fact, receive a financial benefit from declining to take action against Erlich:

As a commercial provider of Internet services, Netcom directly profits from the media and Internet exposure it receives as a result of its refusal to take enforcement action against Erlich and Klemesrud in this situation, and fears it will suffer adverse consequences if it acts on its own to prevent their infringements. Netcom advertises its services as providing easy, regulation-free access to the Internet, access which is not available from its more restrictive competitors such as Compuserve and America Online, Inc. Indeed, Netcom's "NETCOM Info" boasts to its customers that "there is no administration to the Internet" and that "[n]o one person can 'lay down the law' to the rest of the community because there is no law. . . ." It is precisely this hands off approach that will attract to Netcom, rather than to its competitors, subscribers who seek to copy or distribute copyrighted materials. It is not a matter of free speech as Netcom urges, but of profits.

Regarding the First Amendment, Scientology urges that no harm to the public will accrue if an injunction is issued. According to Scientology, "courts have consistently rejected all claims of a First Amendment right to engage in copyright infringement and instead have fully protected the statutory rights granted to authors of creative works." Scientology further asserts that its proposed order takes fair use into account, adding that,

Where a defendant's right to engage in fair use has been accommodated by a court, there is simply no place for a separate First Amendment analysis because 'the fair use doctrine encompasses all claims of first amendment in the copyright field.' (Citation omitted.)

[CyberLaw™ 9/95]

GOVERNMENT RECOMMENDATIONS

I. Closing Loopholes?

In early 1993, President Clinton created the Information Infrastructure Task Force "to articulate and implement the Administration's vision for the National Information Infrastructure (NII)." The Working Group on Intellectual Property Rights, a significant part of this effort, was formed "to examine the intellectual property implications of the NII and make recommendations on any appropriate changes to U.S. intellectual property law and policy." In its report, just published, the Working Group recommends changes in the Copyright Act to recognize that copyright owners can control distribution of copies to the public by transmission, to grant a full public performance right for sound recordings, as well as to make it a criminal offense to willfully infringe a copyright by reproducing or distributing copies with a retail value of $5,000 or more. The Working Group also recommends prohibiting goods and services that defeat technological methods of preventing unauthorized use, and amendment of the Copyright Act to protect the integrity of copyright management information, among other things. (A copy of "The Report of the Working Group on Intellectual Property Rights" can be obtained at http://www.uspto.gov/web/ipnii/.) It remains to be seen whether these recommendations simply close existing loopholes and update the intellectual property system, or change the existing balance in favor of expanded monopoly rights for publishers, resulting in less innovation and creativity in the marketplace.

II. Transmission & Distribution

Examining the adequacy of copyright law to cope with technological change, the Working Group finds the balance of the Copyright Act has changed—in some instances to the benefit of copyright owners, in others to users. While affirming that the Copyright Act is "fundamentally adequate and effective" in providing the necessary copyright protection for the betterment of our society, the Working Group proposes several amendments and changes.

The Working Group recommends that the Copyright Act be amended to "expressly recognize that copies or phonorecords of works can be distributed to the public by transmission, and that such transmissions fall within the exclusive distribution right of the copyright owner." This change would clarify the situation posed by electronic communication systems that transfer copies of a work to others, but leave an original in the hands of the distributor.

Outside the digital world, for example, a purchaser of a book at a bookstore can sell it at a garage sale or otherwise dispose of it. Although the Copyright Act gives the copyright owner the right to control distribution of a work, the "first sale" doctrine stops the owner of a copyrighted work from preventing the purchaser of a particular copy from further distributing ownership of that copy. The Working Group explains that the first sale doctrine would not, however, allow the purchaser to distribute of a copy of the copy purchased through a computer network, "because, under current technology the transmitter retains the original copy of the work while the recipient of the transmission obtains a reproduction of the original copy (i.e., a *new* copy), rather than the copy owned by the transmitter." In this case, there may be copyright infringement because the first sale doctrine does not allow reproduction—only distribution of a particular copy.

The Working Group detects confusion in recent court decisions involving computer bulletin board systems. In a case involving unauthorized downloading of digitized photographs (whose reproduction was prohibited), the court recognized that the owner's right to distribute copies had been "implicated" by the operator of the bulletin board, who supplied a product containing unauthorized copies of copyrighted photographs. *Playboy Enterprises Inc. v. Frena*, 839 F.Supp. 1552 (M.D. Fla. 1993). It is less than clear to the Working Group, however, whether the operator "distributed" or "reproduced" an unauthorized copy of a photograph obtained by a board subscriber.

In another case, a computer bulletin board system was used to "make and distribute" copies of copyrighted video games. The court found "unauthorized copying and distribution" of the games on the bulletin board, and that the defendant profited from the "distribution." *Sega Enterprises Ltd. v. MAPHIA*, 857 F.Supp. 679 (N.D. Cal. 1994). The court held that the reproduction right had been infringed but, notes the Working Group, apparently did not reach a like conclusion with respect to the distribution right."

Difficulties related to electronic communication systems extend to importation of works into the United States—a right given to the copyright owner, with limited exceptions. On transmission of works into the United States through online systems, the Working Group observes that

A data stream can contain a copyrighted work in the form of electronic impulses, but those impulses do not fall within the definition of "copies" or phonorecords. Therefore, it may be argued that the transmission of a reproduction of a copyrighted work via international communication links fails to constitute an "importation" under current law, just as it is less than clear that a domestic transmission of a reproduction of a work constitutes a distribution of a copy under a literal reading of the Copyright Act.

In light of the above and because the "costs and risks of litigation" to define and clarify the issue "would discourage and delay use of the NII," the Working Group proposes to amend the Copyright Act to state that transmissions to the public are included within the distribution right. This is not intended to create a new right, but to make clear that people having a right to reproduce a work do not automatically have the right to distribute it through transmission, "thereby displacing the market for the copyright owner or his distribution licensee." Implementation would entail a number of changes to the Copyright Act, including amendment of the definition of "publication," which currently requires "a material object—a copy of the work—" to change hands.

The Working Group also recommends changing the definition of "publication" to recognize that "a work may be published through the distribution of copies of the work to the public by transmission." (Restricted transmissions of copies, e.g., via private e-mail message or within a company computer network where further distribution is not authorized, would not be regarded as publications.) This definitional change will impact copyright owner, because once works have been published they

(1) [M]ust be deposited in the Library of Congress; (2) are subject to more limitations on the [copyright owner's] exclusive rights, including a broader application of [the fair use doctrine]; (3) must meet certain author nationality or domicile requirements to be eligible for protection; and (4) must bear a copyright notice if published before March 1, 1989.

The Working Group hopes that the change will protect the scholarly and scientific record, by preserving works (by means of the deposit requirement) that otherwise "might be updated or revised on-line, destroying—or at least obscuring—the original published versions."

Similarly, the Working Group recommends amendment of the

Copyright Act to reflect that copies of copyrighted works can be imported into the United States by transmission. Interestingly, the Working Group "recognize[s] that the U.S. Customs Service cannot, for all practical purposes, enforce a prohibition on importation by transmission. . . ."

III. Sound Recordings

The Working Group believes that sound recordings transmission "will certainly supplement and may eventually replace the current forms of distribution of phonorecords." In addition to recommending that the Copyright Act be amended to make clear that sound recordings can be distributed by transmission, the Working Group seeks a full public performance right for sound recordings, "*particularly* with respect to all *digital* transmissions."

Currently, there is no public performance right for sound recordings under U.S. law. To transmit a public performance of a sound recording, observes the Working Group, a person is simply required to obtain a license from, and pay a royalty to, the copyright owner of the underlying musical composition. No permission need be obtained from, and no license fee need be paid to, the copyright owner of the sound recording or the performer. This situation, says the Working Group, is a historical anomaly without strong policy justification "—and certainly not a legal one." Granting that this right will treat creators of these works the same as creators of all other works capable of being performed, and will also "strengthen the hand of Government negotiators and private advocates seeking a fair share of foreign royalty pools."

IV. Criminal Sanctions

Under the Copyright Act, "[c]riminal sanctions are levied against infringers if the infringement was willful and for purposes of commercial advantage or private financial gain." In one recent case, an indictment was dropped against a university student who established computer bulletin boards for the receipt and distribution of unauthorized copies of commercially published, copyrighted software. *U.S. v. LaMacchia*, 871 F.Supp. 535 (D. Mass. 1994). Although the indictment alleged loss of revenue to copyright owners in excess of $1 million during a six-week period, the student could not be charged for criminal violation of copyright law because he sought no profit. To remedy this situation, the Working Group supports changing copyright and criminal laws to make it a criminal offense to willfully infringe a copyright by reproducing or distributing copies with a retail value of $5,000 or more.

V. Technological Protection

As copyright owners will look to technology for protection, the Working Group suggests prohibition of goods and services that defeat technological methods of preventing unauthorized use. Specifically, the Working Group recommends that

the copyright Act be amended to include . . . a provision to prohibit the importation, manufacture or distribution of any device, product or component incorporated into a device or product, or the provision of any service, the primary purpose or effect of which is to avoid, bypass, remove, deactivate, or otherwise circumvent, without authority of the copyright owner or the law, any process, treatment, mechanism or system which prevents or inhibits the violation of any of the [copyright owner's] exclusive rights. . . .

In the face of concerns that the prohibition is incompatible with the fair use privilege, the Working Group notes that the "fair use doctrine does not require a copyright owner to allow or to facilitate unauthorized access or use of a work." In any event, claims the Working Group, "if the circumvention device is primarily intended and used for legal purposes, such as fair use, the device would *not* violate the provision, because a device with such purposes and effects would fall under the 'authorized by law' exemption." Similarly, says the Working Group, "devices whose primary purpose and effect is to defeat the [technological] protection for [copies of works not protected by copyright law] would *not* violate the provision." Acknowledging that a manufacturer could find itself in a situation where a device could fail to be used primarily for the purpose for which it was sold and instead, to the surprise of the manufacturer, to be used primarily for defeating copyright protection technology, the Working Group proposes an "innocent violation" provision, to allow a court to reduce or eliminate altogether any damages for which the manufacturer may otherwise be liable. This limitation requires, however, that the manufacturer bear the burden of proving that it "was not aware and had no reason to believe that its acts constituted a violation."

VI. Copyright Management Information

The Working Group believes that in the future, copyright management information associated with a work "may be critical to the efficient operation and success of the NII." Such information might include the name and other identification of the author and the copyright owner, and the terms and conditions of use. Also included may be the country of origin, the year of creation and first publication, the name and other information about licensees, as well as standardized codes. Reliable information would allow persons to find and make authorized uses of works, as well as facilitate efficient licensing and reduce transaction costs. Accordingly, the Working Group recommends that the Copyright Act be amended to "prohibit the provision, distribution or importation for distribution of copyright management information known to be false and the unauthorized removal or alteration of copyright management information."

Although copyright owners are not required to provide copyright management information, the Working Group would require that such information be accurate if given.

VII. Other Concerns

In addition, the Working Group addresses special exemptions for libraries under the Copyright Act, suggesting that libraries should be permitted to engage in digital copying under certain circumstances. The Working Group also recommends an exemption to allow nonprofit organizations to reproduce and distribute, at cost, Braille, large type, audio, or other editions of previously published literary works in forms intended for the visually impaired, provided that the owner of U.S. distribution rights has not entered the market for such editions in the year following first publication. Regarding patents and trademarks, the Working Group recommends, among other things, obtaining public input relating to measures to ensure the authenticity of electronically disseminated publications.

[CyberLaw™ 11/95]

NOTICE OF INFRINGEMENT

I. Access Providers & Infringement

In the first ruling of its kind, a federal court in California has held that a large Internet access provider may be liable for copyright infringement if it knows or should have known that an unauthorized copy of a copyrighted work is being posted to the Internet through its system and the provider is able to take simple measures to prevent further damage to the copyright owner. *Religious Technology Center v. Netcom On-line Communication Services, Inc.*, No. C-95-20091, Order Denying Netcom's Motion for Summary Judgment (N.D. Cal. 11/21/

95). This ruling comes in a case brought by holders of the copyrights to published and unpublished works of L. Ron Hubbard, founder of the Church of Scientology, against a former church minister, Dennis Erlich (now a vocal critic), and the operator of the computer bulletin board system (BBS) to which Erlich subscribes, Thomas Klemesrud, as well as the Internet access provider that connects Klemesrud's BBS to the Internet, Netcom. The suit alleges copyright infringement by Erlich, who posted portions of plaintiffs' (Scientology's) works on the Internet—the Usenet newsgroup alt.religion.scientology—using access through Klemesrud's BBS. Failing to stop Erlich's continued postings, Scientology contacted Klemesrud and Netcom. Both refused to act. Although the court's ruling states that Scientology has not shown that it will likely prevail on its claims against Netcom or Klemesrud, it reveals to online systems that a simple copyright notice may be sufficient to support a claim of infringement sufficient to compel the system to take steps to prevent further damage to a claimant's copyrighted work.

II. Volition & Automatic Forwarding

Copyright infringement involves unauthorized exercise of one or more of the exclusive rights of a copyright holder, as set out in Section 106 of the Copyright Act. Although intent and a particular state of mind may be relevant to an award of damages, they are not required elements of proof for a finding of direct copyright infringement. This is in contrast to defamation, where an online system may be able to escape liability for a defamatory posting where it can be shown the operator did not know or have reason to know of the defamatory posting.

Netcom urges that Erlich, not Netcom, is directly liable for the unauthorized copying of Scientology's works that found their way onto Netcom's computers. The court observes that

Netcom did not take any affirmative action that directly resulted in copying [Scientology's] works other than by installing and maintaining a system whereby software automatically forwards messages received from subscribers onto the Usenet, and temporarily stores copies on its system. Netcom's actions, to the extent that they created a copy of plaintiff's works, were necessary to having a working system for transmitting Usenet postings to and from the Internet.

According to the court, Scientology's theory that Netcom is liable "because its computers in fact made copies" would result in "liability for every single Usenet server in the worldwide link of computers transmitting Erlich's message to every other computer." There is no need, says the court, to make all these parties infringers. "Although copyright is a strict liability statute, there should still be some element of volition or causation which is lacking where a defendant's system is merely used to create a copy by a third party."

Although Scientology complains that infringing copies of its works were found on Netcom's computer for eleven days, the court recognizes that under Scientology's theory "any storage of a copy that occurs in the process of sending a message to the Usenet is an infringement." Whether Netcom acted after it had warning from Scientology is not relevant to its *direct* liability for copying, but may be relevant to liability to contributory infringement—where knowledge is an element.

Looking to a recent case where unauthorized copies of *Playboy* photographs were found on a BBS, the court notes that there the BBS operator was liable for violating the plaintiff's right to publicly distribute and display copies of the work. The BBS itself was not, as Scientology suggests, held liable for the unauthorized reproduction of plaintiff's work. And, says the court, "the storage on a defendant's system of infringing copies and retransmission to other servers is not a direct infringement by the BBS operator of the exclusive right to *reproduce* the work where such copies are uploaded by an infringing user."

In response to Scientology's claim that Netcom infringed Scientology's exclusive right to publicly distribute and display copies of its works, the Court notes that it "is not entirely convinced that the mere possession of a digital copy on a BBS that is accessible to some members of the public constitutes direct infringement by the BBS operator." According to the court,

Only the subscriber should be liable for causing the distribution of plaintiff's work, as the contributing actions of the BBS provider are automatic and indiscriminate. . . . Where the BBS merely stores and passes along all messages sent by its subscribers and others, the BBS should not be seen as causing these works to be publicly distributed or displayed.

The court points out that accepting Scientology's argument would create "unreasonable liability." "No purpose would be served," observes the Court, "by holding liable those who have no ability to control the information to which their subscribers have access, even though they might be in some sense helping to achieve the Internet's automatic 'public distribution' and the users' 'public' display of files." This result is "unnecessary as there is already a party directly liable to causing the copies to be made." (The court acknowledges that its conclusion is at odds with the Report of the Working Group on Intellectual Property Rights, which recommends a strict liability paradigm for BBS operators.)

III. Contributory Infringement

But even if not liable for direct copyright infringement, Netcom may still be held liable as a contributory infringer. The rule is that "Liability for participation in the infringement will be established where the defendant, 'with knowledge of the infringing activity, induces, causes or materially contributes to the infringing conduct of another.' "

Here, Netcom allegedly knew that Erlich was infringing Scientology's copyright. Scientology's counsel told Netcom that copies of Scientology's works were being posted in a Usenet newsgroup by Erlich through Netcom's system. And, says Scientology, Netcom did nothing—allowing allegedly infringing postings to remain on its system so that Netcom subscribers and Usenet servers could access them. But Netcom responds that

(1) it did not know of Erlich's planned infringing activities when it agreed to lease its facilities to Klemesrud, (2) it did not know that Erlich would infringe prior to any of his postings, (3) it is unable to screen out infringing postings before they are made, and (4) its knowledge of the infringing nature of Erlich's postings was too equivocal given the difficulty in assessing whether [Scientology copyright] registrations were valid and whether Erlich's use was fair.

Reviewing Netcom's argument, the court notes that the relevant time period is not when Netcom entered into its agreement with Klemesrud, but when it "provided its services to allow Erlich to infringe [Scientology's] copyrights."

Netcom points out that all alleged instances of infringement occurred prior to the date it first received notice of Scientology's infringement claim, on December 29, 1994. There is no question of fact therefore, says the court, "as to whether Netcom knew or should have known of Erlich's infringing activities that occurred more than 11 days before receipt of [Scientology's] letter." But there is a genuine question of fact about "whether Netcom knew of any infringement by Erlich before it was too late to do anything about it." Accordingly,

If Scientology can prove the knowledge element, Netcom will be liable for contributory infringement since its failure to simply cancel Erlich's infringing message and thereby stop an infringing copy from being distributed worldwide constitutes substantial participation in Erlich's public distribution of the message.

Netcom claims that Scientology's notice of alleged infringement was too equivocal given the difficulty in assessing whether copyright registrations are valid and whether use is fair. But liability need not be unequivocal, says the court. "Where works contain copyright notices within them, as here, it is difficult to argue that a defendant did not know that the works were copyrighted." Recognizing the problems in verifying claims of infringement because of possible fair use defenses, lack of copyright notices, or failure of the copyright holder to provide "necessary" documentation of a "likely" infringement, the court states that where a BBS operator cannot "reasonably verify a claim of infringement" for such reasons, "the operator's lack of knowledge will be found reasonable and there will be no liability for contributory infringement for allowing the continued distribution of the works on its system."

Here, observes the court, Netcom admits that it did not look at the postings once given notice. Had Netcom viewed the copyright notice and statements regarding authorship, it would have triggered an investigation as to whether there was infringement. According to the court, "these facts are sufficient to raise a question as to Netcom's knowledge once it received a letter from [Scientology] on December 29, 1994."

On the matter of inducing, causing, or materially contributing to the infringing conduct of the primary infringer, the court notes that such participation must be substantial. Netcom did not act like a landlord and completely relinquish control of its system. Says the court,

[I]t is fair, assuming Netcom is able to take simple measures to prevent further damage to [Scientology's] copyrighted works, to hold Netcom liable for contributory infringement where Netcom has knowledge of Erlich's infringing postings yet continues to aid in the accomplishment of Erlich's purpose of publicly distributing the postings.

There is, therefore, a genuine issue of material fact on Scientology's claim of contributory infringement "as to the postings made after Netcom was on notice of [Scientology's] infringement claim."

IV. Vicarious Liability

According to the Court, if Scientology cannot prove contributory infringement by Netcom, Scientology may raise a claim that Netcom is vicariously liable for infringement based on its relationship with Erlich. Vicarious liability for actions of a primary infringer will be found where "the defendant (1) has the right and ability to control the infringer's acts and (2) receives a direct financial benefit from the infringement." Proof of "knowledge" is not required to win a vicarious liability claim.

Although Netcom urges that it has no right to control its users' postings before they occur, Scientology points out that Netcom's terms and conditions specify that it reserves the right to take remedial action against subscribers. Scientology also argues that under "netiquette," violation of copyright is unacceptable and access providers have a duty to prevent this. Where the access provider fails to do so, the next service provider up the transmission stream must act. Other evidence of Netcom's right to control is alleged to be its prohibition of copyright infringement and requirement that subscribers indemnify it for damage to third parties.

Netcom claims, however, that it cannot screen messages before they are posted given the speed and volume of data that passes through its system, and that it has never exercised control over the content of user postings. But Scientology experts believe—although without submitting supporting evidence—that with an easy software modification Netcom could identify postings containing particular words or that come from particular individuals. Scientology also believes that Netcom could deny Erlich access to Usenet without denying access to the five hundred users of Klemesrud's BBS, and notes that Netcom has suspended subscriber accounts on over a thousand occasions and has the ability to delete specific postings. Considering these claims, the court finds that Scientology has a raised a genuine issue of fact "as to whether Netcom has the right and ability to exercise control over the activities of its subscribers, and of Erlich in particular."

On the issue of whether Netcom obtains a direct financial benefit from Erlich's postings, the court observes that Netcom obtains a flat fee and "[t]here is no evidence that infringement by Erlich, or any other user of Netcom's services, in any way enhances the value of Netcom's services to subscribers or attracts new subscribers." The court rejects Scientology's claim that Netcom somehow gains a benefit from refusing to take enforcement actions against subscribers, advertising that compared to competitors like CompuServe and America Online, it provides easy, regulation-free Internet access. Having failed to raise a question of fact on this issue, Scientology's claim of vicarious liability fails.

V. First Amendment

Netcom claims that liability in this case would contravene the First Amendment, "forc[ing] Usenet servers to do the impossible—screening all the information that comes through their systems." But, says the court, it is "not convinced that Usenet servers are directly liable for causing a copy to be made, and absent evidence of knowledge and participation or control and direct profit, they will not be contributorily or vicariously liable." If such were not the case, "this could have a serious chilling effect on what some say may turn out to be the best public forum for free speech yet devised."

VI. Liability for Internet Browsing

Netcom also urges that under Scientology's theories, users might be liable for merely browsing infringing works, as browsing "technically causes an infringing copy of the digital information to be made in the screen memory." In response, the court states that browsing is "the functional equivalent of reading, which does not implicate the copyright laws and may be done by anyone in a library without the permission of the copyright owner." Significantly, the court observes,

Absent a commercial or profit-deriving use, digital browsing is probably a fair use; there could hardly be a market for licensing temporary copying of digital works onto computer screens to allow browsing. Unless such a use is commercial, such as where someone reads a copyrighted work online and therefore decides not to purchase a copy from the copyright owner, fair use is likely. . . .

Additionally, unless a user has reason to know, such as from the title of a message, that the message contains copyrighted materials, the browser will be protected by the innocent infringer doctrine, which allows the court to award no damages in appropriate circumstances. In any event, users should hardly worry about a finding of direct infringement; it would seem highly unlikely from a practical matter that a copyright owner could prove such infringement or would want to sue such an individual.

VII. Fair Use

"Fair use" is a defense to copyright infringement. If Scientology can prove infringement by Netcom, the company may raise a defense focusing on its acts. In considering the fair use defense, courts evaluate four nonexclusive factors:

(1) the nature and purpose of the use, including whether such use is of a commercial nature or is for nonprofit educational purposes;
(2) the nature of the copyrighted work;
(3) the amount and substantiality of the portion used in relation to the copyrighted work as a whole; and
(4) the effect of the use upon the potential market for or value of the copyrighted work.

The first factor weighs in Netcom's favor, says the court. "Although Netcom gains financially from its distribution of messages to the Internet, its financial incentive is unrelated to the infringing activity and [it] receives no direct financial benefit from the acts of infringement."

The second looks to whether a work is published or unpublished, informational or creative. But here, Netcom's use of the works was "merely to facilitate their posting to the Usenet" and, the court notes, their precise nature "is not important to the fair use determination."

On the matter of the amount and substantiality of the portion used, Netcom made available only what was posted by Erlich. (The court previously ruled that Erlich is "not likely entitled to his own fair use defense, as his postings contained large portions of [Scientology's] published and unpublished works quoted verbatim with little added commentary.") Doing so, the court finds, "Netcom copied no more of [Scientology's] works than necessary to function as a Usenet server. . . . Netcom had no practical alternative way to carry out its socially useful purpose [—in allowing for the functioning of the Internet and the dissemination of other creative works, a goal of the Copyright Act]. . . ."

The last factor, the market effect, is the most important consideration. Among other things, Netcom argues there is no evidence that making Scientology's religious scripture and policy letters available on the Internet will harm the market for those works by preventing someone from participating in the Scientology religion. Scientology counters that the wide distribution of the Internet, said to be twenty-five million, multiplies the effect of market substitution, and notes that in the past, groups have stolen Scientology scripture in charging for Scientology-like training. And on this issue, the court finds a genuine issue as to whether Erlich's Internet postings could hurt the market for Scientology works. There is, therefore, a question of fact on the matter of a fair use defense.

VIII. Scientology Not Likely to Prevail

In summary, the court finds that Scientology has raised genuine issues of fact regarding whether Netcom should have known that Erlich was infringing Scientology's copyrights after receiving Scientology's letter, whether Netcom substantially participated in the infringement, and whether Netcom has a valid fair use defense. But Scientology is not entitled to a preliminary injunction against Netcom and Klemesrud. According to the court, Scientology is not likely to prevail on its copyright claims against either, particularly "as they did not receive notice of the alleged infringement until after all but one of the postings were completed. Further, their participation in the infringement was not substantial." In addition, Scientology has not shown that the current injunction against Erlich is not sufficient to avoid any harm to Scientology's intellectual property rights. Importantly, the court observes,

Because [Scientology] seek[s] injunctive relief that is broader than necessary to prevent Erlich from committing copyright infringement, there is a valid First Amendment question raised here. Netcom and Klemesrud play a vital role in the speech of their users. Requiring them to prescreen postings for possible infringement would chill their users' speech.

[CyberLaw™ 1/96]

LOSING DATA

I. Taking Data

Can a company that has made a significant investment in producing a database be compelled to stand by helplessly and watch as a competitor strips out the data and publishes it on the Internet? As reflected in a Wisconsin federal court decision, the answer is "yes." On this case, the Court ruled that it is not unfair or commercially destructive to allow the taking of data assembled with a significant investment of time, effort, and money, albeit in an uncopyrightable form, and to use it for commercial purposes without paying any compensation. The court also ruled that the manufacturer's shrinkwrap license was ineffective, and federal copyright law preempted the manufacturer's claims of misappropriation and unfair competition, as well as violation of a state computer crimes act. See, *ProCD, Inc. v. Zeidenberg*, 1996 U.S. Dist. LEXIS 167 (W.D. Wisc. 1996).

II. Millions of Dollars

ProCD, Inc. is a Massachusetts company that spent millions of dollars to compile ninety-five million residential and commercial listings from about three thousand telephone books. The listings include names, addresses, phone numbers, zip codes, and industry, or "SIC," codes. ProCD sells these listings under the name "Select Phone TM," on a CD-ROM that includes software to access, retrieve, and download data. Each box in which the product is sold contains a "Single User License Agreement," which states,

"Please read this license carefully before using the software or accessing the listings contained on the discs. By using the discs and the listings licensed to you, you agree to be bound by the terms of this License. If you do not agree to the terms of this License, promptly return all copies of the software, listings that may have been exported, the discs and the User Guide to the place where you obtained it."

The license advises that the software is copyrighted. But the box itself only mentions the agreement in one place in small print, and does not provide the specific terms of the license.

Once the product is installed, a message appears on the user's computer screen to remind the user that use of the product and the data is subject to the Single User License Agreement and that use of the product is licensed for authorized use only. Most screens warn, "The user agreement provides that copying of the software and the data may be done only for individual or personal use and that distribution, sublicense, or lease of the software or the data is prohibited."

Matthew Zeidenberg bought a copy of Select Phone TM. In early 1995, he "decided he could download data from Select Phone TM and make it available to third parties over the Internet for commercial purposes." He bought an updated version in March 1995.

In April 1995, Zeidenberg incorporated Silken Mountain Web Services, Inc. to make a database of telephone listings available over the Internet. The database included listings from Select Phone TM. The computer screen warning messages were disregarded, because they were not viewed as being binding.

Zeidenberg downloaded data from Select Phone TM by installing the product onto his PC and making a copy of the software on his computer's hard drive. The software was used to download data into Silken Mountain Web Services' database. Each time data was downloaded, a copy of Select Phone TM software was copied into the random access memory (RAM) of Zeidenberg's computer. But Silken Mountain wrote its own software to search its database. Select Phone TM software was not copied or used by anyone who accessed Silken Mountain's Web site.

In May 1995, Silken Mountain Web Services entered into an agreement with an Internet service provider, Branch Information Systems. Silken Mountain loaded its database onto Branch's computer, which made it available from the Internet. ProCD learned of this and demanded that Silken Mountain and Zeidenberg stop their activities immediately. In response, Zeidenberg admitted copying the listings from Select Phone TM but said that he would continue his project. Branch, however, decided to stop doing business with Silken Mountain and Zeidenberg.

In August, Zeidenberg and Silken Mountain entered into an agreement with another Internet service provider, Ivory Tower Information Services. The agreement provided that Ivory would continue providing Internet access until ordered by a court to stop.

III. No Protection for Raw Data

By September 22, 1995, Silken Mountain Web Services' Internet database was receiving 20,000 hits per day. Each user was able to extract up to 1,000 listings per search. Believing that its ability to sell Select Phone TM was in jeopardy, ProCD sued and obtained a preliminary injunction barring Zeidenberg and Silken Mountain from distributing Select Phone TM listings over the Internet. It was clear then, however, says the federal court hearing the matter, that "[ProCD] had no valid claim to federal copyright protection for the raw data contained on its Select Phone TM CD-ROM discs."

ProCD's claims regarding the Select Phone TM data, says the Court, "boil down to the proposition that it is unfair and commercially destructive to allow defendants to take information [ProCD] assembled with a significant investment of time, effort, and money and use it for commercial purposes without paying any compensation to [ProCD]." But the Supreme Court specifically rejected this proposition in a case in which it ruled that telephone listings are not protected by copyright, denying "the claim of a telephone company that sought to prevent competitors from using the data it had compiled and published in its directories."

IV. Copying Software an Essential Step

ProCD argues that defendants Zeidenberg and Silken Mountain Web Services infringed its copyright by copying Select Phone TM software to Zeidenberg's hard drive for the purpose of distributing the listings on the Internet. While the Copyright Act proscribes unauthorized copying of a copyrighted work, there is an important exception under Section 117 of the Act:

It is not an infringement for the owner of a copy of a computer program to make . . . another copy or adaptation of the computer program provided: (1) that such new copy or adaptation is created as an essential step in the utilization of the computer program in conjunction with a machine and that is used in no other manner.

ProCD and defendants dispute the scope and meaning of the term "essential elements." ProCD would not have it extend to copying Select Phone TM software to a computer's hard drive, on the grounds that defendants "could have utilized the program by booting it into [random access memory (RAM)] memory every time they desired to use it." RAM is volatile memory, so that information stored in it is lost each time a computer is turned off. But, says the court, this interpretation would lead to the conclusion that "any copying of a computer program onto the owner's hard drive would constitute copyright infringement unless the program developer gave the owner specific authorization to a make a hard drive copy." Such an interpretation conflicts with the spirit of the Section 117 exception and is not how people use computers in the 1990s. The court observes, "The day has passed when it was necessary to insert a floppy disk in a disk drive any time a user wanted access to a particular program."

Under Section 117, copies made must be for personal use. "Odd as it may seem, given defendants' subsequent commercial use of the telephone data," remarks the Court, "the undisputed fact is that defendants made no copies of [ProCD's] software except for their own personal use." They only used the software to access and download the telephone listing data. New software was created to allow Internet users to access the data. "In distributing only the uncopyrightable data over the Internet," ruled the Court, "defendants did not disqualify themselves from the infringement exception contained in Section 117."

V. An Ineffective Shrinkwrap License

ProCD apparently realized that there was a potential copyright problem and sought to resolve the issue with an agreement in the Select Phone TM software package. The court described this agreement as a shrinkwrap license, a common feature of mass market software that the court described as follows:

Shrinkwrap licenses are intended to take the place of any bargains or agreements between mass market software producers and users, because the typical software transaction does not involve bargained agreements concerning use limitations, but a purchase made by a computer user at a retail store or through the mail, with little discussion or bargaining between the producer and the user. In placing a shrinkwrap license provision on its software product, the producer seeks to 1) prohibit unauthorized copies; 2) prohibit software rental; 3) prohibit reverse engineering and modification to the software; 4) limit the use of software to one central processing unit; 5) disclaim warranties; and 6) limit liability.

Finding the sale of the Select Phone TM software to be a sale of goods subject to the Uniform Commercial Code, the court went on to rule that the parties entered into a binding contract for that sale when Zeidenberg purchased the off-the-shelf product by paying for it at a retail outlet. At that time, the court observes, the terms of the Select Phone TM user agreement were not presented to Zeidenberg—

The sole reference to the user agreement was a disclosure in small print at the bottom of the package, stating that defendants were subject to the terms and conditions of the enclosed license agreement. Defendants did not receive the opportunity to inspect or consider those terms.

This "mere reference" did not give buyers an adequate opportunity to decide, at the time of contract formation, whether the terms were acceptable. So viewed, the terms did not become a part of the contract and could not constitute a contract modification assented to by Zei-denberg's use of the product. According to the court, "because defen-dants did not have the opportunity to bargain or object to the pro-posed user agreement or even review it before purchase and they did not assent to the terms explicitly after they learned of them, they are not bound by the user agreement."

Interestingly, the court notes that a proposed new Uniform Com-mercial Code provision would make a standard form license enforce-able if the purchaser, prior to or within a reasonable time after begin-ning to use the product, by his or her behavior manifests assent to the license and had an opportunity to review the terms of the license, whether or not he or she actually reviewed the terms. "This pro-posal," says the court, "is evidence that the [drafter of the Uniform Commercial Code] views current law as insufficient to guarantee the enforcement of standard form contracts such as shrinkwrap licenses." The court also believes that if states adopt the draft provision, the issue of federal preemption will be "more prominent."

VI. Preemption of State Law Claims

Under Section 301 of the Copyright Act, federal copyright law pre-empts a state law claim if "1) the work in which the state law right is asserted comes within the 'subject matter' of copyright . . . ; and 2) the state law right asserted is equivalent to any of the rights specified [as exclusive rights of a copyright owner] in [Section 106 of the Copy-right Act]." In this case, the Select Phone TM listings are compilations of fact that would qualify for copyright protection if sufficiently origi-nal. "[T]hat they lack the necessary originality," observes the Court, "does not affect their status as coming within the subject matter of copyright."

An asserted state law right may avoid preemption if it incorpo-rates an "extra element" beyond those necessary to prove copyright infringement by reproduction, performance, distribution, or display. In this case, the court ruled, ProCD's state law claims are all "designed to protect these same reproduction and distribution rights," and are, therefore, preempted. Here, for example, ProCD's contract claim "is nothing more than an effort to prevent defendants from copying and distributing its data." There is no assertion of a qualitatively different element from the underlying copyright claim. And, the court notes pointedly,

Had each of the compilers of the 3,000 directories that [ProCD] used to put together its database attached a set of terms prohibiting further distribution of the information included in its directories, [ProCD] would not have been able to create Select Phone

TM without negotiating with and compensating each compiler for use of its data. . . . It is ironic that after [ProCD] has attained the benefit of copyright law, it wants to prevent others from receiving that same protection. Unfortunately for [ProCD], the rules of the game have not changed.

ProCD also alleged misappropriation and unfair competition claims against the defendants. The elements of a Wisconsin misappropriation claim are, "(1) time, labor, and money expended in the creation of the thing misappropriated; (2) competition; and (3) commercial damage to the plaintiff." But, says the court regarding ProCD's claim, "misappropriation does not serve any qualitatively different purposes from copyright law. . . . Adding competition and commercial damage does not differentiate the underlying protected right." The claim is, therefore, preempted.

The Wisconsin Computer Crimes Act, says the court, "makes it unlawful to modify, destroy, access, take, or copy computer data willfully, knowingly, and without authorization." Although the ProCD listings qualify as data under this act, ProCD's claim is preempted by the Copyright Act because its "efforts to establish a right under the Wisconsin Computer Crimes Act conflicts directly with the federal copyright law's directive to keep unoriginal factual compilations in the public domain. It would undermine the public access to facts and ideas if states could block access with their own legislation."

In light of the above, the court dissolved the preliminary injunction previously ordered, and awarded summary judgment for Zeidenberg and Silken Mountain Web Services.

2

Trademark

The purpose of a trademark[93] is to identify and distinguish the source of a good or service. Trademarks protect words, symbols, slogans, designs, characters, packaging, sounds, smells, and colors, as well as product configurations, as used in commerce.[94] In essence, trademark laws protect against confusion in the marketplace resulting from conflicting use of similar words or symbols, among other things.

Primary trademark protection is found under the Trademark Act, generally known as the Lanham Act.[95] Several states also offer trademark protection.[96] No international treaties protect U.S. trademarks overseas. Companies wishing to protect trademarks outside the United States need to register them in countries important to their business.

The Lanham Act defines the term "trademark" to include

any word, name, symbol, or device, or any combination thereof—

(1) used by any person, or
(2) which a person has a bona fide intention to use in commerce and applies to register on the principal register established by this chapter,

to identify and distinguish his or her goods, including a unique product, from being manufactured or sold by others and to indicate the source of the good, even if that source is unknown.[97]

In recent years, the concept of a trademark has expanded, particularly in the field of "trade dress"—defined as the "total image of a product [, which] may include features such as size, shape, color,

---

[93] The term "trademark" may sometimes be used to indicate a servicemark, which identifies the source of a service.
[94] See, e.g., *Qualitex Co. v. Jacobson Prods. Co.*, __ U.S. __, 131 L.Ed.2d 248, 115 S.Ct. 1300 (1995) (green-gold color of manufacturer's dry cleaning press pad).
[95] 15 U.S.C. §§ 1051–1127.
[96] See, e.g., Cal. Bus. & Prof. Code. § 14340.
[97] 15 U.S.C. § 1127.

or color combinations, texture, graphics, or even particular sales techniques."[98]

Under common law and the Lanham Act, distinctiveness is a key element for protection of a trademark. Marks may be classified as (1) arbitrary and fanciful, (2) suggestive, (3) descriptive, and (4) generic. Arbitrary marks are those that bear no relationship to associated goods, but may include words in common use. Fanciful marks are typically made-up names. Descriptive marks actually describe an aspect of a product or service, such as a characteristic, quality, purpose, or geographic origin. Descriptive marks cannot be registered unless a "secondary meaning" has been developed. Suggestive marks are those that suggest, but do not describe, a good or service. Generic marks are names that describe a common class or group to which a product or service belongs.

Marks within the first two categories can be registered with the U.S. Patent and Trademark Office without showing that a "secondary meaning" has developed in the market, i.e., the mark need not be shown to identify, in the minds of the public, the source of the product rather than the product itself.[99] Being highly distinctive, they are entitled to the highest level of protection.

Under the Lanham Act, a showing of substantially exclusive and continuous use by the applicant in commerce for at least five years is prima facie evidence of distinctiveness.[100]

As generic marks do not identify or distinguish the origin of a product or service, they cannot be registered—even if a secondary meaning can be shown.

A trademark, if not defended, may become a generic name incapable of protection under law. Federal law protects against the dilution or tarnishment of a popular trademark, allowing for the issuance of an injunction against the offending party. The Lanham Act provides that

The owner of a famous mark shall be entitled, subject to the principles of equity and upon such terms as the court deems reasonable, to an injunction against another person's commercial use in commerce of a mark or trade name, if such use begins

---

[98] *John H. Harland Co. v. Clarke Checks, Inc.*, 711 F.2d 966, 980 (11th Cir. 1983) (bank checks); see also *Two Pesos, Inc. v. Taco Cabana, Inc.*, 505 U.S. 763, 120 L.Ed.2d 615, 112 S.Ct. 2753 (1992) (restaurant); *International Jensen v. Metrosound U.S.A.*, 4 F.3d 819 (9th Cir. 1993) (audio speakers).
[99] See *Inwood Laboratories, Inc. v. Ives Laboratories, Inc.*, 456 U.S. 844, 851 n.11, 102 S.Ct. 2182, 72 L.Ed.2d 606 (1982); Restatement (Third) of Unfair Competition § 13, Comment e.
[100] 15 U.S.C. § 1052(f).

after the mark has become famous and causes dilution of the distinctive quality of the mark. . . .[101]

A number of states also have adopted anti-dilution statutes.[102] A notable feature of these statutes is that they may provide protection even where there is no direct competition or likelihood of confusion.[103]

In the United States, an owner may maintain an enforceable trademark simply by using the trademark in commerce.[104] Instead of registering a trademark, an owner may rely on the common law of unfair competition and related state laws. But there are significant benefits that come with federal registration, including nationwide protection and ability to use the federal registration symbol, ®.

If a trademark is arbitrary, fanciful, suggestive, or has become distinctive, it can be registered on the Principal Register. Such registration provides prima facie evidence of the mark's validity, the registrant's exclusive right to use it, and ownership of the mark, among other things.[105] After five years on the Principal Register, the registration becomes conclusive evidence of validity and ownership, and can only be canceled on certain specified grounds.[106] In cases of civil infringement, registration also makes available recovery of a defendant's profits, in addition to damages, treble damages, costs, and attorneys' fees.[107]

A trademark registration on the Principal Register may be based on actual use, or on a bona fide intent to use a mark in commerce. There is a ten-year term of initial registration, but a mark will be canceled at the end of the sixth year if a registrant does not file, in the year preceding that time, an affidavit indicating continuing use of the mark in commerce, or that nonuse is due to certain reasons and there is no intent to abandon the mark.[108] At the end of the ten-year term, the registration may be renewed.[109]

---

[101] 15 U.S.C. § 1125(c)(1); see *Hasbro, Inc. v. Internet Entertainment Group, Ltd.*, No. C96-130WD (W.D. Wash. Feb. 9, 1996) (Preliminary injunction issued prohibiting use of the name CANDYLAND or the Internet domain name "candyland.com" in connection with any Internet site containing sexually explicit material or other pornographic content, among other things).

[102] See e.g., Cal. Bus. & Prof. Code § 14330(a).

[103] See *Hasbro, Inc. v. Internet Entertainment Group, Ltd.*, No. C96-130WD (W.D. Wash. Feb. 9, 1996).

[104] For protection of a mark outside the United States, foreign registration is generally required.

[105] 15 U.S.C. §§ 1072, 1115(a).

[106] Ibid. §§ 1065, 1115.

[107] Ibid. § 1117.

[108] Ibid. § 1058.

[109] Ibid. § 1059.

Marks that distinguish goods and services but cannot be filed on the Principal Register, may be registered on the Supplemental Register.[110] Such registrations, however, cannot be based on an intent to use.[111] Supplemental registration also does not provide many of the advantages of registration on the Principal Register. Most states have adopted their own registration procedures, but the benefits are often not much more than common law protections.[112]

Trademarks are distinct from "trade names," which identify the producer of a good or service and are ineligible for trademark protection because they do not identify a good or service. A trade name cannot be registered under the Lanham Act.[113] But it may be protected by state unfair competition law.[114]

Regarding online systems and the Internet, trademark claims have been raised over the posting of unauthorized copies of copyrighted materials. They have also surfaced over registration of Internet domain names (the element in an electronic address directly following the symbol "@," which serves as the key identifier of a computer or group of computers connected to the Internet).

In one case, a manufacturer of computer video games (Sega) sued a computer bulletin board service (BBS) and one of its operators over the unauthorized uploading of copies of Sega games to, and their downloading from, the BBS. The court found Sega likely to establish that use of Sega's trademark in the BBS's file sections and file descriptors, as well as on programs made available and encouraged for downloading, constitute trademark infringement.[115] The court noted that

[Sega] need not prove that any person actually has been mistaken because of Defendant's use [of Sega's trademark]. . . . Once a product is put into commerce, confusion, mistake, or deception occurring at some future time is sufficient to establish liability for trademark infringement.[116]

In another case, *Playboy* sued the operator of a subscription BBS.[117] Subscribers were able to browse different areas and download high-quality copies of *Playboy* photographs to their own computers. *Playboy* held copyrights on 170 available images.

---

[110] Ibid. § 1091.
[111] Ibid. § 1094.
[112] See, e.g., Cal. Bus. & Prof. Code §§ 14200–342.
[113] See *Safeway Stores, Inc. v. Safeway Discount Drugs, Inc.*, 675 F.2d 1160, 1163 (11th Cir. 1982) ("a trademark identifies and distinguishes a product, a service mark a service, and a trade name a business").
[114] See, e.g., Cal. Bus. & Prof. Code §§ 14400–418.
[115] *Sega Enters. v. MAPHIA*, 857 F.Supp. 679 (N.D. Cal. 1994).
[116] *Ibid.*, 857 F.Supp. 679, 688 (N.D. Cal. 1994).
[117] *Playboy Enters. v. Frena*, 839 F.Supp. 1552 (M.D. Fla. 1993).

Playboy's registered trademarks were used in the file descriptors for 170 images found on the BBS. The BBS operator, George Frena, claimed that he had never placed the words *Playboy* or *Playmate* onto the BBS. Instead, he argued that these words had been uploaded into the BBS's index by subscribers to accompany material uploaded by them. Frena claimed that "he, innocently and without malice, allowed subscribers to upload whatever they wanted onto [the] BBS."[118] But the court ruled that intent or bad faith is unnecessary for a violation of the Lanham Act. In a trademark case, the court observed, the central inquiry concerns "likelihood of confusion."[119] "[L]ack of intent to deceive does nothing to alleviate the confusion precipitated by similarity of trademarks."[120] Here, the court found, "It is likely that customers of Defendant Frena would believe that [*Playboy*] was the source of Defendant Frena's images and that [*Playboy*] either sponsored, endorsed, or approved Defendant Frena's use of [*Playboy*] images."[121] Frena was, therefore, found guilty of trademark infringement.

Frena was also found guilty of "reverse passing off," for removing *Playboy* trademarks from photographs. As noted by the Court, Frena deleted *Playboy*'s text from *Playboy*'s photographs, to some of which he added his own text including his name, Tech Warehouse BBS, and telephone number.[122]

A number of claims have been filed over registration of Internet domain names. Most early case were settled prior to any court decision. In one case, a New York arbitration panel ruled that Princeton Review has no right to establish an Internet address[123] using the name of its chief rival, Stanley H. Kaplan Educational Centers Ltd.[124] In another case, the Council of the Better Business Bureau filed suit against Mark Sloo, dba Clark Publishing, for acquiring registration of "bbb.org" and "bbb.com" allegedly to elicit money from the Bureau (which has used the BBB acronym for years) when it decides to use the Internet. The suit was settled, with the council prevailing.[125] A number of other cases are winding their way through the courts.[126]

---

[118] *Ibid.*, 839 F.Supp. 1552, 1559 (M.D. Fla. 1993).

[119] *Ibid.*, 839 F.Supp. 1552, 1560 (M.D. Fla. 1993).

[120] *Ibid.*, 839 F.Supp. 1552, 1561 (M.D. Fla. 1993).

[121] *Ibid.*, 839 F.Supp. 1552, 1561 (M.D. Fla. 1993).

[122] Perhaps Frena was not the innocent he claimed to be.

[123] kaplan.com.

[124] See *New York Times*, Oct. 10, 1994, C1.

[125] See *San Jose Mercury News*, May 12, 1995, 1C; *Wall Street Journal*, July 27, 1995, B14.

[126] See, e.g., *Knowledgenet, Inc. v. Boone, et al.*, No. 94C-7195 (N.D. Ill. filed 12/2/94) (use of "knowledgenet.com" in transacting business on the Internet); *MTV*

Due to the proliferation of these suits (including one in which civil RICO violations were charged),[127] in July 1995 the company that assigns Internet addresses (Network Solutions, Inc.) said that it will suspend use of a domain name if the first individual to register refuses to relinquish it to the company that owns the trademark.[128] A few weeks later, Network Solutions announced a new policy requiring companies registering a domain name to indemnify Network Solutions in any legal action and cover its legal fees. Network Solutions will also require a company disputing an Internet address to prove that it holds a trademark certificate for the name from the U.S. Patent and Trademark Office.[129]

Networks v. Curry, 867 F.Supp. 202 (S.D.N.Y. 1994) (contract counterclaims over use of Internet address "mtv.com" survive motion to dismiss); *Macromedia, Inc. v. VRHacker*, Case No. C95-1261 (N.D. Cal. filed April 13, 1995); *Fry's Electronics, Inc. v. Octave Systems, Frenchy Frys, Network Solutions, Inc., et al.*, No. C95-2525-CAL (N.D. Cal. filed July 13, 1995) (suit over domain name, "frys.com").

[127] *Fry's Electronics, Inc. v. Octave Systems, Frenchy Frys, Network Solutions, Inc., et al.*, No. C95-2525-CAL (N.D. Cal. filed July 13, 1995) (suit over domain name, "frys.com").

[128] See *Wall Street Journal*, July 27, 1995, B14.

[129] See *New York Times*, August 14, 1995, C5.

APPENDIX

[CyberLaw™ 2/96]

FAMOUS TRADEMARKS

I. Tarnishing Imagery

In late 1995, a Seattle company paid more than $20,000 to acquire the Internet domain name "candyland.com." It then spent a substantial amount of money on the site, including $150,000 for advertising in adult publications. But at the beginning of 1996, it was sued by a world-leading toymaker, Hasbro, Inc., for infringing the trademark of a board game called "Candy Land" that the company sells to young children. Hasbro apparently plans to offer an Internet version of Candy Land. Hasbro claims that "[IEG's] use of the CANDYLAND name in connection with a sexually explicit pornographic Internet site by its very nature tarnishes the pure, sweet, wholesome, and fun imagery associated with Hasbro's CANDY LAND mark, and is certainly likely to undermine or damage the positive association evoked by the mark." For its part, IEG states that it does not compete with Hasbro and notes that "[there are] third party uses of the candyland mark for a wide variety of goods and services, including food, dolls, childcare services, clothing, retail sales of groceries, vending machines, paper goods, wedding supplies and services, and real estate services." But a federal court sided with Hasbro, ruling that it demonstrated a likelihood of prevailing on its claims. The court issued a preliminary injunction requiring IEG to stop using the CANDYLAND name and the Internet domain name candyland.com. *Hasbro, Inc. v. Internet Entertainment Group, Ltd.*, No. C96–130WD (W.D. Wash. Feb. 9, 1996)

II. A Famous Mark

In January 1996, Hasbro, filed suit against Internet Entertainment Group, Ltd. and related persons (collectively, "IEG") over commercial use of the "CANDYLAND" name and the Internet domain name "candyland.com." Hasbro is a world leader in the design, manufacture, and marketing of toys, and claims that one of its "longest selling and most popular toys is a children's board game known as "Candy Land." IEG allegedly "operates and/or provides content for a sexually explicit pornographic Internet site which goes by the name 'CANDY-LAND' and which uses the Internet domain name 'candyland.com."

Hasbro says that it owns the trademark "CANDY LAND," which has been on the Principal Register of the United States Patent and Trademark Office since 1951. The mark has been in continuous use by Hasbro and the Milton Bradley Company on the Candy Land board game and related products since at least 1949. Hasbro also claims the "CANDYLAND" mark, which has been on the Principal Register since no later than 1985.

The Candy Land game was developed in the 1940s by Eleanor Abbott as a way for young children to pass the time while recuperating from polio. Designed for children three years and older, since 1949 it has been advertised as "a child's first game." Candy Land was one of the classic toys featured in the current hit movie "Toy Story."

According to Hasbro, since 1975 about 23 million Candy Land games have been sold worldwide, with 1.4 million sold in each of the past three years. A recent survey found that ninety-four percent of U.S. mothers are aware of Candy Land, and that sixty percent of U.S. households with five-year-old children own the game.

Because of Candy Land's popularity and goodwill, Hasbro uses the name to market other games from its Milton Bradley division—held out to the public as "the maker of Candy Land." Says Hasbro, "Using Candy Land as a foundation, Hasbro has established Milton Bradley as a trusted, dependable maker of games for both children and adults":

By virtue of the continuous and exclusive use made of the CANDY LAND mark by Hasbro and its predecessors in connection with the Candy Land children's game and related products, the name CANDY LAND has become associated with Hasbro's Candy Land game in the minds of consumers and has come to mean and is understood to be related to Hasbro and its products.

III. Infringement & Dilution

Hasbro charges IEG with trademark infringement. Requesting an injunction and money damages, Hasbro accuses IEG of false designation of origin and dilution of a famous mark, under both federal and state law.

In supporting papers, Hasbro notes that "Candy Land's simplicity, its bright colors and its sweet and wholesome imagery have helped the game become one of Hasbro's most popular products...."

Over the past ten years, the company has spent an average of $1 million per year to advertise and promote the game.

Notably, Hasbro discloses that it's launching a new interactive division:

Hasbro is also using Candy Land to help launch a new division, the Hasbro Interactive Group. Hasbro Interactive was formed in the fall of 1995 to promote the development of Hasbro's computer-oriented games and entertainment products, in light of the rapidly increasing popularity of computer CD-ROM games and Internet gaming. As one of Hasbro's popular products, Candy Land is and will be an integral part of Hasbro Interactive's strategy. In fact, Hasbro Interactive has publicly announced that among the first computer CD-ROM games that it will release is a CD-ROM version of Candy Land, which is expected to ship within the next few months. In addition, Hasbro Interactive plans to offer an 'on-line' version of Candy Land which children will be able to play with other children around the world over the Internet.

Hasbro "has already secured the Internet domain name 'games.com' and plans to offer many of its most popular games, including Candy Land, on-line at this site in the next few years." It sent a cease and desist letter to IEG upon learning that

[IEG is] operating a sexually explicit Internet site under the name CANDYLAND which uses the domain name 'candyland.com.' While some of the site's content is accessible only to paying members, any Internet user coming upon this site can see digitized pictures of naked women engaging in various homosexual and heterosexual sex acts and review Phone Sex Yellow Pages. . . .

Federal and Washington State law permits the issuance of injunctive relief to prevent the dilution or tarnishment of a popular trademark. The federal Lanham Act, at Section 43(c), provides that

The owner of a famous mark shall be entitled, subject to the principles of equity and upon such terms as the court deems reasonable, to an injunction against another person's use in commerce of a mark or trade name, if such use commences after the mark has become famous and causes dilution of the distinctive quality of the mark, and to obtain such other relief as is provided in this section.

According to Hasbro, these statutes recognize that "trademarks are powerful marketing tools, and that even non-confusing uses of a mark by others may cause the gradual whittling away or dispersion of the trademark's identity, integrity and value."

There can be no doubt, asserts Hasbro, that CANDY LAND is a famous mark. And it is clear to Hasbro that unless enjoined, IEG's use of the CANDYLAND name will continue to dilute its mark. Says Hasbro,

[IEG's] use of the CANDYLAND name in connection with a sexually explicit pornographic Internet site by its very nature tarnishes the pure, sweet, wholesome and fun imagery associated with Hasbro's CANDY LAND mark, and is certainly likely to undermine or damage the positive association evoked by the mark. This risk is particularly acute with respect to children who may inadvertently access [IEG's] CANDYLAND Internet site in hopes of finding an on-line version of the Candy Land game.

Hasbro also claims that IEG's use of the name CANDYLAND and the domain name "candyland.com" also violates the Lanham Act by causing confusion, suggesting that such use is "likely to lead at least some segment of the public to believe that Hasbro sponsored and otherwise approved [IEG's] use of the mark." "Indeed," says Hasbro, "once someone hears of, sees, or becomes aware of [IEG's] pornographic CANDYLAND Internet site, it is unlikely that the pornographic imagery could ever be disassociated from Hasbro's game."

Hasbro believes that IEG is trading off Hasbro's goodwill. It notes that IEG "has also claimed an intention to use the domain name 'parkerbrothers.com' "—which happens to be the name of a well-known Hasbro division.

IV. Other Uses & Markets

In response, IEG states that in November 1995, it purchased the rights to the Internet domain name "candyland.com" from Scott Peiken, who was listed in an Internet database as its reputed owner. A week later, IEG paid $10,001 to Brent Davis of Candyland, Inc., who also claimed to be the rightful registered owner of candyland.com. IEG has, in fact, "incurred in excess of $700,000 related to the candyland.com address, $150,000 of which is for advertising."

IEG never intended to compete with Hasbro "by making and selling similar goods." IEG markets its services for a fee to adults, and has restricted its advertising to adult publications. IEG does not market its services to "'children aged 3 and older' as is Hasbro's Candy Land board game."

IEG notes that

[There are] third party uses of the candyland mark for a wide variety of goods and services, including food, dolls, childcare services, clothing, retail sales of groceries, vending machines, paper goods, wedding supplies and services, and real estate services. Trademark registrations exist at the state and federal level for Candyland in the name of third parties.

IEG submitted to the court a printout showing twenty-three trademark applications and registrations involving Candy Land and variations, as well as fifty-nine "unregistered (common law) uses of the mark by third parties."

Upon learning of Hasbro's concerns, IEG took a number of precautions "to avoid any possible confusion surrounding the Internet address and the Candy Land name":

(a) Removed what might be considered objectionable graphics and text from the candyland.com guest site. In particular, the Yellow Pages referred to in [Hasbro's] papers are no longer available to non-members.

(b) Inserted a disclaimer and reference at the candyland.com site to this lawsuit, clearly alleviating any possibility of likelihood of confusion.

(c) More prominently displayed its own trade name, IEG, which has always been displayed on its screen in connection with its copyright notices.

In January 1996, IEG offered to give up the candyland.com Internet address to Hasbro, "with a six-month period of time to refer users who respond to current advertising to the new site . . . , [during which time] there will be *no* content in the candyland.com site, except for a referral to a new site and whatever reasonable language Hasbro desires to assure a lack of confusion."

To prevail on a trademark claim, IEG observes that Hasbro must establish a likelihood of confusion. Factors to be considered include

strength of plaintiff's mark and similarity of the marks; evidence of actual confusion; marketing channels used; type of goods and degree of care likely to be exercised by purchaser; defendant's intent in selecting the mark, and the likelihood of the expansion of the product lines.

IEG says that it has not had the opportunity to verify Hasbro's trademark ownership or registration. But it asserts that the trademark is not inherently distinctive—"at best it is merely descriptive of a feature of the game; i.e., a game involving 'lands' named after well-known candies."

There are substantial uncontested third party uses of "candyland," states IEG, many of which are in the service sector. This "calls into question whether the Candy Land mark is 'famous' and the extent or scope of its 'fame.' Certainly," continues IEG, "it does not rise to the level of recognition achieved by Coca-Cola, Disney, Goodyear, etc."

IEG claims that use of the word "candyland" as part of an Internet domain alone in connection with adult entertainment services "does not rise to the level of trademark infringement or false designation." And there is no evidence of any actual confusion, observes IEG.

IEG also remarks that, "Hasbro's attempt to claim an expansion of its trademark rights into online services by planning an 'interactive version' of its Candyland game is questionable because it has not attempted to register for itself the Candyland.com domain name."

Hasbro apparently registered other names, including gijoe.com, over one and one-half years ago.

On Hasbro's trademark dilution claims, IEG replies, "There are substantial questions as to the strength and scope of Hasbro's claim to fame for its Candy Land mark. . . ." IEG argues that Hasbro's mark is merely descriptive of the features of a game, so that it must prove it has acquired distinctiveness. And IEG challenges, among other things, (1) the duration and extent of advertising and publicity of the mark; (2) the geographic extent of the trading area in which the mark is used; (3) the channels of trade for the goods or services with which the mark is used; (4) the degree of recognition of the mark in the trading areas and channels of trade used by Hasbro and IEG; (5) the nature and extent of use of the same or similar marks by third parties; and, (6) whether the mark was actually registered.

IEG also wonders whether Hasbro's game has appeal for children over three years old. IEG also observes that Hasbro did not submit any evidence of substantial usage of the mark in other channels of trade.

V. Referrals Allowed

At the end of January 1996, IEG offered to give up the candyland.com Internet address to Hasbro. But IEG has expended considerable amounts to advertise the Internet site, and says that it is unable to immediately cease advertising for the site or stop word-of-mouth referrals from users. Appealing to fairness, IEG states,

Clearly, IEG stands to lose substantial sums of money it has already invested in advertising if it is not even allowed to inform users accessing the candyland.com address that IEG's restricted online services are available at another site. IEG is not seeking an unlimited right to do so. Rather, it is willing to agree to eliminate all content from the candyland.com address and merely continue it for six months as a change of address notice to another non-candyland address.

In early February 1996, the court issued a ruling on Hasbro's application for a temporary injunction, and the parties agreed that it should be entered as a preliminary injunction. In relevant part, the court found that Hasbro has demonstrated a likelihood of prevailing on its federal and Washington State trademark dilution claims, that IEG's use of the CANDY LAND name and domain name is causing Hasbro irreparable injury, and that probable harm to Hasbro outweighs any inconvenience IEG will experience if required to stop using the CANDYLAND name. The court went on to order IEG immediately to take affirmative steps to stop any previously purchased advertising and to immediately remove all content from the "candy-land.com" site. But IEG is "allowed to post a 'referral notice' at the URL address 'http:[//]www.candyland.com' until May 5, 1996, which shall provide the new location of [IEG's] Internet site. The referral notice shall not contain any hyperlink to [IEG's] new site or sites, or to any other site."

3

Defamation

"Defamation" is a term from the early Middle Ages and Church law, which signified "that evil reputation which is sufficiently notorious to put a man on his trial." [130] Today, it is defined as an invasion of a person's reputation and good name. [131] A complaint for defamation may be based on a false statement, spoken (slander) or written (libel), that exposes a person to hatred, contempt, or ridicule, or which causes a person to be shunned or avoided, or which has a tendency to injure that person in his or her occupation. [132] Because online communication presently consists, for the most part, of the transfer of written text, online defamation claims are considered under libel law. This will change as real-time audio, now available through Internet videoconferencing packages, is incorporated into online systems.

The essence of libel is the publication of a false, defamatory, and unprivileged statement to a third person. [133] An actionable libel need not expressly disclose its subject. A person may prove that he or she was the intended target of the false statement, and understood as such. Importantly, liability is not restricted to the person who originates the defamatory remark—each person who repeats or republishes the defamation may be liable for so doing. [134]

Because of the chilling effect on the free flow of ideas that may be exerted by a libel claim, courts have developed limitations grounded in the First Amendment. The most important limitations concern the

---

[130] T. Plucknett, *A Concise History of the Common Law* (5th ed., 1956), 484.

[131] W. Prosser, *Torts* § 111 (4th ed., 1971).

[132] See Cal. Civ. Code §§ 45 (libel), 46 (slander).

[133] Restatement (Second) of Torts § 558.

[134] See *Stratton Oakmont, Inc. v. Prodigy Servs. Co.*, 1995 N.Y. Misc. Lexis 229, 23 Media L. Rep. 1794 (1995) ("[O]ne who repeats or otherwise republishes a libel is subject to liability as if he had originally published it."); *Hellar v. Bianco*, 111 Cal.App.2d 424, 244 P.2d 757 (1952) (bar owner liable for defamatory remarks written on men's room wall, a bartender having been asked and having failed to remove the remarks).

status of the person who is the subject of the alleged libel. For a public official to win a defamation action, he or she must prove publication with "actual malice," i.e., "with knowledge that it was false or with reckless disregard of whether it was false or not."[135] This standard also applies in cases brought by "public figures,"[136] including "involuntary public figures" and "limited purpose" public figures—those who have "thrust themselves to the forefront of particular public controversies in order to influence the resolution of the issues involved."[137] The Supreme Court explains,

The first remedy of any victim of defamation is self-help—using available opportunities to contradict the lie or correct the error and thereby to minimize its adverse impact on reputation. Public officials and public figures usually enjoy significantly greater access to the channels of effective communication and hence have a more realistic opportunity to counteract false statements than private individuals normally enjoy. Private individuals are therefore more vulnerable to injury, and the state interest in protecting them is correspondingly greater.[138]

In 1994, an Ohio corporation that conducts direct marketing to households (Suarez Corporation) filed a defamation lawsuit against a journalist (Brock N. Meeks) who writes his own news and commentary service published only via computer to a limited audience on the Internet. In his defense, Meeks raised the concept of a "meta-public figure."[139] Looking to considerations that determine whether a libel plaintiff is a public figure, Meeks observed that

First, public figures "invite attention and comment" and thereby "have voluntarily exposed themselves to increased risk of injury form defamatory falsehoods concerning them." [Citation omitted.] Second, public figures "usually enjoy significantly greater access to channels of effective communication and hence have a more realistic

---

[135] *New York Times Co. v. Sullivan*, 376 U.S. 254, 279–80, 11 L.Ed.2d 686, 84 S.Ct. 710 (1964).

[136] So classified because of "the notoriety of their achievements or the vigor and success with which they seek the public's attention." *Gertz v. Robert Welch, Inc.*, 418 U.S. 323, 342, 41 L.Ed.2d 789, 94 S.Ct. 2997 (1974).

[137] See *Gertz v. Robert Welch, Inc.*, 418 U.S. 323, 342, 345, 41 L.Ed.2d 789, 94 S.Ct. 2997 (1974). Notably, a person may be a "public figure" for some issues and not for others. See *Tavoulareas v. Piro*, 817 F.2d 762, 775 (D.C. Cir. 1987), *cert. denied*, 484 U.S. 870 (oil company president held limited purpose public figure regarding management and structure of company); cf. *Rosanova v. Playboy Enters.*, 411 F.Supp. 440, 443 (S.D. Ga. 1976), *aff'd*, 580 F.2d 859 (5th Cir. 1978) ("Defining public figures is much like trying to nail a jellyfish to the wall").

[138] *Gertz v. Robert Welch, Inc.*, 418 U.S. 323, 345 41 L.Ed.2d 789, 94 S.Ct. 2997 (1974).

[139] *Suarez Corp. Industries v, Meeks*, Case No. 267513, Brief In Support of Motion of Defendant Brock M. Meeks for Summary Judgment (Ct. Common Pleas, Cuyahoga County, Oh. August 2, 1994).

opportunity to counteract false statements than private individuals normally enjoy." [*Gertz v. Robert Welch, Inc.*, 418 U.S. 323, 345, 344 (1974).]

Contending that the plaintiffs voluntarily assumed the risk of criticism by soliciting Internet users to examine their products and learn more about them, Meeks asserted that

Like any other Internet user, they have ample ability to rebut that criticism. Just like any other Internet user, plaintiffs could have written any response they desired and posted it to as many persons as they chose. Unlike traditional communications media where editors and news directors control who says what, the Internet provides plaintiffs with unfettered access to its mass audiences. See [*Steaks Unlimited, Inc. v. Deaner*, 623 F.2d 264, 274 (3d Cir. 1980)] (public figure plaintiff had ability to purchase advertising time and therefore had regular and continuing access to effective channels of communication to respond to charges).

There are a number of defenses to libel actions, the primary one being truth. But in some states, truth may not be an absolute defense. A defendant may have to prove that the statement was made for good motives or justifiable ends.[140] Other defenses include "privilege," which may include, among other things, a publication made in the proper discharge of an official duty; a legislative or judicial proceeding; a fair and true report in a public journal of a judicial or legislative meeting; or a verified charge or complaint made to a public official, upon which a warrant has been issued.[141]

A plaintiff has the right to demand a correction on publication of a libel, and sometimes doing so will have legal consequences. Generally, in jurisdictions where there is a correction statute, if a correction is not demanded or is, in fact, published, the plaintiff can lose his or her ability to recover money damages without specific proof of loss, such as damages for loss of reputation, shame, mortification, and hurt feeling.[142]

---

[140] See W. Prosser, *Torts* § 116 (4th ed. 1971).

[141] See, e.g., Cal. Civ. Code § 47; *Shahvar v. Superior Court*, 25 Cal.App.4th 653, 663 (1994) (except for fair reports in public journals, Section 47 privileges are not "designed to protect a party's statements about litigation to someone entirely unrelated to the litigation."); see also *Proctor & Gamble Mfg. Co. v. Hagler*, 880 S.W.2d 123 (Tex. App. 1994) (reversing jury verdict against employer over termination notice posted on internal company bulletin boards, including alleged theft of company telephone as reason for termination, on grounds plaintiff did not meet his burden of showing employer lost qualified privilege by acting with actual malice).

[142] For example, in Wisconsin under § 895.05(2), STATS:

Before any civil suit shall be commenced on account of any libelous publication in any newspaper, magazine or periodical, the libeled person shall first give those alleged to be responsible or liable for the publication a reasonable opportunity to correct the libelous matter. . . . A correc-

In a case over an alleged libel posted on a national electronic online service, a Wisconsin court held that a demand for retraction under state statute was not required because it does not cover computer network bulletin board communications.[143] In this case, a Wisconsin resident, Fuschetto, and a New York resident, Meneau, communicated with each other over SportsNet, a national electronic online service, and by telephone. They agreed to meet in New York. Unfortunately, prior to the trip Fuschetto and his wife became ill. When Fuschetto asked to postpone the trip, Fuschetto and Meneau argued about the price of airline tickets, as well as tickets purchased for the Knicks and the David Letterman show. Fuschetto posted to SportsNet an explanation of his arguments with Meneau, who responded with claims of defamation, negligence, and tortious interference with business relations. The trial court granted a motion for summary judgment in favor of Fuschetto, on the grounds Meneau had not demanded a retraction. But the court of appeals reversed, because SportsNet is not a newspaper, magazine, or periodical. The statute, explained the court of appeals, only relates to publications in print media (personal letters, billboards, and signs are not included). "The nature of bulletin board postings on computer network services," ruled the court of appeals, "cannot be classified as print."[144]

The first major court decision on online defamation was the result of a lawsuit filed against CompuServe, one of the world's largest computer online services. CompuServe provides its subscribers with a number of online forums, including a journalism forum, and electronic libraries. One publication available in the journalism forum contained an allegedly defamatory statement, which led to a suit against CompuServe. Notably, CompuServe had contracted with an independent entity, Cameron Communications, Inc., "to manage, review, create, delete, edit and otherwise control the contents of Journalism Forum in accordance with editorial and technical standards and conventions of style established by Compuserve."

---

tion, timely published, without comment, in a position and type as prominent as the alleged libel, shall constitute a defense against the recovery of any damage except actual damages, as well as being competent and material in mitigation of actual damages to the extent the correction published does not so mitigate them.

See also Cal. Civ. Code § 48a; cf. *Miami Herald Pub. Co. v. Tornillo*, 418 U.S. 241, 41 L.Ed.2d 730, 94 S.Ct. 2831 (1974) ("right of reply" statute requiring newspapers that assail character or record of a political candidate to afford the candidate free space to reply violates First Amendment guarantees of a free press).

[143] *It's in the Cards v. Fuschetto*, 193 Wis.2d 429, 535 N.W.2d 11 (Ct. App. 1995).
[144] Ibid., 193 Wis. 2d 429, 535 N.W. 2d 11, 14 (Ct. App. 1995).

In *Cubby, Inc. v. CompuServe, Inc.*,[145] the court found that CompuServe did not have the opportunity to review the content of the publication at issue before it was uploaded into its computer banks. CompuServe's product, said the court, was an electronic library for profit carrying a vast number of publications, with CompuServe exercising little or no editorial control over publication content. Finding it to be an "electronic news distributor," the court held CompuServe to the lower standard of liability accorded to public libraries, book stores, and newsstands, i.e., whether it had knowledge, or reason to know, of the defamatory content of the publication.[146] Holding that CompuServe could not be held liable for posting the alleged defamatory statement, the court stated:

CompuServe and companies like it are at the forefront of the information industry revolution. High technology has markedly increased the speed with which information is gathered and processed; it is now possible for an individual with a personal computer, modem, and telephone line to have instantaneous access to thousands of news publications from across the United States and around the world. While CompuServe may decline to carry a given publication altogether, in reality, once it does decide to carry a publication, it will have little or no editorial control over that publication's contents. . . .

CompuServe has no more editorial control over [such a publication] than does a public library, book store, or newsstand, and it would be no more feasible for CompuServe to examine every publication it carries for potentially defamatory statements than it would be for any other distributor to do so. . . .

Technology is rapidly transforming the information industry. A computerized database is the functional equivalent of a more traditional news vendor, and the inconsistent application of a lower standard of liability to an electronic news distributor such as CompuServe than that which is applied to a public library, book store, or newsstand would impose an undue burden on the free flow of information. Given the relevant First Amendment considerations, the appropriate standard of liability to be applied to CompuServe is whether it knew or had reason to know of the alleged defamatory . . . statements.[147]

---

[145] 776 F.Supp. 135 (S.D.N.Y. 1991).

[146] See *Church of Scientology v. Minnesota State Medical Asso. Foundation*, 264 N.W.2d 152, 156 (Minn. 1978) ("Those who merely deliver or transmit defamatory material previously published by another will be considered to have published the material only if they knew, or had reason to know, that the material was false and defamatory. It is this rule that protects libraries and vendors of books, magazines, and newspapers."); *Western Union Tel. Co. v. Lesesne*, 182 F.2d 135, 136–37 (4th Cir. 1950) (telegraph company); see also, *Smith v. California*, 361 U.S. 147, 4 L.Ed.2d 205, 80 S.Ct. 215 (1959) (bookseller); *Anderson v. New York Tel. Co.*, 361 N.Y.S.2d 913, 916, 320 N.E.2d 647 (1974) (telephone company is "privileged under its tariff restrictions to terminate service for cause only in certain prescribed circumstances none of which encompass the subscriber's dissemination of defamatory messages").

[147] *Cubby, Inc. v. CompuServe, Inc.*, 776 F.Supp. 135, 140–41 (S.D.N.Y. 1991). On the duty to investigate, see *McBride v. Merrell Dow & Pharmaceuticals*, 613 F.Supp.

(Notably, the court did not rule on the liability of Cameron Communications, Inc., the company managing the journalism forum for CompuServe.)

But this lower standard for "distributors" may not cover all computer online services. Prodigy, for example, is a computer online service with at least two million subscribers. Prodigy's subscribers communicate with each other and "the general subscriber population" using the service's bulletin boards. "Money Talk" is a popular Prodigy bulletin board, where members can post statements about stocks, investments, and other financial matters. Prodigy "contracts with Bulletin Board Leaders, who, among other things, participate in board discussions and undertake promotional efforts to encourage usage and increase users."

In October 1994, an unidentified person posted on Money Talk allegedly defamatory statements about Stratton Oakmont, Inc., a securities investment banking firm. These statements accused Stratton and its president of committing criminal and fraudulent acts in connection with the initial public offering of a particular stock. The offering was described as a "major criminal fraud" and "100% criminal fraud." Stratton's president, the posting alleged, was "soon to be a proven criminal." His firm was characterized as a "cult of brokers who either lie for a living or get fired."

In response, Stratton and its president sued Prodigy and the unidentified person who posted the statements. One claim was for libel. To "advance" the litigation, Stratton requested that the trial court determine (1) whether Prodigy is a "publisher" of the alleged defamatory statements, and (2) whether Money Talk's board leader acted as Prodigy's "agent" for the purposes of the action.

In *Stratton Oakmont, Inc. v. Prodigy Services Co.,*[148] the court held that Prodigy's family orientation—supported by its use of screening software, usage guidelines, and management of contractors hired to run its online discussion forums—gave it "sufficient control over its computer bulletin boards to render it a publisher with the same responsibilities as a newspaper." Distinguishing the *CompuServe* case, the court observed that

---

1349, 1356 (D.D.C. 1985), *aff'd in part and rev'd in part*, 800 F.2d 1208 (D.C. Cir. 1986) ("The courts have required a showing of special circumstances imposing a duty on the distributor to ascertain the defamatory character of the publication."); and compare *Dworkin v. Hustler Magazine, Inc.*, 611 F.Supp. 781, 786–87 (D. Wyo. 1985), with *Spence v. Flynt*, 647 F.Supp. 1266, 1274 (D. Wyo. 1986).

[148] 1995 N.Y. Misc. Lexis 229, 23 Media L. Rep. 1794 (N.Y. Sup. Ct. 1995).

First, PRODIGY held itself out to the public and its members as controlling the content of its computer bulletin boards. Second, PRODIGY implemented this control through its automatic software screening program, and the Guidelines which Board Leaders are required to enforce. By actively utilizing technology and manpower to delete notes from its computer bulletin boards on the basis of offensiveness and "bad taste," for example, PRODIGY is clearly making decisions as to content (see *Miami Herald Publishing Co. v. Tornillo*, [418 U.S. 241 (1974)]), and such decisions constitute editorial control. That such control is not complete and is enforced both as early as the notes arrive and as late as a complaint is made, does not minimize or eviscerate the simple fact that PRODIGY has uniquely arrogated to itself the role of determining what is proper for its members to post and read on its bulletin boards.

The *Prodigy* court also found an interesting comparison to a case where apple growers sued a television network and its local affiliates over an allegedly defamatory report generated by the network and broadcast by local affiliates.[149] In that case, the affiliates had the power to exercise editorial control by virtue of their contract with the network, as well as the technical capacity and opportunity to do so given the three hour time difference between the east and west coasts. In addition, the local affiliates had occasionally censored network programming, albeit not respecting "60 Minutes." But the court did not impose "conduit liability,"

[as this] would force the creation of full time editorial boards at local stations throughout the country which possess sufficient knowledge, legal acumen and access to experts to continually monitor incoming transmissions and exercise on-the-spot discretionary calls or face $75 million dollar lawsuits at every turn. That is not realistic. . . . More than merely unrealistic in economic terms, it is difficult to imagine a scenario more chilling on the media's rights of expression and the public's right to know.[150]

Here, however, says the court, Prodigy has "virtually created" an editorial staff to monitor transmissions and censor notes. By use of automatic scanning, guidelines, and board leaders, observes the court, Prodigy may have chilled freedom of communication in cyberspace— "and it appears that this chilling effect is exactly what PRODIGY wants, but for the legal liability that attaches to such censorship."

These two cases, *Cubby* and *Prodigy*, indicate that where there is a moderated discussion group online, there is potential liability—for the moderator, the online service carrying the discussion group, or both. What the courts do not fully address, as indicated in the "*60 Minutes*" case, is the fact that you cannot realistically screen for defa-

---

[149] *Auvil v. CBS "60 Minutes,"* 800 F.Supp. 928 (E.D. Wash. 1992).
[150] Ibid., 800 F.Supp. 928, 931–32 (E.D. Wash. 1992).

mation. Nor do they recognize that an online system is simply not the same thing as a print (e.g., book or newspaper) distributor or publisher. In many cases, online systems provide the equivalent of a park and areas where people with common interests may congregate and set up their own soapbox. The online system may have wardens that ensure that people wait their turn to get on the box and that nude sunbathers do not scare the children, but that have no real ability to analyze content and determine whether a statement is defamatory. Forced to try to do so, they will simply not allow people to speak their minds—not a good thing in a society that values freedom of speech.

APPENDIX

3

[CyberLaw™ 10/94]

LIBEL & SUPPRESSION

I. A Chilling Decision

Has a decision by a California Court of Appeal undermined a rule ensuring unintimidated access to the courts and the free flow of information concerning public disputes? The decision in *Shahvar v. Superior Court*, 25 Cal.App.4th 653 (6th App. Dist. June 2, 1994), involves irreconcilable differences between founders of a computer company and the ouster of one of them. When the unseated founder sued and his allegations were reported in the local newspaper, the other side replied with a $27 million dollar libel claim based on transmission of a copy of the complaint to the press. The trial court was asked to dismiss the libel claim, on the grounds that both the filing of the original complaint and the publication of the report about the lawsuit were privileged, i.e., immune from claims of libel. But the trial court refused to dismiss the claim, a result that appears wrong. As stated by counsel upon appeal, "Publicly available judicial documents are the proper subject of public dissemination, in turn enabling public discussion. In a democracy this should be an unassailable truism, not a proposition for debate." Appeal of the ruling was rejected, however, and the case settled, so the ruling now stands as law in California's 6th Appellate District. Hopefully, the issues will soon be revisited so that there will be an opportunity to reverse this chilling precedent.

II. Two Stories

ASP Computer Products, Inc. was founded in 1987. The company "designs, manufactures, and provides direct marketing and sales of printer sharing products that permit multiple users of personal computers or LAN networks to share printers." The gross business of ASP grew from $1 million in 1989 to about $14 million in 1992.

Shahvar alleges that virtually all the business plans, product ideas, and marketing strategies were his products. As founder, he elected Amnon Even-Kesef as a codirector of the company and for the next five years ran the company with him as the functional equivalents of copresidents, who acted in concert on all matters of significance. Between 1987 and 1992, Shahvar was ASP's executive vice president and functioned as its chief financial officer. Even-Kesef held the title of president.

In 1992, Shahvar became angry over a campaign by Even-Kesef allegedly intended to deplete ASP's profits. In response to Shahvar's attempts to discuss this with Even-Kesef, Shahvar was told that Even-Kesef was going to run the company. The two other shareholders in ASP, the Sigals (husband and wife), sided with Even-Kesef and laid off Shahvar, allegedly telling Shahvar that he would be terminated if he returned to the company.

Shahvar says that ASP replaced him, canceled promissory notes payable to the company by the defendants, extended the due date on other notes, and reduced Shahvar's severance pay by twenty-five percent (he had been expecting payments of $15,000 per month for eighteen months). Among other things, Shahvar alleges that "defendants [have] plainly demonstrated their intent and majority power to control ASP and to strip [Shahvar] of any opportunity to protect his economic investment in the company."

In early 1993, Shahvar's termination from ASP was confirmed, for asserted failure to report to work, for a "sham position" says Shahvar. He also alleges that "defendants in bad faith curtailed all severance payments because they wanted Shahvar to be cash poor, so he would accede to their tortious efforts to buy his stock at a low price."

Even-Kesef, in a cross-complaint filed against Shahvar, tells a different story. At the end of 1986, Even-Kesef was a "Senior Program Manager in a Silicon Valley computer manufacturing company." Shahvar, on the other hand, was unemployed but experienced as a computer dealer in El Paso, Texas.

After having been terminated from his last position, and suffering from personal family problems, Shahvar was in the Silicon Valley looking for employment. Shahvar was depressed and consumed by his failures. Even-Kesef believed Shahvar had potential and wanted to give him another opportunity in business.

Even-Kesef and Shahvar discussed going into business together. Two other investors joined them and ASP was formed. Even-Kesef alleges that "Shahvar did not understand the market and was an incompetent manager of the marketing of products of ASP." Even-Kesef states that he "assumed control of the marketing of ASP and turned around the failed program of Shahvar." Even-Kesef further alleges that Shahvar was incompetent, obstructionist, and dishonest.

III. Publication & Libel

In April 1992, Shahvar filed suit against Even-Kesef, the Sigals, and ASP. According to the Court of Appeal,

This complaint falsely alleged, among other things, that Ellen and Gerald Sigal submitted invoices to ASP for work they did not do and that Gerald Sigal violated ASP's by-laws by transferring stock to Ellen Sigal for consideration in an effort to avoid shareholder or director liability to Shahvar.

Shahvar's lawyer sent a copy of the complaint to the *San Francisco Examiner* newspaper. Shahvar later sent copies of the resulting *Examiner* article to social and business associates of Even-Kesef, Ellen and Gerald Sigal, both in California and Israel. This conduct led to a cross-complaint for libel.

Shahvar sought to have the counter-claim dismissed as a matter of law, i.e., without having to go to trial. But the trial court dismissed his request without stated reason. Shahvar appealed the ruling to the Court of Appeal.

IV. A Litigation Privilege

Under California law, there exists a "litigation privilege." California Civil Code Section 47 provides generally that a privileged publication or broadcast is, among other things, one made in any judicial proceeding. This Section also privileges "a fair and true report in a public journal" of a judicial proceeding and anything said during its course. California courts have noted that "the obvious purpose of section 47 [is] to afford litigants the utmost freedom of access to the courts to secure and defend their rights without fear of being harassed by actions for defamation."

According to Shahvar's counsel,

California Civil Code Section 47(b) absolutely privileges from liability (under *any* theory) statements spelled out in a pleading, as well as communications "related" not only to actual but to potential litigation.

Indeed, this is the *core* of the privilege—in reality it extends much further. . . .

It protects not only pleadings, draft pleadings, or evidence but *any* communication having "some logical relation to" litigation. "Malice" is irrelevant. The privilege attaches to the statements made before, during, or after the commencement of litigation, so long as they have some "logical relationship" to the litigation. (Citations omitted.)

Shahvar warns that the trial court's decision not to dismiss the libel claim filed against him as a matter of law will have wide-ranging repercussions:

[T]he ruling below would bless—or spawn—the practice of responding to complaints with libel cross-complaints as a standard litigation tactic. Civil Code Section 47's intended purpose will be overthrown, and press access to vital public information thwarted or crippled. Particularly in a court based in the Silicon Valley, newsworthy legal actions are frequently pending. Accurate information about their content is often difficult for the press even under the best of deadline-straitened circumstances. Judicial scrutiny of news articles referring to filed complaints will cause the media to shy away from gathering and reporting on the natural and most direct source for such data—the complaint itself.

(Indeed, the only place to find a digital copy of a complaint is from a party's attorney, as litigants are not required to and do not file copies of their pleadings on a disk.)

In opposition, the defendants argued that allowing the "litigation privilege" to cover "publication to the general public through the press" would be an expansion that swallows the rule that republication to nonparticipants in a legal action is not privileged. "To argue otherwise," they urge, "is to support the 'universally condemned "trial by press," a procedure forbidden to counsel and subversive of the fair and orderly conduct of judicial proceedings.'"

V. Inducing Publication

In considering the parties' arguments, the Court of Appeal observed that the basis for the libel claim against Shahvar was not that a false complaint had been filed. The cross-complaint is based on the communication of a copy of the complaint to a newspaper, "which induced the newspaper to publish an article summarizing the complaint's allegations." The Court of Appeal ruled that "Shahvar's communication of his allegations to [the *Examiner* newspaper] was unrelated to the litigation and therefore not covered by the litigation privilege."

VI. Free Speech & Reputation

In reaching its conclusion, the Court of Appeal rejected a decision by another appellate court, *Abraham v. Lancaster Community Hospital* (1990) 217 Cal.App.3d 796. In *Abraham*, the plaintiff claimed that he had been defamed by the actions of the defendants in causing their allegations, filed in a proposed amended federal court complaint, to be published in the local press and in disseminating those allegations to the local media. Holding that the defendants' actions were privileged, the appellate court stated,

Since the articles were accurate reports of the contents of the federal pleadings . . . they were absolutely privileged as a 'fair and true report in a public journal, of (1) a judicial . . . proceeding.' Since both the pleadings in the federal court and publication in the press of a fair and true report of the pleadings are absolutely privileged, *it would defeat the purpose of section 47, subdivisions 2 and 4 to punish transmittal of the privileged pleadings to the press.* Finally, there is the alleged communication of the allegations within the Antelope Valley and specifically within the medical community. These, too, are privileged communications. First, the local medical community possessed 'a substantial interest in the outcome of the pending litigation' [because the allegations concerned whether a hospital administrator had used the hospital's local monopoly to require health insurers to purchase other services from the hospital and not from competing hospitals] and as such were 'participants' therein. Second, to exclude those alleged communications about a judicial proceeding from the scope of section 47, subdivision 2 would impose a chilling effect on the public's discussion of pending litigation. Would judges or attorneys talking about allegations over lunch with their colleagues or at social dinners be subject to defamation suits? Would there be liability for hospital administrators discussing the fair and true report of allegations they read about in the Antelope Valley Press? It would be anomalous to hold that a litigant is privileged to make a publication necessary to bring an action but that he can be sued for defamation if he lets anyone know that he has brought it. (Citations omitted.)

The Court of Appeal distinguished the factual circumstances in *Abraham* and the court decision on which it relied from those present in *Shahvar*. The Court of Appeal also held that *Abraham* placed undue reliance upon the chilling effect on discussion absent the litigation privilege. In *Shahvar*, the Court of Appeal observed that free speech protections are preserved by governing constitutional rules that statements of opinion are not actionable, only false statements of fact are subject to defamation liability, and that false statements of fact about public figures are subject to liability only for "malice," i.e., when a statement is made with knowledge of falsity or reckless disregard of whether it was false or not. A private person must prove negligence to recover damages and when the matter sued upon is a public concern, cannot recover presumed or punitive damages without proving malice.

The First Amendment balances between social interest in free discussion and private reputation. According to the California Supreme Court,

Society's interest in the value of a private person's reputation weighs against the judicial creation of a privilege (whether by construing a statute or the common law) that would impose burdens greater that those already required under the federal Constitution. (Citation omitted.)

Cloaking itself with this policy, the Court of Appeal decided not to follow what it describes as *Abraham*'s "extension of the litigation privilege beyond its statutory terms." The Court of Appeal also noted that "[a] statement 'to' a public journal is not a statement 'in' a public journal," and described as unwarranted the "bridge" privilege it says *Abraham* "invented" between privileged pleadings and a privileged report. According to the Court of Appeal, except for fair reports in public journals Section 47 privileges are not "designed to protect a party's statements about litigation to someone entirely unrelated to the litigation."

VII. Fear, Uncertainty, & Suppression

While the decision of the Court of Appeal in *Shahvar* may be a product of correct legal logic, it is hard to see that the right result was achieved. Absurdly, in *Shahvar* the Court of Appeal attempts to preserve a balance between private reputation and the right of the public to a fair and true report by relying upon, if not creating, an inefficiency.

Under *Shahvar*, the public's ability to receive a fair and true report of a judicial proceeding is handicapped. If a litigant or a litigant's attorney cannot alert the press to the filing of a case that warrants a public report, whether such report will be made will depend upon whether the resources of the press are sufficient to uncover the noteworthy case or just plain luck.

Suppose the press happens to learn of a case upon which it wishes to report. Someone will be sent to the courthouse to obtain a copy of the pleadings. If the file is not available—maybe the judge has it or someone else is reviewing it—the press will have to wait until the file returns. It would have been more efficient to call a party's lawyer for a copy. But now that lawyer cannot provide a copy for fear of creating the basis for a libel claim.

In any event, if a public report is published, the press will be asked for the source of the underlying documentation. Inevitably, this will result in a tremendous waste of time, money, and resources in case after case as the press defends itself (and inevitably works to protect sources) from parties seeking to determine facts that may allow proof of a defamation claim.

In defense of *Shahvar*, one might cite a concern about civil suits filed as a cheap way to blacken opponents' names and to compel unwarranted money settlements. But one should recognize that the remedy chosen may well have societal implications of greater import—including suppression of important news.

[CyberLaw™ 5/95]

ONLINE DEFAMATION

I. Control & Liability

Will a New York court decision force computer online services to construct full time editorial boards possessing sufficient knowledge, legal acumen, and access to experts to continually monitor postings on their bulletin boards and exercise on-the-spot discretionary calls or face multimillion-dollar lawsuits at every turn? In *Stratton Oakmont, Inc., et al. v. Prodigy Services Company*, 1995 N.Y. Misc. Lexis 229, 23 Media L.Rep. 1794 (1995), the family orientation of the Prodigy Services Company—supported by its use of screening software, usage guidelines, and management of contractors hired to run its online discussion forums—was held to give Prodigy "sufficient control over its computer bulletin boards to render it a publisher with the same responsibilities as a newspaper." In response to the claim that its decision would chill the flow of speech across Prodigy's network, the court commented that a "chilling effect is exactly what PRODIGY wants, but for the legal liability that attaches to such censorship." Will this decision drive online services away from content regulation? Or will the market, as the court supposes, compensate a network for increased control and liability exposure?

II. Money Talk

Prodigy is a computer online service with at least two million subscribers, who communicate with each other and with "the general subscriber population" using Prodigy's bulletin boards. Prodigy "contracts with "Bulletin Board Leaders," who, among other things, participate in board discussions and undertake promotional efforts to encourage usage and increase users." "Money Talk" is a Prodigy bulletin board where members can post statements regarding stocks, investments, and other financial matters. It may be the most widely read financial computer bulletin board in the United States. Charles Epstein is Money Talk's Board Leader.

In October 1994, a still-unidentified person posted on Money Talk allegedly defamatory statements about Stratton Oakmont, Inc., a securities investment banking firm. These statements accused Stratton and its president, Daniki Porush, of committing criminal and fraudulent acts in connection with the initial public offering of stock of Solomon-Page Ltd. This offering was described as a "major criminal fraud" and "100% criminal fraud." Porush, the posting alleged, was "soon to be a proven criminal" and his firm, Stratton Oakmont, was characterized as a "cult of brokers who either lie for a living or get fired."

Stratton Oakmont and Porush (collectively, "Stratton") responded by suing Prodigy and the unidentified person who posted the statements onto Money Talk. One of the claims is for per se libel. To "advance" the litigation, Stratton requested that the trial court determine (1) whether Prodigy is a "publisher" of the alleged defamatory statements, and (2) whether Money Talk's Board Leader, Epstein, acted as Prodigy's "agent" for the purposes of this action.

III. Family Orientation

Stratton's claim that Prodigy is a publisher is based in large measure on its policy (started in 1990 when it commenced operations) that it is a family-oriented computer network. In articles written by Prodigy's director of market programs and communications, the court found that Prodigy "held itself out as an online service that exercised editorial control." In one such article, Prodigy stated,

We make no apology for pursuing a value system that reflects the culture of the millions of American families we aspire to serve. Certainly no responsible newspaper does less when it chooses the type of advertising it publishes, the letters it prints, the degree of nudity and unsupported gossip its editors tolerate.

Prodigy, however, insists that its policies have changed and evolved since 1990. Prodigy claims that "the latest article on the subject, dated February, 1993, did not reflect PRODIGY's policies in October, 1994, when the allegedly libelous statements were posted." But, says the court, consideration of the passage of time goes solely to the weight of the evidence.

To bolster its claim that Prodigy is a publisher, Stratton also points to

(A) promulgation of "content guidelines" . . . in which, inter alia, users are requested to refrain from posting notes that are "insulting" and are advised that "notes that harass other members or are deemed to be in bad taste or grossly repugnant to community standards, or are deemed harmful to maintaining a harmonious online community, will be removed when brought to PRODIGY's attention"; the Guidelines all expressly state that although "Prodigy is committed to open debate and discussion on the bulletin boards . . . this does not mean that 'anything goes'";

(B) use of a software screening program which automatically prescreens all bulletin board postings for offensive language;

(C) the use of Board Leaders such as Epstein whose duties include enforcement of the Guidelines . . . and

(D) . . . a tool for Board Leaders known as an "emergency delete function" pursuant to which a Board Leader could remove a note and send a previously prepared message of explanation "ranging from solicitation, bad advice, insulting, wrong topic, off topic, bad taste, etcetera."

IV. Publisher Liability

"A finding that PRODIGY is a publisher is the first hurdle to overcome in pursuit of [Stratton's] defamation claims," notes the court, because "one who repeats or otherwise republishes a libel is subject to liability as if he had originally published it." Others, such as distributors or deliverers (e.g., bookstores, libraries), may be held liable only if they know or have reason to know of the defamatory statement at issue. The court explains:

A distributor or deliverer of defamatory material is considered a passive conduit and will not be found liable in the absence of fault. However, a newspaper, for example, is more than a passive receptacle or conduit for news, comment, and advertising. The choice of material to go into a newspaper and the decisions made as to the content of the paper constitute the exercise of editorial control and judgment, and with this editorial control comes increased liability. (Citations omitted.)

V. Editorial Control

In this case, states the court, the critical issue is whether Prodigy "exercised sufficient editorial control over its computer bulletin boards to render it a publisher with the same responsibilities as a newspaper." Prodigy answers that it changed its policy of manually reviewing all messages prior to posting long before the posting of the comments at issue. But Prodigy did not submit to the court documentation or detailed explanation, or dissemination of news of such a change.

Prodigy also claims that it is not feasible to review manually the 60,000 messages that are posted each day. And while Board Leaders may remove messages that violate its Guidelines, Prodigy argues they are not "editors." More generally, Prodigy urges "that this Court should not decide issues that can directly impact this developing communications medium without the benefit of a full record." But, observes the court, Prodigy "fails to describe what further facts remain to be developed on this issue of whether it is a publisher."

To avoid publisher liability, Prodigy looks to *Cubby, Inc. v. Compuserve, Inc.*, 776 F.Supp. 135 (S.D.N.Y. 1991). In that case, a computer online service provided subscribers with forums, including a journalism forum, and electronic libraries. One publication available in the journalism forum contained an allegedly defamatory statement about the plaintiff. An independent entity, Cameron Communications, Inc., had "contracted to manage, review, create, delete, edit and otherwise control the contents of Journalism Forum in accordance with editorial and technical standards and conventions of style established by Compuserve."

In *Cubby*, the court found that Compuserve did not have the opportunity to review the content of the publication at issue before it was uploaded into its computer banks. Compuserve's product, said the court, was an electronic library for profit carrying a vast number of publications, with Compuserve exercising little or no editorial control over publication content. Finding it to be an "electronic news distributor," the court held Compuserve to the lower standard of liability accorded to public libraries, book stores, and newsstands (i.e., whether it had knowledge, or reason to know, of the defamatory content of the publication).

Distinguishing between Compuserve and Prodigy, the court here observed,

First, PRODIGY held itself out to the public and its members as controlling the content of its computer bulletin boards. Second, PRODIGY implemented this control through its automatic software screening program, and the Guidelines which Board Leaders are required to enforce. By actively utilizing technology and manpower to delete notes from its computer bulletin boards on the basis of offensiveness and "bad taste," for example PRODIGY is clearly making decisions as to content (see *Miami Herald Publishing Co. v. Tornillo*, [418 U.S. 241 (1974)]), and such decisions constitute editorial control. That such control is not complete and is enforced both as early as the notes arrive and as late as a complaint is made, does not minimize or eviscerate the simple fact that PRODIGY has uniquely arrogated to itself the role of determining what is proper for its members to post and read on its bulletin boards.

The court also found an interesting comparison in a case where apple growers sued a television network and its local affiliates over an allegedly defamatory report generated by the network and broadcast by local affiliates (*Auvil v. CBS "60 Minutes"*, 800 F.Supp. 928 [(E.D. Wash. 1993)]). In that case, the affiliates had the power to exercise editorial control by virtue of their contract with the network, as well as the technical capacity and opportunity to do so given the three-hour time difference between the east and west coasts. In addition, the local affiliates had occasionally censored network programming, albeit not respecting "60 Minutes." In that case, however, the court did not impose "conduit liability,"

[as this] would force the creation of full time editorial boards at local stations throughout the country which possess sufficient knowledge, legal acumen and access to experts to continually monitor incoming transmissions and exercise on-the-spot discretionary calls or face $75 million dollar lawsuits at every turn. That is not realistic. . . . More than merely unrealistic in economic terms, it is difficult to imagine a scenario more chilling on the media's rights of expression and the public's right to know.

But here, says the court, Prodigy has "virtually created" an editorial staff to monitor transmissions and censor notes. By use of automatic scanning, guidelines and board leaders, observes the court, Prodigy may have chilled freedom of communication in cyberspace— "and it appears that this chilling effect is exactly what PRODIGY wants, but for the legal liability that attaches to such censorship."

Publisher status for Prodigy will not compel all computer networks to abdicate control over their networks, explains the court. Fear of such a result "incorrectly presumes that the market will refuse to compensate a network for its increased control and the resulting increased exposure." The court also notes that the issues here may ultimately be preempted by enactment of the Communications Decency Act of 1995 now pending before Congress.

VI. Contractors & Agents

Turning to the status of Epstein, the Board Leader, the court noted that agency "is a legal relationship which results from the manifestation of consent of one person to allow another to act on his or her behalf and subject to his or her control, and consent by the other to so act." Prodigy had attempted to structure its contractual relationship with Epstein so that he could not act as, or be found by a court to be, Prodigy's agent. The written agreement between Prodigy and Epstein provides that, among other things,

[Epstein] indemnify and agree to hold PRODIGY harmless from and against all claims, cost[s], liabilities[, and] judgments . . . arising out of or in connection with anything [Epstein does]. . . .

Being a Board Leader does not make [Epstein] a PRODIGY Services Company employee, representative or agent, and [Epstein] agree[s] not to claim or suggest [he is] one.

The court noted, however, that "talismanic language [in a contract] does not determine an agency relationship." Similarly, "whether one is an independent contractor is not determinative of whether one is an agent." Courts look, instead, to the substance of the relationship and whether "one party retains a sufficient degree of direction and control over another."

For the limited purpose of monitoring and editing the "Money Talk" bulletin board, the court ruled that "PRODIGY directed and controlled Epstein's actions." This conclusion was based on the relationship between Prodigy and its Board Leaders, the obligation of Board Leaders to follow the Guidelines, and Prodigy's "management function" regarding the Board Leaders' activities. The court observed that the agreement between Prodigy and Epstein sets forth eleven acts to be taken by Epstein, including posting a minimum number of notes on the bulletin board each month, providing monthly reports to Prodigy, following additional procedures provided by Prodigy, and obtaining Prodigy's prior approval for promotional efforts. The court also pointed out that a "Bulletin Board Leader Survival Guide" dated October 1994 includes the caveat: "IF YOU DON'T KNOW WHAT SOMETHING IS OR WHAT IT'S SUPPOSED TO DO, LEAVE IT ALONE UNTIL YOU CAN ASK." Accordingly, the court held that Epstein acted as Prodigy's agent for purposes of the acts and omissions alleged in the complaint.

4

Privacy

Rights to privacy are a relatively recent development, the origin of which are traced to a law review article published in 1890.[151] Based on the right to be let alone,[152] the law developed along two lines:

(1) a common law right, supplemented in some instances by statutes, protecting a diverse set of individual interests from interference by nongovernmental entities; and (2) a federal constitutional right, derived from various provisions of the Bill of Rights, that took distinct shape in United States Supreme Court decisions in the 1960s safeguarding the rights of individuals and private entities from government invasion.[153]

A. Common Law Privacy

Four activities give rise to liability for invasion of privacy under common law or state statute:

(1) Intrusion upon seclusion;
(2) Appropriation of name or likeness;
(3) Publicity given to private life; and
(4) Publicity placing a person in a false light.[154]

Some states do not, however, recognize all such claims. For example, New York refuses to recognize false light claims.[155] And some states protect a larger class of persons than others. Private persons, as well as celebrities, are protected by California and New York laws on misappropriation of name or likeness.

The first reported decision on a state privacy claim against an online service resulted from a claim brought by controversial radio talk show host Howard Stern, who had announced his candidacy for governor of the state of New York. Stern sued the Delphi online sys-

---

[151] S. Warren & L. Brandeis, *The Right to Privacy*, 4 Harv. L. Rev. 193 (1890).
[152] Restatement (Second) of Torts § 652A, Comment a.
[153] *Hill v. National Collegiate Athletic Ass'n*, 7 Cal.4th 1, 23, 865 P.2d 633 (1994).
[154] Restatement (Second) of Torts §§ 652B-652E.
[155] See *Howell v. New York Post Co.*, 596 N.Y.S.2d 350, 354, 612 N.E.2d 699 (Ct. App. 1993).

tem for using his photograph without permission in an advertisement for a subscriber-participation debate on his political candidacy, claiming violation of New York privacy laws. The court held against Stern, because "Delphi's bulletin board, like a letter-to-the-editor column of a newspaper, is a protected First Amendment activity," and "[t]he newsworthy use of a person's name or photograph does not give rise to a cause of action under [New York's privacy law] as long as the use is reasonably related to a matter of public interest."[156]

In a case that promises to refine the law of privacy in the workplace on communications among employees, a former McDonald's supervisor is suing McDonald's, a franchise owner, and an employee for $2 million and punitive damages. The former supervisor, Michael Huffcut, alleges that a McDonald's employee copied voice-mail messages between Huffcut and a McDonald's manager with whom he was having an affair, and then transmitted the messages to the franchise owner. The owner played the tape to Huffcut's wife and then fired him.[157]

B. Constitutional Law

A "right to privacy" is not expressly mentioned in the U.S. Constitution or the Bill of Rights. Many privacy decisions have been based on the Fourth Amendment,[158] which provides that

The right of the people to be secure in their persons, houses, papers, and effects, against unreasonable searches and seizures, shall not be violated, and no Warrant shall issue, but upon probable cause, supported by Oath or affirmation, and particularly describing the place to be searched, and the persons or things to be seized.

In 1965, the U.S. Supreme Court ruled that there are "zones of privacy" implicit in the Bill of Rights. This ruling was made in a case in which the Court invalidated a statute prohibiting the use of contraceptive devices and the giving of medical advice on their use.[159] According to the California Supreme Court,

Collectively, the federal cases 'sometimes characterized as protecting "privacy" have in fact involved at least two different kinds of interests. One is the individual interest in

---

[156] *Stern v. Delphi Internet Servs. Corp.*, 626 N.Y.S.2d 694, 698, 700 (Sup. Ct. 1995).
[157] San Jose Mercury News, Jan 21, 1995, 1D; *Huffcut v. McDonald's Corp.*, No. 94-CV-6589 (W.D.N.Y. Dec. 7, 1995).
[158] Applicable to the States through the Fourteenth Amendment. *Mapp v. Ohio*, 367 U.S. 643, 655, 6 L.Ed.2d 1081, 81 S.Ct. 1684 (1961).
[159] *Griswold v. Connecticut*, 381 U.S. 479, 484–86, 14 L.Ed.2d 510, 85 S.Ct. 1678 (1965).

avoiding disclosure of personal matters, and another is the interest in independence in making certain kinds of important decisions.'[160]

In a child pornography case involving seizure of files held by a commercial online service (America Online), a U.S. Air Force court of military appeals ruled that under the Fourth Amendment, the defendant had a right of privacy in "any e-mail transmissions he made so long as they were stored in [an] America Online computer."[161] According to the court,

[The defendant] clearly had an objective expectation of privacy in those messages stored in computers which he alone could retrieve through the use of his own assigned password. Similarly, he had an objective expectation of privacy with regard to messages he transmitted electronically to other subscribers of the service who also had individually assigned passwords.

In that case, the court also affirmed a federal magistrate's determination that there was probable cause "within the intent and meaning of the Fourth Amendment" to support issuance of a warrant authorizing the search of America Online computers.

Notably, federal constitutional privacy rights only apply to prevent governmental or state action.[162] And there have been no court decisions enforcing civil liability claims concerning online systems based on a federal constitutional right of privacy.

California added an express right of privacy to its state constitution in 1972.[163] A number of other state constitutions similarly protect privacy,[164] and may limit private as well as governmental action.[165]

In California, the elements of a claim for invasion of privacy

---

[160] *Hill v. National Collegiate Athletic Ass'n*, 7 Cal.4th 1, 30, 865 P.2d 633 (1994).
[161] *United States v. Maxwell*, 42 M.J. 568 (A.F.C.C.A. 1995).
[162] *Simmons v. Southwestern Bell Tel. Co.*, 452 F.Supp. 392, 394 (W.D. Okla. 1978), *aff'd*, 611 F.2d 342 (10th Cir. 1979); *O'Connor v. Ortega*, 480 U.S. 709, 714, 94 L.Ed.2d 714, 107 S.Ct. 1492 (1987); *K-Mart v. Trotti*, 677 S.W.2d 632 (Tex. App. 1984); see also, *Katz v. United States*, 389 U.S. 347, 350, 19 L.Ed.2d 576, 88 S.Ct. 507 ("[T]he protection of a person's *general* right to privacy—his right to be let alone by other people—is, like the protection of his property and of his very life, left largely to the law of the individual States").
[163] California Const., art. I, § 1.
[164] See, among others, Alaska Const., art. I, § 22 ; Ariz. Const., art. 2, § 8; Fla. Const., art. I, § 23; Haw. Const., art. I, § 6; Ill. Const., art. I, §§ 6, 12; La. Const., art. I, § 5; Mont. Const., art. II, § 10; S.C. Const., art. 1, § 10; Wash. Const., art. I, § 7; see also, *Wilkinson v. Times-Mirror Corp.*, 215 Cal.App.3d 1034 (1989); *White v. Davis*, 13 Cal.3d 757, 775, 533 P.2d 222 (1975). On the application of constitutional free speech rights to private parties, see *Robins v. Pruneyard Shopping Center*, 23 Cal.3d 899, 910 (1979), *aff'd*, 447 U.S. 74, 64 L.Ed.2d 741, 100 S.Ct. 2035 (1980) (shopping center); *Laguna Publishing Co. v. Golden Rain Foundation*, 131 Cal.App.3d 816, 843–44 (1982) (private, residential, walled community).
[165] *Hill v. National Collegiate Athletic Ass'n*, 7 Cal.4th 1, 20, 865 P.2d 633 (1994).

based on the state constitution are "(1) a legally protected privacy interest;[166] (2) a reasonable expectation of privacy in the circumstances; and (3) conduct by defendant constituting a serious invasion of privacy."[167] Several California privacy claims have been filed over company review of employee e-mail. Although a damage award has yet to be won against an employer, there is no reason to suppose that an appropriate claim will not succeed.[168]

C. Federal Statutes

Congress has passed a number of laws affecting online privacy, and it is likely that courts will let such laws define the area rather than expand the contours of implied "zones of privacy."

1. Electronic Communications Privacy Act of 1986

The Electronic Communications Privacy Act of 1986 (ECPA), described below in detail,[169] is the primary federal legal protection

---

[166] According to the California Supreme Court, there are generally two classes of legally recognized privacy interests: "(1) interests in precluding the dissemination or misuse of sensitive and confidential information ('informational privacy'); and (2) interests in making intimate personal decisions or conducting personal activities without observation, intrusion, or interference ('autonomy privacy')." *Hill v. National Collegiate Athletic Ass'n*, 7 Cal.4th 1, 35, 865 P.2d 633 (1994).

[167] *Hill v. National Collegiate Athletic Ass'n*, 7 Cal.4th 1, 39–40, 865 P.2d 633 (1994); see also, *People v. Chapman*, 36 Cal.3d 98, 106, 679 P.2d 62 (1984) (unlisted telephone number); *People v. Blair*, 25 Cal.3d 640, 602 P.2d 738 (1979) (credit card charges and telephone call records); *Valley National Bank of Nevada v. Superior Court*, 15 Cal.3d 652, 542 P.2d 977 (1975) (bank customer information).

[168] See, e.g., *Flanagan v. Epson America, Inc.*, No. BC007036, Ruling on Plaintiff's Motion for Class Certification (Cal. Super. Ct., Los Angeles Cty., July 31, 1992) (denying motion for class certification in lawsuit alleging violation of Cal. Const. Art. 1, Sec. 1, by Epson in allegedly monitoring employee e-mail, but noting that relief may be sought on an individual basis); compare *Shoars v. Epson America, Inc.*, No. B073234, Slip Opinion (Cal. Ct. App., 2d App. Dist., April 14, 1994) (affirming summary judgment against plaintiff on wrongful discharge cause of action in violation of public policy related to downloading of messages as they crossed from an external MCI e-mail system to Epson's internal e-mail system; "'downloading' of messages into storage by Epson's computer software did not constitute reading them or attempting to learn their contents"); *Bourke v. Nissan Motor Co.*, No. YC003979, Complaint for Invasion of Privacy (Cal. Super. Ct., Los Angeles Cty., filed Jan. 3, 1991); *Smyth v. Pillsbury Co.*, 914 F.Supp. 97 (E.D. Penn. 1996) (dismissing action for wrongful termination in violation of public policy in case in which employee was fired for inappropriate and unprofessional e-mail sent over company computer system to supervisor).

[169] See Ch. VI. Criminal Liability, § C, *infra*.

against unauthorized interception and disclosure of electronic communications, while in transit or in storage. The ECPA contains a number of significant exceptions.

While operators of electronic communication services for the public are generally barred from disclosing the content of a message in storage,[170] operators of purely internal e-mail systems are not covered by this prohibition. As many companies operate internal e-mail systems that do not connect to the outside world, they take the position that authorized coworkers, supervisors, and system operators may access and read messages and files on their systems.[171] But they should check that they have not limited their ability to do so by agreement or by establishing a custom, practice, policy, or procedure that gives rise to a reasonable and legally enforceable expectation of employee privacy in their interoffice e-mail and other files.

2. Privacy Protection Act of 1980

The Privacy Protection Act establishes safeguards relating to materials held by "a person reasonably believed to have a purpose" to publish a newspaper, book, broadcast, or similar public communication.[172] Such materials, generally, may not be subject to search or seizure by a government employee unless there is probable cause to believe that the person possessing the materials has committed or is committing the criminal offense to which the materials relate, or immediate seizure is necessary to prevent death or serious bodily injury.[173]

The leading case applying the Privacy Protection Act to electronic publishers arose from a Secret Service raid of a small, Texas publisher of electronic games, named Steve Jackson Games.[174] In the

---

[170] 18 U.S.C. § 2702(a); cf., *Deal v. Spears*, 780 F.Supp. 618 (W.D. Ark. 1991), *aff'd*, 980 F.2d 1153 (8th Cir. 1992) (employer recording of personal phone calls served no legitimate purpose).

[171] See *Flanagan v. Epson America, Inc.*, No. BC007036, Ruling on Demurrer and Motion to Strike of Defendant Epson America, Inc. (Cal. Super. Ct., Los Angeles Cty., Jan. 4, 1991) (generally referring to "ECPA and Online Computer Privacy," 4 Federal Communications Law Journal 17, 39 (1989), wherein the author opines that an employee has no ECPA claim against an employer over examination of stored communications on the company's in-house computer system); J. Podesta & P. Sher, *Protecting Electronic Messaging: A Guide to the Electronic Communications Privacy Act of 1986*, pp.viii, ix, 1.

[172] 42 U.S.C. § 2000aa(a).

[173] 42 U.S.C. § 2000aa(a)(1)–(2).

[174] *Steve Jackson Games v. United States Secret Serv.*, 816 F.Supp. 432 (W.D. Tex. 1993), *aff'd*, 36 F.3d 457 (5th Cir. 1994).

course of the raid, the Secret Service removed the company's computers, including one running the company's BBS. At the time of the raid, the Secret Service apparently did not know that Steve Jackson Games was a publisher. But the court ruled that the Secret Service violated the Privacy Protection Act when it was so informed and refused to return the company's work product.[175]

3. Privacy Act of 1974

Limited privacy protections for government-maintained databases are found in the Privacy Act of 1974.[176] Generally, no government agency may conceal the existence of a personal data record-keeping system. Each agency maintaining such a system must publish a notice of the existence and character of the system, including

(A) the name and location of the system;

(B) the categories of individuals on whom records are maintained in the system;

(C) the categories of records maintained in the system;

(D) each routine use of the records contained in the system, including the categories of users and the purpose of such use;

(E) the policies and practices of the agency regarding storage, retrievability, access controls, retention, and disposal of the records;

(F) the title and business address of the agency official who is responsible for the system of records;

(G) the agency procedures whereby an individual can be notified at his request if the system of records contains a record pertaining to him;

(H) the agency procedures whereby an individual can be notified at his request how he can gain access to any record pertaining to him contained in the system of records, and how he can contest its content; and

(I) the categories of sources or records in the system.[177]

The Privacy Act contains a general restriction on disclosure of records, subject to a number of broad exceptions including civil or criminal law enforcement activity, circumstances affecting the health or safety of an individual, court orders, and consumer reporting agencies acting in accordance with applicable law.[178] The disclosing agency is required to keep records of disclosures and make them avail-

---

[175] Compare *State ex rel. Macy v. One Pioneer CD-ROM Changer*, 891 P.2d 600, 606–07 (Okla. Ct. App. 1994) (no violation of Act where seized equipment contained 500 megabytes of non-obscene material to be pressed into a compact disc to be published).

[176] 5 U.S.C. § 552a.

[177] Ibid. § 552a(e).

[178] Ibid. § 552a(b).

able to the individual named in the record, who may review the records and request correction.[179]

4. Fair Credit Reporting Act of 1970

Information maintained by credit bureaus is regulated by the Fair Credit Reporting Act of 1970.[180] Credit bureaus are required to implement and maintain procedures to avoid reporting obsolete or inaccurate information. Credit reports may only be furnished for (1) credit, (2) insurance, (3) employment, (4) obtaining government benefits, or (5) other legitimate business needs involving a business transaction.[181]

5. Right to Financial Privacy Act

The Right to Financial Privacy Act[182] restricts government access to the financial records of any financial institution customer. Financial institutions may not provide the government "access to or copies of, or the information contained in, the financial records of any customer except in accordance with the provisions of [the Act]."[183] But financial institutions are permitted to notify a government authority that it "has information which may be relevant to a possible violation of any statute or regulation."[184] And they are allowed to release "records as incident to perfection of security interest, proving a claim in bankruptcy, collecting a debt, or processing an application with regard to a Government loan, loan guarantee, etc."[185]

Customers, of course, may authorize disclosure to the government.[186] The authorization may not extend for more than three months[187] and can be revoked at any time before records are disclosed.[188] The government may otherwise gain access to a customer's financial records pursuant to an administrative subpoena or sum-

---

[179] Ibid. §§ 552a(c), (d).
[180] 15 U.S.C. §§ 1681–1681t.
[181] Cf., European Union Directive on the Protection of Individuals with Regard to the Processing of Personal Data and on the Free Movement of Such Data, Appendix IV, *The Privacy Directive*, CyberLaw (Aug. 1995), *infra*.
[182] 12 U.S.C. § 3401 *et seq.*
[183] Ibid. § 3403(a).
[184] Ibid. § 3403(c).
[185] Ibid. § 3403(d).
[186] Ibid. § 3404.
[187] Ibid. § 3404(a)(1).
[188] Ibid. § 3404(a)(2).

mons,[189] search warrant,[190] judicial subpoena,[191] or a formal written request[192] in certain circumstances, and in accordance with specified requirements, as described in the act.

6. Telephone Consumer Protection Act of 1991

The Telephone Consumer Protection Act of 1991 makes it unlawful to place a phone call using any automatic telephone dialing system or an artificial or prerecorded voice to any service for which the called party is charged for the call.[193] A CompuServe subscriber, Robert Arkow, filed suit against CompuServe and CompuServe Visa claiming that they had violated the Telephone Consumer Protection Act by sending advertisements to him via e-mail. The case was settled for an undisclosed amount.[194]

The Telephone Consumer Protection Act also bars, among other things, using "any telephone facsimile machine, computer, or other device to send an unsolicited advertisement to a telephone facsimile machine."[195]

7. Government E-Mail & Public Records

The Federal Records Act[196] governs federal agency record creation, management, and disposal duties. The act's goals include an "[a]ccurate and complete documentation of the policies and transactions of the Federal Government," as well as "[j]udicious preservation and disposal of records."[197]

A document qualifies as a "record" under the Federal Records Act, if it is

(1) "made or received by an agency of the United States Government under Federal law or in connection with the transaction of public business"; and
(2) "preserved or appropriate for preservation by that agency . . . as evidence of the organization, functions, policies, decisions, procedures, operations, or other

---

[189] Ibid. § 3405.
[190] Ibid. § 3406.
[191] Ibid. § 3407.
[192] Ibid. § 3408.
[193] 47 U.S.C. § 227(b)(1)(A)(iii).
[194] The *Kansas City Star*, March 17, 1995.
[195] 47 U.S.C. § 227(b)(1)(C); *Destination Ventures v. F.C.C.*, 46 F.3d 54 (9th Cir. 1995).
[196] 44 U.S.C. §§ 2101 *et seq.*, 2501 *et seq.*, 2701 *et seq.*, 2901 *et seq.*, 3101 *et seq.*, 3301 *et seq.*
[197] Ibid. § 2902.

activities of the Government or because of the informational value of the data in them."[198]

And an agency cannot dispose of a "record" by fiat—the approval of the archivist of the United States is required.[199]

In a case involving the Executive Office of the President and the National Security Council, a federal court of appeals confirmed that government e-mail systems contain records subject to Federal Records Act preservation requirements.[200] The appeals court emphasized that substantive e-mail satisfies the definition of a covered "record,"[201] and concluded that agencies must retain and manage these electronic documents.

Requirements of the Federal Records Act and similar state laws, as well as laws requiring the disclosure of public records, may cause public officials and employees to pause before using e-mail and the Internet. Public employees do not, in general, possess privacy rights that would require their e-mail to be withheld from the public record or disclosure.

The Supreme Court of Florida notes that under its rules, e-mail made or received in connection with the official business of the judicial branch comes within the definition of a "judicial record," which must be directed and channeled so that it can be recorded as a public record.[202] Importantly, many judge/staff communications are excluded from the public records, as they are clearly not official business. Exemptions from public disclosure include proposed drafts of opinions and orders, memoranda concerning pending cases, proposed jury instructions, and certain other e-mail sent and received between judicial employees within a particular court's jurisdiction.

In an Arizona case, a newspaper requested computer backup tapes of a county assessor's office, including e-mail communications.[203] The county resisted disclosure because some of the material might be protected by a deliberative process privilege, or be immune from dis-

---

[198] Ibid. § 3301.

[199] *Armstrong v. Executive Office of the President, Office of Admin.*, 1 F.3d 1274, 1278–79 (D.C. Cir. 1993); 44 U.S.C. § 3303a.

[200] *Armstrong v. Executive Office of the President, Office of Admin.*, 1 F.3d 1274 (D.C. Cir. 1993).

[201] "Not all scribbles and off-the-cuff comments will qualify as federal records." *Armstrong v. Executive Office of the President, Office of Admin.*, 1 F.3d 1274, 1287 (D.C. Cir. 1993).

[202] *In re Amendments to Rule of Judicial Admin., 2.051—Pub. Access to Judicial Records*, 651 So.2d 1185 (Fla. 1995).

[203] *Star Publishing Co. v. Pima County Attorney's Office*, 181 Ariz. 432, 891 P.2d 899 (Ct. App. 1994).

closure in order to protect public employee privacy rights. In the absence of any proof offered to substantiate these claims, the Arizona appeals court noted that a deliberative process privilege might apply were Arizona to adopt one, and that the court "doubt[s] that public employees have any legitimate expectation of privacy in personal documents that they have chosen to lodge in public computer files."[204] The court went on to hold that the records were wrongfully withheld.

As discussed in the Arizona case, courts have recognized a "deliberative process privilege"[205] designed to "protect materials reflecting deliberative or policymaking processes, and not 'purely factual, investigative matters.' "[206]

California also recognizes a "deliberative process" privilege. In a decision refusing a newspaper's request under the California Public Records Act for the state governor's schedules and appointment calendars, the California Supreme Court stated,

> Disclosing the identity of persons with whom the Governor has met and consulted is the functional equivalent of revealing the substance or direction of the Governor's judgment and mental processes; such information would indicate which interests or individuals he deemed to be of significance with respect to critical issues of the moment. The intrusion into the deliberative process is patent. . . .
>
> If the law required disclosure of a private meeting between the Governor and a politically unpopular or controversial group, that meeting might never occur. Compelled disclosure could thus devalue or eliminate altogether a particular viewpoint from the Governor's consideration.[207]

For similar reasons, a California court later refused a newspaper's request for the telephone numbers of persons with whom city council members had spoken. "[R]outine public disclosure of such records," said the court, "would interfere with the flow of information to the government official and intrude on the deliberative process."[208]

In light of the above, it appears that in appropriate circumstances government officials can shield not only the content of e-mail they send and receive, but also the names and e-mail addresses of the persons with whom they correspond.

---

[204] Ibid. 899, 901 (Ct. App. 1994).

[205] Also known as "executive privilege" under the Federal Freedom of Information Act, 5 U.S.C. § 552(b)(5); *NLRB v. Sears, Roebuck & Co.*, 421 U.S. 132, 150, 44 L.Ed.2d 29, 95 S.Ct. 1504 (1975). See also *Computer Professionals for Social Responsibility v. U.S. Secret Service*, 1996 U.S. App. Lexis 14 (D.C. Cir. 1996) (ruling, in part, that Secret Service properly invoked exemptions of the Freedom of Information Act in response to request for records related to possible involvement of Secret Service in breakup of a meeting of young "computer hackers" at a Virginia shopping mall).

[206] See *Rogers v. Superior Court*, 19 Cal.App.4th 469, 478 (1993).

[207] *Times Mirror Co. v. Superior Court*, 53 Cal.3d 1325, 1343–44 (1991).

[208] *Rogers v. Superior Court*, 19 Cal.App.4th 469, 480 (1993).

8. Communications Assistance for Law Enforcement

The Communications Assistance for Law Enforcement Act[209] excepts "information services" and private networks and interconnection services and facilities from requirements that telecommunication carriers ensure that their equipment and services are capable of facilitating authorized communications interception.[210] But the government may require the disclosure of detailed subscriber account information, including identity and address.[211]

D. Anonymity

Not only do people seek to keep the content of their communications private, but many take steps to prevent identification of their message traffic as well. In a number of circumstances, simply identifying the people who communicate with each other can be as important as, or, perhaps, more valuable than, knowing the content of the communication itself.[212] For example, a company that sells baby diapers or parenting magazines may be interested in knowing and paying for a list of names and addresses of women who visit a prenatal care facility. More sinisterly, an antiabortion group may seek the identity of women visiting and staff working at a family planning clinic.[213] And there are many legitimate and appropriate uses of anonymity online. Women posting to battered women support groups, alcoholics posting to a recovering alcoholic newsgroup, and messaging by whistleblowers are just three examples of socially beneficial uses of anonymity. Would such people be inclined to seek help if another person could search and retrieve postings they were compelled to sign?

---

[209] Public Law 103-414, Oct. 25, 1994, 108 Stat. 4279. Congress has authorized $500 million to implement the act for 1995–98 (47 U.S.C. § 1009), but it has not been funded so far. If the attorney general is not in a position to agree to pay for telecommunication carrier compliance costs, it appears that the carriers are deemed in compliance with the act. See 47 U.S.C. § 1008(b)(2).

[210] 47 U.S.C. § 1002(b).

[211] See 18 U.S.C. § 2703.

[212] The O.J. Simpson freeway chase and capture resulted from tracking the ID signal of his cellular phone, which routinely reported its location to the nearest cell. See *The Simpson Murder Case; Fugitive Relied On And Was Undone by Cellular Phone*, Los Angeles Times, June 19, 1994, at A11; *Police Like to Listen In: Crime, Cellular Phones Don't Mix*, San Francisco Chronicle, June 21, 1994, p. A1.

[213] In 1993, a former Anaheim, California, police employee pleaded guilty to disclosing to antiabortion activists confidential state driving record information on four individuals. Three of the four individuals were employees of a family planning clinic, targeted for picketing by antiabortion groups. The former police employee, Lisa Lorraine Villarreal, was sentenced to three years probation and two hundred hours community service.

On both commercial online services and the Internet, it is possible to take steps to provide a measure of anonymity. Many online services allow users to adopt pseudonyms, which accompany the public messages they post on electronic bulletin boards. On the Internet, one can find "anonymous remailers" that receive messages, strip them of identifying information, and send them on to their final destination, be it a private e-mail address or an Internet newsgroup.[214]

There are a number of instances, involving child pornography, copyright infringement, as well as defamation, where people have violated the law using online systems while hiding behind an assumed identity or a layer of anonymity—sometimes successfully.

For example, in October 1994 a yet-unidentified person posted on a Prodigy bulletin board allegedly defamatory statements about a securities investment banking firm. The posting accused the firm and its president of committing criminal and fraudulent acts in connection with the initial public offering of a particular stock. The offering was described as a "major criminal fraud" and "100% criminal fraud." The firm's president, the posting said, was "soon to be a proven criminal." The firm was characterized as a "cult of brokers who either lie for a living or get fired." Unable to identify the person who posted the comments (who used the account of a Prodigy employee who had left the company), the firm and its president sued Prodigy.[215]

The abuses of a few have raised fears that anonymity exacerbates online copyright infringement and defamation, and also creates opportunities for a host of other unlawful activities, such as child pornography and money laundering. It has been suggested that online services and providers be provided a measure of freedom from liability if they are willing and able to produce the identity of people who post material online.[216]

In this debate, it should be noted that society benefits from anonymity. The value in not compelling an individual to be linked to a

---

[214] While anonymous remailers strip elements that identify a sender, such as a message's header, a unique identifying number may be created to allow reply mail to be forwarded to the sender.

[215] See *Stratton Oakmont, Inc. v. Prodigy Servs. Co.*, 1995 N.Y. Misc. Lexis 229, 23 Media L. Rep. 1794 (1995). The case was later settled for an apology by Prodigy that the message had been posted—perhaps in response to indications that Prodigy was preparing to defend the defamation claim on the basis of "truth."

[216] See D. Johnson & K. Marks, *Mapping Electronic Data Communications Onto Existing Legal Metaphors: Should We Let Our Conscience (And Our Contracts) Be Our Guide?*, 38 Vill. L. Rev. 487 (1993) (proposed Electronic Communication Forwarding Act).

comment has been recognized by the U.S. Supreme Court.[217] In case over a school official's complaint that distribution of unsigned leaflets opposing a proposed school tax levy violated state law,[218] the U.S. Supreme Court held the statute unconstitutional. The Court observed that "[a]nonymous pamphlets, leaflets, brochures and even books have played an important role in the progress of mankind," noting that the following authors, among others, used pseudonyms: Samuel Langhorne Clemens (Mark Twain), William Sydney Porter (O. Henry), Benjamin Franklin, François Marie Arouet (Voltaire), Armandine Aurore Lucile Dupin (George Sand), Mary Ann Evans (George Eliot), Charles Lamb, and Charles Dickens.[219]

"The decision in favor of anonymity," said the Court, "may be motivated by fear of economic or official retaliation, by concern about social ostracism, or merely by a desire to preserve as much of one's privacy as possible."[220] Anonymity also "provides a way for a writer who may be personally unpopular to ensure that readers will not prejudge her message simply because they do not like its proponent."[221]

There is a respected tradition of anonymity in politics, with the Federalist Papers being but one famous example. The decision to remain anonymous, says the Supreme Court, is "an aspect of the freedom of speech protected by the First Amendment."[222]

It should be noted, however, that the Supreme Court does not endorse anonymity as a vehicle for transmitting false or libelous matters. In striking the Ohio statute, the Court remarked that a different situation may be posed by a statute that limited its application to "fraudulent, false, or libelous statements."[223]

E. Technology Expanding Privacy Rights

The power of computer systems is increasingly coming to be recognized as a threat to privacy rights. For example, a large commercial online system was warned by a congressman that its practice of selling subscriber lists could pose a new threat to privacy. In response, the

---

[217] See *McIntyre v. Ohio Elections Comm'n*, __ U.S. __, 131 L.Ed.2d 426, 115 S.Ct. 1511 (1995).
[218] Leading to a $100 fine.
[219] *McIntyre v. Ohio Elections Comm'n*, __ U.S. __, 131 L.Ed.2d 426, 115 S.Ct. 1511, 1516 (1995).
[220] Ibid.
[221] Ibid., __ U.S. __, 131 L.Ed.2d 426, 115 S.Ct. 1511, 1517 (1995).
[222] Ibid., __ U.S. __, 131 L.Ed.2d 426, 115 S.Ct. 1511, 1516 (1995).
[223] Ibid., __ U.S. __, 131 L.Ed.2d 426, 115 S.Ct. 1511, 1517 (1995).

online service said that it would suspend the practice until all the issues are satisfactorily resolved and that it would remove names at customers' request.[224]

In a case over a computer recordkeeping error that wrongly informed Arizona police that there was an outstanding arrest warrant for a person they stopped, U.S. Supreme Court justice Stevens noted the "reality that computer technology has changed the nature of threat to citizens' privacy over the past half century."[225] Justice Ginsburg reiterated the Arizona Supreme Court's concern that "As automation increasingly invades modern life, the potential for Orwellian mischief grows."[226]

---

[224] San Jose *Mercury News*, October 5, 1994, p. 1G.
[225] *Arizona v. Evans*, 115 S.Ct. 1185, 1197, 131 L.Ed.2d 34 (1995) (Stevens, J., dissenting).
[226] Ibid., 115 S.Ct. 1185, 1198, 131 L.Ed.2d 34 (1995) (Stevens, J., dissenting).

APPENDIX

The Legal Side [11/90]

EPSON & E-MAIL

Have you ever sent a personal message over your company's computer network? Do you receive personal messages at work on your computer? Would you be mortified if your employer looked through or tracked your messages? Would you be fired on account of some of the information you have stored on your computer? Some employees have never thought about such things. Employees of Epson America, Inc. ("Epson"), however, have filed a lawsuit against Epson that should highlight such concerns for many employees and employers.

Some Epson employees have complained that their electronic mail was regularly intercepted by Epson. Specifically, they allege that an Epson manager for computer operations and data communications placed a "tap" on the electronic mail gateway where Epson's mainframe computer interfaces with the outside MCI E-Mail communications interface.

According to Epson, e-mail is a feature of an elaborate computer system which the company provides to its employees to assist them in the performance of their job duties. Using personal computers connected to a Hewlett-Packard mainframe, Epson employees can exchange, via e-mail, communications with their fellow employees, as well as with outside consultants and others connected to Epson's system.

As part of their action against Epson, these employees allege that by using the "tap," "Epson was systematically printing up and reading all of the E-Mail that was entering and leaving Epson's Torrance facility" in violation of California Penal Code §631. That section of the Penal Code forbids the intentional tapping or unauthorized connection with any telegraph or telephone wire, line, cable, or instrument of any internal telephonic communication system, among other things.

Epson's defense to this charge is basically that the employees have not stated a violation of the Penal Code because the alleged wrongful conduct does not involve the "simultaneous interception of a 'wire, line, cable or instrument' within the meaning of Section 631, and Epson did not try to learn the contents of any telephonic communication while in transit. Epson also claims that Section 631 does not require that a company sponsoring an electronic communications system obtain authorizations from each employee using the system before it connects to its own system. Epson also contends that under California and federal law, it is only the interception of aural, not electronic, communication that is forbidden.

It is notable that the Epson employees only raise claims under California Penal Code §631. At this stage of the legal proceedings, Epson is restricted to accepting, only for the sake of argument, that the allegations made by the employees are true. It is not able to bring out its side of the story.

The issues raise by the Epson lawsuit are novel, and should be of concern to many employees and employers. For example, do employees have a legitimate expectation of privacy in their electronic communications, just as they do in their telephone conversations? In Clifford Stoll's book *The Cuckoo's Egg*, he describes printing out all communications with his employer's computer system in an effort to resolve a 75-cent billing error. Did Stoll violate anyone's privacy rights or the California Penal Code in so doing? If a company is concerned about viruses and sets up an intercept program that reads all electronic communication on its system to prevent the entry of viruses, has it broken the law? Is the law in such a state that a company trying to prevent viruses is exposed to a lawsuit from its employees over this.

At this point, it may be wise for companies to contemplate informing their employees that they have no reasonable expectation of privacy respecting any information found in computers connected to a company-sponsored network, or transmitted on or to that network. Companies may also want to have such a warning displayed when any user, in-house or remote, connects to the network. On the other hand, such warnings may have a negative impact on company culture and other steps should be considered. At a minimum, both employers and employees should give thought to what their expectations are regarding messages and information on the network.

A related issue is whether the electronic communication of data is entitled to free speech and free press protections. The First Amendment clearly covers newsprint. Neither television nor radio have been accorded the same degree of freedom under the First Amendment. The Epson case also bears watching to see what it says about constitutional protections in the electronic medium.

CyberLaw™ [12/92]

PRIVACY [U.S. V. SMITH

An impassioned dispute has been brewing between government agencies seeking to slow the pace of commercial development in the areas of data encryption and telecommunications, and consumer advocates and a range of computer companies arguing for the broad availability of advanced data encryption and telecommunication systems. The government agencies argue that the availability of such systems may threaten national security and crime control. Critics argue that these systems are necessary to protect personal privacy in the "electronic information age." A recent court ruling in a Texas drug trafficking case may provide increased weight to the critics' position. In that case, the U.S. Court of Appeals for the Fifth Circuit ruled that technological advances are capable of expanding the legally-protected range of privacy individuals enjoy. The decision also appears to hold individuals responsible for attaining a level of technical knowledge sufficient to show that any expectation of privacy sought to be preserved is reasonable, both subjectively and objectively. (*U.S. v. Smith*, No. 91–5077 (5th Cir. Nov. 12, 1992).)

In 1990, David L. Smith lived with his girlfriend in Port Arthur, Texas. His next-door neighbor had experienced problems with break-ins to his garage and cars, and suspected Smith. Using a Bearcat scanner designed to scan and intercept 400 "radio-type" channels, the neighbor began to intercept Smith's phone conversations, made in Smith's home over a cordless telephone.

Listening to the conversations, the neighbor did not hear anything to tie Smith to the break-ins, but did discover that he was involved in drug dealing. The neighbor contacted a friend in the local police department, who "instructed and assisted" the neighbor to tape Smith's conversations. Police officers also participated in the interception and recording of Smith's calls.

Based on the intercepted calls, Smith was arrested and charged with drug trafficking. At trial, Smith requested the suppression of evidence obtained through interception of his phone conversations. The request was denied, and Smith was convicted.

On appeal, Smith claimed that the interception and use of the calls in obtaining his conviction was in violation of Title III of the Omnibus Crime Control and Safe Streets Act of 1968 (18 U.S.C. Sections 2510 et seq.) As described by the Fifth Circuit, "Title III essentially prohibits the nonconsensual interception of 'wire,' 'oral,' and 'electronic' communication without prior judicial approval." Smith also argued that the interception and use of his calls violated the Fourth Amendment, which bars unreasonable searches and seizures.

The Fifth Circuit quickly dismissed Smith's Title III claims. Although Title III includes an exclusionary rule barring the introduction into evidence of illegally intercepted communications, the Fifth Circuit noted that cordless phone communication is expressly carved out from Title III's coverage. The exclusion had been made because "some types of cordless communication could be so easily intercepted."

On the Fourth Amendment claim, the Fifth Circuit noted that "what is really involved in Fourth Amendment analysis is our 'societal understanding' about what deserves 'protection from government invasion.'" The court stated that for a defendant to establish a Fourth Amendment violation, he must "show that a government activity intruded upon a reasonable expectation of privacy in such a significant way that the activity can be called a 'search.'" He would also have to show that the intrusion was unreasonable given the particular facts of the case.

Regarding privacy expectations, Smith reminded the Fifth Circuit that the U.S. Supreme Court has ruled that a person in a phone booth has a justifiable expectation of privacy in his conversation, whether measured subjectively or objectively. "Obviously," continued Smith, "one who has a telephone conversation in the privacy of his own home is seeking to keep his personal matters private, unless he knows that the conversation is being heard by others." Because "one has a right to be secure in one's house against unauthorized intrusion against a policeman viewing or seizing tangible property," reasoned Smith, "the home owner's rights are as clearly invaded when the police warrantlessly intrude into the home with a listening device."

Smith further advised the Fifth Circuit that the cordless phone at issue was owned by his girlfriend, that he had never read the owner's manual for the phone or owned such a phone, and that he had never been informed that his conversations would not be private. Although the cordless phone base contained a warning that "privacy of communications may not be insured . . . ," the base was located on a wall and could not be and had not been seen by Smith. Accordingly, Smith argued that he had a subjective expectation of privacy in his conversations, which society should be prepared to recognize as reasonable. Additionally, Smith noted that his calls were "not intercepted unintentionally, or by plain radio, or by another cordless telephone. The interception was an intentional intrusion into [his] privacy through the use of a device specifically designed to intercept transmissions."

In considering these arguments, the Fifth Circuit focused upon the important role that telecommunications play in today's society, observing that "wireless" technology is one of the fastest growing areas in the field of telecommunications, and that cordless phones are threatening to outstrip sales of traditional land line telephones. According to the court, "the decision as to whether cordless telephone conversations are protected by the Fourth Amendment may ultimately determine whether *any* telephone conversation is protected by the Fourth Amendment."

Where a cordless telephone differs from a normal land line phone is in the cordless phone's use of an actual radio signal. A cordless phone transmits the signal from a mobile unit to a base unit, which is attached to a land-based telephone line. A cordless phone also receives radio signals from the base unit. The radio signals carry the actual conversation. Although communications carried over land-based telephone lines are clearly protected by the Fourth Amendment, a conversation broadcast into the air by radio waves has been viewed as "more analogous to carrying on an oral communication in a loud voice or with a megaphone. . . ." In such cases, the person carrying on the call was viewed as knowingly exposing the communication to the public.

Courts had ruled in earlier decisions that cordless phone users could have no reasonable expectation of privacy in their calls because of the ease by which the calls could be monitored. At the time of those decisions, some cordless phones had a range of over seven-hundred feet and were subject to interception by standard radio scanners, radio receivers, and other cordless phones (many of which were pre-set to the same frequency). The Fifth Circuit noted, however, that more recent cordless phones employ an evolved technology; many are limited in range to about sixty feet, "barely beyond the average house or yard," and are no longer pre-set to the same frequency. Since cordless phones now transmit on frequencies not utilized by commercial radio, conventional radios can no longer intercept cordless communications. Although the conversations can be monitored by radio scanners, the court further noted that only a small percentage of the populace own such scanners. In addition, new cordless phones also incorporate the ability to scramble their signals.

Respecting the new technology, the Fifth Circuit discerned that,

"Surely the reasonableness of an expectation of privacy becomes greater when the conversation can only be intercepted using specialized equipment not possessed by the average citizen." "[I]n spite of the fact that a defendant uses a cordless phone," continued the court, "the circumstances may show that he also has a reasonable expectation of privacy." In this case, however, the Fifth Circuit found that although Smith claimed not to know that his conversations would not be private, he had "introduced absolutely no evidence—such as the phone's frequency or range—that would tend to show that his subjective expectation of privacy was reasonable."

In light of the above, the Fifth Circuit found that the trial court erred in assuming that there could never be a reasonable expectation of privacy for a cordless telephone communication. But the court affirmed Smith's conviction, nonetheless, for the reason that "even under a correct application of the law . . . [Smith] failed to carry his burden of showing that his Fourth Amendment rights were violated."

[CyberLaw™ 2/93]

E-MAIL & PRIVACY

According to the Electronic Mail Association, electronic mail (e-mail) usage has experienced explosive growth over the past decade. In the U.S. alone, the number of public and private mailboxes grew from less than one-half million in 1980 to nineteen million in 1991. E-mail can be a valuable tool for businesses to improve responsiveness, enhance productivity, and reduce paper flow and handling, among other things. Individual users also benefit from a reduction in time zone and telephone tag problems, and easy access to up-to-date information. E-mail is susceptible, however, to significant abuse. In California, the use of e-mail systems by private companies has given rise to a number of civil suits. One employer was sued for allegedly engaging in the systematic interception of employee e-mail. Employees of a number of companies have been charged with using e-mail to transfer trade secrets to competitors. Following a profusion of stories widely reported in the media (e.g., the Rodney King case in Los Angeles, where e-mail between police officers was introduced as evidence of their intent), much fear, uncertainty, and doubt has been expressed regarding the rights and obligations of e-mail providers and users, with privacy rights being a matter of considerable interest. Concerned companies and individual users may, however, be able to resolve many of their concerns by reviewing three principal sources of legal rights and obligations concerning e-mail: federal law, the law of the states, and employer policies and practices.

The Electronic Communications Privacy Act of 1986 (ECPA) is the primary source of law concerning e-mail. A comprehensive guide to the ECPA has been written by John Podesta and Michael Sher for the Electronic Mail Association, titled "Protecting Electronic Messaging: A Guide to the Electronic Communications Privacy Act of 1986." As stated by Podesta and Sher,

The [ECPA] has two essential purposes: 1) to protect *all* electronic communications systems, including purely internal electronic mail systems and public systems, from outside intruders; and 2) to protect the privacy of certain messages sent over public service electronic mail systems just as the privacy of telephone calls over public telephone systems is protected. (Protecting Electronic Messaging, p.viii.)

Under the ECPA, it is a federal felony to intentionally intercept wire, oral, and electronic communications while in transmission, among other things. (18 U.S.C.A. Section 2511(1).) Intentionally gaining unauthorized access to an electronic communication service, or intentionally exceeding one's authority to access such service, "and thereby obtain[ing], alter[ing], or prevent[ing] authorized access to a wire or electronic communication while it is in electronic storage in such a system" is similarly prohibited. (18 U.S.C.A. Section 2701(a).) The ECPA, however, neither prohibits the interception or accessing of an electronic communication made through "an electronic bulletin board or communications system that is configured so that it is readily accessible to the public," nor prevents "access to public electronic communication facilities or services." (Protecting Electronic Messaging, pp.4, 26.)

ECPA restrictions on the disclosure of the content of e-mail in transit or while in electronic storage do not appear to apply to operators of "purely private, internal messaging systems." (Protecting Electronic Messaging, p.6.) The law also makes several notable exceptions for providers of electronic mail messaging to the general public. For example, such providers are allowed to divulge the content of communications inadvertently obtained "which appear to pertain to the commission of a crime, if the divulgence is made to a law enforcement agency" (18 U.S.C.A. Sections 2511(3)(b)(iv), 2702(B)). They are further allowed, in the normal course of business, to intercept, disclose, or use communications necessarily incident to the protection of their rights and property. (18 U.S.C.A. Section 2511(2)(a)(i).) With regard to this latter exception, Podesta and Sher explain that

Congress recognized that electronic communication providers may have to monitor a stream of transmissions in order to properly route, terminate or manage individual messages. This type of monitoring is not prohibited because it does not infringe on the privacy of either the sender or recipient. (Protecting Electronic Messaging, p.4.)

Service providers are not allowed, however, to utilize "service observing or random monitoring, except for mechanical or service quality control checks." (18 U.S.C.A. Section 2511(2)(a)(i).) Significantly, the ECPA also sets out a procedures that if followed, will insulate e-mail providers that cooperate with law enforcement officials.

Penalties for violation of the ECPA are severe. The illegal interception or disclosure of e-mail, or use of illegally intercepted e-mail, is punishable as a felony by up to a five-year prison sentence and a fine. (18 U.S.C.A. Sections 2511(4).) Individuals may be subject to fines up to $250,000, and businesses may be subject to fines up to $500,000. (Protecting Electronic Messaging, p.6.) Civil actions for money damages and other relief are also authorized.

Other rights and obligations relating to e-mail may be found under state law. For example, California penalizes a range of computer-related activities, including "knowingly and without permission access[ing] or caus[ing] to be accessed any computer, computer system, or computer network." (Cal. Penal Code Section 502(c)(7).) In this regard, the California Legislature has declared that

protection of the integrity of all types and forms of lawfully created computers, computer systems, and computer data is vital to the protection of the privacy of individuals as well as to the well-being of financial institutions, business concerns, governmental agencies, and others within this state that lawfully utilize those computers, computer systems and computer data. (Cal. Penal Code Section 502(a).)

Similarly, under New York law it is a misdemeanor to "knowingly [use] or [cause] to be used a computer or computer service without authorization and the computer utilized is equipped or programmed with any device or coding system, the function of which is to prevent the unauthorized use of said computer or computer system." (NY Penal Law Section 156.05.)

Aside from computer-specific laws of the type noted above, there are other state laws of more general application that affect e-mail. For instance, the California Constitution includes an express right of privacy, which may be violated by certain actions involving computers and e-mail. Similarly, an unreasonable search by a California employer may also lead to civil liability for violation of rights under the California Constitution. A host of other laws found in California and other states may also affect the use of e-mail, including laws concerning defamation and invasion of privacy.

At the grass-roots level, rights and obligations concerning e-mail may arise by agreement (such as a collective bargaining agreement) or from the policies and practices of an employer that provides an e-mail system for the use of its employees. There has been much discussion on the subject of employee rights concerning e-mail sent over an employer's system. In this regard, it has been widely suggested that companies formulate and implement policies defining parameters concerning access to company e-mail systems, use of such systems, and the monitoring and disclosure of e-mail found on such systems.

Companies interested in developing e-mail guidelines may want to contact the Electronic Mail Association, based in Arlington, VA (703/875-8620). The association publishes a useful guide titled "Access to and Use and Disclosure of Electronic Mail on Company Computer Systems: A Tool Kit for Formulating Your Company's Policy." The tool kit, available to non-members for $45, briefly describes the legal rights and duties regarding the provision of e-mail systems, and presents a number of issues and concerns that should be addressed in the course of developing a company policy. The tool kit describes alternate policies and provides possible text for use in policy statements. Policy topics discussed in the tool kit include disclosure of company policy in advance, permissible uses of the electronic mail system, monitoring for security violations, grounds required for targeted access, and limitations on disclosure and use of information obtained by means of access or monitoring.

[CyberLaw™ 9/93]

PROTECTING PRIVACY

We have reached a point in time at which it is relatively inexpensive to collect, store, sort, and analyze huge amounts of information. But until now, little attention has been paid to the impact this progress may have upon our lives. The compilation of data about the intimate details of our day-to-day existence may impair fundamental rights of association, expression, and privacy guaranteed by the Constitution. Recently, there has been wide criticism voiced about the White House's plan to develop an encryption standard engineered to guarantee government access to the content of encrypted communications. One national organization has pointed out that the plan is based, in substantial part, on the flawed assumption that government has a right to review our private discourse. Many people immediately understand the implications such review might have on their lives and their liberty. But how many realize that similarly intrusive information is currently stored in easily accessible databases and that its review may have equally ruinous effects.

Would you forgo seeking reimbursement for marital counseling if your employer had access to the bills you send to your health insurance carrier? Would you be able to fairly negotiate a salary or a raise if your employer could check your credit information? Are there any purchases you would not make if your employer could review all your expenses? When you consider these questions, can you see that there is a relationship between the amount of data that is collected about you and your freedom as an individual. You may be able to find a new employer; with the government, your options are limited.

The media has really missed the point with recent stories about individuals who break into commercial computer systems and read files. The relatively trivial acts of a handful of individuals are mere symptoms of issues that have yet to be adequately explored, and mainly serve as a distraction. The real issues concern the development of powerful databases that hold detailed information about our lives, who has access to that information, and for what reasons.

Consider, if you will, that one of the largest databases of personal information maintained by the federal government is the Internal Revenue Service's Integrated Data Retrieval System (IDRS). For about twenty years, this has been the primary computer system for accessing and adjusting taxpayer accounts. As this system contains confidential and highly personal information, we should expect that it is protected by extraordinary controls. But substantial weaknesses have been found in IDRS security. An internal IRS report titled "Review of Controls Over IDRS Security," recently made public, notes that "[i]neffective security controls over IDRS allowed employee fraud to occur." In one regional integrity project alone, the IRS "found strong indicators that 368 employees used IDRS to monitor non-work related accounts, including those of friends, relatives, associates, neighbors or celebrities." Six IRS employees were found to have prepared fraudulent returns for taxpayers and then monitored the accounts on IDRS.

These abuses occurred despite public law, Treasury Department directives, and internal guidelines requiring the IRS to protect the "integrity, availability and privacy of taxpayer information on its systems." If these tools are not sufficient to protect the IRS from its own employees, it appears that there is substantial opportunity for abuse of other databases—particularly those maintained by commercial entities.

Information collected in databases can facilitate a wide range of insidious acts. Subversive groups could, for example, buy the names of individuals that subscribe or donate to certain political publications in order to target them, their families, and employers. A deranged fan could locate the home of a celebrity. An employer could uncover sensitive personal information about prospective and current employees.

The increased use of databases has already given rise to a new form of crime: the theft of personal data for the purpose of defrauding third parties. For example, a clerk in a company's human resources department might note personal information of a particular individual (including social security number and names of dependents and relatives) and use that information to obtain one or several credit cards in that individual's name. The crime may go undetected for a long period—until the unfortunate individual from whom the data was taken tries to make a major purchase and discovers that his credit history has been destroyed. In 1975, John Brunner published a novel called *The Shockwave Rider* in which he wrote of the manipulation of interlinked credit-appraisal computers to effect digital mayhem. This fiction has become today's nightmare.

Little has been written about how an individual may protect himself in this age of relational databases and digital superhighways. Consumers receive occasional notices that they may check their credit histories upon the denial of credit. The media publishes infrequent reminders not to disclose telephone numbers to merchants when using credit cards. But there is sparse available material concerning how to safeguard against the acquisition of personal data by regional and national databases, both public and commercial.

One useful resource related to these issues is a FAQ (a discussion of frequently asked questions) on Social Security Numbers written by Chris Hibbert, a member of Computer Professionals for Social Responsibility. The purpose of this FAQ is to "try to help you keep your Social Security Number from being used as a tool in the invasion of your privacy."

As noted by Hibbert, Social Security Numbers (SSNs) were originally intended for use only by the social security program. In 1943, federal agencies were required by Executive Order to use SSNs when creating new record-keeping systems. In 1961, the IRS began using SSNs as taxpayer identification numbers. But the Privacy Act of 1974 required authorization for government agencies to use SSNs in their databases and also that disclosures be made when SSNs are requested. The Tax Reform Act of 1976 allowed certain state and local authorities to use SSNs in order to establish identities. (Interestingly, the Privacy Protection Study Commission in 1977 recommended the revocation of the 1943 Executive Order noted above.)

Under the Privacy Act of 1974, only federal law can mandate the disclosure of an SSN. Any federal, state, or local authority that requests an individual's SSN must disclose the following:

1. Whether the disclosure is optional or mandatory;
2. The statutory or other legal authority for requesting the SSN;
3. How the SSN will be used; and
4. The consequences of failure to provide an SSN.

Mr. Hibbert advises that

anytime you're dealing with a government institution and you're asked for your [SSN], just look for the Privacy Act Statement. If there isn't one, complain and don't give your number. If the statement is present, read it. If it says giving your [SSN] is voluntary, you'll have to decide for yourself whether to fill in the number.

Private organizations are less restricted concerning requests for SSNs. Some institutions are, in fact, required to obtain SSNs. For example, the IRS requires banks to report SSNs of account holders who are paid interest. Account holders who do not disclose SSNs are penalized.

(According to Hibbert, banks send SSN information to a company called ChexSystem, which keeps a database of people whose accounts have been terminated for fraud or chronic insufficient funds in the past five years. Other organizations use SSNs for similar purposes. Hibbert notes that "[m]ost insurance companies share access to old claims through the Medical Information Bureau. If your insurance company uses your SSN, other insurance companies will have a much easier time finding out about your medical history.")

Although SSNs have become popular as an identifier (e.g., as a key in databases), little notice has been paid to the fact they were not designed for many tasks for which they are used. Hibbert observes that SSNs are commonly misunderstood to include the following qualities: uniqueness, universality, security, and identification. But SSNs fail on all four levels.

First, the government does not take sufficient precautions to ensure that SSNs are unique. Upon occasion, different Social Security Administration offices have issued the same social security number to different people. Hibbert reports that a "few numbers were used by thousands of people because they were on sample cards shipped in wallets by their manufacturers." New immigration laws requiring employers to check employee SSNs have led to the increased use of duplicate SSNs. Since you cannot cross-check an SSN against the Social Security Administration database, Hibbert observes that you can expect false SSNs will be used.

Second, not everyone has an SSN. They are not issued at birth.

Even though new tax rules request that children be issued social security numbers early on, this does not occur in all cases. Hibbert states that many children do not get SSNs until they begin school. Foreigners also may not have SSNs.

Third, few requesters ever ask to see an SSN card for identification purposes. With the exception of employment, it is sufficient to simply recite an SSN and write it on a form.

Fourth, respecting security it is notable that SSN cards are not forgery resistant. Hibbert also states that

[SSNs] don't have any redundancy (no check-digits) so any 9-digit number in the range of numbers that have been issued is a valid number. It is relatively easy to copy the number incorrectly, and there is no way to tell that you have done so.

In most cases, there is no cross-checking that a number is valid. [In contrast, credit card and checking account numbers are checked against a database almost every time they are used. If you write down someone's phone number incorrectly, you find out the first time you try to use it.

And why should you resist disclosing your SSN? According to Hibbert,

When you give out your number, you are providing access to information about yourself . . . that you [may not] have the ability or the legal right to correct or rebut. You provide access to data that is irrelevant to most transactions but that will occasionally trigger prejudice. Worst of all, since you provided the key, (and did so "voluntarily") all the info discovered under your number will be presumed to be true, about you, and relevant.

Courts have been open to challenges to requests for SSNs. Chris Hibbert reports,

[A Virginia] resident . . . refused to supply a Social Security Number when registering to vote. When the registrar refused to accept his registration, he filed suit. He also challenged Virginia on two other bases: the registration form lacked a Privacy Act notice, and the voter lists they publish include Social Security Numbers. The Federal court of appeals ruled that Virginia may not allow the disclosure of Social Security [N]umbers as a condition of registering to vote. The court said that the Virginia requirement places an 'intolerable burden' on the right to vote. The case is officially referred to as [*Greidinger v. Davis*, No. 92–1571 (4th Cir. March 22, 1993)].

The *Greidinger* case notwithstanding, there have been few legal challenges aimed at protecting individuals from the publication of personal information. Credit card companies recently have been pressured to forgo selling information about customer purchases, but this is only a small first step.

There is a strong case to be made that the use of personal information disclosed at the request of government or business be strictly limited to the purpose for which it was requested, and that such information not be used for another purpose or sold or otherwise transferred. This position would surely be opposed by business interests, but it is instructive to note that businesses already enjoy protection against disclosure of their private information. For example, companies are able to bring lawsuits against employees for disclosure of information obtained during the course of employment. A sales manager may be sued if he solicits his employer's business contacts in the course of establishing his own business enterprise.

If a company may go to court to protect against the disclosure of private information, an individual should be able to prevent the publication of personal information for reasons unrelated to those for which the information was provided. After all, privacy is a Constitutional right. Should we not insist that the transmission of personal information and its entry in databases be severely restricted unless that transmission or entry is preceded by a voluntary, informed, and express waiver of privacy rights related thereto?

[CyberLaw™ 8/95]

THE PRIVACY DIRECTIVE

I. Protecting Personal Data

On July 25, 1995, the European Union announced adoption of a Directive on the Protection of Individuals with Regard to the Processing of Personal Data and on the Free Movement of Such Data. The directive seeks to prevent abuses of personal data and lays down comprehensive rules, including an obligation to collect data only for specified, explicit, and legitimate purposes, as well as only to hold data if it is relevant, accurate, and up-to-date. The directive requires all data processing to have a proper legal basis and, as noted in the European Commission's announcement of the adoption of the directive, grants data subjects "a number of important rights including the right of access to that data, the right to know where the data originated (if such information is available), the right to have inaccurate data rectified, a right of recourse in the event of unlawful processing, and the right to withhold permission to use their data in certain circumstances." Although an English version of the directive will not be published until later this year, its outline was stated in a Common Position published in February 1995 (http://privacy.org/pi/). As written in that version, it is clear that a number of substantial loopholes exist. Success of the directive will depend upon the commitment of the European Union and its member states to uphold individual privacy against the pressures of commerce, politics, and security concerns.

II. Free Flow of Data

In its preamble, the directive states that free movement of goods, persons, services, and capital requires not only the free flow of personal data from one member state to another, but also that "fundamental rights of individuals should be recognized." Different levels of protection for individual rights and freedoms (particularly the right of privacy) are seen as "an obstacle to the pursuit of a number of economic activities at [European] Community level, distort[ing] competition and imped[ing] authorities in the discharge of their responsibilities under Community law." An objective of the directive, therefore, is a system acceptable to all members, so they no longer have grounds for inhibiting the flow of personal data among them on the ground of protecting individual rights and freedoms.

Importantly, the directive excludes exclusively personal or domestic matters, such as correspondence and holding address records. There are also significant carve-outs for video surveillance carried out for purposes of "public security, defense, State security (including the economic well-being of the State) and the activities of the State in areas of criminal law," as well as for the processing of sound and image data for journalistic, artistic or literary purposes.

III. Privacy & Consent

The directive, in its operative provisions, expressly states that the right to privacy is a fundamental right and freedom of natural persons. The directive covers not only processing of personal data by automatic means, but also other forms of processing personal data which form part of a filing system or are intended to do so. Personal data itself is defined as data relating to a natural person, or a person who can be identified, by an identification number, or by reference to specific factors such as physical, physiological, mental, economic, cultural, or social identity.

Subject to various exceptions, personal data may only be processed if the data subject has given unambiguous consent (meaning a "freely given and informed indication" of a person's "wishes" signifying "his agreement to personal data about him being processed"); necessary to the performance of a contract to which the data subject is a party or at his request on entering into a contract; to protect his vital interests; in compliance with a legal obligation of the person responsible for the processing; or necessary for performance of a task carried out in the public interest. A data subject may object to processing of data related to him "on compelling and legitimate grounds relating to his particular situation."

IV. Data Quality, Notice, & Access

Member states are required, generally, to ensure that personal data is

1. "processed fairly and lawfully";
2. "collected for specified, explicit and legitimate purposes and not further processed in a way incompatible with those purposes";
3. "adequate, relevant and not excessive in relation to the purposes for which they are collected," or further processed;
4. "accurate and, where necessary, kept up to date";
5. "kept in a form which permits identification of data subjects for no longer than is necessary for the purposes for which the data were collected," or further processed.

Member states are also required to prohibit processing of data "revealing racial or ethnic origin, political opinions, religious or philosophical beliefs, trade-union membership, and the processing of data concerning health or sex life." But states may establish exceptions for reasons of important public interest, if suitable safeguards are implemented. Other exceptions include cases where the data subject's explicit consent is obtained, as well as in the field of employment law.

The directive seeks to guarantee fair processing of data. States must notify persons from whom personal data are collected of the following:

1. The identity of the person or company that determines the purposes and means of processing the personal data;
2. "[T]he purposes of the processing for which the data are intended";
3. Other information, including the recipients of the data, whether replies to questions are obligatory, the possible consequence of failure to reply, and "the existence of the right of access to and the right to rectify the data concerning him."

Similar rights exist where the data has not been obtained from the data subject. But the protections may not apply where the provision of information "proves impossible, involves a disproportionate effort," or if recording or disclosure is required by law. Again, adequate safeguards are required.

In addition to notice, a right of access is established. At reasonable intervals and without excessive delay or expense, a data subject has the right to receive confirmation of whether data related to him are being processed and the purpose therefor. He may also learn the categories of data involved, as well as the recipients of the data. Regarding the data, he may receive the data and information about the source and logic involved in the data processing. In addition, a data subject may obtain rectification, erasure, or blocking of incorrect or incomplete data. Unless impossible or involving a disproportionate effort, third parties to whom the incorrect or incomplete data has been disclosed are to be notified of this.

Significantly, broad exemptions and restriction may be established relating to data quality, notice requirements, and rights of access. Member states can adopt legislation to restrict their rights and obligations in order to safeguard national security, defense, and public security; the prevention, investigation, and prosecution of criminal offenses or breaches of professional ethics; "an important economic or financial interest of a member state or of the Economic Union"; and, the data subject or the rights and freedoms of others. Rights of access may also be restricted in the case of data processed for scientific research or creation of statistics.

V. Objections

The data subject's right to object to processing of personal data is not limited to "compelling legitimate grounds." There is also a right to object to data processing for direct marketing purposes. The data subject is given notice of disclosure of data to third parties for the first time, along with the right, on request and free of charge, to object to data processing for direct marketing purposes.

A data subject is granted, generally, the right not to be subjected to decisions producing a legal effect, or significantly affecting him, solely based on "automated processing of data intended to evaluate certain personal aspects relating to him, such as his performance at work, creditworthiness, reliability, conduct, etc." Broad exceptions exist, however, allowing such decisions if pursuant to a contract, if "there are suitable measures to safeguard his legitimate interests, such as arrangements allowing him to defend his point of view; or . . . [if] authorized by a law which also lays down measures to safeguard the data subject's legitimate interests."

VI. Security

Regarding data processing, itself, member states are required to "implement appropriate technical and organizational measures to protect personal data against accidental or unlawful destruction or accidental loss and against unauthorized alteration, disclosure or access, in particular where the processing involves the transmission of data over a network, against all other unlawful forms of processing." Security measures are to be commensurate with the risks represented and the data to be protected. In addition, member states are to be notified of data processing operations. But a state may opt out of this notification by allowing appointment of independent data protection officials, responsible for compliance with the directive and maintaining a register of processing operations.

VII. Third Countries

Under the directive, personal data may be transferred to third countries "only if, without prejudice to compliance with the national provisions adopted pursuant to the other provisions of [the] directive, the third country in question ensures an adequate level of protection." Adequacy of protection will be assessed in light of all the circumstances. Member states and the European Commission are to notify each other of cases where a third country does not ensure an adequate level of protection. But transfers to countries that do not ensure adequate levels of protection may occur, if, among other things, "the data subject has given his consent unambiguously to the proposed transfer."

VIII. Remedies

Violation of the directive's provisions, as enacted by member states, may lead to a judicial remedy for breach of rights. Compensation for damage suffered may be recovered. Member states are also required to provide for independent, public authorities responsible for monitoring implementation of the directive. Such authorities shall be able to investigate, intervene, engage in legal proceedings or to bring violations to the attention of judicial authorities, and to hear claims.

5

Duty of Care

A. Negligence

Negligence is "conduct which falls below a standard established by the law for the protection of others against unreasonable risk of harm."[227] A negligence claim may be brought where there exists a legal duty of care, and breach of that duty to a person injured as a result.[228] The "duty" is based upon a relationship between the actor and the injured party giving rise to a legal obligation on the actor's part for the benefit of the injured person.[229] That relationship may be created by contract, statute, judicial decision, or "the interdependent relationship of human society."[230]

Negligence is defined by an objective, not subjective standard. Liability may exist, therefore, even where a person "has considered the possible consequences carefully, and has exercised his own best judgment."[231] It may be based on an act or a failure to act.

Notably, professionals and those engaged in any work or trade requiring special skill may be held to a higher, professional, standard of care. For example, a computer system consultant may be liable for failing to act reasonably in light of his or her superior knowledge in the area of computer systems.[232]

Publishers have been subject to negligence liability for, among other things, publishing materials that subject the public to a clearly identifiable, unreasonable risk of harm from violent criminal ac-

---

[227] W. Prosser, *Torts* §31 (4th ed. 1971).
[228] See 57A Am. Jur. 2d *Negligence* §78.
[229] Ibid. §89.
[230] Ibid. §90.
[231] W. Prosser, *Torts* §31 (4th ed. 1971).
[232] Compare *Diversified Graphics, Ltd. v. Groves*, 868 F.2d 293 (8th Cir. 1989) (computer consultant held to professional standard of care), with *Hospital Computer Systems, Inc. v. Staten Island Hosp.*, 788 F.Supp. 1351, 1361 (D. N.J. 1992) (cause of action for professional negligence against computer consultant would not be recognized by New York courts).

tivity.[233] In a Georgia case involving a suit against *Soldier of Fortune* magazine over a "Gun for Hire" ad that resulted in murder, the court stated that "[a] risk is unreasonable if it is 'of such magnitude as to outweigh what the law regards as the utility of the defendant's alleged negligent conduct.'"[234]

B. Negligent Misstatement

Many online systems provide newsfeeds and other third-party information streams for the benefit of their subscribers. In so doing, online systems run a risk that subscribers will receive false or misleading information.

The U.S. Supreme Court has held that the press would be unconstitutionally chilled in violation of the First Amendment if it were subject to sanctions for either innocent or negligent misstatement, "especially when the content of the speech itself affords no warning of prospective harm to another through falsity."[235] Advertising is also covered by First Amendment protections, albeit in a limited form, "so long as it concerns a lawful activity and is not misleading or fraudulent."[236]

In a case decided under New York law,[237] the court ruled that there was no special relationship between an online news service and a subscriber to support a negligent misstatement claim. In that case, a securities investor subscribed to the Dow Jones News Service, an interactive online system that allowed him to search for news information. Through Dow Jones, the investor received a report on a Canadian corporation, which failed to mention that the prices shown were in Canadian, not U.S., dollars. Having relied on the information to his detriment, the investor filed suit against Dow Jones, alleging that it negligently published false and misleading statements.

But the court noted that news services have long been held free

---

[233] *Braun v. Soldier of Fortune Magazine, Inc.*, 968 F.2d 1110, 1114 (11th Cir. 1992), *cert. denied*, 506 U.S. 1071, 122 L.Ed.2d 173, 113 S.Ct. 1028 (1993); but see *Eimann v. Soldier of Fortune Magazine, Inc.*, 880 F.2d 830 (5th Cir. 1989), *cert. denied*, 493 U.S. 1024, 107 L.Ed.2d 748 110 S.Ct. 729 (1990) (rejecting standard "requir[ing] publishers to recognize ads that 'reasonably could be interpreted as an offer to engage in illegal activity' based on their words or 'context' and refrain from printing them.")
[234] *Braun v. Soldier of Fortune Magazine, Inc.*, 968 F.2d 1110, 1115 (11th Cir. 1992), *cert. denied*, 506 U.S. 1071, 122 L.Ed.2d 173, 113 S.Ct. 1028 (1993).
[235] *Time, Inc. v. Hill*, 385 U.S. 374, 389, 17 L.Ed.2d 456, 87 S.Ct. 534 (1967).
[236] *Posadas de Puerto Rico Associates v. Tourism Co. of Puerto Rico*, 478 U.S. 328, 340, 92 L.Ed.2d 266, 106 S.Ct. 2968 (1986).
[237] *Daniel v. Dow Jones & Co.*, 137 Misc.2d 94, 520 N.Y.S.2d 334 (Civ. Ct. 1987).

from liability to their readers for negligent false statements. Both federal and New York courts require a "special relationship" between the parties for negligent misstatement liability. Here, the relationship between the investor and Dow Jones is "functionally identical to that of a purchaser of a newspaper," observed the court, and "[t]he 'special relationship' required to allow an action for negligent misstatements must be greater than that between the ordinary buyer and seller."

The court also ruled the investor's claim barred by the U.S. and New York constitutions. "The societal right to free and unhampered dissemination of information," says the court, "precludes liability absent proof of knowing falsity or reckless disregard for the truth." Dow Jones, as provider of, "in essence, a 'wire service'," should "be treated as a 'media' defendant, entitled to the fullest protection of the First Amendment." Dismissing the investor's claim, the court held that Dow Jones' service "is one of the modern, technologically interesting ways the public may obtain up-to-the-minute news. It is entitled to the same protection as more established means of news distribution."

C. Equipment Malfunctions

System failures are always a concern to online system operators, and occur with some frequency. Failure to anticipate such failures and to provide for appropriate backup may lead to negligence liability.[238]

D. Economic loss may not be recoverable

Where negligence liability is established, a claimant may recover money damages for physical injury or property damage. Whether economic loss, such as lost earnings or profits, may be recovered in a negligence suit depends on the state law that controls the case. In an Illinois lawsuit, for example, a company sued the sellers of a computer and a software package for negligent misrepresentation, seeking to recover economic losses consisting of lost profits, salaries, offices supplies, and accounting and leasing expenses. The court dismissed the claim, on the grounds that it is not one in which Illinois law permits

---

[238] See *Blake v. Woodford Bank & Trust Co.*, 555 S.W.2d 589 (Ky. Ct. App. 1977) (circumstances causing delay in bank bookkeeping department, including breakdown of two posting machines, were foreseeable, and did not excuse bank from meeting a midnight deadline for revoking provisional "settlement" of checks under the Uniform Commercial Code).

recovery of economic loss.[239] In contrast, California courts find that economic losses, such as an interest in prospective economic advantage, "may be protected against an injury occasioned by negligent as well as intentional conduct."[240]

E. Contractual Limitations of Liability

In an effort to reduce risk, online services have included limitation of liability clauses in their subscription agreements. Similar contractual limitations of liability have been enforced by courts.[241] In a notable case, an auto dealership's advertising was omitted from the classified section of a telephone directory. This was caused by the telephone company's erroneous deletion of the dealership's data from its computer system and the company's failure to follow its own standard operating procedures. But the auto dealership was not permitted to recover for lost profits, injury to business reputation, or loss of goodwill. Instead, the court found applicable and upheld a contractual limitation of liability in the Directory Advertising Agreement between the parties, limiting damages to amounts not exceeding monthly charges for advertising or listings involved.[242]

It should be noted, however, that contractual limitations of liability may not be upheld in all circumstances. Limitations of remedy to repair or replacement of defective parts, for example, may be avoided where a manufacturer or seller is unable to make repairs within a reasonable period of time. In such a case, the exclusive or limited remedy is said to have failed of its essential purpose, allowing consequential damages (such as lost profits) to be recovered.[243] A disclaimer of consequential damages may also be avoided if found to be unconscionable.[244]

---

[239] *Black, Jackson & Simmons Ins. Brokerage, Inc. v. International Business Machines Corp.*, 109 Ill.App.3d 132, 440 N.E.2d 282 (1982). See also, *Transport Corp. of America v. International Business Machines Corp.*, 30 F.3d 953 (8th Cir. 1994) (Minnesota law).

[240] *J'Aire Corp. v. Gregory*, 24 Cal.3d 799, 803, 598 P.2d 60 (1979).

[241] *Primrose v. Western Union Tel. Co.*, 154 U.S. 1, 38 L. Ed. 883, 14 S.Ct. 1098 (1894) (telegraph co. may limit its contractual and tort liability to an amount, such as transmission price); *Dubovsky & Sons, Inc. v. Honeywell, Inc.*, 89 A.D.2d 993, 454 N.Y.S.2d 329 (1982) (on installation and maintenance of alarm system, exculpatory clause upheld in case of ordinary negligence).

[242] *Ed Fine Oldsmobile, Inc. v. Diamond State Tel. Co.*, 494 A.2d 636 (Del. 1985).

[243] See Uniform Commercial Code § 2–719; *Milgard Tempering v. Selas Corp. of America*, 902 F.2d 703, 709 (9th Cir. 1990).

[244] See Uniform Commercial Code § 2–719(3); *Transport Corp. of America v. International Business Machines Corp.*, 30 F.3d 953, 960 (8th Cir. 1994) ("An exclusion

There has been widespread concern that preprinted limitations of liability found on the outside of computer software packages or in documents inside the sealed packages are not effective. There has been little judicial guidance on this matter,[245] and it would seem the wisest course for sellers to bring such limitations conspicuously to the attention of purchasers at the time of sale. From a business standpoint, it is to be hoped that shrinkwrap licenses will be upheld, since in virtually all cases it is not economically efficient or practical to obtain and retain copies of signed agreements entered into at the point of sale.

The National Conference of Commissioners on Uniform State Laws is working to "develop tailored and effective contract principles related to licensing and other transactions involving digital transactions."[246] Proposed amendments to the Uniform Commercial Code include a section on "mass market licenses" that provides that

a party adopts the terms of a mass market license if, before or within a reasonable time after beginning to use the digital information pursuant to an agreement, the party

(1) signs or otherwise by its behavior manifests assent to a mass market license; and
(2) had an opportunity to review the terms of the license before manifesting assent, whether or not the party actually reviewed the terms.[247]

To guard against surprise, a term may be excluded from a mass market license if it "creates an obligation or imposes a limitation that is

---

of consequential damages set forth in advance in a commercial agreement between experienced business parties represents a bargained-for allocation of risk that is conscionable as a matter of law.")

[245] Compare *ProCD, Inc. v. Zeidenberg*, No. 96-1139, Slip Opinion (7th Cir. June 20, 1996) ("Shrinkwrap licenses are enforceable unless their terms are objectionable on grounds applicable to contracts in general. . . .") with *Arizona Retail Sys. v. Software Link*, 831 F.Supp. 759, 764 (D. Ariz. 1993) (in initial transaction, buyer accepted seller's terms when it opened envelope containing software on which was printed a license agreement, but in subsequent phone orders the license agreement was not discussed and did not become part of the agreement, despite being printed on packaging attached to the product); *Step-Saver Data Systems, Inc. v. Wyse Technology*, 939 F.2d 91 (3rd Cir. 1991) (where purchaser ordered computer software by phone, receiving an invoice with terms essentially identical to purchaser's purchase order, but on each package of software was printed disclaimer of warranty and limitation of remedies provisions, the court held the terms of the box-top license did not become part of the parties' agreement, the disclaimer not being expressed until after the contract was formed and substantially altering the distribution of risk between the parties); cf., *Vault Corp. v. Quaid Software, Ltd.*, 655 F.Supp. 750 (E.D. La. 1987), *aff'd*, 847 F.2d 255 (5th Cir. 1988) (license agreement prohibiting decompilation or disassembly of computer software held unenforceable contract of adhesion, not supported by state statute preempted by Copyright Act).
[246] National Conference of Commissioners on Uniform State Law, Uniform Commercial Code Article 2B. Licenses, at p.i. (December 1, 1995, Draft)
[247] Proposed Uniform Commercial Code § 2B-308(a) (December 1, 1995, Draft).

not consistent with customary industry practices and that the licensor should know would cause most licensees in transactions of similar type to refuse the license if the term were brought to the attention of the licensee."[248]

---

[248] Ibid. § 2B-308(b) (December 1, 1995, Draft).

6

Criminal Liability

Until 1990, the online world was an electronic frontier that law enforcement rarely noticed. But "[i]n 1990, there came a nationwide crackdown on illicit computer hackers, with arrests, criminal charges, one dramatic show trial, several guilty pleas, and huge confiscations of data and equipment all over the United States."[249] Politics and police now are an entrenched feature of the electronic landscape, as are novel prosecutions and defenses that challenge a legal system that did not anticipate the development of cyberspace.

A. Computer Fraud & Abuse Act

The Computer Fraud and Abuse Act is largely aimed at protecting federal government as well as financial and medical institution computers.[250] The act prohibits unauthorized access in order to obtain sensitive information,[251] such as defense-related information and financial and consumer credit records, among other things. Trafficking in passwords for computers used by or for the U.S. government is also barred.[252]

Notably, the Computer Fraud and Abuse Act prohibits the transmission of "a program, information, code, or command to a computer or computer system" with intent to damage, or cause damage to, or to withhold or deny the use of, a computer, computer services or network, information, data, or program.[253] Such transmission is

---

[249] B. Sterling, *The Hacker Crackdown* (1992), p. xiii.
[250] 18 U.S.C. § 1030.
[251] See *United States v. Pedersen*, 3 F.3d 1468 (11th Cir. 1993) (police detective unlawfully accessed and solicited others to access FBI's NCIC database, as well as Social Security Administration computer records); cf., *State v. Olson*, 47 Wash.App. 514, 735 P.2d 1362, 1364 (1987) (unauthorized use of computer data by police officer not prohibited by Washington State computer trespass law).
[252] 18 U.S.C. § 1030(a)(6).
[253] Ibid. § 1030(a)(5)(A).

also prohibited if done with reckless disregard of a substantial and unjustifiable risk of the same effect.[254]

A widely-observed prosecution under the Computer Fraud and Abuse Act concerned a first-year graduate student in Cornell University's computer science Ph.D program. He wrote, and in 1988 released into the Internet, a computer program known as a "worm," which spread through the network, causing computers to "crash" at leading universities, military installations, and medical research facilities.[255] The student, Robert Morris, intended the program to demonstrate inadequate computer network security measures. The "worm" was supposed to spread across the Internet without drawing attention to itself or interfering with the normal use of computers. But design defects caused the worm to duplicate at an unanticipated rate, crashing computers around the country and clogging network routes so that instructions on how to kill the worm and prevent reinfection could not be transmitted. The cost of dealing with the worm at each installation affected ranged from $200 to more than $53,000. Morris was found guilty of violating the Computer Fraud and Abuse Act, sentenced to three years probation and four hundred hours of community service, and fined $10,500 plus costs of supervision.

B. Wire Fraud

Wire fraud[256] consists of "1) a scheme to defraud by means of false pretenses, 2) the defendant's knowing and willful participation in the scheme with intent to defraud, and 3) the use of interstate wire communications in furtherance of the scheme."[257] Notably, wire fraud is a predicate act for a RICO (Racketeer Influenced and Corrupt Organizations) prosecution.[258] The wire fraud statute has been applied to the use of computers.[259]

In 1988, Robert Riggs was indicted for allegedly using a home computer to gain unauthorized access to a Bell South Telephone Company computer and downloading a text file describing its enhanced

---

[254] Ibid. § 1030(a)(5)(B).

[255] *United States v. Morris*, 928 F.2d 504 (2d Cir.), *cert. denied*, 502 U.S. 817, 116 L.Ed.2d 46, 112 S.Ct. 72 (1991)

[256] 18 U.S.C. § 1343.

[257] *United States v. Cassiere*, 4 F.3d 1006, 1011 (1st Cir. 1993).

[258] 18 U.S.C. § 1961 *et seq.* Penalties under RICO include fines, imprisonment, and forfeiture.

[259] See also *United States v. Kelly*, 507 F.Supp. 495 (E.D. Pa. 1981).

911 system for handling emergency phone calls. Riggs allegedly placed a copy of the text file on an Illinois computer bulletin board, so that it could be available to another person, Craig Neidorf, who then edited the file to conceal its theft from Bell South and later uploaded it back onto the BBS. This led to charges of wire fraud.[260]

Neidorf asked the court to dismiss the wire fraud charges in the indictment, on the grounds that the wire fraud statute did not apply to him. But the court denied his request. Riggs allegedly used fraudulent means to access Bell South's computers and disguised his entry. Neidorf allegedly furthered the scheme by redacting identifying information from the 911 document, among other things. The court also held that the 911 document was considered by Bell South to be valuable, confidential information that can constitute "'property,' the deprivation of which can form the basis of a wire fraud charge under [Section] 1343."[261] (Neidorf's prosecution collapsed at trial, when it was shown that the 911 document was publicly available for $13, and Riggs testified that Neidorf was not a hacker—just the publisher of a magazine.)[262]

In 1994, David LaMacchia, a twenty-one-year old student at the Massachusetts Institute of Technology, was indicted by a federal grand jury on one count of conspiring "with persons unknown" to violate the wire fraud statute. He had established a BBS on which he encouraged others to upload computer software applications and games. He transferred uploaded programs to a second BBS. Those with password access to the second BBS could download the programs. The indictment did not allege that LaMacchia sought or derived any personal benefit,[263] but that he

devised a scheme to defraud that had as its object the facilitation "on an international scale" of the "illegal copying and distribution of copyrighted software" without payment of license fees and royalties to software manufacturers and vendors.[264]

Upon LaMacchia's request, the court dismissed the charge against him. LaMacchia had not engaged in any "fraudulent scheme," said

---

[260] Riggs and Neidorf were also charged with violation of the National Stolen Property Act, 18 U.S.C. § 2314, prohibiting interstate transfer of stolen property, and the Computer Fraud and Abuse Act of 1986, 18 U.S.C. § 1030(a)(6)(A).

[261] U.S. v. Riggs, 739 F.Supp. 414, 419 (N.D. Ill. 1990).

[262] See B. Sterling, *The Hacker Crackdown* (1992), p. 275–81.

[263] LaMacchia could not be charged under the criminal copyright statute, 17 U.S.C. § 506(a), which requires that a defendant be shown to have sought to personally profit from the scheme to defraud. See *United States v. LaMacchia*, 871 F.Supp. 535, 541–42 (D. Mass. 1994).

[264] *United States v. LaMacchia*, 871 F.Supp. 535, 536 (D. Mass. 1994).

the court. And illegal conduct alone, observed the court, cannot satisfy the fraud element of the wire fraud statute.

The court also rejected the government's argument that the wire fraud statute should apply to intangible property interest (such as copyright) as well as tangible property interests. The court based this ruling on a decision in which the U.S. Supreme Court reversed an interstate transportation of stolen property conviction for sale of bootleg Elvis Presley recordings,[265] on grounds that "a copyrighted musical composition impressed on a bootleg phonograph record is not property that is 'stolen, converted, or taken by fraud' within the meaning of the Stolen Property Act."[266]

Although reasonable people may agree that LaMacchia's conduct deserves punishment, continued the court, Congress has "chosen to tread cautiously" in determining where criminal copyright sanctions are necessary. Congress is sensitive to the "special concerns implicated by the copyright laws," and courts should leave it to the legislature to define crimes and prescribe penalties. The court also noted that

[The government's] interpretation of the wire fraud statute would serve to criminalize the conduct of not only persons like LaMacchia, but also the myriad of home computer users who succumb to the temptation to copy even a single software program for private use. It is not clear that making criminals of a large number of consumers of computer software is a result that even the software industry would consider desirable.[267]

Copyright prosecutions should be limited, said the court, to Section 506 of the Copyright Act and other incidental statutes that refer explicitly to copyright and copyrighted works.

C. Electronic Communications Privacy Act of 1986

The Electronic Communications Privacy Act of 1986 (ECPA)[268] prohibits unauthorized interception and disclosure of the content of electronic communications. Fines and imprisonment are prescribed for anyone who "intentionally intercepts, endeavors to intercept, or procures any other person to intercept or endeavor to intercept, any wire,

---

[265] Ibid.
[266] See *Dowling v. United States*, 473 U.S. 207, 216, 87 L.Ed.2d 152, 105 S.Ct. 3127 (1985).
[267] *United States v. LaMacchia*, 871 F.Supp. 535, 544 (D. Mass. 1994).
[268] 18 U.S.C. §§ 1367, 2232, 2510 *et seq.*, 2701 *et seq.*, 3117, 3121 *et seq.*

oral, or electronic communication."[269] It is also a felony to use the content of an unlawfully intercepted e-mail message if the person doing so knows or has reason to know it was wrongfully obtained.[270] It is generally permissible, however, for a party to a message to intercept it or to give prior consent to its interception, if for a proper and lawful purpose.[271] And, of course, it is not illegal to access a message on a public BBS.[272]

Providers of electronic communication services may, in the normal course of business, intercept, disclose, or use communications while engaged in an activity necessarily incident to the rendition of the service, or to the protection of their rights and property.[273] They are not permitted, however, to utilize service monitoring or random monitoring, except for mechanical or service quality control checks.[274]

Disclosure of the content of a message may be made by providers of electronic communication services to the public, with the consent of the originator or any addressee or intended recipient.[275] The content may also be disclosed to another service that will forward the communication to its destination. Communications inadvertently obtained that appear to pertain to the commission of a crime may be

---

[269] 18 U.S.C. § 2511(1)(a); *Steve Jackson Games v. United States Secret Serv.*, 816 F.Supp. 432, 441–42 (W.D. Tex. 1993), *aff'd*, 36 F.3d 457 (5th Cir. 1994) (Secret Service did not "intercept" communication stored on an electronic BBS, on grounds that only contemporaneous acquisition of a communication is prohibited); *State ex rel. Macy v. One Pioneer CD-ROM Changer*, 891 P.2d 600, 606 (Okla. Ct. App. 1994); *U.S. v. Maxwell*, 42 M.J. 568 (A.F.C.C.A. 1995) (ECPA applies to e-mail transmission; defendant had objective expectation of privacy in e-mail messages stored on America Online, which he alone could retrieve through the use of his own assigned password).

[270] 18 U.S.C. § 2511(1)(d).

[271] 18 U.S.C. § 2511(2)(d); compare, Cal. Pen. Code §§ 631–32 (requiring consent of all parties to a confidential communication); *Coulter v. Bank of America*, 28 Cal.App.4th 923 (1994) (employee held liable under California law for secretly recording phone and face-to-face conversations with coworkers, supervisors, and officers of employer).

[272] 18 U.S.C. § 2511(2)(g)(i).

[273] 18 U.S.C. § 2511(2)(a)(i). Pending cases over alleged disclosure of trade secrets by an executive who departed a computer software company for a competitor may shed light on this section of the ECPA. See *Borland International, Inc. v. Eubanks, et al.*, Civ. Case No. 123059 (Cal. Super. Ct., Santa Cruz Cty., filed Sept. 3, 1992); *People v. Eubanks*, Crim. Case No. 6748 (Cal. Super. Ct., Santa Cruz Cty., filed Feb. 26, 1993); *People v. Wang*, Crim. Case No. 6749 (Cal. Super. Ct., Santa Cruz Cty., filed Feb. 26, 1993).

[274] 18 U.S.C. § 2511(2)(a)(i); *United States v. Christman*, 375 F.Supp. 1354 (N.D. Cal. 1974) (random monitoring is forbidden to "communications common carriers," but not to private telephone installations).

[275] 18 U.S.C. § 2511(3)(b)(ii).

disclosed, but only to a law enforcement agency.[276] Disclosure can also be made pursuant to proper government authorization.[277]

Although some people appear to believe that there is no protection for communication over cellular phones, cellular calls are, in fact, protected by the ECPA.[278] Previously, the ECPA did not cover communications over cordless telephones of the type where a radio signal is transmitted between the telephone handset and base unit, but this exception was removed in 1994.[279]

The ECPA prohibits unauthorized access to stored communications. Section 2701 of the ECPA prohibits intentional unauthorized access to an electronic communications service facility, as well as intentionally exceeding authorized access to such a facility, and obtaining, altering, or preventing authorized access to a wire or electronic communication in electronic storage.[280] This bar operates, therefore, against unauthorized outsiders as well as persons who have their own accounts but hack into other users' directories and files, or into other prohibited areas of the system. There is no indication in the ECPA that it would prohibit a person from accessing a file placed in public area of a system, such as in a public ftp, gopher, or World Wide Web directory. System operators should be careful not to leave important files, such as an encrypted password file, in a public area.

Subject to a number of exceptions similar to those covering disclosure of the content of messages in transit, operators of electronic communication services for the public are barred from disclosing the content of a message in storage.[281] Section 2702(b)(5) of the ECPA does state an exception to the general rule of nondisclosure, allowing a company to disclose the contents of a communication "as may be necessarily incident to the rendition of the service or to the protection of the rights or property of the [service] provider. . . ." Operators of purely internal e-mail systems are not covered by this prohibition, and it is widely believed that authorized coworkers, supervisors, as well as

---

[276] Ibid. (iv).

[277] Ibid. (i).

[278] See 18 U.S.C. § 2511(4)(b).

[279] See *United States v. McNulty (In re Askin)*, 47 F.3d 100, 103 (4th Cir.), *cert. denied*, 133 L.Ed.2d 305, 116 S.Ct. 382 (1995) ("Congress has since extended Title III's coverage to include the radio portion of cordless communications. . . .").

[280] Compare *Sega Enters. v. MAPHIA*, 857 F.Supp. 679, 689 (N.D. Cal. 1994) (employee of video game company did not violate 18 U.S.C. § 2701 by accessing BBS through use of a pseudonym, where BBS was open to the public and normally accessed by use of an alias or pseudonym, the employee was authorized by a BBS user, and identification of the employee would have defeated the investigation of copyright or trademark infringement).

[281] 18 U.S.C. 2702(a).

system operators generally may read internal messages and files without liability under the ECPA, despite the fact that the law does not contain express authorization therefor.[282] But agreement, company custom, policy, or procedure may give rise to a reasonable and legally enforceable expectation of employee privacy restricting a company's ability to review internal messages and files communicated via its internal e-mail system.

The ECPA does contain exceptions that may assist employers with a business reason to be concerned about employee messaging. Section 2510(5) of the ECPA looks to devices that can be used to monitor electronic communications, and excepts from coverage components furnished to a subscriber or user "by a provider of wire or electronic communication service in the ordinary course of its business and being used by the subscriber or user in the ordinary course of its business," among other things. Although there are no reported court decisions related to employee e-mail, a number of cases have considered this exception (commonly known as the "extension phone exception" or the "business extension exemption") and allowed certain employer monitoring of employee phone calls.[283]

Section 2511(2)(d) of the ECPA permits interception of wire communications by one party to the communication or where one party has given prior consent to such interception. Arguably, this ex-

---

[282] See *Flanagan v. Epson America, Inc.*, No. BC007036, Ruling on Demurrer and Motion to Strike of Defendant Epson America, Inc. (Cal. Super. Ct., Los Angeles Cty., Jan. 4, 1991) (generally referring to "ECPA and Online Computer Privacy," (1989) 4 Federal Communications Law Journal 17, 39, wherein the author opines that an employee has no ECPA claim against an employer over examination of stored communications on the company's in-house computer system); J. Podesta & P. Sher, *Protecting Electronic Messaging: A Guide to the Electronic Communications Privacy Act of 1986*, pp.viii, ix, 1.

[283] See *Epps v. St. Mary's Hospital, Inc.*, 802 F.2d 412, 417 (11th Cir. 1986) (in case in which intercepting device was a dispatch console and a double reeled tape recorder was used to record a conversation between employees, the court held the "potential contamination of a working environment is a matter in which the employer has a legal interest"); *Briggs v. American Air Filter Co.*, 630 F.2d 414, 420 (5th Cir. 1980) ("[w]hen an employee's supervisor has particular suspicions about confidential information being disclosed to a business competitor, has warned the employee not to disclose such information, has reason to believe that the employee is continuing to disclose the information, and knows that a particular phone call is with an agent of the competitor, it is within the ordinary course of business to listen in on an extension phone for at least so long as the call involves the type of information he fears is being disclosed."); *James v. Newspaper Agency Corp.*, 591 F.2d 579, 581 (10th Cir. 1979) (affirming judgment against employee in case where employer installed a telephone monitoring device, notifying all affected personnel, with purpose to give employees training and instruction as to how better to deal with the general public, and also to serve as some protection for employees from abusive calls).

ception may assist employers who notify employees that e-mail sent across the company-provided system is subject to inspection.[284] But it should be noted that a state—California, for example—may require the consent of all parties to a confidential communication if the content is to be recorded.[285]

ECPA allows law enforcement officials to intercept electronic communications, both in transit and storage, if proper procedures are followed.[286] Generally, a court order is required. But there are exceptions for emergency situations, where authorization can be obtained from high-level federal and state attorneys.[287] A governmental entity may gain access to communications stored for 180 days or less by obtaining a warrant.[288] Messages stored for a longer period are easier to obtain, including, for example, by use of a trial subpoena and prior notice to the subscriber or customer.[289]

One case under the ECPA arose when the Secret Service raided a Texas company named Steve Jackson Games, Inc., searching for evidence of a Bell South "911" program document taken by an "intrusion" into Bell South's computer network. A federal court ruled that the Secret Service violated the ECPA by seizing and removing the company's BBS, named "Illuminati." The seized BBS contained stored public and private electronic communications and e-mail, and was not returned until months later. Although it contained messages that had been sent to but not yet read by the intended recipients, the seizure was not found to be an "interception" proscribed by the ECPA.[290] If it had been an interception, the authorizing court order would have required it be executed "in such a way as to minimize the interception

---

[284] See *Watkins v. L.M. Berry & Co.*, 704 F.2d 577 (11th Cir. 1983) (plaintiff consented to a policy of monitoring sales calls, including the inadvertent interception of a personal call, but only for as long as necessary to determine the nature of the call).
[285] See Cal. Penal Code §§ 631–32.
[286] See, e.g., 18 U.S.C. §§ 2516–18, 2703.
[287] See, e.g., 18 U.S.C. § 2518(7).
[288] 18 U.S.C. § 2703(a).
[289] Ibid. § 2703(b).
[290] Ibid. § 2511(1)(a). The ECPA did not extend the Federal Wiretap Act's statutory exclusion to the interception of electronic communications. See 18 U.S.C. § 2515; *Steve Jackson Games v. United States Secret Serv.*, 36 F.3d 457, 461 n.6 (5th Cir. 1994); *United States v. Meriwether*, 917 F.2d 955, 960 (6th Cir. 1990) ("The ECPA does not provide an independent statutory remedy of suppression for interceptions of electronic communications."). If the government is involved, defendants seeking to suppress evidence must look to the Fourth Amendment. See *Katz v. United States*, 389 U.S. 347, 19 L.Ed.2d 576, 88 S.Ct. 507 (1967) (government violated privacy upon which defendant justifiably relied while using a telephone booth and government eavesdropping therefore constituted a "search and seizure" within the meaning of the Fourth Amendment).

of communications not otherwise subject to interception,"[291] and other limitations would have applied.

Here, the Secret Service wanted to seize and read all stored communications. But the ECPA permits issuance of a disclosure order "only if the governmental entity offers specific and articulable facts showing that there are reasonable grounds to believe that the contents of a[n] . . . electronic communication . . . are relevant and material to an ongoing criminal investigation."[292] Here, the requesting Secret Service agent did not tell the judge that the BBS contained private electronic communications between users, or how the disclosure of their content could relate to his investigation. As the application and affidavit for the search warrant were sealed, the plaintiffs were not on notice that the search and seizure order was pursuant to the ECPA, and that Steve Jackson Games "could move to quash or modify the order or eliminate or reduce any undue burden on it by reason of the order."[293] Accordingly, the court ruled that the Secret Service had "virtually eliminated the safeguards contained in the [ECPA]." Statutory damages of $1,000 were awarded to each plaintiff.[294]

The ECPA also contains procedures and provisions on government requests for customer records and information. In appropriate circumstances, the government may apply for an order prohibiting a service provider from notifying a person of the existence of a warrant, subpoena, or court order.[295]

D. Extortion & Threats

Federal law prohibits interstate or foreign transmission of communications regarding kidnapping, extortion, or threat to injure.[296]

In a suit over failure to make lease payments for computer hardware, a defendant counterclaimed for extortion, based on alleged wrongful deactivation of computer software. But the defendant had

---

[291] 18 U.S.C. § 2518(5).
[292] Ibid. § 2703(d); *Steve Jackson Games v. United States Secret Serv.*, 816 F.Supp. 432, 443 (W.D. Tex. 1993), *aff'd*, 36 F.3d 457 (5th Cir. 1994).
[293] *Steve Jackson Games v. United States Secret Serv.*, 816 F.Supp. 432, 443 (W.D. Tex. 1993), *aff'd*, 36 F.3d 457 (5th Cir. 1994).
[294] Ibid.
[295] 18 U.S.C. § 2705(b); compare, *Gibson v. Florida Legislative Investigative Committee*, 372 U.S. 539, 9 L.Ed.2d 929, 83 S.Ct. 889 (1963) (contempt conviction for refusal to divulge information contained in NAACP membership lists violated rights of association protected by the First and Fourteenth Amendments).
[296] 18 U.S.C. § 875.

signed a software license agreement providing that the software could be canceled upon default. When the defendant stopped making payments, the software was deactivated. The licensor had a legal right to do so, ruled the court, so the extortion statute did not apply.[297]

In early 1995, a University of Michigan student, Jake Baker, was arrested and held without bail for publishing a sexually violent piece of fiction in an Internet newsgroup. The reason for the arrest seemed to be an unfortunate choice in naming the story's victim—giving her the name of a student in one of Baker's classes.[298] While many wondered how anyone could be arrested and held for such a thing, Baker spent twenty-nine days in jail. Not surprisingly, the government soon abandoned prosecution based on the story, focusing instead on Baker's private e-mail exchanges with a person named Gonda. A superseding indictment, which did not mention the story, charged Baker with five counts of transmitting threats in interstate commerce. A U.S. district Court judge later dismissed the indictment against Baker, ruling that the First Amendment barred his prosecution.[299]

E. Exports

The Arms Export Control Act authorizes the government to control the export of defense articles and services to foreign countries. To further "world peace and the security and foreign policy of the United States," the president is given the power to designate restricted articles and services and to issue regulations for their import and export.[300]

The regulations implementing the Arms Export Control Act are the International Traffic in Arms Regulations (ITAR).[301] Defense articles and services subject to ITAR are listed on the U.S. Munitions List. To export an item on the Munitions List, a person must be registered with the State Department prior to submitting an export license application.[302] Before each export, an individually validated license must be obtained.[303]

Unclassified technical data not in the "public domain"[304] may be subject to export license requirements. A license is required regardless

---

[297] *American Computer Trust Leasing v. Jack Farrell Implement Co.*, 763 F.Supp. 1473, 1493 (D. Minn. 1991).
[298] See Appendix VI., *True Threats*, CyberLaw (July 1995), *infra*.
[299] *United States v. Baker*, 890 F.Supp. 1375 (E.D. Mich. 1995).
[300] 22 U.S.C. § 2778(a)(1).
[301] 22 C.F.R. Subchapter M, Part 120 *et seq*.
[302] 22 C.F.R. § 122.1.
[303] Ibid. § 123.1.
[304] Ibid. § 120.11 ("public domain" defined).

of the manner in which the data is transmitted, and must be obtained before even an oral disclosure (e.g., in a seminar) to a foreign national visiting the United States.[305]

Criminal penalties for violating the Arms Export Control Act or ITAR include fines up to $1 million and ten years imprisonment.[306] Substantial additional civil penalties are authorized.[307]

Cryptography equipment and software are on the U.S. Munitions List.[308] Excepted from regulation are decryption functions specifically designated to allow the execution of copy-protected software, provided that the decryption functions are not user-accessible; hardware or software specially designed for use in machines for banking or money transactions, and restricted to use only in such transactions; and hardware and software only employing analog techniques to provide cryptographic processing to ensure information security in a limited range of applications, including facsimile equipment and restricted audience broadcast equipment.

Encryption technology not covered by ITAR is, with few exceptions, covered by a companion statute, the Export Administration Act, and the Commerce Department's Export Administration Regulations.[309] Items governed by the Export Administration Regulations are found on the Commerce Control List (CCL).[310] Except for exports to Canada, generally, exports of items on the CCL require a general or validated license,[311] or other export authorization granted by the Office of Export Licensing.[312] Violation of the Export Administration Act is subject to criminal and civil penalties similar to those under the Arms Export Control Act and ITAR.[313]

In 1992, the government agreed to relax and streamline export controls on mass-market software with encryption capabilities. Control of such software, when limited to certain functions, was transferred by the State Department to the Commerce Department, and expedited procedures were established to review requests to transfer commodity jurisdiction to the Commerce Department.[314] Export controls on encryption using RSA Data Security Inc.'s RC2 and RC4 pro-

---

[305] Ibid. § 125.2(c).
[306] 22 U.S.C. § 2778(c).
[307] 22 C.F.R. § 127.10(a); 50 U.S.C. App. 2410(c).
[308] Ibid. § 121.1, Category XIII—Auxiliary Military Equipment.
[309] 15 C.F.R. Part 768 et seq.
[310] 15 C.F.R. § 799.1.
[311] Ibid. §§ 772.1–72.2.
[312] 22 C.F.R. § 770.3(a).
[313] See 50 U.S.C. App. § 2410.
[314] Interim Final Rule, Amendment to ITAR, the U.S. Munitions List, 57 Fed. Reg. 32148, July 20, 1992.

prietary algorithms, which support asymmetric ("public-key") encryption using 40-bit keys, were also relaxed.[315] (But the 56-bit Data Encryption Standard, a symmetric—"private-key"—encryption system using a 56-bit algorithm, remains unavailable for export.)

In 1995, the Commerce Department approved the export of Cybercash Inc. encryption technology. Although similar to an encryption program approved previously for transfer of financial data among international banks, the Cybercash system only encrypts a small section of a transaction message—not the entire message.[316]

In early 1995, Dr. Daniel Bernstein, a scientist, challenged ITAR in a legal action to have declared unconstitutional prohibitions preventing him from publishing, publicly discussing, or circulating a scientific paper, algorithm, or computer program in the field of cryptology.[317] Under ITAR, says Bernstein,

1. [He] cannot even teach his ideas to his students in a classroom without government permission, unless he ensures that none of his students is a "foreign person."
2. [He] would export his ideas if he were to disclose them at an academic conference, because said publication would surely disclose his ideas to a "foreign person."
3. [He] would export his ideas if he were to post a message containing them to the sci.crypt newsgroup. Export includes distributing the ideas over the Internet by posting them to internationally available newsgroups, since this might disclose them to a "foreign person."

Bernstein claims "he cannot even stand on a street corner and talk about his ideas, because this might 'export arms' if a foreign person was listening."

According to Bernstein, the Justice Department concluded in a 1978 memorandum that "existing provisions of the ITAR are unconstitutional insofar as they establish a system of prior restraint on the disclosure of cryptographic ideas and information developed by scientists and mathematicians in the private sector." It is highly likely that the ITAR prohibitions at issue will be found inconsistent with and in violation of the First Amendment.[318]

Bernstein's valid concerns over the risks posed by export controls are also faced by persons who maintain Web sites or online systems that can be accessed by foreigners and contain restricted information,

---

[315] Export approval for software using RSA Data Security Inc.'s RC2 and RC4 algorithms without key management may be granted within seven days of request.
[316] See San Jose *Mercury News*, May 9, 1995, p.3E.
[317] *Bernstein v. United States*, No. C-95-0582 MHP (N.D. Cal. filed Feb. 21, 1995).
[318] In a preliminary ruling, the court held that "source code is speech" and that Bernstein alleged "facts sufficient to state a nonfrivolous First Amendment claim." *Bernstein v. United States*, No. C-95-0582 MHP, Slip Opinion (N.D. Cal. April 15, 1996).

such as encryption programs subject to export controls.[319] For example, Netscape Communications Corp. will not distribute the domestic version of Navigator 2.0 (which uses a 56-bit algorithm) by posting it on the Internet because doing so may be viewed as engaging in the export of a restricted item.[320]

Because of concerns that U.S. citizens and residents traveling abroad with a notebook computer equipped with mass-market software, such as Lotus Notes, may be in violation of the Arms Export Control Act unless they have a Department of State license, there is now a limited exemption for temporary export for personal use of certain cryptographic products. Among other things, the exemption requires that the "exporter" takes normal precautions to ensure the security of the laptop by locking it in a hotel room, safe, or other comparably secure location. While in transit, the "exporter" is required to keep the laptop "in his/her carry-on luggage or locked in baggage accompanying the exporter which has been checked with the carrier."[321]

F. Sexual Exploitation of Children

Federal law prohibits employing, using, persuading, inducing, enticing, or coercing a minor to engage in any sexually explicit conduct for the purpose of producing any visual depiction of such conduct.[322] Also barred is the knowing transmission or receipt by computer of visual depictions involving the use of a minor engaged in sexually explicit conduct,[323] as well as the knowing publication of a notice or advertisement seeking or offering to receive, exchange, buy, produce, display, distribute, or reproduce such visual depictions.[324] Knowing possession with intent to sell visual depictions that have been transmitted by computer, or just knowing possession of three or more items containing such depictions that may have been transmitted by

---

[319] An example of a restricted program is PGP (Pretty Good Privacy). Developed by Philip Zimmermann, PGP is a public-key cryptosystem. Zimmermann put his first version of PGP onto BBS's and gave a copy to a friend who posted it on the Internet. See S. Levy, "Crypto Rebels," *Wired* 1, no. 2 (May/June 1995): 57.
[320] Because Netscape cannot mail patches and upgrades to eight to ten million domestic users, they are compelled to use the 40-bit export version.
[321] See 22 C.F.R. § 123.27.
[322] 18 U.S.C. § 2251(a).
[323] Ibid. § 2252.
[324] Ibid. § 2251(c).

computer, is a criminal offense.[325] Penalties for violation range from fines and imprisonment to civil and criminal forfeiture of personal property. Operators of computer bulletin boards and online systems should take immediate action when they discover or have reason to suspect that any of these activities are occurring on or through their systems.

G. Obscene & Indecent Transmission

1. Obscenity

Obscenity is not an area of constitutionally protected speech or press.[326] But the definition of obscenity is neither clear nor predictable. In 1973, the Supreme Court issued the following test:

(a) whether the "average person, applying contemporary community standards" would find that the work, taken as a whole, appeals to the prurient interest . . . ;
(b) whether the work depicts or describes, in a patently offensive way, sexual conduct specifically defined by the applicable state law; and
(c) whether the work, taken as a whole, lacks serious literary, artistic, political, or scientific value.[327]

Defining the relevant "community" to determine patent offensiveness and appeal to "prurient interest"[328] is not a simple matter.[329] In mail order and phone sex cases, the relevant "community" may be the geographic community into which the communication arrives.[330] In

---

[325] Ibid. § 2252(a)(2), (a)(4).
[326] Roth v. United States, 354 U.S. 476, 484 1 L.Ed.2d 1498, 77 S.Ct. 1304 (1957) ("[I]mplicit in the history of the First Amendment is the rejection of obscenity as utterly without redeeming social importance.").
[327] Miller v. California, 413 U.S. 15, 37 L.Ed.2d 419, 93 S.Ct. 2607 (1973) (Citations omitted).
[328] That which appeals to a shameful or morbid interest in sex. See Brockett v. Spokane Arcades, Inc., 472 U.S. 491, 504, 86 L.Ed.2d 394, 105 S.Ct. 2794 (1985).
[329] See Smith v. United States, 431 U.S. 291, 313–16, 52 L.Ed.2d 324, 97 S.Ct. 1756 (1977) (Stevens, J., dissenting) ("The diversity within the Nation which makes a single standard of offensiveness impossible to identify is also present within each of the so-called local communities . . . In my judgment, the line between communications which 'offend' and those which do not is too blurred to identify criminal conduct.")
[330] United States v. Thomas, Nos. 94-6648, 94-6649, 1996 U.S. App. Lexis 1069 (6th Cir. 1996) (community standards of judicial district to which computer-generated images were electronically transmitted); Sable Communications of California, Inc. v. F.C.C., 492 U.S. 115, 125–26, 106 L.Ed.2d 93, 109 S.Ct. 2829 (1989); United States v. Easley, 927 F.2d 1442, 1449–50(8th Cir. 1991); United States v. Bagnell, 679 F.2d 826 (11th Cir. 1982), cert. denied, 460 U.S. 1047, 75 L.Ed.2d 803, 103 S.Ct. 1449 (1983).

contrast, where an individual travels to another state to purchase a book alleged to be obscene and takes it back home, an obscenity prosecution would be based on the standards of the community where the bookstore is located.[331] The "community" need not always correspond to a particular geographic area. A nongeographic standard may, for example, be applied to radio and television broadcasts.[332]

Importantly, an individual has the right to possess obscene materials in the privacy of his or her own home.[333] But prosecutions have been allowed for transport of obscene matter, whether intended for home use or not.[334] According to the Supreme Court, "States have a legitimate interest in prohibiting dissemination or exhibition of obscene material when the mode of dissemination carries with it a significant danger of offending the sensibilities of unwilling recipients or of exposure to juveniles."[335] Notably, obscenity is a "continuing offense" that may be "inquired of and prosecuted in any district from, through, or into which [it] moves."[336]

Federal law also prohibits the interstate and foreign transportation of obscene matters for sale or distribution[337]—by mail,[338] importation or transport via common carrier,[339] broadcast,[340] and private

---

[331] See *Kaplan v. California*, 413 U.S. 115, 37 L.Ed.2d 492, 93 S.Ct. 2680 (1973).

[332] See *In re Liability of Sagittarius Broadcast Corp.*, 7 FCC Rcd 6873 (1992) (nongeographical standard applied for measuring whether Howard Stern broadcast was patently offensive); *In re Infinity Broadcast Corp. of Pennsylvania*, 2 FCC Rcd 2705 (1987), *aff'd in relevant part, Action for Children's Television v. F.C.C.*, 852 F.2d 1332 (D.C. Cir. 1988).

[333] *Stanley v. Georgia*, 394 U.S. 557, 565, 22 L.Ed.2d 542, 89 S.Ct. 1243 (1972) ("If the First Amendment means anything it means that a State has no business telling a man, sitting alone in his own house, what books he may read or what films he may watch. Our whole constitutional heritage rebels at the thought of giving government the power to control men's minds.")

[334] *United States v. Thomas*, Nos. 94-6648, 94-6649, 1996 U.S. App. Lexis 1069 (6th Cir. 1996) ("'[The Supreme Court] has . . . recognized that the right to possess obscene materials in the privacy of one's home does not create a correlative right to receive it, transport it, or distribute it in interstate commerce even if it is for private use only."); *United States v. Maxwell*, 42 M.J. 568 (A.F.C.C.A. 1995) (e-mail); *United States v. 12 200-Ft Reels of Super 8mm Film*, 413 U.S. 123, 37 L.Ed.2d 500, 93 S.Ct. 2665 (1973) (importation of obscene matter for private, personal use and possession); *United States v. Orito*, 413 U.S. 139, 37 L.Ed.2d 513, 93 S.Ct. 2674 (1973) (plane); *United States v. Reidel*, 402 U.S. 354, 28 L.Ed.2d 813, 91 S.Ct. 1410 (1971) (mail); *Sable Communications of California, Inc. v. F.C.C.*, 492 U.S. 115, 106 L.Ed.2d 93, 109 S.Ct. 2829 (1989) (phone).

[335] *Miller v. California*, 413 U.S. 15, 18–19, 37 L.Ed.2d 419, 93 S.Ct. 2607 (1973).

[336] 18 U.S.C. § 3237.

[337] Ibid. § 1460 *et. seq.*

[338] Ibid. §§ 1461, 1463.

[339] Ibid. § 1462.

[340] Ibid. § 1464.

conveyance.[341] Up to five years' imprisonment is prescribed for knowing interstate or foreign transport of any obscene, lewd, lascivious, or filthy book, pamphlet, picture, film, paper, letter, writing, print, silhouette, drawing, figure, image, cast, phonograph recording, electrical transcription, or other article capable of producing sound or any other matter of indecent or immoral character.[342] Transport of two or more copies of any publication or two or more of any article of such character, or a combined total of five such publications and articles, creates a presumption that such publications or articles are intended for sale or distribution.

In a landmark prosecution, a couple living in Milpitas, California, were convicted by a Memphis, Tennessee, jury for transmitting obscene computer-generated images (GIF files) in interstate commerce.[343] Robert Thomas was sentenced to thirty-seven months in prison and his wife, Carleen, was sentenced to thirty months.

The case centered on the "Amateur Action Bulletin Board System," a BBS operated from the Thomases' home since 1991. It featured a collection of adult computer files. Robert Thomas scanned pictures from sexually explicit magazines purchased in California public bookstores, creating GIF files organized in binary code format on the BBS (which had to be downloaded and then decoded to become viewable images). Access to the GIF files was limited to BBS members. Robert Thomas also purchased videotapes in adult bookstores, which he sold to BBS members.

To become a member of the Amateur Action BBS, an applicant was required to pay a fee and complete a signed application form, stating the applicant's age and the following: "I am a legal adult and request adult file access, I will use Amateur Action GIF files for my private use . . ." Applicants also had to designate an individual password.

In 1993, a Tennessee postal inspector, David Dirmeyer, allegedly received a complaint from a Tennessee resident named Mr. Crawley about the Amateur Action BBS. Using the pseudonym "Lance White," Dirmeyer joined the BBS from Memphis. As "Lance White," Dirmeyer downloaded GIF files and ordered videotapes. According to Robert Thomas's counsel on appeal, there was no evidence that the BBS had any members in Tennessee other than Dirmeyer or that Robert Thomas ever solicited subscribers from Tennessee. (Mr. Crawley was not called as a prosecution witness and did not testify at trial.)

---

[341] Ibid. § 1465.
[342] Ibid.
[343] *United States v. Thomas*, Nos. 94-6648, 94-6649, 1996 U.S. App. Lexis 1069 (6th Cir. 1996).

In 1994, Dirmeyer sent Robert Thomas an envelope containing three child pornography magazines. Dirmeyer claims that he sent Thomas an e-mail message stating that he had "hardcore sex magazines featuring young girls having sex with adults and other children," proposing to let Thomas scan the magazines and create GIF files. The government claims that Thomas was "interested," and Dirmeyer then sent the child pornography magazines—which formed the basis for a federal search warrant.[344] At trial, Robert Thomas denied requesting the magazines, and the jury acquitted him on the child pornography charges.

On appeal of the conviction for transporting obscene material in interstate commerce,[345] it was argued, among other things, that the operative statute does not cover computer transmissions at all, relying on a Tenth Circuit ruling that it prohibits transportation of tangible objects, not intangible computer impulses.[346] It was also claimed that the statute covers travel by private conveyance, not by phone lines, and is, therefore, inapplicable to computer exchange of information. But the U.S. Court of Appeals for the Sixth Circuit rejected these and other claims, and affirmed the Thomases' convictions.[347] The Sixth Circuit, relying on a case on electronic funds transmission, ruled

---

[344] According to The Society for Electronic Access, local law enforcement authorities did not bring any charges against the Thomases and returned the computer equipment. In its amicus curiae brief, the society notes, "Mr. Thomas and Mrs. Thomas have sworn under oath and without contradiction that the San Jose Police Department provided them with a written release affirming that the materials stored on the [Amateur Action BBS] were legal and not obscene." *United States v. Thomas*, Nos. 94-6648, 94-6649, Brief of Amicus Curiae The Society for Electronic Access, at 7 n.2 (6th Cir. filed Apr. 18, 1995).

[345] See *United States v. Thomas*, Nos. 94-6648, Brief of Appellant Robert Alan Thomas (6th Cir. dated Apr. 24, 1995).

[346] See *United States v. Carlin Communications, Inc.*, 815 F.2d 1367 (10th Cir. 1987) (in case over Utah calls to New York telephone number with sexually-suggestive prerecorded messages, the Court dismissed charges of transporting obscene matter under 18 U.S.C. § 1465); cf. *United States v. Maxwell*, 42 M.J. 568 (A.F.C.C.A. 1995); *United States v. Riggs*, 739 F.Supp. 414, 422 (N.D. Ill. 1990) (in wire fraud prosecution, court ruled that "[t]he accessibility of the information in readable form from a particular storage place also makes the information tangible, transferable, salable and, in this court's opinion, brings it within the definition of 'goods, wares, or merchandise' under § 2314."); *United States v. Gilboe*, 684 F.2d 235, 238 (2d Cir. 1982), *cert. denied*, 459 U.S. 1201, 75 L.Ed.2d 432, 103 S.Ct. 1185 (1983) (electronic money transfers). Notably, Congress amended 18 U.S.C. § 2251 (child pornography) to specifically cover computers, but did not make a similar amendment to 18 U.S.C. § 1465. Congress also amended the "Wire and Electronic Communications Intercept and Interception of Communications Act," 18 U.S.C. § 2510 *et. seq.*, to include "electronic communication."

[347] *United States v. Thomas*, Nos. 94-6648, 94-6649, 1996 U.S. App. Lexis 1069 (6th Cir. 1996).

that the defendants "erroneously concluded that the GIF files are intangible."[348]

The Sixth Circuit also rejected the Thomases' claim that Tennessee's community standards should not be applied when determining whether the GIF files are obscene. Prosecutions for obscenity, said the court, lie in any district from, through, or into which allegedly obscene material moves. "This may result," said the court, "in prosecutions of persons in a community to which they have sent materials which is obscene under that community's standards though the community from which it is sent would tolerate the same material."[349] The court did note, however, that

This is not a situation where the bulletin board operator had no knowledge or control over the jurisdictions where materials were distributed for downloading or printing. Access to the Defendants' [BBS] was limited. Membership was necessary and applications were submitted and screened before passwords were issued and materials were distributed. Thus, Defendants had in place methods to limit user access in jurisdictions where the risk of a finding of obscenity was greater than that in California. They knew they had a member in Memphis; the member's address and local phone number were provided on his application form. If Defendants did not wish to subject themselves to liability in jurisdictions with less tolerant standards for determining obscenity, they could have refused to give passwords to members in those districts, thus precluding the risk of liability.[350]

The scope of the same statute[351] was also argued in a child pornography case involving an America Online subscriber. In that case, the U.S. Air Force Court of Military Appeals ruled that electronic transmission of visual images through use of an online computer service is a statutory violation, finding it "clear Congress intended to stem the transportation of obscene material in interstate commerce regardless of the means used to effect that end."[352]

2. Indecency

The rising popularity of the Internet has spurred a host of proposals to regulate its content. The Communications Decency Act of 1996,[353]

---

[348] United States v. Gilboe, 684 F.2d 235 (2d Cir. 1982), cert. denied, 459 U.S. 1201, 75 L.Ed.2d 432, 103 S.Ct. 1185 (1983).

[349] United States v. Thomas, Nos. 94-6648, 94-6649, 1996 U.S. App. Lexis 1069 (6th Cir. 1996). Also see discussion of community standards, Ch. VI. Criminal Liability, § G.1., supra, and of Sable Communications of California, Inc. v. F.C.C., 492 U.S. 115, 106 L.Ed.2d 93, 109 S.Ct. 2829 (1989), another telephone line case, in Ch. VI. Criminal Liability, § H, infra.

[350] United States v. Thomas, Nos. 94-6648, 94-6649, 1996 U.S. App. Lexis 1069 (6th Cir. 1996).

[351] 18 U.S.C. § 1465.

[352] United States v. Maxwell, 42 M.J. 568 (A.F.C.C.A. 1995).

[353] 47 U.S.C. § 223(c).

enacted with the purported purpose of protecting children from exposure to indecent material, is the most successful and controversial of these efforts. The act is widely denounced[354] as so vague and overbroad that it stifles communications of "significant educational, political, medical, artistic, literary, and social value that deal with issues such as sexuality, reproduction, human rights, and civil liberties."[355] Critics also charge that the act will reduce the level of discourse on the Internet to a level fit only for children.

The Communications Decency Act

prohibits a person in interstate or foreign communications who uses a "telecommunications device"[356] from knowingly making, creating, or soliciting "any comment, request, suggestion, proposal, image, or other communication which is obscene or indecent, knowing that the recipient of the communication is under 18 years of age, regardless of whether the maker of such communication placed the call or initiated the communication."[357]

Regarding "interactive computer services" in particular, the act prohibits their use to send or "display in a manner available to" a person under eighteen

any comment, request, proposal, suggestion, proposal, image, or other communication that, in context, depicts or describes, in terms patently offensive as measured by contemporary community standards, sexual or excretory activities or organs, regardless of whether the user of such service placed the call or initiated the communication.[358]

---

[354] Prior to passage of the Communications Decency Act, the Justice Department commented that the indecency standard is "constitutionally problematic." Letter from Andrew Fois, U.S. Department of Justice, to Rep. Howard Berman, December 20, 1995. A Federal judge also noted that the Senate's passage of the Communications Decency Act "suggests that the First Amendment's applicability to on-line communications has not been well considered." *United States v. Baker*, 890 F.Supp. 1375, 1387 n.19 (E.D. Mich. 1995).

[355] *A.C.L.U. v. Reno*, Civ. No. 96-963, Plaintiffs' Memo. of Law in Support of a Motion for a Temporary Restraining Order and Preliminary Injunction (E.D. Penn. Feb. 8, 1996). The plaintiffs in this case other than the American Civil Liberties Union are Human Rights Watch, Electronic Privacy Information Center, Electronic Frontier Foundation, Journalism Education Association, Computer Professionals for Social Responsibility, National Writers Union, ClariNet, Institute for Global Communications, Stop Prisoner Rape, AIDS Education Global Information System and Critical Path AIDS Project, Safer Sex Page, BiblioBytes, Wildcat Press, Queer Resources Directory, Justice On Campus, Cyberwire Dispatch, The Ethical Spectacle, and Planned Parenthood Foundation of America.

[356] According to the government, "[w]hatever meaning is encompassed by th[e] term ["telecommunications device"], it specifically 'does not include an interactive computer device.'" *A.C.L.U. v. Reno*, Civ. No. 96-963, Defendant's Opposition to Plaintiffs' Motion for a Temporary Restraining Order (E.D. Penn. Feb. 14, 1996)

[357] *A.C.L.U. v. Reno*, Civ. No. 96-963, Defendant's Opposition to Plaintiffs' Motion for a Temporary Restraining Order (E.D. Penn. Feb. 14, 1996); 47 U.S.C. § 223(a)(1)(B).

[358] 47 U.S.C. § 223(d).

The act also bars permitting a telecommunication facility to be used for such activity with the intent that it be so used.[359]

A surprise to many who were not aware of it prior to passage, the act prohibits the sending and receiving of information by any means regarding "where, how, or of whom, or by what means any [drug, medicine, article, or thing designed, adapted, or intended for producing abortion] may be obtained or made."[360]

Penalties under the Communications Decency Act include fines of up to $100,000 and 2 years' imprisonment.[361]

As noted by the government, the act seeks to establish a safe harbor for access providers:

In establishing liability for indecent communications to minors over an interactive computer service, the Act distinguishes between those entities that provide access to information online ("access software provider")[362] and those who provide the content of that information ("content provider"). . . .[363]

Based in part on the foregoing distinctions, the Act establishes statutory defenses to [liability]. The target of criminal penalties under the [Act] are "content providers who violate [the Act] and persons who conspire with such content providers, rather than entities that simply offer general access to the Internet and other online content." [Citation omitted.] Those who solely provide access or connection to a computer network, and are not involved in the creation of the content of the communication, are not liable for violations of Sections 223(a) and (d) of the [Act]. 47 U.S.C. Section 223(e)(1).

More importantly . . . the [Act] also establishes a defense for a person that

(A) has taken, in good faith, reasonable, effective, and appropriate actions under the circumstances to restrict or prevent access by minors to a communication specified in such subsections, which may involve any appropriate measures to restrict minors from such communications, including any method which is feasible under available technology; or

(B) has restricted access to such communication by requiring use of a verified credit card, debit account, adult access code, or adult personal identification number.

47 U.S.C. Section 223(e)(5). The conference report states that the word "effective" under the good faith defenses "is given its common meaning and does not require an absolute 100% restriction of access to be judged effective."

In connection with the good faith defense, the statute also provides that the Federal Communications Commission "may describe measures which are reasonable, effective, and appropriate to restrict access to prohibited communications under sub-

---

[359] Ibid. § 223(d)(2).
[360] 18 U.S.C. § 1462, as amended by the Communications Decency Act of 1996; see *A.C.L.U. v. Reno*, Civ. No. 96-963, Plaintiffs' Memo. of Law in Support of a Motion for a Temporary Restraining Order and Preliminary Injunction (E.D. Penn. Feb. 8, 1996).
[361] 47 U.S.C. § 223(d).
[362] See 47 U.S.C. § 230(e)(4).
[363] Ibid. § 230(e)(3).

section (d)." 47 U.S.C. Section 223(e)(6). "The use of such measures shall be admitted as evidence of good faith efforts for purposes of paragraph (5) in any action under subsection (d). Id.[364]

Upon enactment, a coalition of civil rights organizations and on-line publishers immediately challenged the Communications Decency Act on First Amendment grounds, seeking "emergency relief to stop the enforcement of provisions of the Act that criminalize their expression of constitutionally protected information and ideas over computer communication systems."[365]

According to opponents of the Communications Decency Act,

the very nature of the online medium puts control of information and content in the hands of the users. In addition, there are an increasing number of devices that assist users in screening and blocking access to certain kinds of information. . . .

[T]he various blocking mechanisms [,though not foolproof,] are much more effective than a government ban in keeping minors away from materials that their parents and teaches deem inappropriate. Particularly given the inability of any government to ban material posted outside its borders, blocking mechanisms are a more effective alternative than censorship.[366]

These critics note that "indecent" speech, unlike obscenity, is constitutionally protected and "often has substantial social value."[367] Under the act, they complain, any reference to sexual activity or body parts is targeted if considered "offensive," "even if the ideas or information in question undeniably has serious literary, artistic, scientific, or educational value."[368] Assuming for the sake of argument that the government (in place of parents) is the appropriate agency to determine what is suitable to expose to children, the government cannot show, as required by the Supreme Court, that "a total ban on indecency is a 'narrowly tailored' way"[369] to restrict children's access to indecent materials. "Had Congress bothered to hold hearings on various ways to restrict access to communications with sexual content or vulgar words," complain the critics, "it would have learned of a myriad of ways in which all online users, including parents, can control the information they receive." "While not foolproof," the critics

---

[364] A.C.L.U. v. Reno, Civ. No. 96-963, Defendant's Opposition to Plaintiffs' Motion for a Temporary Restraining Order (E.D. Penn. Feb. 14, 1996) (Citations to Conference Report omitted).

[365] Ibid. Plaintiffs' Memo. of Law in Support of Motion for a Temporary Restraining Order and Preliminary Injunction (E.D. Penn. Feb. 8, 1996).

[366] Ibid.

[367] Ibid.

[368] Ibid.

[369] See Sable Communications of California, Inc. v. F.C.C., 492 U.S. 115, 126, 106 L.Ed.2d 93, 109 S.Ct. 2829 (1989).

continue, "these methods put responsibility for making choices about minors' access to sexually explicit material 'where our society has traditionally placed it—on the shoulders of the parent.'"

Among many other points of contention, Communication Decency Act opponents note that a federal court of appeals has ruled "that requiring adults to obtain an advance identification code in order to obtain access to sexually explicit phone messages failed the least restrictive means test and thus violated the First Amendment." [370] The act's "indecency" provisions are clearly more restrictive than that. The critics add that the concerns supporting broadcast media restrictions do not readily translate to "the cyberspace medium."

More fundamentally, the critics warn that the act is vague, violating two fundamental principles of due process:

(1) [T]hey leave the public guessing as to what actions are proscribed; and (2) they invite arbitrary and discriminatory enforcement by giving unbridled discretion to law enforcement offices. [371]

The Communications Decency Act is also overbroad, "ban[ning] much expression that is protected even for minors." [372] It will result in the outright exclusion of minors from the online medium, as most online information providers and other users cannot currently know whether they are communicating with a minor, and it is too expensive to create a separate version of an online system for minors. Also, the act "impermissibly burdens minors' First Amendment right to ideas and information about sexuality, reproduction, and the human body—subjects of interest not only to humanity generally, but of special interest to maturing adolescents." [373]

Free speech rights of adults are violated by the enactment of a total ban on "indecent" expression. And why, ask the critics, should educational and other materials be proper for distribution in print, but disqualified from online communication. The discrimination between online and print speakers makes no sense. [374]

---

[370] See *Fabulous Assoc., Inc. v. Pennsylvania Pub. Util. Comm.*, 896 F.2d 780, 788 (3d Cir. 1990) ("the statutory requirement of access codes to hear sexually suggestive telephone messages imposes a burden on the exercise of the callers' First Amendment rights and chills the message services' protected speech.")

[371] *A.C.L.U. v. Reno*, Civ. No. 96-963, Plaintiffs' Memo. of Law in Support of Motion for a Temporary Restraining Order and Preliminary Injunction (E.D. Penn. Feb. 8, 1996).

[372] Ibid.

[373] Ibid.

[374] On June 11, 1996, a panel of judges for the U.S. Court of Appeals for the Third Circuit granted a preliminary injunction in a challenge to the Communications Decency Act, ruling that "[p]laintiffs have established a reasonable probability of even-

H. Obscene & Indecent Telephone Calls

The extent to which the government may regulate the content of on-line communications will certainly be guided by experience with laws in related mediums. Of particular relevance is a federal law that generally prohibits interstate telephone communication in which a person makes "any comment, request, suggestion or proposal which is obscene, lewd, lascivious, filthy, or indecent."[375] Also prohibited is permitting a telephone facility to be used for such purposes.

Defenses to prosecution include limiting access to prohibited communications to persons over eighteen years of age.[376] To establish this defense, access needs to be restricted in accordance with procedures prescribed by the Federal Communications Commission, such as requiring payment by credit card prior to sending messages, or issuing an identification code after "reasonably ascertaining through receipt of a written application that the applicant is not under eighteen years of age," or message scrambling with appropriate notification, among other things.[377]

In April 1988, Congress banned indecent as well as obscene interstate commercial telephone communications directed to any person, *regardless of age*. The constitutionality of this law was challenged by Sable Communications, Inc., a company offering sexually-oriented prerecorded messages over a telephone network ("dial-a-porn"). Sable claimed that the law "creates an impermissible national standard of obscenity, and that it places message senders in a 'double bind' by compelling them to tailor all their messages to the least tolerant community." But the Supreme Court held that "there is no constitutional stricture against Congress' prohibiting the interstate transmission of *obscene* commercial telephone recordings." (Emphasis added.) The Court continued:

Furthermore, Sable is free to tailor its messages, on a selective basis, if it so chooses, to the communities it chooses to serve. While Sable may be forced to incur some costs

---

tual success in the litigation by demonstrating that Sections 223(a)(1)(B) and 223(a)(2) are unconstitutional on their face to the extent that they reach indecency. Sections 223(d)(1) and 223(d)(2) of the [Act] are unconstitutional on their face." *A.C.L.U. v. Reno*, No. 96-1458, Slip Opinion (3rd Cir. June 11, 1996).

[375] 47 U.S.C. § 223. The U.S. Court of Appeals for the Sixth Circuit ruled that this statute does not apply to "computer bulletin boards that use telephone facilities for the purpose of transmitting obscene computer-generated images to approved members." *United States v. Thomas*, Nos. 94-6648, 94-6649, 1996 U.S. App. Lexis 1069 (6th Cir. 1996).

[376] 47 U.S.C. § 223(b)(3).

[377] 47 C.F.R. § 64.201.

in developing and implementing a system for screening the locale of incoming calls, there is no constitutional impediment to enacting a law which may impose such costs on a medium electing to provide these messages. Whether Sable chooses to hire operators to determine the source of the calls or engages with the telephone company to arrange for the screening and blocking of out-of-area calls or finds another means for providing messages compatible with community standards is a decision for the message provider to make. There is no constitutional barrier under *Miller* to prohibiting communications that are obscene in some communities under local standards even though they are not obscene in others. If Sable's audience is comprised of different communities with different local standards, Sable ultimately bears the burden of complying with the prohibition on obscene messages.[378]

The Supreme Court did agree, however, that the statute violated the First Amendment in its effort to protect children from exposure to *indecent* dial-a-porn messages by implementing a complete ban and criminalization of indecent commercial telephone communications with adults as well as minors. The Court noted that sexual expression that is indecent, but not obscene, is protected by the First Amendment. To protect children from exposure to indecent messages, the government is required to choose the "least restrictive means to further [that] interest."[379] An insufficiently tailored law, such as one that denies adults their free speech rights by allowing them to read only what is acceptable for children, will be struck. It is not satisfactory, says the Supreme Court, to "burn the house to roast the pig."[380]

I. Copyright

It is a criminal offense to infringe a copyright "willfully and for purposes of commercial advantage or private financial gain."[381] Fraudulent removal of a copyright notice is also a crime,[382] as is use of a fraudulent copyright notice[383] and making a false representation in a copyright registration.[384]

---

[378] *Sable Communications of California, Inc. v. F.C.C.*, 492 U.S. 115, 125–26, 106 L.Ed.2d 93, 109 S.Ct. 2829 (1989); compare 47 C.F.R. § 64.201 (providing a defense to prosecution for the provision of indecent communications under § 223(b)(2) of the Communications Act of 1934 where specified steps are taken to restrict access to prohibited communications to persons eighteen years of age or older).
[379] *Sable Communications of California, Inc. v. F.C.C.*, 492 U.S. 115, 126, 106 L.Ed.2d 93, 109 S.Ct. 2829 (1989).
[380] Ibid.
[381] 17 U.S.C. § 506.
[382] Ibid. § 506(d).
[383] Ibid. § 506 (c).
[384] Ibid. § 506(e).

Penalties include up to five years' imprisonment (ten years for a subsequent offense) and fines.[385] The highest level of punishment is reserved for reproducing or distributing, within any 180 day period, at least ten copies of one or more copyrighted works, with a retail value of more than $2,500.[386] Upon conviction, courts are authorized to order the "forfeiture and destruction or other disposition of all infringing copies . . . and all implements, devices, or equipment used in the manufacture of such infringing copies. . . ."[387]

Because the criminal copyright statute requires a showing that the defendant sought to personally profit, the government could not use it as the basis for the prosecution of a student at the Massachusetts Institute of Technology,[388] who established a BBS and encouraged others to upload computer software applications and games. Uploaded programs were transferred to a second board, where persons with passwords could download the programs. Faced with this problem, the government instead tried to prosecute him for wire fraud. But the court dismissed the indictment, holding that the wire fraud statute does not reach copyright infringement.[389]

J. State Computer Crime Laws

Virtually all states have passed computer crime laws.[390] For example, under the Wisconsin Computer Crimes Act it is unlawful to modify, destroy, access, take, or copy computer data willfully, knowingly, and without authorization.[391] under that statute, a computer software programmer was convicted for destroying data stored on the computer of his former employer by inserting "booby traps into programs he had written for the employer."[392] In a civil action based on the same statute, but in another case (later reversed), a federal court ruled that the Copyright Act preempted the Wisconsin act, because the data the defendant was accused of copying could not be protected by copyright,

---

[385] See 18 U.S.C. § 3571, which provides for a fine of up to $250,000 for an individual, and up to $500,000 for an organization found guilty of an offense.

[386] 18 U.S.C. § 2319(b)(1).

[387] 17 U.S.C. § 506(b).

[388] See Appendix VI., *Cryptography & Speech*, CyberLaw (Oct. 1995), *infra*.

[389] *United States v. LaMacchia*, 871 F.Supp. 535 (D. Mass. 1994).

[390] See, e.g., Cal. Penal Code § 502; N.Y. Penal Law § 156.00 *et seq.*

[391] Wis. Stat. § 943.70(2)(a).

[392] *State v. Corcoran*, 186 Wis.2d 616, 522 N.W.2d 226 (Ct. App. 1994). A similar case under Texas law is *Burleson v. Texas*, 802 S.W.2d 429 (Tex. App. 1991).

and the "plaintiff [sought] merely to prohibit the copying and distribution that it could not prevent under Federal copyright law." [393]

K. Stalking

Stalking may be committed by a person who "willfully, maliciously, and repeatedly follows or harasses another person and who makes a credible threat with the intent to place that person in reasonable fear for his or her safety, or the safety of his or her immediate family." [394] In California, a stalker may be subject to criminal and civil penalties, including punitive damages.

There is no reason to suppose that harassment on online systems or the transmission of threats by electronic messaging is not as harmful as any other forms of written communication that may subject a person to liability for stalking.[395] With due respect to constitutional rights, in States that prohibit stalking a victim should be able to seek a restraining order to halt such online conduct.[396]

---

[393] *ProCD, Inc. v. Zeidenberg*, No. 95-C-0671-C, 1996 U.S. Dist. Lexis 167 (W.D. Wisc. 1996), *rev'd*, No. 96-1139, Slip Opinion (7th Cir. June 20, 1996).

[394] See, e.g., Cal. Penal Code § 646.9; Cal. Civ. Code § 1708.7. The California anti-stalking law was the first in the nation, passed following the murder of actress Rebecca Schaefer. A list of states with anti-stalking legislation is found in "Comment, Anti-Stalking Legislation: A Comparison of Traditional Remedies Available for Victims of Harassment Versus California Penal Code" § 646.9, 24 Pacific L.J. (1993) 1945, 1946 n.6.

[395] In 1994, a Michigan man was charged with violating Michigan's anti-stalking laws for continuing to send e-mail after a woman and police told him to stop. San Jose *Mercury News*, May 27, 1994, 2C.

[396] See also Conn. Gen. Stat. §§ 53a-182b, 53a-183 (criminalizing harassment by computer).

APPENDIX

The Legal Side [8/91]

THE INTERNET WORM

Robert Tappan Morris began graduate school at Cornell University in 1988. His goal was to obtain a Ph.D. in computer science. Previously, he attended Harvard, "published several technical papers, and had lectured on computer security at the National Computer Security Center of the National Security Agency, and the United States Naval Research Laboratory." His goal might have been to succeed his father as chief scientist at the National Computer Security Center of the National Security Agency. But whatever Morris's dreams may have been, they must have crashed around his feet on the night of November 2, 1988, when a computer programming experiment he designed went out of control and slowed down or stopped computers at numerous universities and research facilities connected to the Internet computer network.

In the fall of 1988, Morris began work on a program that would demonstrate the inadequacies of security measures on computer networks. According to Morris's legal counsel, he designed a program that would expose security defects by means of a "worm," a program that travels from one computer to another without attaching itself to the operating system of the computer it infects. (A "virus" differs from a "worm" in that a virus attaches itself to a computer's operating system, and can later infect the operating system of any computer that uses a file taken from the infected computer.) Morris sought to have his worm spread across the Internet, a group of national networks that connect military, government, and university computers.

To guard against both the possibility that the worm would be detected and that it would crash targeted computers, Morris designed the worm to determine whether a computer it encountered already was infected with a copy of the worm program. If a negative response was received, the worm would be copied onto the target system. If a positive response was received, the worm would ignore the target and find a new one. Morris also programmed the worm to ignore every seventh positive response, and duplicate itself anyhow. Morris' legal counsel explains that this was done because "Morris was concerned that other programmers could kill the worm by programming their own computers to falsely respond [with a positive response]." Morris, however, did not intend for the worm to exist forever; it would "die" when the infected computer was shut down (typically, once every week or two).

On November 2, 1988, Morris released the worm from a computer at MIT. It quickly went out of control, replicating and reinfecting computers at a catastrophic rate. Morris had underestimated the number of times that a target computer would be asked whether it had been infected by the worm.

When Morris realized what had happened, he tried to send an anonymous message over the Internet with instructions on how to kill the worm and prevent reinfection. But the message could not get through the interference caused by the worm. The result was a widespread loss of computer time and money expended to deal with the worm. The episode also triggered a national uproar.

On January 22, 1990, Morris was found guilty of violating Section 1030(a)(5) of the Computer Fraud and Abuse Act of 1986, which provides punishment (as a felony) by fine or imprisonment, or both, for one who

(a) intentionally accesses a Federal interest computer without authorization, and by means of one or more instances of such conduct alters, damages, or destroys information in any such Federal interest computer, or prevents authorized use of any such computer or information, and thereby—

(5) causes loss to one or more others of a value aggregating $1,000 or more during any one year period.

One month later, the United States Court for the Northern District of New York rejected Morris's request for an acquittal or new trial. On May 16, 1990, he was sentenced to three years probation, with the condition that he perform four hundred hours of community service.

Nearly a year later, on March 17, 1991, the United States Court of Appeals for the Second Circuit denied Morris's appeal. Shortly thereafter, Morris filed a petition to the United States Supreme Court, asking it to review his case on the following narrow question: "Does 18 U.S.C. § 1030(a)(5) permit conviction in the absence of proof that a defendant intended to cause the resulting injury."

Briefly stated, Morris's appeal to the Supreme Court is based on the argument that "the government had to prove not only that he intended the unauthorized access of a federal computer, but also that he intended to prevent others from using it, and thus cause a loss." Against the government's argument looking to plain reading of the law, Morris argues, among other things, that Congress intended only to penalize those who intentionally alter, damage, or destroy another's computer data.

Further information concerning Morris's conviction and post-trial arguments is published in the opinion of the United States Court of Appeal for the Second Circuit in *United States v. Robert Tappan Morris*, 928 F.2d 504 (2d Cir. 1991). Morris's Petition for a Writ of Certiorari is filed at the United States Supreme Court under No. 90-1876.

CyberLaw™ [5/92]

DIGITAL TELEPHONY

In an article published in the *New York Times*, the director of the F.B.I., William S. Sessions, has claimed that "Advances in telecommunications technology promise to deprive Federal, state and local law enforcement officers and the public of the incalculable benefits that can be obtained by court-authorized wiretapping." (*New York Times*, March 27, 1992, A19). To combat the perceived threat, the F.B.I. has proposed legislation on digital telephony to compel "the telecommunications industry to come to the aid of law enforcement." According to Mr. Sessions, "The cost to telecommunications companies would not be so substantial as to outweigh the consequences of an inability of law enforcement to act."

The F.B.I. proposal has been widely criticized. According to Janlori Goldman, director of the privacy and technology project at the American Civil Liberties Union, "The proposal makes the [F.B.I.] look like Luddites, the 19th century English weavers who smashed new machines that they claimed put them out of work. . . . The F.B.I. is not only asking the industry to dumb down existing software, it wants to prohibit it from developing new technologies. . . ." (New

York Times, March 27, 1992, A19). William Safire comments that "The trouble with both our Federal law enforcement and intelligence services is that they have become hooked on yesterday's technology. Electronic surveillance for cops and spooks has become central to their lives; their reaction to the inexorable improvement in encryption is to say to the world of science: slow down." (*New York Times*, May 11, 1992, A15). In defense, the Director of the F.B.I. responds that

Describing [F.B.I.] guidelines for legislation as "unclear, open to abuse and possibly retarding the pace of technological innovation" is off the mark. . . . The proposed legislation requires only that telephone companies, if ordered by a court, make available the "digital bit stream" associated with a specific telephone number used to conduct criminal activity. (*New York Times*, April 26, 1992, E18).

According to an F.B.I. press release dated March 6, 1992, the proposed amendment to the Communication Act of 1934 would provide the following:

1. The FCC, in consultation with the Attorney General, shall determine the technical interception needs of the Government and issue regulations which will preserve the Government's ability to conduct lawful electronic surveillance.
2. The FCC shall issue regulations within 120 days after enactment *requiring the modification of existing telecommunications systems* if those systems impede the Government's ability to conduct lawful electronic surveillance.
3. Requires compliance by service providers and private branch exchanges within 180 days of the issuance of regulations and *use of nonconforming equipment is prohibited* thereafter.
4. Gives FCC the authority to compensate through the rate structure telecommunications systems operators under FCC jurisdiction for reasonable costs associated with required modifications of existing telecommunications equipment or technology.
5. Gives the Attorney General specific authority in addition to that already vested in the FCC to seek civil penalties and injunctive relief for non-compliance. (Emphasis added.)

With regard to the specific regulations to be issued by the FCC, the proposed amendment reads as follows:

(b) The regulations issued by the [FCC] shall:

(1) *establish standards and specifications* for telecommunications equipment and technology employed by providers of electronic communication services or private branch exchange operators as may be necessary to maintain the ability of the government to lawfully intercept communications. . . ." (Emphasis added).

An F.B.I. analysis accompanying the proposal states that such regulations would, among other things, "require that equipment or technologies currently used by such providers or operators that impede this interception ability not be expanded so as to further impede such ability until brought into compliance with the regulations."

According to the F.B.I., last year there were 1,083 court-authorized wiretaps by federal, state and local law enforcement authorities. Mr. Sessions has admitted to Congress that no warrant has been issued that could not be executed. (*New York Times*, March 27, 1992, A19). The F.B.I.'s chief of technology, James K. Kallstrom, has also conceded that the agency already has access to technology that allows it to tap digital lines. According to Mr. Kallstrom, the F.B.I. is more worried about emerging technologies like personal communications networks and services like call forwarding, cellular telephones, and wireless data transfer, all of which would defeat wiretaps. (*New York Times*, April 19, 1992, §4, p.2).

The costs of the proposed legislation have been the subject of extensive comment. The *New York Times* notes that the proposed legislation

would, in effect, require the licensing of new telephone equipment by the Federal government so the [F.B.I.] could wiretap it. Telephone companies would have to modify computers and software so that agents could decipher the digital bit stream. The cost of the modifications would be passed on to rate payers.

Jerry Berman, director of the Electronic Frontier Foundation, cautions that requiring the F.C.C. to clear new technology could slow innovation, and that the proposed legislation does not impact only local and long-distance calls. According to Mr. Berman, "We're talking about CompuServe, Prodigy and other computer services, electronic mail, automatic teller machines and any changes in them." (*New York Times*, April 19, 1992, §4, p.2).

David Bellin, professor of computer science at the Pratt Institute, has focused on an additional concern. Noting the analogous efforts of the N.S.A. to "stymie adoption of developed encryption standards that it considers too difficult for it to decode," Mr. Bellin asserts that "In the electronic age, freedom to speak and freedom of association can only be guaranteed with high-tech methods. We need to have the strongest safeguards on the privacy of our words that computer scientists can offer." (*New York Times*, April 22, 1992, A14).

In light of the above, the F.B.I.'s proposal on digital telephony should be the subject of vigorous review. Questions to be addressed include the following: (1) How difficult/costly would it be for a telecommunications company to make available a digital bit stream associated with a specific telephone number? (2) What is the projected total cost to the market to comply with the proposed regulations? (3) What is the cost to the government to develop the technology the F.B.I. seems to require? (4) What type of crimes does the government seek to impact by wiretapping, and how effective have its prior efforts been? (5) How does the F.B.I. proposal fit in the administration's efforts to free industry from regulation and promote competitiveness in the marketplace?

[CyberLaw™ 4/93]

SEARCH & SEIZURE

Three years ago, a small publisher of role-playing games in Texas was raided by the United States Secret Service. Government agents carted away computers, one of which ran the company's computer bulletin board system (BBS), hundreds of floppy disks, and drafts of a soon-to-be-published book and of magazine articles. The seized material was held for months, which led to the layoff of a number of the company's employees. No one at the company was arrested or charged with a crime. The owner of the company, Steve Jackson, appealed for help and managed to gain the attention of some prominent members of the computer community. The case came to be viewed by many as a struggle for civil liberties in the new electronic frontier, known as Cyberspace. Steve Jackson and his supporters were vindicated recently, when a federal district court ruled that the Secret Service had violated federal statutes protecting publishers and the privacy of electronic communications with regard to its raid of the company.

The saga of Steve Jackson and his company began in the summer of 1989, when the Secret Service was contacted by a representative of BellSouth (a Regional Bell Operating Company), who advised that there had been a theft of sensitive data from BellSouth's computer system. The stolen data was described as "an internal, proprietary document that described the control, operation and maintenance of BellSouth's 911 emergency system." This report led the Secret Service and the U.S. Attorney's office in Chicago into a larger investigation, concerning a national group of computer hackers called the "Legion of Doom" (LOD).

A member of LOD had allegedly entered a BellSouth computer and copied the 911 document to his own computer. The 911 document was then allegedly sent to a BBS in Illinois, from which it was downloaded by a student named Craig Neidorf and edited for and distributed in a publication named *Phrack*. One person who received *Phrack* was Lloyd Blankenship, also a member of LOD.

Notably, the 911 document is not a computer program and has

nothing to do with accessing a 911 system. It simply details who does what in the telephone company bureaucracy regarding customer complaints and equipment failures, among other things. For the Secret Service, BellSouth estimated the cost of the 911 document at $79,449. But in July 1990, during Neidorf's trial, it was disclosed that the 911 document was available to the public directly from BellSouth for about $20. (Upon this disclosure, the prosecution of Neidorf collapsed—leaving him owing over $100,000 in legal fees.)

In early 1990, the Secret Service learned that another LOD member had posted a message on a BBS maintained by Blankenship, allegedly "inviting other BBS participants to send in encrypted passwords stolen from other computers, which Blankenship and [the other member of LOD] would decrypt and return. . . ." After seeking additional information, the Secret Service decided to obtain search warrants to obtain evidence against them, including a search warrant for the offices of Blankenship's employer, Steve Jackson Games, Inc.

Steve Jackson Games, as described by its lawyers, "publishes role-playing games in book form, magazines, a book about game theory, boxed games, and game-related products. The company's games are played *not* on computers, but with dice, a game book or books, and lots of imagination." As part of its business, the company runs a BBS (the "Illuminati" BBS) that allows outside callers to dial in and, as outlined by Steve Jackson, "read messages left by [the company], read public messages left by others who have called the bulletin board, leave public messages for other callers to read, send private electronic mail to other persons who called the bulletin board, and 'download' computerized files to their own computer." Like the typical BBS, the Illuminati BBS stored electronic mail, including mail that had been sent but not yet received. In February 1990, there were 365 users of the Illuminati BBS and, according to the trial court, Blankenship was a "co-sysop" of the BBS.

On March 1, 1990, Steve Jackson Games was raided by the Secret Service. They seized and carried away a computer found on Blankenship's desk, a disassembled computer next to his desk, the computer running the Illuminati BBS, over three hundred computer disks, and various documents and other materials. Among the seized items were drafts of a book titled *GURPS Cyberpunk*, which was to be published within days or weeks of the raid, and drafts of magazines and magazine articles. ("GURPS" stands for "Generic Universal Game Role Playing System.") According to the company's attorneys, a Secret Service agent called *GURPS Cyberpunk* "'a handbook for computer crime' in Mr. Jackson's presence, (although the government now claims that the book was not the target of the search and admits it was not evidence of any crime)."

For Steve Jackson Games, the raid was a calamity. It was suffering severe cash flow problems, and the seizure caused substantial delays in publication and the termination of eight employees. The bulk of the seized material was not made available to the company until late June 1990, and no printed copies of *GURPS Cyberpunk* were ever returned.

The raid also caused wide concern across the United States. From the outset, as noted by the company's lawyers, many saw the case as one in which

The Secret Service, on exceedingly weak pretense, invaded the office of an upstanding, hard-working small businessman, and nearly put him out of business. The Secret Service shut down a working BBS—a new, powerful means of public and private communication—with *no* evidence that anything unlawful was transpiring there. Shutting down the "Illuminati" was like clearing or closing down a park or meeting hall, simply because one of hundreds of the people gathered there was under vague suspicion.

This view was later validated by the trial court, which found that

prior to March 1, 1990, and at all other times, *there has never been any basis for suspicion* that [Steve Jackson Games, Steve Jackson, or any of the other individuals who subsequently sued the Secret Service as a result of the raid] have engaged in any criminal activity, violated any law, or attempted to communicate, publish, or store any illegally obtained information or otherwise provide access to any illegally obtained information or to solicit any information which was to be used illegally. (Emphasis added.)

After the raid, Steve Jackson Games, Steve Jackson, and three users of the Illuminati BBS filed suit against the United States Secret Service, the United States of America, and several government employees who had been involved in the raid. The plaintiffs brought causes of action for violation of the following: the Fourth Amendment to the U.S. Constitution; the Privacy Protection Act, 42 U.S.C. 2000aa *et seq.*; the Wire and Electronic Communications Interception and Interception of Oral Communication Act, 18 U.S.C. 2510 *et seq.*; and the Stored Wire and Electronic Communications and Transactional Records Act, 18 U.S.C. 2701 *et seq.* (The latter two statutes are part of the Electronic Communications Privacy Act, or ECPA).

With respect to the Fourth Amendment, the plaintiffs argued that "probable cause to believe that a crime has occurred . . . does not automatically give license to search every place that a suspect may frequent," and also that "there must be probable cause to believe that the *type* of materials sought are located at the place to be searched." "The search warrant," continued the plaintiffs, "did not establish probable cause that evidence of any crime would be found at [Steve Jackson Games]," and the search of the company "was broader than justified by any facts in the warrant." In response, the government argued that even if the plaintiffs were correct, they still had to prove that "these defects were so obvious that no reasonable officer could have believed the warrant to be valid, in light of the information [the officer] possessed." Because a court determination in favor of the plaintiffs could have resulted in an immediate appeal that would delay the balance of their case, the plaintiffs dropped their Fourth Amendment claims to focus their case on the Privacy Protection Act and ECPA claims.

The Privacy Protection Act concerns the investigation and prosecution of criminal offenses and, in relevant part, prohibits government employees from searching for or seizing any "work product materials" possessed by a person reasonably believed to have a purpose to disseminate to the public a newspaper, book, broadcast, or other similar form of public communication. "Work product materials" are defined to include materials, not including contraband, the fruits of a crime, or things used as the means of committing a crime, created or prepared for the purpose of communicating such materials to the public.

At the time of the raid on Steve Jackson Games, the Secret Service was advised that the company was in the publishing business. No significance was attached to this information, however, as the Secret Service agents involved in the raid were oblivious of the provisions of the Privacy Protection Act.

Notwithstanding the fact that the Secret Service had failed to make a reasonable investigation of Steve Jackson Games "when it was apparent [its] intention was to take substantial properties belonging to the [company], the removal of which could have a substantial effect on the continuation of business," the trial court declined to find that on March 1, 1990, any government employee had reason to believe that the property to be seized would be "work product material" subject to the Privacy Protection Act. But during the raid, the Secret Service had been advised of facts that put its agents on notice of probable violations of that act. Indeed, the Secret Service continued to detain the company's property through late June 1990 despite the fact that as observed by the trial court, "[i]mmediate arrangements could and should have been made on March 2, 1990, whereby copies of all information seized could have been made." The refusal of the Secret Service to return the company's information and property violated the Privacy Protection Act, and the court awarded Steve Jackson Games its expenses ($8,781) and economic damages ($42,259).

The trial court did not find, however, that the Secret Service had violated the Electronic Communications Interception and Interception of Oral Communication Act. According to the trial court, "the Secret Service intended not only to seize and read [the communications stored on the Illuminati BBS], but in fact did read the communications and thereafter deleted or destroyed some communications either intentionally or accidentally." But the Secret Service had not "intercepted" communications within the meaning of the latter act, ruled the court, apparently on the grounds that only the contemporaneous acquisition of a communication is prohibited thereby.

In support of this ruling, the court looked to the Congressional enactment of the Stored Wire and Electronic Communications and Transactional Records Act, among other things. This statute protects the content of electronic communications in electronic storage and sets out specific requirements for the government to follow to obtain the "disclosure" of such communications. One such requirement is that there be "reason to believe the contents of a[n] . . . electronic communication . . . are relevant to a legitimate law enforcement inquiry." Although the Secret Service wanted to seize, review, and read all electronic communications, public and private, on the Illuminati BBS, the Secret Service did not advise the magistrate judge who issued the warrant for the raid on Steve Jackson Games "that the Illuminati board contained private electronic communications between users or how the disclosure of the content of these communications could relate to [the] investigation." The court commented that it was not until June 1990 that the plaintiffs were able to determine the reasons for the March 1, 1990, seizure, "and then only with the efforts of the offices of both United States Senators of the State of Texas." Simply stated, "[t]he procedures followed by the Secret Service in this case virtually eliminated the safeguards contained in the statute." Lacking sufficient proof of compensatory damages, the court assessed statutory damages in favor of the plaintiffs, in the amount of $1,000 for each plaintiff.

Further information concerning this case may be found in the opinion of the United States District Court in *Steve Jackson Games, Inc., et al. v. United States Secret Service, et al.*, No. A-91-CA-346-SS (W.D. Tex. 3/12/93). For background information on this case and other related cases, see B. Sterling, *The Hacker Crackdown* (1992), and John Perry Barlow, *Crime & Puzzlement* (1990).

[CyberLaw™ 1/95]

COPYRIGHT & PROPERTY

I. A Different Property

Copyright is a shorthand term that describes a set of enforceable rights to prevent unauthorized persons from making a copy of a "work" for a period of time. The person entitled to exercise these rights may choose not to do so and donate the work to the public domain, thereby allowing all comers to freely copy. If a work is not donated to the public domain, during the period in which copyright is enforceable there are a number of circumstances in which persons may freely copy the work, the copyright notwithstanding. The "fair use" privilege defines a set of circumstances in which copies may be freely made, as does the First Amendment. After a time, copyright expires and a work enters the public domain. Given the limited nature of the grant of rights that define copyright, is the classification of copyright as intellectual property simply a rhetorical exercise to assist publishers in their efforts to strengthen their monopoly rights? Questions concerning the nature of copyright as a "property" interest were recently addressed by a federal court in Massachusetts considering wire fraud charges against the owner of a pirate computer bulletin board, *United States v. LaMacchia*, Crim. No. 9410092-RGS (D.Mass. December 28, 1994). Following a decision by the U.S. Supreme Court over bootleg Elvis Presley recordings, the district court ruled that rights of copyright owners in their protected property are different from ownership interests in other types of property. In so ruling, the court emphasized that the limited nature of property rights conferred by copyright stem from "an overriding First Amendment concern for free dissemination of ideas" and the constitutional mandate to promote "the Progress of Science and useful Arts."

II. LaMacchia is Charged

David LaMacchia, a twenty-one-year-old student at the Massachusetts Institute of Technology, set up a bulletin board on which he encouraged others to upload computer software applications and games. He transferred uploaded programs (e.g., Excel 5.0, Word-

Perfect 6.0, Sim City 2000) to a second board. Those with password access to the second board could download the programs.

In early 1994, LaMacchia was indicted by a federal grand jury on one count of conspiring "with persons unknown" to violate the wire fraud statute, 18 U.S.C. Section 1343. The indictment did not allege that LaMacchia sought or derived any personal benefit, but that he

devised a scheme to defraud that had as its object the facilitation "on an international scale" of the "illegal copying and distribution of copyrighted software" without payment of license fees and royalties to software manufacturers and vendors.

LaMacchia requested that a U.S. District Court in Massachusetts dismiss the charge, on grounds that the government "had improperly resorted to the wire fraud statute as a copyright enforcement tool in defiance of [a U.S. Supreme Court decision titled] *Dowling v. United States*, 473 U.S. 207 (1985).

III. Dowling & Stolen Property

As described by the district court, in *Dowling* the Supreme Court reviewed the conviction of Paul E. Dowling for interstate transportation of stolen property. Dowling and others sold bootleg Elvis Presley recordings by soliciting catalogue orders from post office boxes in California. Infringing recordings were shipped interstate to Maryland and Florida. Dowling was convicted of conspiracy, interstate transportation of stolen property, copyright violations, and mail fraud. Affirming Dowling's convictions (he appealed all but the copyright conviction), the Ninth Circuit U.S. Court of Appeals ruled that "rights of copyright owners in their protected property were indistinguishable from ownership interest in other types of property and were equally deserving of protection under the [stolen property] statute."

Dowling's conviction for interstate transportation of stolen property was reversed, the Supreme Court ruling that "a copyrighted musical composition impressed on a bootleg phonograph record is not property that is 'stolen, converted, or taken by fraud' within the meaning of the Stolen Property Act." Dowling had not, in fact, stolen the records on which the recordings were imprinted.

In *Dowling*, the government argued that "unauthorized use of the underlying musical composition was itself sufficient to render the offending phonorecords property 'stolen, converted or taken by fraud.'" Justice Blackmun noted, however, that the property interest protected by copyright is limited by the First Amendment interest in free expression, and that copyright's goal not to reward authors but "[t]o promote the Progress of Science and Useful Arts." "[I]nterference with copyright," stated Justice Blackmun, "does not easily equate with theft, conversion or fraud." Although Dowling clearly violated copyright by unauthorized use of performances of copyrighted compositions on his bootleg albums, he had "not assume[d] physical control over the copyright; nor . . . wholly deprive[d] the owner of its use."

The law governing interstate transportation of stolen property is rooted in jurisdictional problems arising when stolen property crosses state lines. No such issues exist concerning copyright infringement; federal law controls, so there is no conflict among the states. Congress has taken "a great deal of care" in the development of serious criminal penalties for copyright infringement, observed Justice Blackmun, and there is no room to presuppose a congressional decision to bring to bear on the problem of copyright infringement the felony provisions of the interstate transportation of stolen property statute. Accordingly, the Supreme Court reversed Dowling's convictions for interstate transportation of stolen property.

IV. Criminal Copyright Infringement

Under the Copyright Act, since 1897 criminal (as opposed to civil) copyright violation has been based on a purpose of commercial exploitation. In *LaMacchia*, the district court noted that through the 1976 revision of the Copyright Act, criminal infringement was a misdemeanor, except in the case of repeat offenders who were subject to a maximum two-year prison term and $50,000 fine. Penalties were increased in 1982, when certain first-time offenses were made punishable as felonies depending on the time period involved and the number of copies reproduced or distributed. Proof that a defendant's conduct was for the purpose of "commercial advantage or private commercial gain" remained an element of the offense, and "[m]ost criminal infringements remained misdemeanor offenses despite the new penalty structure." When Congress passed the 1992 Copyright Felony Act, which extended felony provisions to criminal infringement of all copyrighted work including computer software, the intent element stayed the same—"requiring prosecutors to prove that the defendant infringed a copyright 'willfully and for purpose of commercial advantage or private financial gain.'"

V. A Scheme to Defraud

The wire fraud statute under which LaMacchia was indicted (18 U.S.C. Section 1343) provides that

Whosoever, having devised or intending to devise any scheme or artifice to defraud, or for obtaining money or property by means of false or fraudulent pretenses, representations, or promises, transmits or causes to be transmitted by means of wire, radio, or television communication in interstate or foreign commerce, any writings, signs, signals, pictures, or sounds for the purpose of executing such scheme or artifice, shall be fined not more than $1,000 or imprisoned not more than 5 years, or both. If the violation affects a financial institution, such person shall be fined not more than $1,000,000 or imprisoned not more than 30 years, or both.

This statute was designed to reach fraudulent activity conducted by means of radio and television, not within the reach of the mail fraud laws. Under both the wire and mail fraud statutes, a scheme to defraud is the defining concept. Federal courts, observes the district court, have split mail and wire fraud into two separate offenses: "the first, the devising of a scheme to defraud, the second, the devising of a scheme to obtain money or property by false pretenses." The latter comports with common law fraud, while the former has come "to prohibit a plan, that is, to forbid a state of mind, rather than physical conduct."

[A]n especially pleasing feature from the government's perspective" in LaMacchia's case, observed the District Court, is that

"Unlike the criminal copyright statute, 17 U.S.C. Sec. 506(a), the mail and wire fraud statutes do not require that a defendant be shown to have sought to personally profit from the scheme to defraud.

In *Dowling*, the defendant's conviction for mail fraud had been left undisturbed and the district court focused on whether the mail fraud analysis in that case applies to LaMacchia's. Dowling had brought himself within the "orbit" of the mail fraud statute by mailing advertising catalogues. LaMacchia brought himself within the wire fraud statute, claimed the government, by advertising infringing software via computer transmission.

But in *Dowling*, the defendant had engaged in a "fraudulent scheme"—the basis for which, ruled the Ninth Circuit, may include active misrepresentation, nondisclosure, or concealment. According to the Ninth Circuit,

"a non-disclosure can only serve as a basis for a fraudulent scheme when there exists an independent duty that has been breached. . . ." This duty . . . could be fiduciary in nature, or it could "derive from an independent explicit statutory duty created by legislative enactment."

Dowling was found to have breached a "duty implicit in the compulsory licensing scheme of the Copyright Act, 17 U.S.C. Sec. 115, which requires vendors to notify copyright owners of the intention to manufacture and distribute infringing records." LaMacchia, on the other hand, was not in a fiduciary relationship or subject to any statutory duty of disclosure such as that which "snared" Dowling.

VI. Conduct, Property, & Congress

The district court also ruled that illegal conduct alone cannot satisfy the fraud element of the wire fraud statute. And even if it could, the district court had not been shown, or even alleged by the government, that LaMacchia violated Section 506(a) of the Copyright Act, which requires proof of copyright infringement "willfully and for purpose of commercial advantage or private financial gain."

On further consideration of the government's claim that the wire fraud statute should apply here, particularly its argument that intangible as well as tangible property interests are protected by the mail and wire fraud statutes, the district court stated,

The issue . . . is whether the 'bundle of rights' conferred by copyright is unique and distinguishable from the indisputably broad range of property interests protected by the mail and wire fraud statutes. I find it difficult, if not impossible, to read Dowling as saying anything but that it is.

Although reasonable people may agree that LaMacchia's conduct deserves punishment, the district court continued, Congress has "chosen to tread cautiously" in determining where criminal copyright sanctions are necessary. Congress is sensitive to the "special concerns implicated by the copyright laws" and courts should leave it to the legislature to define crimes and prescribe penalties. The district court observed that

[The government's] interpretation of the wire fraud statute would serve to criminalize the conduct of not only persons like LaMacchia, but also the myriad of home computer users who succumb to the temptation to copy even a single software program for private use. It is not clear that making criminals of a large number of consumers of computer software is a result that even the software industry would consider desirable.

Copyright prosecutions should be limited, said the district court, to Section 506 of the Copyright Act and other incidental statutes that refer explicitly to copyright and copyrighted works.

In light of the above, the district court held that *Dowling* precludes LaMacchia's prosecution under the wire fraud statute. Describing LaMacchia's conduct as at best "heedlessly irresponsible, and at worst as nihilistic, self-indulgent, and lacking in any fundamental sense of values," the district court suggested that "[c]riminal as well as civil penalties should probably attach to willful, multiple infringements of copyrighted software even absent a commercial motive on the part of the infringer." But, cautioned the district court, it is the legislature's role, not that of the judiciary, "to define a crime and ordain its punishment."

[CyberLaw™ 7/95]

TRUE THREATS

I. Bad Judgment

In early February 1995, a University of Michigan student named Jake Baker was arrested and held without bail for publishing a sexually violent piece of fiction in an Internet newsgroup. At the time, the reason for the arrest seemed to be an unfortunate choice in naming the story's victim—giving her the name of a student in one of Baker's classes. While many wondered how anyone could be arrested and held on such charges, Baker spent twenty-nine days in jail. Not surprisingly, the government soon abandoned prosecution based on the story, focusing instead on Baker's private e-mail exchanges with a person named Gonda. On June 21, 1995, a U.S. district count judge dismissed the indictment against Baker, ruling that the First Amendment barred his prosecution. *U.S. v. Baker, et al.*, Crim. No. 95–80106, 1995 U.S. Dist. LEXIS 8977 (E.D. Mich. 6/21/95). The court commented that the justification for Baker's arrest seemed farfetched, and expressed doubt as to whether Baker's prosecution resulted from the exercise of good judgment.

II. Sex & Violence

Between November 29, 1994, and January 25, 1995, Jake Baker exchanged e-mail messages with Arthur Gonda. Baker was living in Ann Arbor, Michigan, at the time. Gonda, whose identity and location remain unknown, sent and received mail through a computer in Ontario, Canada. The correspondence between Baker and Gonda "express[es] a sexual interest in violence against women and girls."

III. Danger to the Community

On February 9, 1995, Baker was arrested on a criminal complaint based on a story Baker posted to an Internet newsgroup titled "alt.sex.stories" and on e-mail Baker sent to Gonda. The story posted to the Internet "graphically described the torture, rape, and murder of a woman who was given the name of a classmate of Baker's at the University of Michigan."

After his arrest, Baker was detained overnight and brought before a magistrate, who ordered him held as a danger to the community. A federal judge affirmed the detention the following day. On March 8, 1995, a psychological evaluation was ordered. Received on March 10, 1995, the evaluation concluded that Baker posed no threat. He was released that day—after twenty-nine days' detention.

Notably, a report by the University of Michigan states that a January 20, 1995, psychological evaluation concluded that Baker did not display any risk factors for potential violence. Another evaluation on February 7, 1995, concluded that there was "no evidence that [Baker] is a danger to himself or others." Two days later, on the same day as his arrest, a further psychological evaluation reported that Baker "presented no clear and present danger to [the student whose name he had used in the story] or anyone, at the time of the interview." According to U.S. district court judge Avery Cohen,

Why Baker was arrested and taken into custody on February 9, 1995, is inexplicable. The government indicated in its supplemental brief that Baker's arrest was justified as preventing "Jake Baker and other like-minded individuals from acting on their violent impulses and desires." In light of the information available at the time of Baker's arrest, this justification seems farfetched.

(On May 26, 1995, the government acknowledged that it had abandoned the story as a basis of prosecution because it did not constitute a threat.)

IV. True Threats

In March 1995, the government charged Baker and Gonda with a superseding indictment that did not mention the story. The indictment consists of five counts of violating 18 U.S.C. Section 875(c), which reads,

Whoever transmits in interstate or foreign commerce any communication containing any threat to kidnap any person or any threat to injure the person of another, shall be fined under this title or imprisoned not more than five years, or both.

According to the court, such a threat "need not be communicated to the person or group identified as its target." But because "pure speech" is involved, the First Amendment is implicated and to pass constitutional muster, the government must prove a "true threat"—one that "on its face and in the circumstances in which it is made is so unequivocal, unconditional, immediate and specific as to the person threatened, as to convey a gravity of purpose and imminent prospect of execution." "A statement which would not be interpreted by any foreseeable recipient as expressing a serious intention to injure or kidnap simply is not a threat under the statute."

(The court notes that initial passage of Section 875(c) was motivated by the unproblematic case of the kidnapping of Charles Lind-berg's son and the use of the mail to convey the kidnappers' threats and demands. In that case, the communication was "so interlocked with violent conduct as to constitute for all practical purposes part of the [proscribed] action itself."[7] Today, a threat that is neither coercive nor extortionate may satisfy the constitutional test.)

V. E-Mail Examined

The government argues here that e-mail between Gonda and Baker reflects "the evolution of their activity from shared fantasies to a firm plan of action." However, messages constituting "shared fantasies," ruled the court, fall short of the required standard and are not "true threats":

Statements expressing musings, considerations of what it would be like to kidnap or injure someone, or desire to kidnap or injure someone, however unsavory, are not constitutionally actionable under Section 875(c) absent some expression of an intent to commit the injury or kidnapping.

The court also noted that the constitutional test is "not satisfied by finding that the desires expressed in a statement are so deviant that the person making the statement must be unstable, and therefore likely to act in accordance with his or her desires at any moment."

The court states that the language for which Baker is charged was contained in private e-mail messages sent to Gonda, not available in any public forum. (The public only knows of the content as a result of the prosecution and ensuing publicity.) While Baker and Gonda exchanged messages concerning violence against women and girls, the court finds that "[i]t would be patently unreasonable after reading [Gonda's] messages to think that Baker's communications caused their only foreseeable recipient, Gonda, to fear violence, or caused him any disruption due to fear of violence."

The government alleges that messages between Baker and Gonda evolved into a "firm plan of action." But, says the court, Section 875(c) covers transmitting threats, not planning crimes. Although the government characterized Baker and Gonda as co-conspirators, to prove a conspiracy one has to prove an overt act in furtherance of the conspiracy—something not alleged by the government. According to the court, "[t]he only actions involved in this prosecution are Speech—'the outward expression of what a person thinks in his mind.'"

Even if Baker and Gonda were conspiring, they are not necessarily guilty under Section 875(c). Fear of serious injury is not sufficient to justify suppression of speech—"there must be reasonable ground to fear that serious evil will result if free speech is practiced. There must be a reasonable ground to believe that the danger apprehended is imminent."

(Interestingly, the court observes that the Senate's passage of the Exon amendment to the telecommunications bill, criminalizing the distribution of "filthy" material over computer networks, "suggests that the First Amendment's application to on-line communications has not been well considered.")

Count I of the indictment concerns e-mail between Baker and Gonda discussing hurting women and sexually abusing "a really young girl." At one point, they discuss kidnapping a girl. Gonda says, "I will keep my eye out for young girls, and relish the fantasy . . . BTW how about your neighbour at home, you may get a chance to see her . . . ? . . . ?" Baker responds, "Yeah. I didn't see her last time I was home. She might have moved. But she'd be a great catch."

The government alleges that the targets of Baker's and Gonda's statements are thirteen- and fourteen-year-old girls living in Baker's neighborhood in Ann Arbor, Michigan, as well as teenage girls living in his neighborhood in Boardman, Ohio. But Count I does not meet the "true threat" requirement. "In reality," says the court, "the only class of people to whom the messages can be taken to refer is 13 or 14 year old girls, anywhere." This class is too indeterminate to meet the constitutional requirement of specificity as to the person threatened. Further, Baker's message, while discussing a predilection toward young girls, is not more than a "a simple expression of desire." According to the court, it is not constitutionally permissible to infer an intention to act on a desire from a simple expression of the desire. And "[d]iscussion of desires, alone, is not tantamount to threatening to act on those desires. Absent such a threat to act, a statement is protected by the First Amendment."

Counts II and III are based on a Baker e-mail message and charge him with making a threat to kidnap and injure. In the message, Baker discusses abduction of a woman from "the girl's bathroom" that is across from his room, and sexual abuse. The government alleges that the targets of Baker's message are female college students who lived in Baker's dormitory at the University of Michigan. "[D]iscussion of a method of kidnapping or injuring a person," notes the court, "is not punishable unless the statement includes an unequivocal and specific expression of intention immediately to carry out the actions discussed." But, rules the court, Baker's message "cannot reasonably be read as satisfying this standard." "Discussing the commission of a crime," explains the court, "is not tantamount to declaring an intention to commit the crime."

Count IV charges transmission of a threat to injure. In part of an exchange, Baker states, "When I lay down at night, all I think of before I sleep is how I'd torture a bitch I get my hands on. I have some pretty vivid near dreams too. I wish I could remember them when I get up." The government identifies the class of targets as women Baker discussed on the Internet.

This is the weakest of the government's charges, states the court. The class of targets is not sufficiently specific, as nothing in the e-mail limits the class to women Baker discussed on the Internet. As Baker often refers to "a girl" in his e-mail and stories, the court states that the class of targets would apparently include "any woman or girl about whom Baker has ever thought." Further, the First Amendment does not permit the inference of an intention to act on the thoughts and dreams expressed here.

Count V focuses on e-mail in which Baker and Gonda discuss torture. Baker writes, "Just thinking about it anymore doesn't do the trick . . . I need TO DO IT." They discuss meeting in the summer. Baker says, "Pickings are better then too. Although it's more crowded." The government identifies the same class of targets as in Count IV.

Again, the court notes that the class of targets is "far too vague." There is also lacking any "unequivocal, unconditional and specific expression of intention immediately to inflict injury." There is only an expression of a strong desire. Says the court,

Baker . . . indicates, at most, an intention to meet Gonda at some indefinite point in the future—in the next week, month, or several months later. This statement does not express an unequivocal intention immediately to do anything. Also, nothing in the language on which the Count is based indicates any intention to commit specific acts if Baker and Gonda ever were to meet.

Dismissing Count V, the court observes that "[t]his prosecution presents the rare case in which, in the government's words, 'the language set forth . . . is so facially insufficient that it cannot possibly amount to a true threat.'"

VI. Insufficient Proof

Accordingly, the court dismissed the indictment against Baker, ruling that in the light most favorable to the prosecution, there is no case for the jury here because the factual proof is insufficient as a matter of law. "The government's enthusiastic beginning," says the court, "petered out to a salvage effort once it recognized that the communication which so alarmed the University of Michigan officials was only a rather savage and tasteless piece of fiction."

"Whatever Baker's faults, and he is to be faulted," observed the court, "he did not violate 18 U.S.C. Section 875(c). This case would have been better handled as a disciplinary matter. . . ." Regarding the government, the court added,

The Court is very skeptical, and about the best thing the government's got going for it at this moment is the sincerity of purpose exhibited by [the Assistant United States Attorneys prosecuting the case]. I am not sure that sincerity of purpose is either synonymous with a good case under the law, or even the exercise of good judgment.

[CyberLaw™ 10/95]

CRYPTOGRAPHY & SPEECH

I. Restricting Access

Dr. Daniel Bernstein has some ideas about cryptography, the art and science of keeping messages secure, that he wants to share. In particular, he wants to publish his ideas and research in an Internet discussion group named sci.crypt, as well as in print. But the government has told Bernstein that he cannot "export" a document or source code describing the encryption system he developed, called Snuffle, without registering as an arms dealer and obtaining an arms license from the State Department. The government says that these items are on the U.S. Munitions List and are covered by the International Traffic in Arms Regulations. But Bernstein claims that the government's actions prevent U.S. citizens from engaging in private electronic communications with foreign persons and, as a practical matter, will restrict private domestic electronic communications. Bernstein also argues that by "restricting access to the tools which allow anonymity and privacy, the government puts the communications of all of its citizens at risk." According to Bernstein,

Without cryptography, what people send via computers is the electronic equivalent of a postcard, open to view by many people while the message is in transit. With cryptography, people can put both messages and money into electronic 'envelopes,' secure in the knowledge that what they send is not accessible to anyone except the intended recipient.

. . . Continued development of cryptography promises to make it possible for the worldwide computer Internet to offer private, secure and protected communication among billions of people worldwide.

II. Ideas as Munitions

While a Ph.D. candidate in mathematics at the University of California at Berkeley, Daniel Bernstein worked in the field of cryptography and developed an encryption algorithm, or recipe, which he calls 'Snuffle.' He described Snuffle in English and in mathematical equations, as well as in the "C" computer programming language (Snuffle.c and Unsnuffle.c). Bernstein wants to publish his cryptographic ideas and research results "as part of the normal process of academic, scientific and political exchange of ideas and information," and, in particular, in "text journals as well as in an online discussion group about the science of cryptography, called sci.crypt."

"Aware of the [government's] civil and criminal restrictions on cryptography export," Bernstein says he, "asked the Office of Defense Trade Controls (OTDC), an arm of the State Department, to find out whether he could publish his ideas." He told OTDC that he wanted to export the document "The Snuffle Encryption System," and the Snuffle.c and Unsnuffle.c source files.

Bernstein filed five different commodity jurisdiction requests. OTDC determined that each of the items is on the U.S. Munitions List and covered by the International Traffic in Arms Regulations (ITAR), so he may not "export" them without registering as an arms dealer and obtaining an arms license from the State Department. Bernstein then filed a lawsuit so that he might publish his own scientific ideas without such restriction: *Bernstein v. U.S.*, C95–00582 MHP (N.D. Cal.).

In response, the government asked the court to dismiss Bernstein's complaint. The government notes that the Arms Export Control Act (17 U.S.C. Section 2778(h)) expressly prohibits judicial review of the determination that cryptographic software should be designated a "defense article" on the U.S. Munitions List. Here, Snuffle 5.0 software was designated a defense article under statutory authority, "[i]n furtherance of world peace and the security and foreign policy of the United States." According to the government, both the Arms Export Control Act and the Constitution prevent the court from second-guessing the designation—whether an item should be placed on the Munitions List possessing nearly every trait that would render the question "political." In addition, claims the government,

No satisfactory or manageable standards exist for judicial determination of the issue, as [the government itself] acknowledge[s] the disagreement among experts as to whether [the particular item] belongs on the list. Neither the courts nor the parties are privy to reports of the intelligence services on which this decision, or decisions like it, may have been based. The consequences of uninformed judicial action could be grave. Questions concerning what perils our nation might face at some future time and how best to guard against those perils "are delicate, complex, and involve large elements of prophecy. They are and should be undertaken only by those directly responsible to the people whose welfare they advance or imperil. . . ." (Citations omitted.)

Bernstein claims that the Court of Appeals for the Ninth Circuit has stated that colorable constitutional claims may be reviewed by courts despite the seemingly absolute preclusion of the Arms Export Control Act (AECA). However, he has not raised colorable claims here, asserts the government, because (1) this case involves not "speech" covered by the First Amendment, "but the conduct of exporting a functioning defense article," and (2) even if "speech" were incidentally involved in the State Department's control of the export of cryptographic software, "such an incidental infringement easily passes First Amendment muster. . . ."

III. Regulation of Conduct

Bernstein claims that the State Department seeks to regulate his right to "publish" a "scientific paper" or "to engage in academic inquiry" and "to openly discuss" ideas related to cryptography. But, says the government, the State Department did "no such thing." The State Department simply determined that Bernstein cannot export his cryptographic software without an export license. As explained by Bernstein and confirmed by the National Security Agency, Snuffle 5.0 is a functioning cryptographic product—software capable of maintaining the secrecy or confidentiality of data.

The government observes that "conduct" is protected by the First Amendment only if it is or could be "sufficiently imbued" with elements of communication. The Supreme Court looks for "[a]n intent to convey a particularized message . . . and [whether] the likelihood was great that the message would be understood by those who viewed it." Here, export of cryptographic software is not sufficiently imbued with communicative elements, says the government, and does not "'convey a particularized message' to its foreign recipients." Despite claims that this case involves Bernstein's right to publish a paper, the government argues that Bernstein did not submit to the State Department an academic discourse on algorithmic theories—he submitted "source code for data encryption, along with instructions on how to make it operational on a computer so that users could have an interactive, zero-delay, encrypted conversation." The dissemination of Snuffle would have a functional—not communicative—purpose, and its designation as a defense article "does not," therefore, "constitute the regulation of expression upon which a colorable constitutional claim may be based."

IV. Incidental Restriction of Speech

Even if the First Amendment applied to Bernstein's export of crypto-graphic software, the government argues that "[t]he State Department's commodity jurisdiction determinations do not run afoul of First Amendment principles because any impact on [Bernstein's] 'speech' would be incidental to the government's regulation of the conduct of exporting cryptographic software."

According to the Supreme Court, an incidental restriction on speech will be supported if

(i) it is within the constitutional power of the government; (ii) it furthers an important or substantial governmental interest; (iii) the governmental interest is unrelated to the suppression of free expression; and (iv) the incidental restriction on alleged First Amendment freedoms is no greater than is essential to the furtherance of that interest.

Here, says the government, the first two elements are readily met. Regulation of the export of defense articles is within the power of Congress to provide for the common defense and regulate foreign commerce. And there is a substantial governmental interest in "control[ling] the availability of cryptography from the United States so that critical foreign intelligence gathering functions are not harmed. . . ." Further, "the determination that cryptographic software like [S]nuffle should be considered a 'defense article' subject to export control '[i]n furtherance of world peace and the security and foreign policy of the United States,' 22 U.S.C. Section 2788(a)(1), is not one for courts to evaluate."

On the third element, the government also believes that the regulation of the export of defense articles and services under ITAR (22 C.F.R. Subchapter M, Parts 120–130) does not suppress free expression. The U.S. Munitions List (USML) and ITAR cover Snuffle software, asserts the government, because of its function and capability to encrypt information, and is, therefore, "unrelated to the suppression of speech."

Fourth, the government claims that the inclusion of certain cryptographic software on the USML is an incidental restriction on alleged First Amendment freedoms no greater than is essential "in furtherance of a substantial national security interest to protect the United States's signals intelligence capabilities that are utilized to provide essential information to national security policymakers and military commanders." ITAR, in fact, "excludes certain cryptographic software that does not maintain data confidentiality or secrecy (such as for data authentication and financial functions), as well as mass market software products with limited encryption capabilities." In so doing, ITAR excludes cryptographic software that does not pose a risk to national security, and "responds precisely to the substantive security problems which legitimately concern the [government]." Looking to a decision by the Ninth Circuit Court of Appeals, *U.S. v. Elder Industries*, 579 F.2d 516 (9th Cir. 1978), the government argues that

[I]f the government may incidentally restrict the transmission of technical data by making it unlawful to assist a foreign national in the development of a functioning defense article, it may, consistent with the First Amendment, regulate the exportation of the functioning defense article itself, even if such regulation may, in certain cases, incidentally inhibit 'expression.'

V. A Misinterpretation?

To the extent that Bernstein claims the government's actions constitute a "prior restraint" on the "publication of scientific papers," the government argues that the claim is "the product of his own misinterpretation of the facts and the ITAR." According to the government,

[N]owhere do the commodity jurisdiction determinations indicate that [Bernstein] is barred from publishing a scientific paper concerning the theory of [S]nuffle, or expressing ideas about cryptography in general. What [Bernstein] cannot do is export [S]nuffle software without first obtaining a license from the State Department.

Control of the export of Snuffle software does not implicate the First Amendment, says the government, because the software functions to encrypt data and "control of its export is unrelated to any incidental restriction on expression that such an export may entail."

Bernstein's claim that the government restrained publication of explanatory information fails, says the government, because the State Department's determination did not assess the explanatory information separately for export control purposes. The government believes that Bernstein only sought a determination for Snuffle and certain technical data. The State Department advised Bernstein that it reviewed the explanatory information only to evaluate the software. To the extent that technical data was included, the State Department advised that Bernstein would need a license to export the data if his objective were to assist a foreign person or enterprise in obtaining or developing his cryptographic software.

In response to Bernstein's claim that the AECA and ITAR violate the First Amendment on overbreadth grounds, particularly because they prevent him from "discussing or revealing his ideas in any public forum in the United States on the grounds that it might have the effect of disclosing the information contained therein to a foreign person," the government urges that the Ninth Circuit Court of Appeals has already ruled that the relevant ITAR provisions are not unconstitutionally overbroad. Bernstein's overbreadth claim is, therefore, foreclosed. The government notes that the definition of technical data under ITAR excludes "information concerning general scientific, mathematical, or engineering principles commonly taught in schools, colleges, and universities," as well as information in the "public domain."

The government also rejects Bernstein's claim that the AECA and ITAR are impermissibly vague. In part, the government observes, "[t]he definition of cryptographic software as that 'with the capability of maintaining secrecy or confidentiality' is surely susceptible to common understanding by 'a person of ordinary intelligence.'"

VI. First Amendment Violation

In opposition to the requested dismissal, Bernstein notes that the definition of "export" under ITAR includes "disclosing (including oral or visual disclosure) or transferring technical data to a foreign person, whether in the United States or abroad." Under this definition, says Bernstein,

1. [He] cannot even teach his ideas to his students in a classroom without government permission, unless he ensures that none of his students is a "foreign person."
2. [He] would export his ideas if he were to disclose them at an academic conference, because said publication would surely disclose his ideas to a "foreign person."
3. [He] would export his ideas if he were to post a message containing them to the sci.crypt newsgroup. Export includes distributing the ideas over the Internet by posting them to internationally available newsgroups, since this might disclose them to a "foreign person."

Bernstein claims that "he cannot even stand on a street corner and talk about his ideas, because this might 'export arms' if a foreign person was listening."

Bernstein agrees that he cannot challenge the designation of an item on the USML, but notes that his challenge is, in fact, to the constitutionality and *ultra vires* nature of the entire regulatory scheme, on grounds that it restrains his right to communicate without meeting the constitutional standards for such restraints. Here, says Bernstein, it is not conduct that ITAR restricts, but disclosure and communication. No export license is required under ITAR to actually use encryption.

VII. Government Sleight-of-Hand

According to Bernstein, the government is "attempting a bit of sleight-of-hand here, hoping to narrow the scope of this lawsuit." The government wrongly construes the State Department's determinations as referring only to "cryptographic software, deliberately ignoring his other submissions, and then argue that publishing 'software' never can be protected expression." But, says Bernstein, the government "did extend . . . control to both the code and non-code items submitted by [him]."

ITAR controls much more than encryption software. The definition of "software" under ITAR, says Bernstein, "includes but is not limited to the system functional design, logic flow, algorithms, applications programs, operating systems and support software for design, implementation, test, operation, diagnosis and repair." As non-code items arguably include logic flow and algorithms that are part of Bernstein's ideas, they could be included within the definition of "software." And even if non-code items do not constitute defense articles, they still may be controlled as technical data or to the extent that they may furnish "assistance" to persons in the use of controlled cryptographic software. In light of the above, Bernstein claims that he has presented colorable constitutional claims that the government's action "constituted a prior restraint on his right to publish non-software expressions of his ideas, as well as those written in computer code."

Bernstein notes that in a 1978 memorandum, the Justice Department concluded that "existing provisions of the ITAR are unconstitutional insofar as they establish a system of prior restraint on the disclosure of cryptographic ideas and information developed by scientists and mathematicians in the private sector."

Bernstein explains that he is a scientist and an academic who seeks to publish his ideas for scientific and academic discussion. He seeks discussion by the worldwide community. His communication meets the First Amendment value of the search for truth through the "marketplace of ideas." His desire for peer review fulfills the First Amendment value of self-expression. Bernstein's activities, therefore, fall within First Amendment protections for academic discourse.

Bernstein also seeks to engage in political speech. He observes,

There has been considerable public debate over the role of cryptography in society and whether the government's current regulatory scheme is appropriate. Government agencies are major players in this debate. When the agencies which administer laws and regulations which can act as a prior restraint are also involved in policy formulation about the same subject, there is a clear risk that these agencies may interfere with that process of political and social change, and 'raise[s] the specter that the Government may effectively drive certain ideas or viewpoints from the marketplace.' Here, [Bernstein's] speech contributes to the cryptography policy debate by demonstrating that nonrestricted hash functions are in truth as powerful as the most heavily restricted items, and that one may be easily converted to the other. To [Bernstein's] audience of scientists and cryptography policymakers, his speech argues that the government's policy is arbitrary and ineffective, rebutting the government's public assertions to the contrary.

VIII. Controlling Speech

The government cannot avoid the traditional tests of prior restraints simply by labeling the publication of computer code as "conduct of export," says Bernstein. Here it is disclosure that is regulated. Bernstein desires to communicate his ideas, and there must not be a Constitutionally cognizable distinction between communication of ideas in English or mathematical symbols and the communication of those ideas written in the language of computer code. Among other things, Bernstein recalls that "software" is treated as expression under copyright law, and that the Supreme Court holds that the First Amendment prohibits the government from restricting the languages used by its citizens.

Notably, Bernstein argues that the government's scheme has the effect of controlling private speech by controlling the tools necessary for it. But, "the Supreme Court has long held that the government cannot target the tools of expression in order to improperly restrict expression itself." Claims Bernstein,

The First Amendment includes the right to speak confidentially. It prevents 'compelled speech,' and preserves the autonomy to control one's own speech. It protects anonymous speech. It prevents compelled disclosure of those with whom one associates and speaks. It requires . . . that the government allow people to speak in any language they choose. It extends to a person's right to communicate with foreigners.

If the government is successful here, it will undermine all of these protections. It will prevent U.S. citizens from engaging in private, electronic communications with foreign persons. As a practical matter, it will also restrict private domestic electronic communications. . . . By restricting access to the tools which allow anonymity and privacy, the government puts the communications of all of its citizens at risk. (Citations omitted.)

IX. Real Issues

Bernstein argues that the Government has exceeded its authority in applying ITAR to him, as Congress "never intended that the AECA be applied to the academic or scholarly publication of scientific and technical information." Neither the statutory language nor legislative history reflects an intent to control academic publications, as noted by the Justice Department in its 1978 memorandum.

In further detail, Bernstein argues that judicial review is not precluded under the political question doctrine, noting that the Supreme Court struck an injunction against publication of the Pentagon Papers even though the Vietnam War was still in progress. Bernstein also claims that jurisdiction here is proper under the Administrative Procedures Act, 5 U.S.C. Section 704.

Accordingly, Bernstein concludes that his claims are sufficient to prove that jurisdiction exists. "Real constitutional issues are at stake; [Bernstein's] communication, not his conduct, was restrained. . . . The appropriate test for judging the prior restraint of [Bernstein's] speech here is laid out in the Pentagon Papers case: whether publication of the items 'will surely result in direct, immediate, and irreparable damage to our Nation or its people.'"

[CyberLaw™ 12/95]

INDECENT COMMUNICATION

I. Communications Decency

A preliminary draft of the final Telecommunications Deregulation Bill (S. 652/H.R. 1555) has been released by a House-Senate conference committee. It includes a provision that prohibits the knowing use of an "interactive computer service" to display in a way available to minors any "indecent" comment, request, suggestion, proposals, or image. Service providers that permit their facilities to be used for such purposes may also be penalized. This prohibition of indecent material is part of the bill commonly known as the Communications Decency Act or the Exon Amendment (after its leading sponsor in the Senate). Notably, the Communications Decency Act provides only a vague definition of "indecency." Under the act, an indecent communication is one "that, in context, depicts or describes, in terms patently offensive as measured by contemporary community standards, sexual or excretory activities or organs." Over the past six months, a range of prominent critics have opposed the Communications Decency Act. They warn that it will seriously hinder development of the Internet and reduce its content to only what is fit for children according to "most narrow of community standards found in the most socially limiting of locations." The act is also viewed as "an unwarranted, unconstitutional intrusion by the federal government into the private lives of all Americans," which overlooks the fact that there now exist free or inexpensive protections that can be used by parents to guard against the problems the Congress chooses to attack by legislation.

II. A New Age of Comstockery

The Cato Institute (http://www.cato.org/), for example, warns that instead of moving communications into the future, the Communications Decency Act "threatens to lobotomize the Internet." And it ushers in "a new age of Comstockery in America." (See http://www.cato.org/pa-232.html.) The Institute explains,

"The term 'Comstockery,' coined by George Bernard Shaw, refers to overzealous moralizing like that of Anthony Comstock, whose Society for the Suppression of Vice censored literature in America for more than 60 years. Under the so called Comstock laws, classic works by such authors as D. H. Lawrence, Theodore Dreiser, Edmund Wilson, and James Joyce were routinely suppressed. Other targets of the society's crusades included such literary giants as Tolstoy and Balzac."

The legal standard for the Comstock laws came from an English case, *Regina v. Hicklin*, which, says the Cato Institute, "held that the test for obscenity turned on whether the material tended to corrupt the morals of a young or immature person." Early feminists, such as Margaret Sanger, were notable targets of Comstock and the Comstock laws, as they banned the mailing of information on contraception and abortion.

Illustrating the excesses under the Comstock laws, the Institute points to the campaign to censor James Joyce's Ulysses:

"The first obscenity prosecution of that now-classic work resulted from publication of installments in the Little Review, a literary magazine. The publishers were arrested and prosecuted in 1920 because of the book's sexual themes. They were convicted and fined $500. But the real loss was beyond the courtroom—no American publisher would even consider printing the book for the next 11 years."

In 1932, a federal court of appeals affirmed a ruling that the book was not obscene and rejecting the prevailing legal test. The appeals court held that a book must be judged as a whole, not by the effect that selected passages might have on vulnerable populations. "As a result," says the Cato Institute, "the sensibilities of the most tender reader were no longer the measure of the obscenity of a work of literature. Instead, the sensitivities of the average reader became the yardstick."

Years later, the Supreme Court ruled that obscenity "must be limited to works which, taken as a whole, appeal to the prurient interest in sex, which portray sexual conduct in a patently offensive way, and which . . . do not have serious literary, artistic, political, or scientific value." As noted by the Cato Institute, the Court relied "on local community standards to determine which portrayals of sexual conduct "appeal to the prurient interest in sex" and consequently are 'patently offensive.'"

III. Indecency Lite

Indecency, says the Cato Institute, may be thought of as "obscenity lite." In a case over the radio broadcast of George Carlin's monologue on the "Seven Dirty Words", the U.S. Supreme Court approved the Federal Communication Commission's legal definition of indecency, which focuses on "the exposure of children to language that describes, in terms patently offensive as measured by contemporary community standards for the broadcast medium, sexual or excretory activities and organs at times of the day when there is a reasonable risk that children may be in the audience." But in a later case over dial-a-porn (sexually-oriented telephone messages), the Supreme Court acknowledged that sexual expression that is "indecent but not obscene is protected by the First Amendment," and held that the government may regulate indecent speech to protect children if it does so "by narrowly drawn regulations . . . without unnecessarily interfering with First Amendment freedoms." The Court also distinguished between radio listeners and callers to dial-a-porn services, who could not be characterized as unwilling listeners.

Regarding the Communications Decency Act, the Cato Institute urges,

If the bill is adopted, it will be extremely bad news for the First Amendment. Nothing in the history of indecency enforcement suggests that the Exon amendment or any similar legislation can be made compatible with a culture of free expression, no matter how narrowly it may be tailored. Indecency rules are based on the central assumptions of obscenity law as it existed under Anthony Comstock's reign, when great works of literature were suppressed routinely. Applying that body of law to cyberspace would be like unleashing a virus that could transform the essential character of the net.

And, among other things, the Cato Institute asks,

"How will the Exon bill affect a service such as Project Gutenberg, which makes electronic texts of books freely available on the World Wide Web? Even a cursory examination of the books provided by that remarkable service turns up authors, such as D. H. Lawrence, who are likely to lead to trouble, just as they did under Anthony Comstock. The only option under the law may be for services like Project Gutenberg to screen their materials and in some way limit access. Even if such a thing can be accomplished, it defeats the purpose of Project Gutenberg, which was created 'to make information, books and other materials available to the general public in a form . . . people can easily read, use, quote, and search.'"

IV. Only What is Fit for Children

These views are echoed in a publication by Voters Telecommunications Watch (http://www.vtw.org), which argues that "[t]he Communications Decency Act (CDA) is a poorly thought-out piece of legislation intended to restrict the access of minors to indecent and obscene material on the Internet." (See, http://www.vtw.org/pubs/cdafaq.) The Communications Decency Act would chill free speech, observes VTW, and dilute the level of Internet communication to a level acceptable to children. "Furthermore, its whole approach is to treat computer communications as a broadcast medium, which fails to take into account the unique possibilities for parental control and 'self-filtering' that are available to us in this medium."

"Indecent" expression, observes VTW, is defined by what is considered inappropriate for children, but retains First Amendment protection so long as it clears the obscenity test. Any regulation of indecent material must use the "least intrusive means" for accomplishing the government's goal of protecting children. And those restrictions, notes VTW, cannot have the effect that they "reduce the adult population to only what is fit for children."

Examples of material that may be found indecent and barred from the Internet, says VTW, include the "Seven Dirty Words" that cannot be uttered in broadcast media, passages from John Updike or Erica Jong novels, certain rock lyrics, and Dr. Ruth Westheimer's sexual-advice column. Under the proposed legislation, says VTW,

[I]it would be criminal to "knowingly" publish such material on the Internet unless children were affirmatively denied access to it. It's as if the manager of a Barnes & Noble bookstore could be sent to jail simply because children were able to wander the store's aisles and search for the racy passages in a Judith Krantz or Harold Robbins novel.

V. The Most Narrow of Community Standards

The American Civil Liberties Union (gopher://gopher.nyc.pipeline. com:70/11/society/aclu/) also argues that proposals to impose regulatory control over the content of speech in cyberspace would "violate free speech, violate the rights of adults to communicate with each other, and establish new government control over what we say and see in the online world." (See http://www.epic.org/free_speech/censorship/hyde_letter.txt; gopher://gopher.nyc.pipeline.com:70/00/society/aclu/speaks/other/exon.) Not only do some of the proposals fail to use the "least restrictive means" to obtain their goals, but they also fail "to take into account the particular characteristics of interactive media in the online environment." All Americans may unfairly be subjected to the "most narrow of community standards found in the most socially limiting of locations." The ACLU observes that

Indecency is essentially a meaningless term, and the [Exon A]mendment's censorial sweep could well cover speech that has nothing to do with sex. Any content that is outside the mainstream or potentially offensive could be banned. Everything from news photos of starving, emaciated children in Somalia to 'gangster rap' has been labeled by some segment of society as indecent or filthy.

Commenting on proposed defenses that may be established by service providers under the Communications Decency Act, the ACLU warns that they might be too vague and limited to help. Corporations with in-house legal departments may fare better, but smaller companies will be "effectively frozen out of the defenses, with a profound chilling effect on their own speech for fear of offending the vague prohibitions and being sent to prison." Individuals will face the same pressures, with the result that the act "will harm the very people who have made cyberspace the incredibly rich source of information it is today."

In response to worries that computers will "somehow begin projecting offensive (and unbidden) images," the ACLU observes that the "nature of online communications requires that the user seek out material by use of descriptors and identifiers." Technology exists today to prevent children from accessing Internet sites with sexual content or to shut down a computer if a child receives an unacceptable question online. The ACLU states,

[T]hese free or inexpensive protections exist today and can be used at the parent's option. There is simply no need for new federal criminal law to address these concerns, especially when such a law would also interfere with the freedom of adults to communicate with each other.

VI. Second-Class Free Speech Rights

The Center for Democracy and Technology (CDT) strongly opposes the Communication Decency Act. (See http://www.cdt.org/cda.html.) It views the current proposal as "threaten[ing] the very existence of the Internet as a means for free expression, education, and political discourse." CDT also sees the act as "an unwarranted, unconstitutional intrusion by the federal government into the private lives of all Americans."

In its analysis of an earlier version of the Communications Decency Act, CDT observed that it "amounts to a total ban on all 'indecent' information in public areas of the Internet, since all users of the Internet know that public areas are accessible to minors." The act also gives second-class free speech rights to all interactive media. For example, print publications that can be sold freely in bookstores will be barred from the Internet.

There are "defenses to prosecution" included in the Communications Decency Act. A service provider or other entity may take "good faith acts" to restrict the flow of prohibited communication. CDT states that a prudent service provider will more likely wait until the Federal Communications Commission issues regulations explaining what procedures are necessary and sufficient to provide a defense. CDT objects to giving the FCC control over Internet content, noting

The FCC took 8 years to get blocking rules settled just for 900# services, and that was one relatively simple technology. Giving the FCC authority to set child-access standards for every piece of the Net, and all new Net services that develop[,] is a disaster for the medium and will have a sweeping, chilling effect on both the technology and free expression online.

CDT recalls that a major criticism of the legislation introduced by Senator Exon "was that it placed criminal liability on online service providers and Internet access providers for any content that traveled across their networks." Senator Exon changed his proposal in response, "to assure that service providers would not be held responsible for content on their network unless they exercised editorial control." But before his bill was passed by the Senate, the provisions were changed—"a service provider would have to show that it has no control over the service which carried indecent content to a particular minor." There is no "editorial control" defense for online providers and, says CDT, "access providers, and thus Internet users, [are left] in a state of great uncertainty as to their responsibility under th[e] bill."

CDT claims that "[i]n sharp contrast to older media, government content regulation is simply not necessary in order to shield children from possibly inappropriate information." And it suggests that "[a]ny legislative action in this area must identify ways to promote greater parental and user control."

7

Procedural Issues

A. Jurisdiction

The term "jurisdiction" refers to the power of a court to judge a particular case. The question of jurisdiction is important, because a judgment rendered by a court lacking personal jurisdiction over a defendant is void.[397]

Previously, the law commonly required the presence of a person involved in a legal action within the territorial boundaries of the court hearing the matter. But notions of physical presence have given way to fairness, reasonable nexus with a dispute, adequate notice, and opportunity to defend. This means that in proper circumstances, a state court can adjudicate a matter involving a nonresident who, for example, "does business" in a particular state but has not consented to be sued in the state, never opened an office, or visited the state.

Federal courts can assert jurisdiction over persons within the territorial limits of the state in which the courts sit. Federal courts can also take advantage of state jurisdictional laws over nonresidents (called "long-arm statutes"), so that they have the same reach available to local state courts.[398] Specific federal statutes may extend the reach of federal courts in particular cases. For example, obscenity is a "continuing offense" that may be "inquired of and prosecuted in any district from, through, or into which [it] moves."[399]

According to the U.S. Supreme Court, a person may be subject to a court's jurisdiction and judgment if "he [has] certain minimum contacts with [the territory of the forum] such that the maintenance of the suit does not offend 'traditional notions of fair play and substan-

---

[397] See *Burnham v. Superior Court*, 495 U.S. 604, 608–09, 109 L.Ed.2d 631, 110 S.Ct. 2105 (1990).
[398] Fed. R. Civ. P. §§ 4(e), 4(f).
[399] 18 U.S.C. § 3237.

tial justice.' "[400] In determining whether a foreign court may exercise jurisdiction, "foreseeability" is a critical consideration. And "foreseeability," in turn, is determined by looking to whether a "defendant's conduct and connection with the forum State are such that he should reasonably anticipate being haled into court there."[401]

On the requirement that individuals have "fair warning that a particular activity may subject [them] to the jurisdiction of a foreign sovereign,"[402] the Supreme Court explains,

> Where a forum seeks to assert specific jurisdiction over an out-of-state defendant who has not consented to suit there, [the] "fair warning" requirement is satisfied if the defendant has "purposefully directed" his activities at residents of the forum, and the litigation results from alleged injuries that "arise out of or relate to" those activities.[403]

A foreign business comes under a court's jurisdiction when it "purposefully avails itself of the privilege of conducting activities within the forum State."[404] In such a case, the company has clear notice that it is subject to suit there, can alleviate the risk of burdensome litigation by procuring insurance, passing expected costs on to customers, or, if the risks are too great, severing its connection with the state.

Simply using interstate communication facilities is not sufficient to establish jurisdiction over the sender.[405] But, foreign jurisdiction

---

[400] *International Shoe Co. v. Washington,* 326 U.S. 310, 316, 90 L. Ed. 95, 66 S.Ct. 154 (1945).

[401] *World-Wide Volkswagen v. Woodson,* 444 U.S. 286, 297, 62 L.Ed.2d 490, 100 S.Ct. 559 (1980); *Perkins v. Benguet Consol. Mining Co.,* 342 U.S. 437, 445–47, 96 L. Ed. 485, 72 S.Ct. 413 (1952) (defendant may be haled into a forum state's courts to defend against causes of action unrelated to its conduct there if its activities in the state are "substantial" or "continuous and systematic").

[402] *Shaffer v. Heitner,* 435 U.S. 186, 218, 53 L.Ed.2d 683, 97 S.Ct. 2569 (1977) (Stevens, J., concurring).

[403] *Burger King Corp. v. Rudzewicz,* 471 U.S. 462, 85 L.Ed.2d 528, 105 S.Ct. 2174 (1985) (citations omitted).

[404] *Hanson v. Denckla,* 357 U.S. 235, 253, 2 L.Ed.2d 1283, 78 S.Ct. 1228 (1958); see also *Quill Corp. v. North Dakota,* 504 U.S. 298, 119 L.Ed.2d 91, 112 S.Ct. 1904 (1992) ("[I]f a foreign corporation purposefully avails itself of the benefits of an economic market in the forum State, it may subject itself to the State's *in personam* jurisdiction even if it has no physical presence in the State."); but see *Asahi Metal Ind. Co. v. Superior Court,* 480 U.S. 102, 112, 94 L.Ed.2d 92, 107 S.Ct. 1026 (1987) ("The 'substantial connection' between the defendant and the forum State necessary for a finding of minimum contacts must come about by *an action purposely directed toward the forum State.* . . . But a defendant's awareness that the stream of commerce may or will sweep the product into the forum State does not convert the mere act of placing the product into the stream into an act purposefully directed toward the forum State.").

[405] *Thos. P. Gonzalez Corp. v. Consejo Nacional de Produccion de Costa Rica,* 614 F.2d 1247, 1254 (9th Cir. 1980) ("use of the mails, telephone, or other international

may be based on electronic contacts that are "purposefully directed" and have a significant connection to the litigation.[406] The Supreme Court comments,

It is an inescapable fact of modern commercial life that a substantial amount of business is transacted solely by mail and wire communications across state lines, thus obviating the need for physical presence within a State. . . . So long as a commercial actor's efforts are "purposefully directed" toward residents of another State, we have consistently rejected the notion that an absence of physical contacts can defeat personal jurisdiction there.[407]

In a Florida case, the operator of a computerized airline reservation system filed suit against a New York travel agency over failure to make contract lease payments. The travel agency used computer terminals to obtain telephone access to plaintiff's computer database in Miami. A Federal appeals court held that the case should be dismissed for lack of jurisdiction.[408] According to the appeals court,

[A] contrary decision would, we think, have far-reaching implications for business and professional people who use 'on-line' computer services for which payments are made to out-of-state companies where the database is located. Across the nation, in every state, customers of 'on-line' computer information networks have contractual

---

communications simply do not qualify as purposeful activity invoking the benefits and protection of the state"); *Peterson v. Kennedy*, 771 F.2d 1244, 1262 (9th Cir. 1985), *cert. denied*, 475 U.S. 1122, 90 L.Ed.2d 187, 106 S.Ct. 1642 (1986); *Interdyne Co. v. SYS Computer Corp.*, 31 Cal.App.3d 508 (1973) ("When a California business seeks out purchasers in other states—purchasers who are not 'present' in California for general purposes—deals with them only by out-of-state agents or by interstate mail and telephone, it is not entitled to force the customer to come to California to defend an action on the contract."); *CompuServe v. Patterson*, 1994 U.S. Dist. Lexis 20352 (S.D. Ohio 1994), *rev'd*, 1996 FED App. 0228P (6th Cir. July 22, 1996) (defendant's electronic links to Ohio, where CompuServe is based, are too tenuous to support personal jurisdiction—despite the fact he is a CompuServe subscriber and shareware provider) [in EFF archive, http://www.eff.org/pub/Legal/Cases/cis_v_patterson.notes]; see also, *Ticketmaster-New York v. Alioto*, 26 F.3d 201 (1st Cir. 1994) (Massachusetts based court may not assert jurisdiction over a California resident alleged to have made a defamatory comment during an unsolicited telephone interview with a reporter for a Massachusetts newspaper).
[406] See *Edwards v. Associated Press*, 512 F.2d 258, 267 (5th Cir.) (in libel case over publication on wire services, the court noted that "defendant's transmission was purposefully and specifically aimed at Mississippi, as surely as if the proverbial gunman had stood in Alabama and fired into a crowd in Mississippi."); *Brown v. Flowers Industries, Inc.*, 688 F.2d 328, 333 (5th Cir. 1982), *cert. denied*, 460 U.S. 1023, 75 L.Ed.2d 496, 103 S.Ct. 1275 (1983) (single defamatory telephone call sufficient to support jurisdiction).
[407] *Burger King Corp. v. Rudzewicz*, 471 U.S. 462, 476, 105 S.Ct. 2174, 85 L.Ed.2d 528 (1985).
[408] *Pres-Kap, Inc. v. System One, Direct Access*, 636 So.2d 1351 (Fla. App. 1994).

arrangements with out-of-state supplier companies, putting such customers in a situation similar, if not identical, to the defendant in the instant case. Lawyers, journalists, teachers, physicians, courts, universities, and business people throughout the country daily conduct various types of computer-assisted research over telephone lines linked to supplier databases located in other states. Based on the trial court's decision below, users of such 'on-line' services could be haled into court in the state in which supplier's billing office and database happen to be located, even if such users, as here, are solicited, engaged, and serviced entirely instate by the supplier's local representatives. Such a result, in our view, is wildly beyond the reasonable expectations of such computer-information users, and, accordingly, the result offends traditional notions of fair play and substantial justice.[409]

Jurisdiction was found, however, in a case in which a business was sued for allegedly using a nationwide computer bulletin board service to make false statements about another company's right to market a software program. Here, California could properly assert jurisdiction over both the nonresident who posted the message and his company. They had "made tortious statements which, though directed at third persons outside California, were expressly calculated to cause injury in California. . . . [T]he defendants knew that plaintiffs would feel the brunt of the injury, i.e., the lost income, in California."[410]

This decision, founded on directed speech, mirrors the rule for print publications. In a case over a newspaper article written and edited in Florida, the Supreme Court held that the Florida writer and editor could be sued for defamation in California, the home of the article's subject.[411] The story concerned the California activities of a California resident, whose career was centered in California. The Court observed,

[T]heir intentional, and allegedly tortious, actions were expressly aimed at California. Petitioner South wrote and petitioner Calder edited an article that they knew would have a potentially devastating impact upon respondent. And they knew that the brunt of that injury would be felt by respondent in the State in which she lives and works and in which the National Enquirer has its largest circulation. Under the circumstances, petitioners must "reasonably anticipate being haled into court there" to answer for the truth of the statements made in their article. An individual injured in California need not go to Florida to seek redress from persons who, though remaining in Florida, knowingly cause the injury in California. (Citations omitted.)

---

[409] *Pres-Kap, Inc. v. System One, Direct Access*, 636 So.2d 1351, 1361 (Fla. App. 1994).
[410] *California Software Inc. v. Reliability Research, Inc.*, 631 F.Supp. 1356, 1361 (C.D. Cal. 1986).
[411] *Calder v. Jones*, 465 U.S. 783, 79 L.Ed.2d 804, 104 S.Ct. 1482 (1984).

B. Venue

The U.S. Constitution provides that "The Trial of all Crimes . . . shall be held in the State where the said Crimes shall have been committed. . . ."[412] This provision is buttressed by the Sixth Amendment, which requires trial "by an impartial jury of the State and district wherein the crime shall have been committed. . . ."

As stated by the U.S. Supreme Court,

> The Constitution makes it clear that determination of proper venue in a criminal case requires determination of where the crime was committed. . . . The provision for trial in the vicinity of the crime is a safeguard against the unfairness and hardship involved when an accused is prosecuted in a remote place.[413]

Venue cannot be solely based on the acts of government agents.[414] But, in a case over shipment of allegedly obscene films to Florida requested by an F.B.I. agent as part of a nationwide investigation, a federal court of appeals affirmed a conviction for interstate transportation of obscene materials. In so doing, the court of appeals rejected the claim that as "the government chose to have him ship materials into the southern district of Florida because it believed that a jury applying the community standards of that district would probably find the materials were obscene,"[415] venue did not properly lie in the southern district of Florida. The court of appeals reserved judgment, however, "on the case in which an obscenity prosecution is brought in a judicial district through which allegedly pornographic [sic] material passes en route to another destination."[416]

Important constitutional issues arise in obscenity prosecutions, which can be prosecuted "in any district from, through, or into which" allegedly obscene material moves.[417] Material that constitutes expression is entitled to First Amendment protection except where it

---

[412] U.S. Const., Art. III, § 2, cl. 3.

[413] *United States v. Cores*, 356 U.S. 405, 407, 2 L.Ed.2d 873, 78 S.Ct. 875 (1958); *Platt v. Minn. Mining & Mfg. Co.*, 376 U.S. 240, 245, 11 L.Ed.2d 674, 84 S.Ct. 769 (1964).

[414] See *United States v. Lewis*, 676 F.2d 508, 511 (11th Cir. 1982); see also *United States v. Archer*, 486 F.2d 670, 685 (2d Cir. 1973) (call manufactured by the Government cannot transform a local bribery offense into a federal crime).

[415] *United States v. Bagnell*, 679 F.2d 826, 830 (11th Cir. 1982), *cert. denied*, 460 U.S. 1047, 75 L.Ed.2d 803, 103 S.Ct. 1449 (1983).

[416] Ibid. 679 F.2d 826, 832 n.8 (11th Cir. 1982), *cert. denied*, 460 U.S. 1047, 75 L.Ed.2d 803, 103 S.Ct. 1449 (1983).

[417] 18 U.S.C. § 3237; *United States v. Peraino*, 645 F.2d 548, 551 (6th Cir. 1981); *United States v. Thomas*, Nos. 94-6648, 94-6649, 1996 U.S. App. Lexis 1069 (6th Cir. 1996) ("Section 1465 does not require the Government to prove that Defendants had specific knowledge of the destination of each transmittal at the time it occurred.")

violates community standards. So, should the operator of a BBS or Internet site with adult content well within acceptable standards of the community in which he or she is physically located—and therefore not obscene there—be worried about being hauled in front of a jury in another state, judged under a foreign community's standards? Unfortunately, the first authoritative answer provides real cause for concern.

The Amateur Action Computer Bulletin Board System, operated by Robert and Carleen Thomas, was located in Milpitas, California. The Thomases bought sexually-explicit magazines from California public bookstores, scanned the images, and converted them to graphical computer files (GIFs). A U.S. postal inspector, David Dirmeyer, joined the BBS by dialing into it from Tennessee, as well as by sending in an application form and $55. Dirmeyer then downloaded GIF files from the BBS by dialing in from Memphis. These GIFs, which depicted images of bestiality, oral sex, incest, sadomasochistic abuse, and sex scenes involving urination, in addition to six sexually explicit video-tapes that Dirmeyer ordered, led to a twelve-count Tennessee federal grand jury indictment of Robert and Carleen Thomas. They were tried in Memphis, found guilty on various obscenity counts, and sentenced to thirty-seven and thirty months incarceration, respectively.

On appeal, the Thomases challenged venue in Tennessee on the charges related to the GIF files. As noted by the court, they assert that "it was Dirmeyer, a government agent, who, without their knowledge, accessed and downloaded the GIF files and caused them to enter Tennessee." But the court ruled that the operative federal obscenity statute[418] only requires that the government "prove that a defendant knowingly used a facility or means of interstate for the purpose of distributing obscene materials"—"[the statute] does not require the Government to prove that Defendants had specific knowledge of the destination of each transmittal at the time it occurred."[419]

The propriety of venue, said the court, is examined by taking "into account a number of factors—the site of the defendant's acts, the elements and nature of the crime, the locus of the effect of the criminal conduct, and the suitability for accurate fact finding. . . ."[420] Obscenity cases, noted the court, generally involve acts in more than one jurisdiction, and "there is no constitutional impediment to the

---

[418] 18 U.S.C. § 1465.
[419] *United States v. Thomas*, Nos. 94-6648, 94-6649, 1996 U.S. App. Lexis 1069 (6th Cir. 1996).
[420] Ibid.

government's power to prosecute pornography dealers in any district into which the material is sent."[421] Venue in such a case, ruled the court, lies in any judicial district from, through, or into which allegedly obscene material moves.[422]

Here, the Thomases' BBS was "set up so members located in other jurisdictions could access and order GIF files which could then be instantaneously transmitted in interstate commerce." Robert Thomas himself "knew of, approved, and had conversed with a [BBS] member in [the western district of Tennessee] who had his permission to access and copy GIF files that ultimately ended up there."[423] The court noted that some GIF files were marked "Distribute Freely." "The effects of Defendants' criminal conduct," ruled the court, "reached the Western District of Tennessee, and that district was suitable for accurate fact-finding. Accordingly, [the court] conclude[d] venue was proper in that judicial district."[424]

C. Conflict of Laws

In the usual case, the rights and liabilities of parties to a suit can be determined under the law of a particular state. This would be true in the case of a simple automobile accident in San Francisco involving California drivers, for example, where one failed to stop for a red light. But what if the parties live in separate states and suit is brought in a state other than the one in which the injury occurs? Such a case might arise from a defamatory comment posted on an Ohio-based online system by a Nebraska resident about a New York native. If the New York plaintiff files suit in Ohio and there are different rules in each state that apply to such suits, how do you determine which laws to apply? CONFLICT OF LAWS is the area of law that tries to sort out such problems, including "which law ([a state's] own local law or the local law of another state) shall be applied by it to determine the rights and liabilities of the parties resulting from an occurrence involving foreign elements."[425]

---

[421] Ibid.

[422] It is unclear that the court realized the implications of what it was saying, particularly given the way messages are transmitted across the Internet—broken into small packages individually routed to the destination.

[423] *United States v. Thomas*, Nos. 94-6648, 94-6649, 1996 U.S. App. Lexis 1069 (6th Cir. 1996).

[424] Ibid.; see also Ch. VI., § G.1. Obscenity, *supra*.

[425] Restatement (Second) of Conflicts § 2, comment a.

1. Torts

In tort cases, in the absence of a local statute determining the matter, the respective rights and liabilities of parties regarding a particular issue may be determined by "the local law of the state which, with respect to that issue, has the most significant relationship to the occurrence and the parties. . . ."[426] In considering this issue, a number of factors are considered:

(a) the needs of the interstate and international systems,
(b) the relevant policies of the forum,
(c) the relevant policies of other interested states and the relative interests of those states in the determination of the particular issue,
(d) the protection of justified expectations,
(e) the basic policies underlying the particular field of law,
(f) certainty, predictability and uniformity of result, and
(g) ease in the determination and application of the law to be applied.[427]

The following contacts are also reviewed:

(a) the place where the injury occurred;
(b) the place where the conduct causing the injury occurred;
(c) the domicile, residence, nationality, place of incorporation and place of business parties, and
(d) the place where the relationship, if any, between the parties is centered.[428]

In the case of a personal injury, such as defamation, the local law of the state where the injury occurred may control, "unless, with respect to the particular issue, some other state has a more significant relationship . . . to the occurrence and the parties, in which event the local law of the other state will be applied."[429]

In a decision on enforcement of an English libel judgment against the New York operator of a news service that transmits only to a news service in India, a New York court barred enforcement on grounds the standards deemed appropriate in England are "antithetical to the protections afforded the press by the U.S. Constitution."[430] The story at issue said that a Swedish newspaper had reported that Swedish authorities had frozen an account belonging to the plaintiff, holding money paid by an arms company that was previously charged with paying kickbacks to obtain a large Indian government munitions contract. Plaintiff sued in London and obtained a money judgment,

---

[426] Ibid. § 145.
[427] Ibid. § 6.
[428] Ibid. § 145(2).
[429] Ibid. § 146.
[430] *Bachchan v. India Abroad Publications, Inc.*, 154 Misc. 2d 228, 585 N.Y.S.2d 661, 665 (Sup. Ct. 1992)

which he sought to enforce in New York. But the New York court noted that U.S. law provides that a private person cannot recover damages, without showing fault, for defamation against a media defendant who publishes speech of a public concern. Enforcing a foreign judgment where the media defendant was required to prove truth, said the court, would produce a "chilling" effect on speech and violate the First Amendment.

2. Contracts

In the case of agreements, contractual rights and obligations may be determined by the law of the state chosen by the parties.[431] In the absence of an effective choice, the parties' respective rights and duties may by determined by the local law of "the state which, with respect to that issue, has the most significant relationship to the transaction and the parties."[432] The following factors may be considered in analyzing the issue:

(a) the needs of the interstate and international systems,
(b) the relevant policies of the forum,
(c) the relevant policies of other interested states and the relative interests of those states in the determination of the particular issue,
(d) the protection of justified expectations,
(e) the basic policies underlying the particular field of law,
(f) certainty, predictability and uniformity of result, and
(g) ease in the determination and application of the law to be applied.[433]

In determining the applicable law, consideration may also made of the parties' contacts with

(a) the place of contracting,
(b) the place of negotiation of the contract,
(c) the place of performance,
(d) the location of the subject matter of the contract, and
(e) the domicile, residence, nationality, place of incorporation and place of business of the parties.[434]

---

[431] See Restatement (Second) of Conflicts §§ 186, 187.
[432] Restatement (Second) of Conflicts § 188.
[433] Ibid. § 6.
[434] Ibid. § 188.

8

Electronic Contracts & Digital Signatures

A. Are Electronic Agreements Enforceable?

A "contract" may be described as a "promise, or group of promises, which the law will enforce, or the performance of which it in some way recognizes as a duty."[435] An enforceable contract may be established by "a bargain in which there is a manifestation of mutual assent to the exchange and a consideration,"[436] or, in the case of the sale of goods, "[a] contract . . . may be made in any manner sufficient to show agreement, including conduct by both parties which recognizes the existence of such a contract."[437]

In certain cases, the law imposes formal requirements. For example, for a contract for the sale of goods for $500 or more, the Uniform Commercial Code requires "some writing sufficient to indicate that a contract for sale has been made between the parties and signed by the party against whom enforcement is sought. . . ."[438] A signed writing is also required for contracts that by their terms cannot be completed within one year from the time they are made. There are a number of other circumstances in which a signed writing is required.[439]

Can an electronic document satisfy the formal requirements of a signed writing? At this time, there is no clear answer. A number of compelling arguments have been made in support of the validity of wholly electronic agreements, but courts have not resolved the issue.

The requirement of a writing does not appear hard to satisfy. All that may be required is an "intentional reduction to tangible form."[440] The form of the writing is immaterial.[441] The requirement of a writing

---

[435] Murray, Contracts § 2 (1974).
[436] Restatement (Second) of Contracts § 17(1).
[437] Uniform Commercial Code § 2–204(1).
[438] Ibid. § 2–201(1); see also Restatement (Second) of Contracts § 110.
[439] E.g., 17 U.S.C. § 204 (transfer of copyright).
[440] Restatement (Second) of Contracts § 131, Comment (d).
[441] Murray, Contracts § 321 (1974).

has been satisfied, either in the context of contract formation or in other cases where a "written instrument" was required, by letters, telegrams, telexes, mailgrams, faxes, and the recording of data on a computer disk.[442]

Regarding a signature, no particular form or kind is required.[443] A signature may be printed, typed, or made by some other mark, "so long as it has been put there, or adopted by the defendant or his agent, for the purpose of authenticating the writing."[444] While it may be thought that the requirement of a signature is intended to prevent fraud, courts have been so liberal in finding signed writings[445]—even where several documents are involved and a signature is placed on less than all of them—that this cannot be a very serious consideration. There is, in fact, a movement to repeal the statute of frauds, supported by the claim by some that the statute of frauds stimulates rather than deters fraud.[446] A proposal for a new section of the Uniform Commercial Code that would govern transactions involving digital information includes an option on contract formation that would dispose with the statute of frauds, providing generally that a contract may be "enforceable, whether or not there is a record signed by a party against whom enforcement is sought. . . ."[447]

B. Public Key Encryption & Digital Signatures

A wide range of people beginning to use electronic communications worry about the enforceability of agreements exclusively evidenced by electronic files. Security concerns combined with the lack of authori-

---

[442] Murray, Contracts § 321 (1974); B. Wright, The Law of Electronic Commerce §§ 16.4.1—16.4.2 (2d ed. 1995).

[443] Murray, Contracts § 323 (1974).

[444] Ibid.; see also Restatement (Second) of Contracts § 134 ("The signature to a memorandum may be any symbol made or adopted with an intention, actual or apparent, to authenticate the writing as that of the signer."); Uniform Commercial Code § 2-201, Comment 1 ("any authentication which identifies the party to be charged").

[445] See Murray, Contracts § 323 (1974); B. Wright, The Law of Electronic Commerce § 16.3.2 (2d ed. 1995) ("At any rate, the signing requirement's purpose is to elicit some objective indication of assent, some action on the part of the party to be bound.")

[446] National Conference of Commissioners on Uniform State Laws, Uniform Commercial Code Article 2B. Licenses (December 1, 1995, Draft) § 2B-201, Reporter's Note 4.

[447] See National Conference of Commissioners on Uniform State Laws, Uniform Commercial Code Article 2B. Licenses (December 1, 1995, Draft) § 2B-201(a)[Option 1].

tative guidance from courts over issues such as the enforceability of electronic signatures have proved an obstacle to increased business use of electronic communication systems.

Authentication and integrity are two special problems associated with electronic communications.[448] Authentication refers to assurance that a message originated from the person who purportedly sent it. Integrity refers to assurance that a message has not been altered or otherwise damaged during transmission. People fear, and perhaps with good reason given media attention to security issues, that electronic messages they receive have been intercepted in mid-transmission and altered, or that they have been sent by a third party impersonating the purported originator.

Encryption is a popular means of protecting communications transmitted through a potentially hostile environment, such as a computer network that does not provide robust security.[449] Encryption takes a message and converts it, by use of a key, into information that commonly appears random and unintelligible.

In a simple encryption system, the key used to encrypt the information is transmitted to the intended recipient, who uses the same key to convert the encrypted message back to its original form. This is commonly known as a private or symmetric key system.[450] There are a number of drawbacks to such a system, including the cost and risk of sending the key to the intended recipient. Security depends on how well the key is protected.

The problem of key security is minimized in public, or asymmetric, key systems.[451] These systems are based on two keys, one public and one private, that are mathematically related. Using a private key, a person can send a message that can only be decrypted with that person's public key and no other, thereby ensuring the integrity and authentication of the original message.[452]

Several States are considering legislation that would enforce elec-

---

[448] A third is privacy or confidentiality.

[449] See C. Merrill, *Monogamous, Promiscuous, and Polygamous Models of Cryptographic Electronic Commerce* (1995).

[450] The Data Encryption Standard (DES), approved by the Department of Commerce as the official method for protecting unclassified data in computers of U.S. government agencies, is an example of a system that uses a private key. See D. Russell & G.T. Gangemi Sr., *Computer Security Basics* (1991).

[451] PGP (for Pretty Good Privacy) is a popular public-key encryption system that is freely available on the Internet.

[452] If privacy is desired, a person encrypts a message with the recipient's public key. The message can only be decrypted with the recipient's private key.

tronic transactions based on the use of encryption technology. Utah and California have enacted legislation that will enforce certain types of electronic transactions. At the federal level, there is movement

(1) [to allow individuals] the maximum .possible choice in encryption methods to protect the security, confidentiality, and privacy of their lawful wire or electronic communications; and

(2) to establish privacy standards for key holders who are voluntarily entrusted with the means to decrypt such communications, and procedures by which investigative or law enforcement officers may obtain assistance in decrypting such communications.[453]

1. Utah Digital Signature Act

The purpose of Utah's Digital Signature Act[454] is

(1) to minimize the incidence of forged digital signatures and enable the reliable authentication of computer-based information;

(2) to enable and foster the verification of digital signatures on computer-based documents;

(3) to facilitate commerce by means of computerized communications; and

(4) to give legal effect to [certain technical] standards. . . . [455]

Under the Digital Signature Act, Utah allows the establishment of licensed certification authorities, who may issue certificates identifying a particular subscriber. The authority also may certify that "each digital signature affixed by means of the private key corresponding to the public key listed in the certificate is a legally valid signature of the subscriber," and that "an unauthorized person does not have access to the private key."[456]

By accepting a certificate, a subscriber "assumes a duty to exercise reasonable care in retaining control of the private key and keeping it confidential."[457]

A verified digital signature is "presumed to have been affixed with the intention of the subscriber to authenticate the message and to be bound by the contents of the message. . . ."[458] Of course, the presumption only holds if "the certificate [verifying the signature] was not revoked, suspended, or expired at the time of [the] signature."[459]

---

[453] "Encrypted Communications Privacy Act of 1996," 104 S. 1587, §2; see also "Security and Freedom Through Encryption (SAFE) Act," 104 H.R. 3011.
[454] Utah Code Ann. § 46-3-102 et seq.
[455] Ibid. § 46-3-102.
[456] Ibid. §§ 46-3-302(1), 46-3-401(1).
[457] Ibid. § 46-3-303(1).
[458] Ibid. § 46-3-401(3).
[459] Ibid. § 46-3-401(2).

Time-stamps are also presumed valid if appropriate conditions hold. But these presumptions may be rebutted

(a) by evidence indicating that a digital signature cannot be verified by reference to a certificate issued by a licensed certification authority;
(b) by evidence that the rightful holder of the private key by which the digital signature was affixed had lost control of the private key, without violating any duty . . . , at the time when the digital signature was affixed;
(c) by evidence showing a lack of evidence of a signature at common law; or
(d) by a showing that reliance on the presumption was not commercially reasonable under the circumstances.[460]

If the presumptions are not rebutted, "[a] digitally signed document is as valid as if it had been written on paper."[461] (Utah does not, however, allow a digital signature to make a negotiable instrument payable to bearer, except in certain specified situations relating to the transfer of funds.)[462]

2. California

California's digital signature law is less ambitious than Utah's—limited to written communications with public entities, with the exception of those regarding environmental reports.[463] A digital signature used in such communications has the same force and effect as a manual signature if it is

(1) unique to the person using it;
(2) capable of verification;
(3) under the sole control of the person using it;
(4) linked to data in such a manner that if the data are changed, the digital signature is invalidated; and
(5) conforms to regulations adopted by the Secretary of State (due no later than January 1, 1997).[464]

3. Proposed Encrypted Communications Privacy Act of 1996

To promote economic growth, privacy, and meet the needs of American citizens and businesses, there have been proposals to revise re-

---

[460] Ibid. § 46-3-401(5).
[461] Ibid. § 46-3-402(1).
[462] Ibid. § 46-3-403.
[463] Under Cal. Pub. Res. Code § 71066, the California secretary for environmental protection is authorized to prescribe one or more techniques by which a report may be signed electronically.
[464] Cal. Gov. Code § 16.5.

strictions on encryption technology. One notable proposal is the "Encrypted Communications Privacy Act of 1996."[465]

Under the proposed act, persons within the United States, and those traveling abroad, would be permitted to use any form of encryption. This freedom would not be limited by any key escrow requirement. But investigative and law enforcement officers would be able to gain access to decryption keys and assistance by securing a court order or through other proper legal process. Unauthorized release of a key is punishable by imprisonment and fines. Civil penalties are also provided.

---

[465] 104 S. 1587; also see, "Security and Freedom Through Encryption (SAFE) Act," 104 H.R. 3011.

APPENDIX

8

[CyberLaw™ 1/94]

ELECTRONIC COMMERCE

When you send a business letter by fax, do you also mail the original? If your company exchanges purchase orders electronically, has it implemented a comprehensive set of audit and archiving procedures? The widespread adoption of electronic messaging technology gives rise to many legal questions and issues. To assist in their analysis and resolution, a Texas lawyer named Benjamin Wright has written a book titled *The Law of Electronic Commerce* (Little, Brown & Co. 1991). Intended for both lawyers and business people, *Electronic Commerce* discusses fax, e-mail, and electronic data interchange (EDI), and their application in the business world. Wright also reviews traditional legal issues in the light of electronic messaging technology. "The book's theme," explains Wright, "is that, if implemented intelligently, electronic communication can confidently be used for legal transactions. It rejects the attitude that technology deserves suspicion."

In *Electronic Commerce*, Wright observes that to be legally enforceable, certain transactions are required—under what is known as the statute of frauds—to be evidenced by a "document," a "writing," and a "signature." (The legal requirement of a "writing," notes Wright, ensures that a record is created, "makes the agreement more psychologically binding, and forces careful thinking." The requirement of a "signature" reflects the desire for a "legal and ritualistic symbol of finality, assent, and authenticity.") For example, under the Uniform Commercial Code (U.C.C. Section 1–201(1)),

[A] contract for the sale of goods for the price of $500 or more is not enforceable by way of action or defense unless there is some writing sufficient to indicate that a contract for sale has been made between the parties and signed by the party against whom enforcement is sought or by his authorized agent or broker.

Regarding telegraph, telex, and mailgram, Wright states that courts have "decidedly recognized" that these media are capable of satisfying the statute of frauds. On faxes, Wright states, "It will be difficult to argue that a conventional fax bearing a facsimile signature is not a signed writing." Concerning purely electronic messages, Wright believes that a message "fixed" in a record should satisfy the requirement of a "writing." There is, however, a substantial concern arising from the fact that absent controls it is relatively easy to change an electronic record to which a "signature" is attached or to forge the "signature" itself. Wright notes,

One observer contends electronic contracts should be enforceable under the statute of frauds only if created with "commercially reasonable security" measures, which presumably would ensure the gathering and preservation of forensic evidence sufficient to prevent fraud.

Wright suggests a number of strategies for handling statute of frauds concerns, including agreement between trading parties (under an ABA Model) that "a properly transmitted message is deemed 'written,' and a designated symbol(s) or code(s) within the message is deemed a 'signature.'"

Some industries have already established their own standards for message confirmation, record making, and control. ANSI X12, for example, is an EDI standard set by the American National Standards Institute. According to Wright,

ANSI X12 standards contemplate two acknowledgment types. The first addresses communications, and, if used, issues automatically upon message receipt. It could be a 'transmission acknowledgment,' which confirms receipt; or it could be a 'functional acknowledgment,' which confirms message receipt and intelligibility. The second is an 'application acknowledgment,' such as a purchase order acknowledgment. It responds to the prior message's content—acceptance, rejection, and so on.

Among private customs now in common use is the fax-then-mail procedure, designed to ensure a paper record of an agreement. Wright notes, however, that this procedure invites a different legal problem:

The welsher could argue the fax was not the final communication and the deal was open until the original paper was mailed. The parties may need to clarify which is the operative communication.

Communications integrity is another pressing consideration in electronic business transactions. The implementation of well-designed control and security standards can overcome many problems. For example, a company may restrict access to software used to transact business and register all uses of the software (including unsuccessful access attempts) in an audit log. Wright also lists a number of techniques for ensuring reliable transmission, including the following: a professionally operated network supported by disaster recovery methods; communications protocols, network control and management software, and data checking and preservation techniques; employment of cryptography; and use of auditors.

On message authentication (defined in *Electronic Commerce* as "the ability to prove to a court the source and integrity of a message"), Wright explores the use of notarized faxes, the employment of a "trusted recordkeeper," and other authentication schemes that may protect the parties from fraud. Interestingly, Wright relates that in the Iran-Contra trial of John Poindexter (the former national security advisor), the court accepted as authentic and reliable an incriminating message sent through the White House internal e-mail system to Oliver North. According to Wright, the record was accepted by the court because a trusted recordkeeper—a system operator outside the control of Poindexter or his prosecutors—"had securely created the record and was able, by analyzing system audit information, to confirm to the court that the message came from Poindexter."

Wright also discusses archiving data and preserving records from technical threats, mistakes, and fraud, as well as designing records for audit. Wright cautions that

A special problem with fax records bears mention: Many conventional fax machines print on thermal paper, which yellows and deteriorates. The practical solution is to photocopy the fax onto plain paper. The copying should be done with care so that all marks are preserved, using routine, controlled, and documented procedures. Abundance of caution also advises that the original fax be attached to and stored with the plain paper copy.

In a section titled "Legal Proof Issues," Wright examines principles of evidence law that developed around paper documents and analyzes how evidence rules may be applied to electronic transactions. These issues, explains Wright, arise as follows:

In the classic trial, one party, the 'proponent,' seeks to 'admit' a bit of evidence (such as a record of an invoice) to prove a point that matters in the trial. Typically the proponent must 'lay a foundation' for the evidence to show its admissibility under evidence law (or the rules of evidence). The other party, the 'opponent,' may object if there is a basis for doing so under the law. If the judge allows the admission, the 'trier of fact' (normally the jury but sometimes the judge) may consider the evidence in deciding the case. A trier of fact generally decides a case only on the basis of evidence that is admitted.

(If you cannot have your evidence admitted, you cannot prove your case and you lose.)

For evidence of an electronic message to be admitted at trial, a party needs to be able to show relevance and authenticity (that the evidence is what it is purports to be). Although there is no relevancy problem specific to computer records, a number of objections can be raised on the grounds of authenticity. And authenticity may be the key to a legal dispute.

In a case decided in Europe, for example, a corporation had sold equipment believing payment was secured by a bank guarantee transmitted by telex. When the corporation tried to collect on the guarantee, the bank denied having issued the guarantee. At trial, an expert testified that one telex user can masquerade as another. There was also evidence of a banking custom to secure binding telexes with a test key (a type of code that attaches to a message to display its origin and the integrity of its content). No test key accompanied the guarantee in question and the court ruled that the bank was not responsible for the guarantee.

To prove authenticity, Wright states that the proponent must show origin and integrity. "He must show who or what originated the message and whether its contents are complete and in the form intended, free from error or fabrication." To do so, the proponent may rely on its policies and procedures manuals, logs of message transmission and acknowledgment, evidence of system reliability in maintaining message integrity, and circumstantial evidence relating to a message's content.

Fraud is a particular concern regarding electronic records. As noted by Wright, "[d]ata processing history is rich with legends of corporate insiders fraudulently falsifying computer records and circumventing controls." There is, of course, a range of civil and criminal liabilities for misconduct that arise under state and federal law and regulation. For example, the federal wire fraud statute (18 U.S.C. Section 1343) covers the transmission of fraudulent electronic records over the interstate telephone system. Other statutes reach false and fraudulent entries in the books and records of federal banking institutions and "almost any electronic dealings with the government, including electronic filings and electronic contracting with the government." The Computer Fraud and Abuse Act of 1986 (18 U.S.C. Section 1030), the Electronic Communications Privacy Act of 1986 (18 U.S.C. Section 2701), and statutes in many states protect against unauthorized use of or access into computers as well as the unauthorized alteration or destruction of data.

In *Electronic Commerce*, Wright examines many other practical issues and legal considerations, including general recordkeeping and control requirements, industry codes and model trading agreements, liability for deficient service, confidentiality and control of data, and electronic funds transfer. In a 1993 supplement, Wright also writes about electronic health care information, including recordkeeping regulations and privacy. The material on privacy law and outside parties is particularly interesting. According to Wright,

All manner of remote or outside parties aspire to accumulate, use, and resell health data after they have been collected by providers and insurers: clearing houses working for insurance companies, researchers working for employers, medical supply marketing firms, firms wishing to sell products or services to consumers, and so on. The law of privacy is not very clear as it applies to remote holders of health information.

As stated in *Electronic Commerce*, "one of the primary reasons businesses implement computer technologies such as EDI and databases is that the new technologies—albeit not perfect—are vastly superior to the systems they replace." The legal issues confronting use of the new technologies are not very different from those that arose with the introduction of the telegraph, telephone, and telex. As noted by Wright, "those problems were solved once legal authorities had time to think carefully about the technologies." But due to the considerable benefit afforded by computer technology, it is highly likely that businesses will be compelled to adopt policies and procedures before answers to legal uncertainties arrive from courts or legislatures. *Electronic Commerce* will assist pioneering businesses with a clear explanation of the issues along with historical perspective and common-sense suggestions as to their resolution.

9

Misappropriation of Information

A great strength of the Internet is that it allows users to make a wealth of information available to a broad audience. Companies can build interfaces between in-house databases and the Internet, generating public interest in their products and services. But this potentially lucrative step entails a serious risk—that a current or prospective competitor will obtain an advantage by gaining access to information compiled at the company's expense. An even more serious risk is posed when the information placed online comprises the company's product.

Illustrating the problem is the case of ProCD, which spent millions of dollars to compile a comprehensive, national directory of residential and commercial listings, including full names, street addresses, telephone numbers, zip codes, and industry or "SIC" codes. ProCD sells the directory on CD-ROM, accompanied by a user agreement that permits copying of the data only for individual or personal use, and prohibits distribution, sublicense, or lease of the software or the data. The user agreement also provides:

You will not make the Software or the Listings in whole or in part available to any other user in any networked or time-shared environment, or transfer the Listings in whole or in part to any computer other than the computer used to access the Listings.

In late 1994, Matthew Zeidenberg purchased a ProCD CD-ROM. Early the following year, he incorporated Silken Mountain Web Services, Inc. to offer a database of telephone listings over the Internet. The database was compiled by copying ProCD and other data. Silken Mountain Web Services wrote its own software to allow users to search the database.

Zeidenberg and Silken Mountain Web Services published the Internet database until September 1995, when stopped by a court-ordered injunction issued at the request of ProCD. At the time, the database was receiving about 20,000 "hits" a day. (Each visitor to the Internet site was permitted to extract up to 1,000 listings.) ProCD sought the injunction because it believed that its ability to sell its product was jeopardized, as the public could search the database on the Internet for free.

Upon review of the parties' arguments, the court concluded that ProCD could not prevail on copyright or state law claims.[466] As described by the court,

> Plaintiff's arguments boil down to the proposition that it is unfair and commercially destructive to allow defendants to take the information plaintiff assembled with a significant investment of time, effort and money and use it for commercial purposes without paying any compensation to plaintiff. Although the proposition has substantial equitable appeal, it is one that the United States Supreme Court rejected specifically in a nearly identical context four years ago. In *Feist Publications, Inc. v. Rural Telephone Service Co., Inc.*, 499 U.S. 340, 113 L. Ed. 2d 358, 111 S.Ct. 1282 (1991), the court held that telephone listings are not protected by copyright law and denied the claim of a telephone company that sought to prevent competitors from using the data it had compiled and published in its directories. If this result seems perverse, the remedy lies with Congress.

Because there was no copyright protection for the listings,[467] the court would not allow the ProCD to use contract, misappropriation and unfair competition law, or claims under the Wisconsin Computer Crimes Act, "to succeed on its underlying copyright claim by dressing it in other clothing."

A few months later, the U.S. Court of Appeals for the Seventh Circuit reversed the court's decision in favor of ProCD, holding enforceable the shrinkwrap license limiting use of the ProCD application program and listings to noncommercial purposes. In a widely criticized decision, the Seventh Circuit also ruled that the two-party contract including the shrinkwrap license is not "equivalent to any of the exclusive rights within the general scope of copyright" and therefore may be enforced.[468]

While the Seventh Circuit's ProCD decision may or may not survive as authority in this area, the case aptly serves to illustrate the perils of online publishing. Publishers of similar online products would be well served by discussing with qualified counsel the risk factors involved and measures that may be taken to reduce them.

---

[466] *ProCD, Inc. v. Zeidenberg*, No. 95-C-0671-C, 1996 U.S. Dist. Lexis 167 (W.D. Wisc. 1996), *rev'd*, No. 96–1139, Slip Opinion (7th Cir. June 20, 1996).

[467] Pointedly, the court noted that, "Had each of the compilers of the 3,000 directories that [ProCD] used to put together its database attached a set of terms prohibiting further distribution of the information included in its directories, [ProCD] would not have been able to create Select Phone TM without negotiating with and compensating each compiler for use of its data."

[468] *ProCD, Inc. v. Zeidenberg*, No. 96-1139, Slip Opinion (7th Cir. June 20, 1996.)

A large legal publisher, West Publishing Co., confronted a similar problem but avoided problems encountered by ProCD because it was undisputed that West owns a valid copyright in editorial enhancements it publishes that accompany otherwise uncopyrightable Florida legal decisions.[469] West was challenged by On Point Solutions, Inc., a company that created, marketed, and licensed a CD-ROM database including unannotated case reports of the Florida Courts of Appeals and the Florida Supreme Court. On Point obtained its pre-1948 cases from Florida Reports, published by the State of Florida but including annotations[470] licensed from West. On Point also used a scanner and optical character recognition software to obtain court decisions published by West. In the process, On Point made copies of West's annotations in RAM and also on its hard drives. But the annotations were deleted prior to creation of On Point's CD-ROM. Interestingly, On Point "acknowledge[d] that those intermediate copies infringed West's copyrights in the annotated case reports scanned by On Point. And a Federal Court issued a permanent injunction barring the sale and distribution of the On Point CD-ROM resulting from that copying and ordering On Point to destroy any remaining copies of it.

The *On Point* decision does not provide much guidance. The court notes that On Point acknowledged infringing West's copyright by making intermediate copies of West publications in order to extract the uncopyrightable court decisions. There is no indication that On Point raised a defense on this issue. But On Point could have claimed a fair use defense on the grounds that it was entitled to make the intermediate copies to access the uncopyrightable court decisions.[471]

A company that cannot or does not choose to rely on copyright law to protect its data may find an alternative avenue of protection in trade secret law. A "trade secret" is defined under the Uniform Trade Secrets Act (adopted by many states)[472] as information that

---

[469] *West Publ. Co. v. On Point Solutions, Inc.*, No. 1:93-CV-2071-MHS, 1994 U.S. Dist. Lexis 20040 (N.D. Ga. 1994) (permanent injunction based, among other things, on intermediate copying of West cases scanned by On Point, with West headnotes and syllabi temporarily stored on On Point's computers and then deleted prior to creation of On Point disks).

[470] Brief summaries of the facts and the court's decision, as well as headnote paragraphs summarizing topic designations and indicating the West "Key Number Classifications" assigned to each headnote.

[471] See *Sega Enters. v. Accolade, Inc.*, 977 F.2d 1510, 1527 (9th Cir. 1992); *Atari Games Corp. v. Nintendo of America, Inc.*, 975 F.2d 832, 843–44 (Fed. Cir. 1992).

[472] By California, Colorado, Ohio, Utah, Washington, and Virginia, for example, but apparently not by Massachusetts, New York, New Jersey, or Texas.

(i) derives independent economic value, actual or potential, from not being generally known to, and not being readily ascertainable by proper means by, other persons who can obtain economic value from its disclosure or use; and

(ii) is the subject of efforts which are reasonable under the circumstances to maintain its secrecy.[473]

Once information is disclosed or sold to a buyer, without thought of keeping it secret, it no longer constitutes a trade secret.[474] But even information that does not qualify as a trade secret may be protected if the information is "disclosed in confidence and later used in a manner that breaches the confidence."[475]

In very narrow circumstances, unfair competition law may also provide comfort. "Unfair competition" includes "unlawful, unfair or fraudulent business act[s] or practice[s] and unfair, deceptive, untrue or misleading advertising," among other things.[476]

A seminal unfair competition case arose at the beginning of the twentieth century, in a suit between competing businesses that gathered and distributed news for their members to publish in newspapers. In that case, the Associated Press complained that the International News Service copied news from bulletin boards and early editions of Associated Press member newspapers to sell as its own, publishing them in its western papers at the same time, or sometimes earlier, than Associated Press papers. Upon review, the U.S. Supreme Court held that the Associated Press had a protectable interest in the news it had gathered for publication, viewing the defendant as "endeavoring to reap where it has not sown" and "appropriating to itself the harvest of those who have sown."[477]

---

[473] Unif. Trade Secrets Act § 1(4). Another definition of a trade secret is "any information that can be used in the operation of a business or other enterprise and that is sufficiently valuable and secret to afford an actual or potential economic advantage over others." Restatement (Third) of Unfair Competition § 39.

[474] *Razorback Oil Tools Int'l v. Taylor Oil Tools Co.*, 626 So.2d 28, 33 (La. App. 1993); *Eli Lilly & Co. v. Environmental Protection Agency*, 615 F.Supp. 811, 820 (S.D. Ind. 1985) ("Property rights in a trade secret are extinguished when a company discloses its trade secrets to persons not obligated to protect the confidentiality of such information."); see also *Religious Technology Center v. Lerma*, 908 F.Supp. 1362 (E.D. Va. 1995) ("Once a trade secret is posted on the Internet, it is effectively part of the public domain, impossible to retrieve.")

[475] *Lehman v. Dow Jones & Co.*, 783 F.2d 285, 299 (2d Cir. 1986).

[476] See, e.g., Cal. Bus. & Prof. Code § 17200; 15 U.S.C. § 1125, forbidding false designations of origin and false description; *Playboy Enters. v. Frena*, 839 F.Supp. 1552 (M.D. Fla. 1993) (Frena violated 15 U.S.C. § 1125(a) by falsely inferring and describing the origin of Playboy's photographs and making it appear that Playboy had authorized his product; removal of Playboy's trademarks from photographs held to constitute "reverse passing off.")

[477] *International News Service v. Associated Press*, 248 U.S. 215, 239–40, 63 L. Ed. 211, 39 S.Ct. 68 (1918)

Courts have refused to extend the *International News* decision beyond its particular type of facts, or

[cases] where there was manifest unjust enrichment, for example, where rights in private enterprises or events for which the investor had granted exclusive TV or Radio licenses were involved—unique situations where the primary purpose of an investor to charge the public for the privilege of watching an event, would be frustrated or defeated through exhibition by others than itself or its exclusive licensees.[478]

Conversion is another cause of action that may protect a company's rights in certain data. It has been defined as "a distinct act of dominion wrongfully exerted over another's personal property in denial of or inconsistent with his title or rights therein, or in derogation, exclusion, or defiance of such title or rights, without the owner's consent and without lawful justification."[479] Importantly, some courts have expanded conversion to cover intangible property, such as business information.[480] But courts may limit conversion actions to *International News* type information.[481]

Overseas, there have been efforts by the European Community to establish legal protections for databases.[482] It remains to be seen whether further development of protections in Europe will lead to a similar effort in the United States.

---

[478] See *Intermountain Broadcasting & Television Corp. v. Idaho Microwave, Inc.*, 196 F.Supp. 315, 323 (D. Idaho 1961).

[479] 18 Am. Jur. 2d *Conversion* § 1.

[480] See *FMC Corp. v. Capital Cities/ABC, Inc.*, 915 F.2d 300, 304–5 (7th Cir. 1990) ("[E]ven if the retention of mere copies of documents did not constitute conversion, we think that FMC would also have a valid claim for conversion on the grounds that ABC is essentially depriving FMC of the *use* of its own business information"); *Conant v. Karris*, 165 Ill. App. 3d 783, 117 Ill. Dec. 406, 520 N.E.2d 757, 763 (1987) (holding that trial court erred in dismissing claim for conversion of bid information, on the grounds that release of the information to competitors destroyed its confidentiality and deprived plaintiff of its benefits); but cf., *Miles, Inc. v. Scripps Clinic & Research Found.*, 810 F.Supp. 1091, 1095 (S.D. Cal. 1993) (refusing to recognize a cause of action for conversion of right to commercialize a cell line).

[481] *Pearson v. Dodd*, 410 F.2d 701, 708 (D.C. Cir.), *cert. denied*, 395 U.S. 947, 23 L.Ed.2d 465, 89 S.Ct. 2021 (1969) (information copied from plaintiff's files was not subject to action for conversion, on grounds, among others, that "it does not appear to be information held in any way for sale by appellee, analogous to the fresh news copy produced by a wire service.")

[482] See Proposal for a Council Directive on the Legal Protection of Databases: initial proposal COM (92) 24 final, 13 May 1992; OJ C 156/4, 23 June 1992; modified proposal COM (93) 464 final, 4 Oct. 1993, OJ C 308/1, 15 Nov. 1993. See also *European Commission Greenpaper on Copyright and Related Rights in the Information Society*, 43 J. Copr. Soc'y 50, 75 (1995); P. Geller, *The Universal Copyright Archive: Issues in International Copyright*, 25 Int'l Rev. Indus. Prop. & Copyright L. 54, 66–68 (1994).

10

Civil Rights

Electronic communications may provide evidence of violations of civil rights laws, and may even constitute the violation itself. In one widely reported instance, the establishment of gender-segregated bulletin boards was challenged as a violation of civil rights laws.

In 1992, a journalism teacher named Roger Karraker gave his students at Santa Rosa Junior College some experience online. At the request of female students, he established a women-only computer bulletin board conference. He also started a men-only conference. Some of the participants in the men-only conference posted derogatory (personal and sexual) remarks about two female students, Lois Arata and Jennifer Branham. Arata was the subject of comments because she had protested and organized a boycott over what she regarded to be a sexist advertisement[483] in the college's student newspaper. Branham worked with the men who posted the messages and had dated one of them.

Violating a confidentiality agreement that was a condition for participating in the single-sex conferences, one male participant, Dylan Humphrey, saw fit to let the women know what had been said about them. His access to the system was removed when Karraker discovered the confidentiality violation. Arata and Branham complained to Karraker and the college administration. The women wanted access to the men-only conference to see what had been said about them and to confront those who had said it. Their request was denied. By this time, Karraker had closed both single-sex conferences. And Karraker and the college felt that they would violate the confidentiality obligations attached to the conference if access to the postings were allowed.

Humphrey, Arata, and Branham filed a complaint over the episode with the U.S. Department of Education's Office for Civil Rights. They alleged that the college had violated Title IX of the Educational Amendment of 1972 by creating gender-segregated computer bulletin

---

[483] A picture of the rear end of a women in a bikini.

board conferences and excluding the two women from the men-only conference.

Title IX provides that

No person in the United States shall, on the basis of sex, be excluded from participation in, be denied the benefits of, or be subjected to discrimination under any educational program or activity receiving Federal financial assistance. . . .[484]

Regulations implementing this law bar a recipient from providing a course or educational program or activity "separately on the basis of sex, or require or refuse participation therein by any of its students on such basis. . . ."[485]

The women also complained to the Office for Civil Rights[486] that the posted messages created a hostile educational environment on the basis of gender, and that the college had failed to respond to their complaints. In addition, all three alleged that the college had retaliated against them for engaging in activities protected by Title IX.

In June 1994, the Office for Civil Rights notified the college that it had found a probable violation of Title IX by the college in establishing the gender-segregated bulletin board conferences, "in that the College provided educational programs separately on the basis of sex and excluded women from the [men-only conference] on the basis of sex." The Office for Civil Rights said that it anticipated finding that the posted messages about one of the women constituted a hostile educational environment on the basis of sex, as they used anatomically explicit and sexually derogatory terms and were written by three men students with whom she worked on the college newspaper staff, with the result that after her discovery of the messages she was unable to work effectively with them. The college had remained in compliance with Title IX, however, by investigating and taking appropriate action to remedy the harm that occurred on the men-only board and to prevent future sexual harassment.

But the Office for Civil Rights also said that it anticipated finding that the college had retaliated against the two women. The college had notice of and failed to take steps to stop retaliation against Lois Arata, which took the form of comments attacking her after she protested the advertisement in the student newspaper, made in a public computer conference as well as the men-only conference. The college also failed effectively to deal with harassment (angry remarks and personal

---

[484] 20 U.S.C. § 1681; 34 C.F.R. § 106.1.
[485] 34 C.F.R. § 106.34.
[486] Docket No. 09-93-2202.

attacks) suffered by Jennifer Branham at the hands of fellow students as a result of her complaint about the men-only conference.

Instead of engaging in protracted litigation with the three students, Sonoma County Junior College District settled with them for $15,000 each. This settlement did not, however, end the involvement of the Office for Civil Rights, which proposed a remedial plan covering use of computer networks and bulletin boards established or operated by Santa Rosa Junior College.

The following provisions were proposed by the Office for Civil Rights as part of the Remedial Action Plan:

V. SRJC [Santa Rosa Junior College] shall promulgate guidelines of appropriate conduct for users of the Super Oak Leaf Online (SOLO) computer network and any other computer networks or bulletin board established or operated by SRJC. The Guidelines shall also notify users of their right to be free from harassment on the basis of race, color, national origin, or disability and of their right to be free from retaliation for protesting such harassment. In particular, the SRJC proposed computing procedures shall be amended to read as follows:

A. Paragraph 4 of the SRJC "Administrative Computing Procedures: shall be amended to read as follows:

The computing facilities at Santa Rosa Junior College are provided for the use of Santa Rosa Junior College students, faculty, and staff in support of the programs of the College. All students, faculty, and staff are responsible for seeing that these computing facilities are used in an effective, efficient, non-discriminatory, and lawful manner.

B. A new paragraph 14.2 shall be added to the SRJC "Administrative Computing Procedures" to read as follows:

14.2 Non-discrimination—All users have the right to be free from any conduct connected with the use of SRJC computer systems which discriminates against any person on the basis of race, color, national origin, sex, or disability. Discriminatory conduct includes, but is not limited to, written or graphic conduct that satisfies both the following conditions: (1) harasses, denigrates, or shows hostility or aversion toward an individual or group based on that person's gender, race, color, national origin, or disability, AND (2) has the purpose or effect of creating a hostile, intimidating, or offensive educational environment. "Harassing conduct" and "hostile educational environment" are defined below.

"Harassing conduct" includes, but is not limited to, the following: epithets, slurs, negative stereotyping, or threatening, intimidating, or hostile acts that relate to race, color, national origin, gender, or disability. This includes acts that purport to be "jokes" or "pranks" but are hostile or demeaning. A "hostile educational environment" is established when harassing conduct is sufficiently severe, pervasive, or persistent so as to interfere with or limit the ability of an individual to participate in or benefit from the SRJC computing system.[487]

---

[487] Quoted in, M. Godwin, *SOLO Contendre: Free Speech vs. Sex Discrimination Online*, Internet World at 92 (Feb. 1995).

According to Roger Karraker, the journalism teacher who found himself at the center of the controversy, the Office for Civil Rights's "preliminary report" was filled with factual inaccuracies. The college, says Karraker, advised that it would "fight [the Office for Civil Rights] in court rather than accept the agency's anticipated findings and its insistence that the college police speech on its computer networks."[488] The college and its attorney also demanded that any hate speech language recognize the primacy of the First Amendment.

When the college unilaterally adopted the proposed language, it did so adding that the prohibition against speech had to be read in light of the First Amendment. This addition, says Karraker, "effectively gutted the hate speech code for all but the most egregious conduct."[489]

By letter dated January 30, 1995, the Office for Civil Rights closed the case. It noted that the college was implementing a remedial action plan "virtually identical with the proposal that [the Office for Civil Rights] first promulgated. . . ."

---

[488] R. Karraker, *An Indictment of the OCR*, Program of The Fifth Conference on Computers, Freedom and Privacy at 83 (March 1995).
[489] R. Karraker, *An Indictment of the OCR*, Program of The Fifth Conference on Computers, Freedom and Privacy at 83 (March 1995).

11

Tax

Because the traditional structure of state sales and use taxes distinguishes between tangible personal property, which is typically taxable, and sales of services and intangibles, which are not usually taxable,[490] many online providers and subscribers have not confronted the issue of state taxation of online services. However, online providers may want to review the various state tax laws that might apply, in addition to the federal tax code, when structuring a new business.

While state taxation of online services faces a number of substantial challenges,[491] there is no federal law or legal doctrine of general application that prevents the imposition of an equitable and intelligently implemented state tax regime.[492] There have, in fact, been a

---

[490] See R. Scot Grierson, *State Taxation of the Information Superhighway: A Proposal for Taxation of Information Services*, 16 Loyola L.A. Ent. L.J. 200 (1996).

[491] See *Quill Corp. v. North Dakota*, 504 U.S. 298, 313, 102 L.Ed.2d 607, 109 S.Ct. 582 (1992) (in case over attempt to require out-of-state mail-order company with no outlets or sales representatives in state to collect and pay use tax on goods purchased for use within state, the court ruled that "a corporation may have the 'minimum contacts' with a taxing State as required by the Due Process Clause, and yet lack the 'substantial nexus' with that State as required by the Commerce Clause."); *Goldberg v. Sweet*, 488 U.S. 252, 119 L.Ed.2d 91, 112 S.Ct. 1904 (1989) (holding that Commerce Clause is not violated by state tax on interstate telecommunications originated or terminated in Illinois and charged to an Illinois address, where a credit is provided upon proof a tax has been paid in another state on the same phone call); *Complete Auto Transit v. Brady*, 430 U.S. 274, 279, 51 L.Ed.2d 326, 97 S.Ct. 1076 (1977) (four-part test governing validity of state taxes under the Commerce Clause, requiring the "tax [1] is applied to an activity with a substantial nexus with the taxing State, [2] is fairly apportioned, [3] does not discriminate against interstate commerce, and [4] is fairly related to the services provided by the State.").

[492] See *Amerestate, Inc. v. Tracy*, 72 Ohio St.3d 222, 648 N.E.2d 1336 (Ohio 1995) (transactions taxable because "true object" of customers was to obtain access to compiled objective information in company's PaceNet computer database); *Reuters Am. v. Sharp*, 889 S.W.2d 646 (Tx. App. 1994) (upholding constitutionality of applying sales tax to information services but not newspapers); *Quotron Sys., Inc. v. Limbach*, 62 Ohio St.3d 447, 584 N.E.2d 658 (Ohio 1992) (computer online service subject to use tax, which does not burden interstate commerce); *cf., Dept. of Revenue v. Quotron Sys., Inc.*, 615 So.2d 774 (Fla. App. 1993) (transmission of electronic images to

number of proposals for taxation of online systems and Internet sites that could be applied on a comprehensive, multistate basis.[493]

In one case, an online service unsuccessfully challenged state taxation on the grounds of free speech and equal protection. While recognizing that computer online services have the same protections as newspapers in a number of different circumstances, a Texas court ruled that Reuters was properly subject to a state scheme imposing sales and use taxes on information services but not newspapers.[494]

Reuters argued that its content is the same as that of newspapers, such as the *Wall Street Journal*, and that it is part of the newspaper medium. Reuters claimed that the tax is unconstitutionally applied because it alone is singled out from among other members of the press. But the court rejected this argument, on the grounds that "Reuters and newspapers convey their messages through different means,"[495] and any discrimination is on the basis of format, not message content.

---

video display screens of subscribers does not constitute a sale of tangible property subject of sales tax notwithstanding fact that the images could be printed at the subscriber's option).

[493] See e.g., R. Scot Grierson, *State Taxation of the Information Superhighway: A Proposal for Taxation of Information Services*, 16 Loyola L.A. Ent. L.J. 200 (1996); Multistate Tax Commission, Nexus Guideline for Application of a Taxing State's Sales and Use Tax to a Remote Seller (draft 01/25/95).

[494] *Reuters Am. v. Sharp*, 889 S.W.2d 646 (Tx. App. 1994).

[495] Ibid. 889 S.W.2d 646, 651 (Tx. App. 1994).

12

Records & Evidence

The opportunities offered by electronic communication also presents risks that need to be understood not only by information system specialists, but also by system users, as well as operations and management executives. For example, computer systems routinely record multiple copies of data. A user may delete one copy, unaware that other copies persist and remain available. There are many examples of stored copies of e-mail that have been uncovered and used to establish liability claims against employees and their companies.[496] Companies are well advised to study the risks posed by computer systems and to develop policies that protect their interests related thereto, particularly on employee use (including provisions on whether employee can expect any measure of privacy regarding any data maintained, transmitted, or received on the company system) and record retention issues.

Notably, electronic files and data are subject to production and discovery in litigation.[497] Key limitations concern whether the files or data are relevant or reasonably calculated to lead to the discovery of admissible evidence, the existence of privilege (e.g., attorney-client), and undue burden.

There are a number of circumstances in which a company or person may not delete or destroy computer records and data. Parties to a lawsuit, for example, are under a duty to preserve certain information. As stated by one court,

---

[496] See *Strauss v. Microsoft Corp.*, 814 F.Supp. 1186, 1194 (S.D.N.Y. 1993) (e-mail created issue of fact as to whether sex played a part in denial of promotion); *Donley v. Ameritech Services, Inc.*, No. 92-72236, 1992 U.S. Dist. Lexis 21281 (E.D. Mich. 1992) (dismissing reverse discrimination claim of employee terminated after he drafted and sent an offensive and disrespectful e-mail message to a co-worker about a company client); M. Patrick, *An Attorney's Guide to Protecting, Discovering and Producing Electronic Information* (1995).
[497] See Fed. R. Civ. P. 34(a).

While a litigant is under no duty to keep or retain every document in its possession once a complaint is filed, it is under a duty to preserve what it knows, or reasonably should know, is relevant in the action, is reasonably calculated to lead to the discovery of admissible evidence, is reasonably likely to be requested during discovery, and/or is the subject of a pending discovery request.[498]

This duty to preserve evidence may be triggered before a lawsuit is filed, extending back to when a party knew or should have known files, documents, or records were relevant to a potential litigation.[499]

---

[498] *William T. Thompson Co. v. General Nutrition Corp.*, 593 F.Supp. 1443, 1456 (C.D. Cal. 1984) (default and dismissal held to be proper sanctions in view of defendant's willful destruction of documents and records that deprived plaintiff of the opportunity to present critical evidence on its key claims to the jury).

[499] See *Capellupo v. FMC Corp.*, 126 F.R.D. 545, 551 (D. Minn. 1989) ("Defendant's purge was intentionally tailored to make forever unavailable records and documents which defendant knew or should have known would be pertinent to this gender discrimination lawsuit.")

13

Ethics

Many professions have established ethical rules and standards governing the conduct of their members. The advent of online technology has required those responsible for developing these rules and standards to educate themselves about the new tools and media and to determine how they fit into the existing scheme and whether some changes are necessary. The legal profession faces a number of challenges related to online technology, and the ethical concerns they are wrestling with are not limited to attorneys only. The issues they face are shared by a number of other professions.

Use of online systems, including large commercial services and smaller BBSs, raises questions, among others, of whether attorneys can respond publicly to posted legal questions and whether responding to persons in other states may constitute the unauthorized practice of law. The answer to both seems to hinge on whether the response creates an attorney-client relationship. According to one bar association, an attorney can participate in online discussions and discuss legal topics generally, "without the giving of advice or the representation of any particular client." [500] If an attorney steps over the line and into an attorney-client relationship due to a publicly-posted response, the attorney may have also violated rules of professional conduct by disclosing to the public what should be a confidential and privileged communication. If the attorney, instead, replies by private e-mail and the addressee is in another state, the attorney faces the danger of being charged with practicing law in a state in which he or she is not admitted or authorized to practice.

E-mail messaging between lawyers and clients has raised a number of specific issues concerning confidentiality. Generally, attorneys are required to maintain the confidentiality of their communications with clients. In California, for example, attorneys are obligated "[t]o maintain inviolate the confidence, and at every peril to himself or her-

---

[500] South Carolina Bar Advisory Opinion 94-27 (01/95).

self to preserve the secrets, of his or her client."[501] In light of the duty to maintain confidentiality, can an attorney communicate with a client via an online system of the Internet? One bar association believes that "the very nature of on-line services is such that the system operators of the on-line service may gain access to all communications that occur on the on-line service." The association opines that "unless certainty can be obtained regarding the confidentiality of communications via electronic media, that representation of a client, or communication with a client, via electronic media, may violate [ethical rules] absent an express waiver by the client."[502] This view seems extreme in light of the protections afforded by the Federal Electronic Communications Privacy Act, but it illustrates the level of concern and anxiety in the profession.

A number of states strictly regulate attorney advertising. The subject of Internet sites has not escaped their attention. Some have ruled that attorney Internet sites are advertising, subject to attorney advertising regulations and, in some cases, review and approval by bar associations. For example, the Florida Bar Ethics Department has announced that "[i]nformation that a lawyer makes available to the public about the lawyer or the lawyer's services via the Internet, or similar computer-based technology, is considered a form of lawyer advertising."[503] If an electronic-media ad (which includes a Florida attorney or firm's Web site or home page) contains an illustration and more than limited, basic information ("name, address, telephone number, area of practice, fees schedule, etc."), it must be filed for review with the Standing Committee on Advertising. The Florida Bar notes that the following rules, among others, are applicable to Florida attorney Web sites:

- Ads may not be *false or misleading*, may not *create unjustified expectations* about results the lawyer can achieve, and may not *contain testimonials*.
- Ads may not contain *dramatizations*.
- Ads may not contain *self-laudatory illustrations* or statements that are merely self-laudatory.
- Ads may not compare *the lawyer's services* with the services of other lawyers, unless the comparison can be *factually substantiated*.

---

[501] Cal. Bus. & Prof. Code § 6068(e).

[502] South Carolina Bar Advisory Opinion 94-27 (01/95). A number of states have said that attorneys should refrain from discussing confidential matters over cellular phones, absent informed client consent. See Illinois Ethics Opinion 90-7; Massachusetts Advisory Opinion 94-5; New Hampshire Advisory Opinion No. 1991-92/6; New York City Advisory Opinion No. 1994-11

[503] Ethics Update, The Florida Bar News, Jan. 1, 1996.

- Ads must *disclose the geographic location*, by city or town, or the office in which the advertising lawyer *principally practices law*.
- In the case of ads using audio, the information in the ad must be articulated by *a single voice*, with *no background sound* other than instrumental music. The voice may be that of a full-time employee of the firm but *shall not be that of a celebrity* whose voice is recognizable.[504]

Texas has similar rules, including a general requirement of review by the Texas Bar's Advertising Review Committee.[505] California, on the other hand, since the beginning of 1995 has relied on, among other things, a consumer protection statute aimed at attorney electronic media advertising,[506] which provides that the message of attorney electronic advertising "as a whole may not be false, deceptive, or misleading, and must be capable of verification by a credible source."[507]

Bar association regulation of Internet sites and home pages has been criticized as an unwarranted intrusion, as well as a violation of First Amendment rights. To the extent that most bar associations issue advertising regulations to protect the public from unscrupulous solicitation of prospective clients, through the practice commonly known as "ambulance chasing" and similar efforts, it appears that the risk of such problems arising from Internet sites and home pages is minimal and, therefore, not appropriately subject to regulations that "chill" speech and are meant to guard against real problems that exist in other mediums. Some have suggested that attorney Internet sites and home pages are subject to regulation in any state from which an interested person may access the site. But if the attorney has no office in a particular state and is not actively soliciting clients in that state, the suggestion seems too broad and violative of First Amendment rights. To accede to such an interpretation would compel attorneys to "dumb down" their sites to comply with the most restrictive regulations of the most insular communities, in which they have not chosen to practice or solicit clients, because of the risk that a member of the public might access their site from such a location.

---

[504] Ibid.

[505] See Texas Bar Association Advertisement/Written Solicitation Review Checklist.

[506] Cal. Bus. & Prof. Code §§ 6157–59.2.

[507] K. Betzner, *New Regulations on Electronic Media Advertising*, 2 Ethics Hotliner 2 (Spring 1995).

APPENDIX

13

The Legal Side [12/90]

REVLON v. LOGISTICON

In early October 1990, a major client of a Santa Clara software company complained that it was dissatisfied with the software company's performance on a contract, and the client announced its intention to terminate the contract. On October 15, 1990, the software company responded that it was disappointed with the decision to terminate the contract. It also complained that it had not received payments due under the contract and announced its intention to repossess the products developed for the client. Early the next morning, the software company disabled the client's computerized product distribution system, and sent a letter to the client stating that the action had been taken in an effort to gain leverage in their contract dispute. Within days, attorneys for the client, Revlon, Inc. (the cosmetics giant), filed suit against the software company, Logisticon, Inc.

Documents filed in Santa Clara County Superior Court reveal that in February 1989, Revlon entered into a contract with Logisticon for the design, development, and installation of two computer-based systems for use in connection with the distribution of cosmetic products. The agreement envisaged a two-phase, two-site installation procedure over the course of eighteen months. For its efforts, Logisticon was to receive over $1.2 million.

Revlon alleges that it was to pay Logisticon about $600,000 upon completion of work on "Phase I," scheduled for January 1990. Revlon admits that it withheld $180,000 of that amount, but alleges that it did so because Logisticon failed to meet its obligations to complete Phase I in accordance with the contract. Revlon also complains that Logisticon did not, among other things, meet "several of the Agreement's most important functional and operational specifications." Revlon claims that between March and October 1990, it repeatedly notified Logisticon of such problems, and that it tried to work with Logisticon to cure them.

On October 9, 1990, Revlon announced to Logisticon that it was prepared to terminate their agreement and to release Logisticon from its obligations pursuant to certain terms and conditions. By letter dated October 15, 1990, Logisticon responded, complaining that Revlon had used the system that had been developed under the contract during the course of the year. In that letter, Logisticon also announced its intention to repossess its source and object code.

Early in the morning of October 16, 1990, Revlon personnel began to report a system-wide breakdown of the Logisticon-installed computer system. Later in the day, Revlon received a letter from the president and CEO of Logisticon, stating that "Logisticon disabled the operation of its Dispatcher™ System software last night but took great care as to do it in an orderly fashion and not violate or corrupt your DATA." The letter also explained that Logisticon had been "forced into using the only leverage available" to it.

A few days later, Revlon sued and claimed that Logisticon had activated a data-scrambling virus placed into Revlon's inventory management system. Revlon also alleged that Logisticon "caused a catastrophic failure of Revlon's inventory data base, to which Logisticon was not permitted access"; that Logisticon paralyzed Revlon's product distribution system from October 16, 1990, through October 19, 1990; that Revlon's daily sales from its New Jersey and Arizona distribution facilities (normally millions of dollars) were brought to a standstill; and that hundreds of Revlon workers were sent home.

Revlon's suit contains numerous causes of action, including breach of contract, trespass, conversion, interference with contractual relations, and misappropriation of trade secrets. Revlon seeks monetary damages, punitive damages, and other relief. Revlon has also sought a court order to prevent Logisticon from interfacing with or accessing Revlon's computer system, alleging that it has suffered irreparable harm and that Logisticon has plans for another "assault" on Revlon.

In response, Logisticon stated that there were no viruses in Revlon's computer system and that Logisticon has no plans to have any further contact with Revlon. A sworn statement by Logisticon's product manager reveals that Revlon owed Logisticon $175,080, and that Logisticon disabled Revlon's system so that it would not function until payment was made. The product manager also admitted that Logisticon had entered Revlon's system by a remote access modem, and that the encoding of a file in Revlon's system, not a virus, rendered the system inoperable.

While Logisticon's actions brought smiles to the faces of many who look upon this situation in David versus Goliath terms, the fact is that Logisticon's actions have only brought it an extremely expensive lawsuit. Logisticon's legal fees alone may be more than Logisticon could ever have hoped to have received from Revlon. Further, Logisticon has to confront the prospect of paying enormous sums of damages to Revlon. In hindsight, the best that can be said is that the tactics used by Logisticon were counterproductive. Who will ever do business with a company that thinks it is ethical (not to mention legal) to shut down its own client's business for a few days over a simple contract dispute.

14

A Context: Legal Developments Late 1990 to Early 1996 [508]

Late 1990

- Operation Sun Devil, which involved raids on "hackers" in fourteen cities and the seizure of forty-two computers and thousands of disks, raised fears of a McCarthy-style witch hunt. In response, Mitchell Kapor and Stephen Wozniac started the Electronic Frontier Foundation to defend the civil liberties of computer users. That foundation has also provided funds to a Palo Alto group, Computer Professionals for Social Responsibility, to aid in its similar efforts.

- One individual targeted by Operation Sun Devil was indicted and tried for allegedly publishing classified phone company information relating to "911" (emergency response) computers. The criminal prosecution was suddenly halted, however, when the prosecutor discovered that the supposedly classified information is disseminated by the phone company's own customer relations department.

- Epson was sued by three former employees for invasion of privacy. The suit is novel because it alleges that Epson illegally tapped its employees' e-mail.

- Congress enacted a law banning the rental of computer software other than video game cartridges.

- Prodigy Services Co. offered to reinstate a dozen subscribers who were cut off for protesting Prodigy's decision to charge fees for electronic mail, on the condition that the former subscribers agree to abide by certain guidelines.

- The National Security Agency blocked the export of an IBM coprocessor for its System 390 mainframe computers that encodes data based

---

[508] Sources include *New York Times*, *Wall Street Journal*, *San Jose Mercury News*, *Marin Independent Journal*, *Los Angeles Times*, The [San Francisco] *Recorder*, *San Francisco Chronicle*, and *Financial Times*.

on the Data Encryption Standard (D.E.S.), and also blocked the export of an encryption system for personal computers also based on D.E.S. that is manufactured by Secures Communications Technologies.

■ In *Lasercomb America Inc. v. Reynolds and Holiday Steel*, the 4th Circuit Court of Appeals held that the owner of a computer program cannot enforce its registered copyright against an admitted copier if the owner has a software license agreement that includes terms preventing a licensee from using the *ideas* embodied in the software in its own independent expression of the program.

1991

■ Revlon, Inc. and Logisticon, Inc. settled the lawsuit filed by Revlon after Logisticon shut down two Revlon warehouses in October, 1990, by "repossessing" software in the middle of the night.

■ Apple Computer, Inc. asked the FCC to set aside radio frequencies to allow personal computers to receive and transmit data without wires.

■ Steve Jackson Games, Inc. filed suit in Austin, Texas, against the Secret Service, two of its agents, and an assistant U.S. attorney, seeking unspecified monetary damages and return of equipment and materials (including a computer bulletin board containing private mail) seized by the Secret Service on March 1, 1990, as part of Operation Sun Devil. The lawsuit is being funded by the Electronic Frontier Foundation, an organization founded by Mitchell D. Kapor to support civil liberties for computer users. The Secret Service raid on Steve Jackson Games, Inc. did not result in the filing of any charges. Computer Professionals for Social Responsibility (based in Palo Alto, California) also filed suit, alleging that the Secret Service failed to respond to a Freedom of Information Act request filed in September 1990 requesting documents concerning Operation Sun Devil.

■ Restrictions on the export of software are to be tightened in the wake of the Persian Gulf war. The Coordinating Committee for Multilateral Export Controls (COCOM) is to formalize new controls on, among other things, software that makes computer networks reliable and resistant to attack by rerouting messages automatically after any single link has been destroyed.

■ The U.S. Supreme Court held, in *Feist Publications v. Rural Telephone Service*, that an alphabetical listing of names and addresses in the white pages of a telephone directory is not entitled to copyright protection. An important aspect of the Court's ruling was its rejection of the "sweat of the brow" doctrine. Under this doctrine, it was argued that a publisher's efforts and investment was sufficient to entitle a work to copyright protection.

- The European Community proposed a set of rules to restrict how computerized information, such as medical records, insurance records, and airline reservation records, can be used by businesses and governments. The proposals, known as the Privacy Directive, are intended to make privacy laws uniform within the European Community and to restrict the flow of information to countries without strict privacy laws. The Directive requires, among other things, the approval of the individual concerned before information about him or her could be collected, processed, or transferred. The directive also would require the registration of all databases containing personal information.

- Prodigy users sued the online service for defrauding subscribers by charging twenty-five cents for each message over thirty messages sent per month. In April 1991, these new charges brought Prodigy under investigation by the consumer protection division of the L.A. County district attorney's office.

- Prodigy discovered that a quirk in its software allowed Prodigy employees to view stray snips of private user files.

- A federal court judge held that the "386" designation used by Intel Corp. is a *generic* description not entitled to trademark protection.

- AT&T warned a number of computer makers and software publishers that they are infringing a 1985 Bell Laboratories patent that covers basic software technology for running several programs simultaneously on a computer screen.

- Leonard Rose, Jr., of Middletown, Maryland, once a member of the group of hackers called the Legion of Doom, pleaded guilty to wire fraud in connection with his efforts to illegally obtain information to permit him secretly to modify an AT&T Unix software program, in order to allow access to Unix programs and to gather passwords. Authorities learned of Rose's efforts during the Secret Service's computer crime investigation named "Operation Sun Devil."

- Kevin Lee Poulson, also known as "Dark Dante," was arrested by the FBI and charged with eighteen counts of telecommunications and computer fraud. Authorities allege that Poulson stole Pacific Bell equipment and access codes to penetrate an Army computer network called MASNET, listen to a girlfriend's phone calls, and listen to FBI agents investigating Ferdinand Marcos.

■ Robert E. Gilligan, a programmer at Sun Microsystems, Inc., charged under a 1986 computer crime law, admitted to obtaining a phone company directory that included codes for free calling, free computer time, and confidential customer information. Gilligan, charged along with Kevin Lee Poulsen and Mark K. Lotter with a conspiracy to engage in high-tech eavesdropping, was sentenced to three years probation and ordered to pay $25,000 restitution to Pacific Bell.

■ Federal district court judge Harold Green issued an order allowing regional Bell telephone companies to enter the information services market.

■ Leonard Rose, Jr., having pleaded guilty to charges of transmitting AT&T software to friends, was sentenced to a year and a day in prison for wire fraud. Rose modified Unix software to allow the collection of identification codes and passwords of legitimate Unix users. As part of his sentence, Rose agreed to sell his computers.

■ A data encryption program written by Colorado programmer Phil Zimmerman, who protests government attempts to force data security systems made in the U.S. to include "trap doors" that would allow access to government agencies, has been sent to computer networks around the country. Zimmerman's program uses a patented method called the Rivest-Shamir-Adelman cryptosystem (a "public key" cryptographic system), sold by RSA Data Security. Zimmerman has advised anyone using it to first obtain a license from RSA.

■ Sun Microsystems and Microsoft Corp. agreed to license computer security techniques from RSA Data Security. Other RSA licensees include Digital Equipment, Lotus Development, and Novell. The National Institute of Standards and Technology, however, has selected a different technique (the "El Gamal" method) as the basis for a new standard for the government's nonsecret computer data.

■ Mitsubishi International is suing AT&T as a result of infiltration of a phone system by hackers. The hackers allegedly made 30,000 calls, and Mitsubishi is seeking dismissal of the $430,000 phone bill they ran up and $10 million in punitive damages. Mitsubishi alleges that AT&T failed to provide a secure phone system or to warn of the potential for unauthorized use.

■ Thrifty Tel, based in Garden Grove, California, is a long-distance carrier that has a special rate for hackers. Unauthorized users of its long-distance lines are charged a $3,000 "set-up" fee, a $3,000 daily line fee, and $200 for labor and the cost of prosecuting offenders. The charges were approved by the California Public Utilities Commission.

■ Federal district court judge Fern Smith ruled in favor of Lewis Galoob Toys, Inc. in a suit brought by Nintendo for copyright infringement. The ruling will allow Galoob to resume manufacture and sale of Game Genie, a device that plugs into Nintendo game cartridges and permits the user to electronically alter the games.

■ The California Assembly passed a bill allowing state transportation authorities to use state-supplied funds to help employers set up telecommuting programs. Los Angeles County already has such a program.

■ Equifax, Inc., the credit-reporting giant, announced that it will no longer sell to junk-mailers target lists drawn from confidential credit files. This move was apparently in reaction to public concern "that electronic databases of sensitive information are used in ways that threaten personal privacy."

■ The Department of Defense proposed new controls on the export of workstations, costing as little as $20,000, that can have military uses. The new controls "would require hardware and software changes that would restrict the applications that could run on inexpensive engineering work stations, audit all programs run on the machines, and limit their ability to connect to computer networks. Government officials are apparently concerned that the workstations could be "chained together to run some weapons design software at supercomputer speeds."

■ An Australian court ordered a twenty-year-old hacker to stand trial on charges of breaking into U.S. computer systems (including that of the Lawrence Livermore National Laboratory) by telephone and altering or deleting data, and for allegedly shutting down a NASA network for twenty-four hours.

■ Two California companies, Zack Electronics and Data Processing and Accounting Services, have filed a lawsuit to overturn San Francisco's Video Display Terminal ordinance. The companies allege that only the state of California, not individual cities or counties, have the right to pass laws concerning worker safety. The companies also complain that the law puts them at a competitive disadvantage with businesses in other parts of the state.

■ Unix System Laboratories of Summit, New Jersey, invited security experts and hackers to try to break into its computer operating system.

■ A federal appeals court gave the seven Bell telephone companies permission to provide information services. Under the antitrust consent decree that broke up AT&T in 1984, the seven companies, known as the "Baby Bells," were barred from owning information services, manufacturing equipment, and providing long-distance service.

■ The Anti-Defamation League of B'Nai Brith charged that Prodigy Services Company allowed its electronic bulletin board to be used to spread anti-Semitism.

■ A federal appeals court in Manhattan ruled that listings in yellow-page telephone directories can be copied by competitors as long as changes are made in the organization of the material. Earlier this year, the United States Supreme Court ruled that white-page telephone directory listings of names and telephone numbers are not protectable under copyright law, for the reason that copyright law does not protect facts.

■ The United States Supreme Court refused to review Robert Morris's conviction for sending a "worm" through the INTERNET computer network.

■ Apple Computer, Inc. and Apple Corps, the holding company for the Beatles, settled Apple Corps's lawsuit relating to the use of the Apple name.

■ The Supreme Court denied a request to block a ruling by a federal appeals court allowing regional Bell telephone companies to enter the news, computer data, and information businesses.

■ Two former employees of Mentor Graphics, in San Jose, California, filed a lawsuit claiming a privacy right concerning electronic mail. One of the former employees alleges that Mentor used records of his electronic mail to justify its claim that he was stealing trade secrets.

■ A federal judge ruled that CompuServe Information Service is insulated from liability in a libel suit based on material in an independent newsletter distributed on CompuServe's network. The judge found, among other things, that CompuServe neither knew nor had reason to know what was in the newsletter.

■ Federal auditors informed the Senate Governmental Affairs Committee that a group of Dutch teenagers was able to tap into sensitive information in Defense Department computers using the simplest of hacking techniques. One of the systems that had been penetrated directly supported Operation Desert Storm.

■ A nonprofit IBM-MCI venture, known as Advanced Network and Services, which manages a computer network called NSFnet, has come under fire from critics who claim that the government has given it unfair control over access to the network. NSFnet connects hundreds of research centers and universities, and manages links to foreign countries. Together, these networks are known as the Internet.

1992

- A California administrative law judge recommended that Caller ID, as proposed by Pacific Bell, GTE-California, and Contel, not be authorized. The judge found that Caller ID would constitute an unwarranted invasion into customers' privacy.

- A coalition of businesses, including IBM, have given support to two small San Francisco businesses that are seeking to overturn San Francisco's Video Display Terminal Ordinance on the grounds that only the state, not individual cities or counties, have the right to pass worker safety laws.

- The government proposed legislation requiring telephone companies to provide help with law-enforcement agency telephone surveillance. Under the proposed legislation, the Federal Communications Commission would issue regulations requiring telephone companies to modify phone systems "if those systems impede the Government's ability to conduct lawful electronic surveillance."

- San Francisco's Video Display Terminal ordinance has been struck down. A San Francisco judge ruled that the city had intruded upon the state's jurisdiction in enacting the law, which aimed at regulating the purchase and use of video display terminals and workstations in private business.

- Logisticon Inc., the company that "repossessed" its inventory control software from Revlon during a dispute over contract payments, has laid off much of its staff and is negotiating with a buyer.

- In an article published by the *New York Times*, the director of the Federal Bureau of Investigation, William S. Sessions, says that the F.B.I. does not want "the new digital technology that is spreading across America to impair [wiretapping.]" Accordingly, the F.B.I. has proposed legislation that would compel the telecommunications and computer industry to accommodate the F.B.I.'s wiretapping needs.

- Novell Corp. has been sued for patent infringement by Roger E. Billings, who claims to hold a 1987 patent for a "Functionally Structured Distributed Data Processing System." Billings claims as his the overall idea of a file server feeding data to a group of desktop computers, and is seeking $672 million in royalties and damages.

- The U.S. District Court for the Northern District of California ruled unprotectable a large number of elements of the graphical user interface that is the basis of Apple Computer, Inc.'s lawsuit against Microsoft Corporation and Hewlett-Packard, Inc. The court stated that it will next, in May 1992, address the issue of whether the "look and feel" of the Apple work is not the necessary result of the grafting of unprotectable elements onto the "look and feel" of Windows 1.0, which was licensed to Microsoft by Apple. According to the court, if such a showing can be made by Apple, infringement may be found.[509]

■ The U.S. District Court for the Northern District of California issued a preliminary injunction against a small video-game maker that markets games compatible with the popular Genesis video-game console manufactured by Sega Enterprises, Ltd. In the court's ruling, it held that, "If the process of reverse engineering software entails the duplication of the copyrighted work and the recasting or transformation of the object code into a form more intelligible to humans, it may infringe upon the copyright owner's exclusive rights."[510]

■ The U.S. Department of Commerce said it will remove remaining export restrictions on certain products, ranging from semiconductor manufacturing equipment to sophisticated computers, to be sold in Western Europe, Australia, and Japan.

■ Police in San Diego, California, cracked a network of as many as 1,000 young computer hackers between the ages of fourteen and twenty-five who allegedly gained unlawful access to major computer networks, such as Telenet, Signet, and Sprintnet and were able to make fraudulent credit card purchases and break into confidential credit card files.

■ A scientist was convicted, fined $225,000, and sentenced to prison for two and one-half years and an additional four years probation for selling and exporting classified computer programs, known as the CONTAM system, used in "star wars" research and in satellites that detected Iraqi Scud missile launches during the Persian Gulf War. The scientist had sold the software to four Japanese companies and to U.S. Customs agents posing as South Africans.

■ A congressional report prepared by the Office of Technology Assessment warns that the quality, price, and availability of computer software are threatened by serious deficiencies in the copyright law and "institutional problems" in the Patent and Trademark Office.

■ AT&T announced that it will introduce a service for corporate customers called Net Protect, which will include increased surveillance to detect

---

[509] *Apple Computer, Inc. v. Microsoft Corp.*, Civil No. C-88-20149-VRW (N.D. Cal. April 14, 1992).
[510] *Sega Enters. v. Accolade, Inc.*, Civil No. C-91-3871 BAC (N.D. Cal. April 13, 1992)

unusual calling patterns. AT&T will monitor the destination of the calls, but will not listen in on them. AT&T also offers a related service, a computer program called Hacker Tracker, which will cost about $2,000.

■ The Federation of American Scientists obtained data from the Patent and Trademark Office showing that the number of secrecy orders imposed by that office under the 1951 Invention Secrecy Act increased steadily from 290 in 1979 to 774 in 1991; 5,893 secrecy orders were in effect in 1991. These secrecy orders block patents from being issued and may prohibit inventors from selling or licensing their inventions to anyone except the government. The orders may also prohibit the publication of information developed entirely by private individuals.

■ A federal judge in San Francisco dismissed Atari Corporation's suit against Nintendo Co. following a jury verdict that Nintendo did not deliberately seek to create a monopoly in home video games, although it did achieve one. Atari's suit centered around Nintendo's former practice of requiring private game developers to grant Nintendo exclusive rights to new games for two years in return for a license to use the Nintendo system. The jury found that Atari had suffered no harm as a result of this practice. Atari was ordered to pay Nintendo's legal costs, estimated to exceed $1 million.

■ The American Society of Magazine Photographers, Inc. will establish a copyright licensing agency for the purpose of licensing photographs for use in electronic media.

■ A federal circuit court of appeals in New York rejected the theory that the packaging of a new product is protected under copyright and trademark law while it is gaining consumer recognition.[511]

■ The United States Circuit Court of Appeals for the Second Circuit ruled, in a case between Computer Associates International Inc. and Altai Inc., that programs incorporating the structure of existing software do not violate copyrights in many cases.

■ The F.B.I. raided a computer bulletin board, called "Davy Jones Locker," in a Millbury, Massachusetts home. F.B.I. agents seized several computers, six modems, the program used to run the bulletin board, and a listing of users of the board. No arrests were made, but the Software Publishers Association (SPA) filed civil suit against the operator of the bulletin board, alleging violation of copyright laws. SPA alleges that the bulletin board contained more than two-hundred copyrighted programs.

---

[511] *Laureyssens v. Idea Group*, 964 F. 2d 131 (2d Cir. 1992)

- A federal judge ordered the consolidation in a single court of dozens of legal actions for repetitive-stress injuries, including carpal tunnel syndrome, a wrist disorder believed to be caused by the use of computer keyboards. The lawsuits allege improper design of data-processing equipment leading to injuries, and failure to warn workers. The companies affected by the ruling include Northern Telecom, Inc., Apple Computer, Inc., AT&T and NCR Corp., Eastman Kodak Co., and Wang Laboratories, Inc.

- The Computer Ethics Institute circulated for comment the following "Ten Commandments of Computer Ethics": I. Thou shalt not use a computer to harm other people; II. Thou shalt not interfere with other people's computer work; III. Thou shalt not snoop around in other people's computer files; IV. Thou shalt not use a computer to steal; V. Thou shalt not use a computer to bear false witness; VI. Thou shalt not copy or use proprietary software for which you have not paid; VII. Thou shalt not use other people's computer resources without authorization or proper compensation; VIII. Thou shalt not appropriate other people's intellectual output; IX. Thou shalt think about the social consequences of the program you are writing or the system you are designing; X. Thou shalt always use a computer in ways that ensure consideration and respect for your fellow humans.

- A federal grand jury in New York indicted five young men, said to be members of a group called the "Masters of Deception," or "MOD." They are charged with computer tampering, computer fraud, wire fraud, illegal wiretapping, conspiracy, and breaking federal privacy laws. The accused allegedly targeted computer systems at phone companies, credit reporting services, and other companies and universities. Two accused allegedly destroyed most of the information on a computer system owned by WNET-TV in New York, and also allegedly sold credit reporting service account numbers and passwords to a New York man, who has pleaded guilty to using them to obtain at least 176 credit reports he sold to private investigators. Federal investigators, including agents from the Secret Service and the F.B.I., said they used court-approved wiretaps of computer data transfers, in analog form. The five men indicted use the names "Outlaw," "Corrupt," "Phiber Optik," "Acid Phreak," and "Scorpion."

- Equifax, Inc., one of the nation's three largest credit-reporting services, agreed to furnish credit reports to consumers within four days of receiving a complaint, investigate information disputed by consumers in thirty days, and ensure that the information it deletes does not reappear.

- Bellcore, the research arm of the regional phone companies, threatened legal action against *2600 Magazine: The Hacker Quarterly* for future publication of information that *2600* has reason to believe is "proprietary to Bellcore or has not been made publicly available by Bellcore," among other things. The editor of *2600* speculates that this threat resulted from an article in *2600* discussing a feature in the phone system called Busy Line Verification (BLV), which can be exploited by telephone networks and others to allow remote monitoring of telephone conversations.

- The Federal Communications Commission proposed setting aside a portion of the radio spectrum for "personal communication services" that would be carried on hand-held computers, among other things.

- A former technical writer at Sun Microsystems, Inc. filed a lawsuit, alleging that he was fired by Sun after sending a series of e-mail messages using his terminal at Sun, including what he describes as "some very, extremely nasty stuff" on a bulletin board used primarily to exchange sarcastic insults and vitriolic humor. The former employee says he would take whatever position was unpopular on bulletin boards, and claims that Sun violated his right to free expression.

- U.S. district court judge Vaughn Walker dismissed most of Apple Computer, Inc.'s lawsuit against Microsoft Corporation and Hewlett-Packard Corporation.

- The National Security Agency eased restrictions on exports of encrypted software and agreed to notify software producers within seven days as to whether a particular product is exportable.

- The U.S. 9th Circuit Court of Appeals lifted an injunction issued against Accolade, Inc. that prohibited it from developing or selling certain video games for consoles manufactured by Sega Enterprises Ltd. The injunction was issued by a lower court after ruling that Accolade had violated Sega copyrights by reverse engineering parts of the Sega console to determine how to open an electronic lock designed to allow only Sega-licensed games to work on its consoles.

- Borland International Inc. filed suit against Symantec Corp., its chairman, and a former Borland executive for allegedly pirating Borland trade secrets. Borland alleges that a former Borland executive, who was vice president and general manger of its programming language business unit, transferred confidential company information at the behest of Symantec and its chairman in the days before the executive left Borland for a similar high-level position at Symantec. Some of the information was allegedly transferred via the executive's company-sponsored account on MCI Mail, and Borland read the messages when it attempted to close the account. Borland also alleged that a former secretary, who resigned with the executive to go with him to Symantec, returned to Borland twice to steal trade secrets and pass them to Symantec. Scotts Valley, California, police are conducting a criminal investigation into the alleged theft.

■ Computer Professionals for Social Responsibility filed suit against the F.B.I., seeking information about reasons for the F.B.I.'s digital telephony proposal that the F.B.I. failed to make public.

■ Logitech Inc., a manufacturer of computer mice and hand-held scanners in Fremont, California, reports that telephone crackers entered its voice-mail system, erased customer messages, and left rude greetings for incoming callers. Logitech is now requiring its employees to select passwords that are longer than the four-digit length of a phone extension and to change them every ninety days.

■ Congress passed a law, now awaiting President Bush's signature, that makes software piracy a felony. According to the law, a person who for commercial profit makes at least ten illegal copies of a computer program or makes copies worth at least $2,500 at retail has committed a felony. A first offense may bring five years in prison and a $250,000 fine; repeat offenses can bring a ten-year sentence.

■ A federal appeals court ruled that in certain circumstances the Copyright Act permits reverse engineering of a copyrighted computer program in order to gain an understanding of the unprotected functional elements of the program. According to the appeals court, "disassembly of copyrighted object code is, as a matter of law, a fair use of the copyrighted work if such disassembly provides the only means of access to those elements of the code that are not protected by copyright and the copier has a legitimate reason for seeking such access." [512]

■ The director of the International Communications Association, a nonprofit group, requested that the government help telephone companies to develop phone systems that are less susceptible to piracy. Lawrence Gessini, testifying before the Federal Communications Commission, said that a survey of association members revealed 550 cases in the past three years of hackers breaking into company lines to make long-distance calls worth more than $73.5 million.

■ The National Security Agency declassified a four-volume book on military code-breaking published during World War II and written by a founder of NSA, Lieut. Col. William F. Friedman. The declassification follows a Freedom of Information Act request by a California cryptographer, John Gilmore, and the filing of a lawsuit after the government failed to respond to

---

[512] *Sega Enters. v. Accolade, Inc.*, No. 92-15655 (9th Cir. Oct. 20, 1992).

that request. Gilmore is still contesting the government's refusal to release the third volume of a later work by Friedman and a student, Lambros D. Callimahos, titled "Military Cryptanalytics." Gilmore would like more to be known about code-breaking so that it will be easier to design codes that will protect personal privacy in the "electronic information age."

- The U.S. attorney in Seattle, Washington, accused a twenty-one-year-old local resident and a nineteen-year-old student at the University of Washington of conspiracy to defraud the government. The charges are based on the alleged use of a home computer to break into data systems at a federal court and at the Boeing Company. According to the federal agent in charge of the investigation, the two accused were "network navigating." These charges follow their conviction for theft of a variety of computer equipment belonging to the University of Washington.

- A federal judge issued a temporary restraining order preventing the Bush White House from destroying computer records, including copies of electronic mail. This action came in response to a suit by the National Security Archive (a private organization), the American Library Association, and the American Historical Association, who argue that the Bush administration does not have adequate guidelines for federal employees to decide which records must be saved.

- The Fifth U.S. Circuit Court of Appeals ruled in a criminal case that a cordless phone user may have a privacy right in his conversation if such user can show that he held a reasonable expectation of privacy. In the case at issue, however, the court upheld the conviction of a Texas man on drug trafficking charges, caught because of cordless-phone conversations tapped into and recorded by his neighbor, since the accused had introduced no evidence on the issue—such as his phone's frequency or range.

- Under FCC rules implementing the Telephone Consumer Protection Act of 1990, which go into effect in December 1992, telemarketers using autodialers are required to make it easier for consumers who object to unsolicited calls to sign up for "do not call" lists. Autodialers are also barred from calling emergency lines, cellular telephones, pagers, or other numbers for which the called party may be charged. The rules also bar recorded messages from use in unsolicited advertisements.

- In a lawsuit concerning whether the copyright to software written on the job by a freelance computer programmer is owned by the programmer or the business for which it was written, the U.S. Court of Appeals for the Second Circuit held that among the most important factors to be weighed are whether the business paid health benefits and Social Security taxes on behalf of the programmer, and the level of expertise involved in writing the program.

- VPL Research, Inc., one of the U.S. leaders in the field of virtual reality, lost basic virtual reality patents to France's Thompson CSF SA. Thompson gained the rights to the patents after VPL failed to repay a series of loans totaling about $1 million; the patents had been pledged as collateral for the loans.

- Kevin Lee Poulsen has been charged with violating a federal espionage law prohibiting the gathering of classified military secrets. There has been no allegation that Poulson intended to distribute the information to any foreign power. Poulson has previously been charged with a number of crimes, and it is alleged that he broke into telephone company offices and penetrated phone company computers, among other things.

- California utility companies have reportedly been voluntarily giving police confidential personal information about consumers. Information disclosed by the utilities includes electricity and gas use figures, as well as Social Security numbers, places of employment, driver's license numbers, and other information provided by consumers to utilities. In some instances, the utilities agreed to tap consumer utility lines to gather evidence on suspected drug labs.

- Two young members of a group known as the "Masters of Deception," Julio Fernandez and John Lee, have pleaded guilty to conspiring to possess or use unauthorized access devices to affect the operation of computer systems involved in interstate commerce. Members of the Masters of Deception allegedly broke into corporate and university computer systems. The two face up to five years in prison and a $250,000 fine.

- Federal Trade Commission staff attorneys reportedly suggested that the FTC seek a preliminary injunction against Microsoft Corp.

- Bell Atlantic Corp., a regional Bell company, filed suit claiming that its right to free speech is violated by the Cable Act of 1984, which prohibits a telephone company from owning a cable television system in a city where it provides phone service. Bell Atlantic is seeking to build an advanced communications network in Alexandria, Virginia, that would provide hundreds of channels of television over fiber-optic lines, as well as new two-way communication services.

1993

- The Federal Trade Commission moved to stop two of the largest credit-reporting companies (TRW Inc. and Trans Union Corp.) from using confidential financial data to create target lists for junk mailers. TRW agreed to stop using credit data in its mailing-list business, but Trans Union did not.

The FTC has issued a complaint against Trans Union for violation of the 1970 Fair Credit Reporting Act.

■ The U.S. Court of Appeals for the District of Columbia allowed the Bush Administration to erase White House and National Security Council computer files so long as it preserved identical electronic copies of what was deleted. Previously, a federal district court judge ruled that electronic mail on those computer systems is protected under the Federal Records Act and could not be immediately destroyed. The rulings are the result of a lawsuit filed in 1989 by Public Citizen, a Ralph Nader group.

■ The General Services Administration released a May 1992 criticism of the F.B.I.'s Digital Telephony proposal, in which it called the proposed legislation unnecessary. The intent of the proposal is to make the nation's telephone lines easier to wiretap. According to the G.S.A., the proposal could hurt the nation's competitiveness in the international trade arena, and could pose a possible danger to national security. The document was obtained under a Freedom of Information Act request filed by Computer Professionals for Social Responsibility.

■ A Florida widower, David Reynard, appearing on the CNN talk show "Larry King Live," alleged that the brain tumor that killed his wife was caused by the emission of radio waves from the pocket cellular phone that she often held to her ear. Reynard has filed suit against NEC Corp., which made the phone, and a GTE subsidiary that provided the service. McCaw Cellular Communications Inc., the nation's largest cellular phone service company, is commissioning a study on how cellular phone antennas affect users' exposure to radio waves.

■ An indictment for a felony count of trafficking in counterfeit goods and two misdemeanor counts of violating copyright law have been issued against two men who lost a 1991 lawsuit brought by Microsoft Corp. for selling bootleg copies of the MS-DOS operating system. The two face only misdemeanor charges for copyright infringement because the alleged acts occurred prior to the passage of a law last year that increases the penalty for certain first-time offenses to a felony, with a five-year prison sentence and a $250,000 fine.

■ A forty-four-year-old Campbell, California, man has been arrested for allegedly distributing adult and child pornography to young boys by means of a "compu-sex" computer bulletin board, then trying to murder the fifteen-year-old boy who turned him in to police.

■ The F.B.I. is reportedly seeking to revive its proposed legislation on digital telephony, which has been widely criticized as an attempt to dumb down advances in telecommunication systems so that law enforcement will have an easier time intercepting and reading messages sent over those systems.

■ The chairman of the House Subcommittee on Telecommunications and Finance, Sen. Edward J. Markey, warned computer industry officials that they need to participate more actively in the development of federal standards regarding the establishment of a national "data superhighway," or risk falling victim to other interests and suffer restricted access to the proposed network.

■ The U.S. Patent & Trademark Office issued a preliminary determination denying Microsoft Corp. a trademark for the word "Windows," which the government considers to be a generic term in the computer industry in use long before Microsoft introduced its product in 1983.

■ The Federal Trade Commission, having received a report by the commission's Bureau of Competition recommending that the commission seek an injunction against Microsoft Corp., rejected that recommendation by a 2–2 vote and deferred taking action against Microsoft. Microsoft has been accused by its rivals of unfair competition relating to its licensing practices and other tactics. One principal complaint concerns the fact that Microsoft offers a sixty percent discount on its MS-DOS operating system to computer manufacturers who agree to pay a fee based on every computer they sell. Another complaint is that Microsoft creates built-in incompatibility in its software, allowing its Windows program only to be compatible with MS-DOS.

■ A municipal court judge in Santa Clara County, California, ruled that a cable company cannot collect fines from customers it suspects of pirating premium programs unless the individual customers are first found guilty in a criminal proceeding.

■ Southwestern Bell Corp., which provides phone service in Southwestern states, agreed to buy two cable television systems in the Washington D.C. area. This will be the first acquisition of a cable system by a telephone company. Southwestern Bell already owns a cellular telephone franchise in the Washington area.

■ The U.S. Second Circuit Court of Appeals reversed itself, upon a motion for reconsideration by Computer Associates International Inc., and ruled that the Copyright Act does not preempt a cause of action based on state common law trade secret rights if that cause of action contains elements of proof additional to or qualitatively different from those required to prove copyright infringement. In the Computer Associates action, an alleged breach of a duty of confidentiality under state law foreclosed preemption.[513]

---

[513] *Computer Assocs. Intern'l v. Altai, Inc.*, Nos. 91-7893, 91-7935 (2d Cir. December 18, 1992.

■ A federal court in Austin, Texas, ruled that the United States Secret Service violated the Privacy Protection Act of 1980 and the Electronic Communications Privacy Act of 1986 in its raid against Steve Jackson Games, a role-playing games publisher, by seizing an electronic bulletin board, electronic mail, and computer records, and by reading, disclosing, and erasing messages on the bulletin board it seized. The court ordered the Secret Service to pay the company $50,000, and noted that there never was any basis for suspecting that the company or its owner, Steve Jackson, had broken any laws. The raid on Steve Jackson Games was part of a nationwide crackdown on computer hackers, and nearly put the company out of business, but no one at Steve Jackson Games was ever arrested or accused of a crime, and no charges were filed.

■ The chairman and chief executive officer of Symantec Corp., Gordon E. Eubanks, Jr., and a vice president who resigned from Borland International Inc. to go to Symantec, Eugene Wang, have been indicted for alleged theft of trade secrets from Borland. Both men have stated that they are innocent and have pleaded not guilty.

■ Two computer hackers, Paul Stira (known as "Scorpion") and Elias Ladoupoulos (known as "Acid Phreak"), both twenty-three years old, pleaded guilty to breaking into computer systems operated by telephone companies and credit-reporting agencies. They face maximum prison terms of five years and fines of $250,000. According to prosecutors, their case marked the first one in which court-authorized wiretaps had been used to obtain conversations and data transmissions of computer hackers.

■ An FBI official stated that the agency will not back off its effort to obtain legislation that would force computerized telephone and communication systems to be vulnerable to wiretaps, and said that the agency expects a proposal to be introduced in Congress by the summer.

■ A subscriber to the Prodigy information service, Peter DeNigris, has been sued by a small New Jersey company, Medphone, which alleges that comments by DeNigris posted on Prodigy helped cause a sixty percent decline in Medphone's stock. Among other things, DeNigris's posting allegedly stated his opinion that the company was having a "difficult time" and would probably "cease operations soon."

■ The Clinton administration called for a program to require applicants for new radio frequency allocations to outbid competing applicants.

■ Teleport Communications Group of Staten Island complained to the Federal Communications Commission that local carriers are seeking to impede competition in local telephone service by charging exorbitant connection rates. Last year, the FCC voted to encourage competition in local telephone service by allowing smaller communications companies to connect directly to the nation's local phone network and thereby cut their costs.

■ The chief executives of AT&T, MCI Communications, Sprint, each of the seven regional Bell companies, and major independent local telephone companies released a statement calling on President Clinton to let private companies build and manage most of the proposed national high-speed fiber-optic network.

■ Law enforcement officials served thirty-one search warrants in fifteen states in the course of an investigation into child pornography. The officials seized equipment allegedly used to transmit Danish-generated porn on computer bulletin boards.

■ The Ninth Circuit Court of Appeals ruled that an independent service provider violated copyright laws by loading operating software licensed to its client into the random access memory of its client's computer in the course of fixing the computer.[514]

■ The White House announced the development of a computer chip, called the "Clipper Chip," that encodes voice and data transmissions using a secret algorithm. The chip is to work with an 80-bit, split key escrow system. Two escrow agents would each hold 40-bit segments of a user's key, which would be released to law enforcement agents upon presentation of a valid warrant or other lawful authority. After the announcement, several groups expressed concern that, among other things, the algorithm used cannot be trusted unless it is public and open to testing.

■ The CIA warned U.S. high-tech companies that the French government may be spying on them.

■ Kevin Poulsen, a hacker already scheduled to be tried on fourteen federal felonies, has been indicted on nineteen more felony counts in which he is accused of using telephone and computer skills to ensure that he and two alleged accomplices would win radio station call-in contests. Prizes in those contest included a pair of Porsche cars and more than $20,000 in cash.

■ InterDigital Communications Corp. filed suit for patent infringement against Oki Electric Industry Co., of Tokyo. The suit concerns a data communication technique called code division multiple access (CDMA), developed by a San Diego–based company, and CDMA-based phones that Oki plans to manufacture, among other things. InterDigital holds many patents on a rival technique called time division multiple access, used by several cellular phone companies.

---

[514] *MAI Sys. Corp. v. Peak Computer*, 991 F.2d 511 (9th Cir. April 9, 1993), *cert. denicd.*, 114 S. ct. 671 (1994).

■ Twenty Japanese telecommunications companies announced that they will join Motorola's Iridium project, a planned digital cellular telephone network linked by sixty-six orbiting satellites.

■ The nation's local phone companies offered to build the "information superhighway" promoted by Vice President Al Gore if they are allowed to go back into the long-distance phone business, to manufacture equipment, and to provide video programming over phone lines.

■ High-tech thieves installed a bogus ATM machine in a shopping mall in Connecticut, using it to record the card numbers and personal identification numbers (PINs) of hundreds of customers that sought to use the machine. Using counterfeit cards and the stolen numbers, the thieves later took at least $50,000 from an ATM network in New York. In an earlier case in Brooklyn, New York, thieves used a video camera to record PINs and match them with discarded receipts.

■ The copyright infringement case brought by Apple Computer, Inc. against Microsoft Corp. and Hewlett-Packard Corp. was removed from the court's trial calendar after the court narrowed the case to whether the appearance of Microsoft's Windows program is virtually identical to that of Apple's Lisa, the predecessor to the Macintosh.

■ A federal appeals court ruled that regional Bell telephone companies are allowed to own information services and to offer them over their phone lines.

■ A federal court ruled that the Telephone Consumer Protection Act's ban on automated calls to deliver prerecorded commercial messages is unconstitutional, violating the First Amendment guarantee of free speech.

■ The Digital Privacy and Security Working Group, a coalition of computer and communications companies and consumer and privacy advocacy groups, presented to White House officials and key members of Congress detailed technical and civil liberties questions about the Clipper Chip and the government's policy regarding the encryption of digital communications. The twenty-eight-member Computer and Business Equipment Manufacturers Association also issued a statement criticizing the economic viability of the Clipper Chip proposal, saying it would effectively handicap American computer and telecommunications equipment makers overseas.

■ A federal court cited the White House and the acting archivist of the United States for civil contempt for failure to protect and preserve the computer records of the Bush and Clinton Administrations. Fines starting at $50,000 and rising to $200,000 a day will last until the Administration takes action to preserve those records.

- The nation's largest computer companies, advocating a "progressive scanning" system for high-definition television, warned the Federal Communications Commission that they would develop a separate standard if the government endorsed the interlaced systems favored by broadcasters.

- Accolade, Inc. and Sega of America, Inc. settled out of court a legal action that looked to whether companies may reverse engineer each other's software.

- A federal court ruled that Atari Games infringed a copyright and patent by copying and using software codes built into Nintendo of America games.

- Apple Computer, Inc. conceded the few remaining points in its copyright suit against Microsoft Corp. and Hewlett-Packard Co. so that Apple might hasten its appeal of rulings in the case that, among other things, treat the graphical user interface of the Macintosh computer as a purely functional arrangement.

- Two computer hackers, Charles Anderson and Costa George Katsaniotis, who illegally entered computers at Boeing Corp. and a U.S. district court, have each been sentenced to five years probation and 250 hours of community service and also have been ordered to pay a combined $30,000 in restitution. In addition, the two residents of Seattle, Washington, are barred from owning computers or holding computer accounts without the permission of their probation officer.

- A Commerce Department advisory committee, the Computer System Security and Privacy Advisory Board, raised serious concerns about the Clinton Administration plan to standardize a high-technology coding system that would allow law enforcement officials to tap telephone calls and computer data transmissions. The advisory committee called for extensive public hearings and urges that the new technology, known as the "Clipper Chip," not be deployed until after the public review is completed.

- The Federal Communications Commission set aside a portion of the public airwaves to be divided into eleven channels for use by a new type of two-way communications network that will operate with wireless computers. Mobile Telecommunications Technologies Corp. of Jackson, Mississippi, has been granted a "pioneer's preference" by the FCC, which will allow it a license when the FCC develops licensing procedures for other companies interested in the business.

- According to unconfirmed reports, the Federal Trade Commission (FTC) will take up the investigation of Microsoft Corp. at its July 21 meeting. The FTC has been "informally" investigating whether Microsoft enjoys an unfair advantage in selling applications programs because it also designs and sells the operating systems that competing software programmers need to make their applications work.

- Mark Abene, also known as Phiber Optik, pleaded guilty in New York to charges that he was part of a group that broke into telephone and credit reporting service company computers.

- Sun Microsystems Inc. shut down all modems attached to its computer network to block a hacker who appeared to be seeking the program code for Solaris, the latest version of the operating system for Sun workstations.

- Federal officials announced the arrest of two men suspected of installing a bogus bank teller machine in a Connecticut shopping mall and using customer codes acquired through the machine to raid customers' accounts. They have been charged with credit card fraud, wire fraud, interstate transportation of stolen property, and conspiracy to commit a felony. If convicted, they face prison terms ranging from ten to thirty years on each charge and fines in excess of $250,000.

- Digital Equipment Co. pulled two computers off the Internet out of concern that foreigners could connect to them from abroad and illegally export data. The computers were later reconnected, but access to the system is now limited to persons who are screened by the company. Last year, Digital shut down a computer bulletin board featuring access to programs for encoding computer data, the export of which would violate federal regulations. In 1991, Digital was fined $2.4 million by the Commerce Department for violations of export laws.

- The Federal Trade Commission again deadlocked on whether to charge Microsoft Corp. with engaging in anti-competitive business practices. The Justice Department decided, however, to review complaints of anti-competitive practices made against Microsoft.

- Gregory Steshenko, who says that he fled the former Soviet Union for the freedom of the West, claims that he was fired from his position at Microsoft Corp. because he spread his political views on Russia and neighboring countries over the Internet.

- A federal jury found that Atari Games Corp. infringed a Nintendo patent on a lock-out system that bars game cartridges from working in the Nintendo system without its permission.

- The U.S. attorney's office in San Francisco announced the first indictments under the new federal felony copyright law. The indictments were issued in two cases in which it is alleged that the defendants made thousands of copies of Microsoft Corp.'s MS-DOS and Windows software.

■ Nearly 370 IRS employees have been investigated or disciplined for using government computers to create fraudulent tax returns or browse taxpayer accounts.

■ Two former police officers in San Jose, California, face sentencing after pleading no contest to felony conspiracy charges involving the sale of confidential "rap sheet" and driver information to a private investigator. Under California law, police officers are allowed to access criminal background information only for official investigations.

■ A federal court ruled unconstitutional a provision of the 1984 Cable Act banning phone companies from providing video services in areas in which they own monopoly phone systems. The decision, based on the First Amendment, would allow telephone companies to establish their own cable systems.

■ AT&T will acquire McCaw Cellular Communications, the nation's largest cellular telephone company.

■ The Justice Department's Antitrust Division is launching an investigation into complaints by software companies that Microsoft Corp. used its size, market practices, and product design to thwart competition. The investigation follows the closing of a Federal Trade Commission investigation of Microsoft.

■ A federal appeals court ruled that the government must save electronic mail and memoranda under the same standards used for paper communications. The case relates to efforts of the Bush administration to erase computer files containing electronic communications between officials during the Reagan presidency.

■ A California judge removed the Santa Cruz district attorney's office from a prosecution concerning alleged theft of Borland International, Inc. trade secrets by top executives of a competitor, Symantec Corp. According to the court, more than $13,000 of prosecution expenses had been paid by Borland. Independent attorneys state that the payments were not illegal, but gave the appearance of undue influence and impropriety. The California attorney general's office will take two weeks to review the case and decide how to proceed.

■ The tax bill passed by Congress includes a proposal to auction part of the nation's airwaves. The frequencies, about 340 million hertz of the radio frequency spectrum, will be used for personal communications services.

■ The Clinton administration is preparing to ease export restrictions on U.S. computer goods. Ashton Carter, assistant secretary of defense, said that the United States is talking with its allies about dissolving the Coordinating Committee for Multilateral Export Controls (COCOM), and "replacing it with a smaller, leaner regime."

■ A federal grand jury in San Jose, California, issued subpoenas to two software publishers selling versions of a software program named PGP (for Pretty Good Privacy), which is used to encrypt computer data. The grand jury investigation appears to focus on whether PGP has been exported in violation of State Department regulations that control the export of cryptographic software without a special munitions export license. The legitimacy of the export regulations in this case has been disputed, particularly by those who argue that they restrict freedom of expression guaranteed by the First Amendment. The companies receiving the subpoenas are Viacrypt, in Phoenix, Arizona, and Austin Code Works, in Austin, Texas.

■ Berkeley Systems, publisher of the After Dark screen saver program, filed a copyright and trademark infringement suit against Delrina Corp. The focus of the suit is a rival product by Delrina featuring a screen saver in which the cartoon character Opus the Penguin uses a shotgun to shoot down flying toasters, a popular image in the After Dark program. Delrina claims that its "Death Toasters" screen saver is a parody, but Berkeley Systems is not amused.

■ Administration officials informed congressional staff members that the two escrow agents for the Clipper plan will be officials of the Commerce Department's National Institute of Standards and Technology and of a non-law-enforcement section of the Treasury Department. The Clinton administration is promoting the Clipper plan, a national standard for encrypting data and voice communications, to discourage the use of highly capable encryption programs that the U.S. National Security Agency reportedly cannot pierce. Industry and civil liberties groups criticized the choice of escrow agents.

■ The Federal Communications Commission announced rules for an auction of blocks of radio spectrum for wireless communication services, more than three times the size of bands used by cellular services today. The first auctions will take place before June 1994.

■ President Clinton announced broad changes in U.S. trade policy that will scrap controls on certain computers and other technology products. Effective immediately, the U.S. will no longer restrict computers able to perform up to 194 million theoretical operations per second (MTOPS). Later, the U.S. will seek to have Western industrial allies raise the threshold to 500 MTOPS.

■ The Federal Trade Commission issued a rule requiring that merchandise ordered by phone, fax, and computer be shipped within thirty days or the time specified in an advertisement, and allowing consumers the option of canceling orders and receiving refunds for products that cannot be shipped promptly. The new regulation will not be effective until March 1994.

■ A Michigan jury rejected a suit filed against Nintendo, in which a woman claimed that a video adventure game gave her an epileptic seizure. The woman, who sought more than $10,000 in damages, argued that Nintendo should have warned of the danger of light-induced seizures.

■ Epitope Inc., based in Oregon, filed suit alleging that a Kansas City stockbroker short-selling its stock (hoping the price would fall) damaged the company by posting derogatory information about Epitope on the Prodigy computer network under a pseudonym.

■ The National Science Foundation is financing a project to make corporate filings with the Securities and Exchange Commission available over the Internet. This support signifies a shift in policy away from favoring the sale of government data by private companies.

■ Motorola Inc. asked the Federal Communications Commission to bar Comsat Corp. from the global satellite-phone market, on the grounds that the congressional act that established Comsat does not allow it to participate in satellite-phone systems. Motorola, which owns thirty-four percent of a consortium (Iridium Inc.) that is building a $3.4 billion satellite system, also alleges that the International Maritime Satellite Organization (Inmarsat), which plans to build a similar system and is twenty-five percent owned by Comsat, would have an unfair advantage over non-Inmarsat members in providing such a system.

■ Mark Abene (aka Phiber Optik), 21, was sentenced to one year and one day in prison after pleading guilty in federal court to one felony count of conspiracy for membership in a group of computer hackers named MOD, or Masters of Deception. Abene apologized for his deeds, noting that he was dismayed that they were misconstrued as malicious. According to prosecutors, only two members of MOD (John Lee and Julio Fernandez) made any money from their misdeeds—$800 from another hacker for phony information on how to break into the TRW system. Prosecutors state that MOD members obtained access to a number of computer networks, cheated phone companies and the Tymnet computer network out of hundreds of thousands of dollars worth of services, and obtained phone numbers and credit reports of celebrities, among other things.

■ Microsoft announced the first prison sentence of a convicted software pirate. Benny S. Lee of Freemont, California, began a one-year federal sentence after pleading guilty to a misdemeanor. A co-defendant received a six-month home-detention sentence. The case began when Microsoft sued Lee and others for selling 25,000 bootleg copies of MS-DOS, valued at $1.8 million. Lee and the co-defendant lost a civil case and were fined $5.3 million—Lee, however, was found liable by the jury for only $18,000 in damages. Both men declared bankruptcy and did not pay the fine. The matter was referred to the U.S. Attorney's Office, which filed criminal proceedings.

- Michael Lafaro, president of MJL Design, of New York, and one of MJL's technicians face up to seven years in jail and fines of $10,000 and $5,000, respectively, under a new New York state law for computer tampering. After a client became engaged in a payment dispute with MJL, the men allegedly infected the client's computer with a virus that would automatically shut down the business's access to information.

- Compton's New Media, of Carlsbad, California, announced that it received a patent (No. 5,241,671) that extends to virtually any database that uses more than just text to retrieve information, such as on-line services and interactive television. The patent holds that Compton's invented the "multimedia search system using a plurality of entry path means which indicate interrelatedness of information." Compton's also announced that it intends to collect royalties of as much as three percent from rival multimedia software makers.

- MFS Communications Inc. of Omaha, Nebraska, asked the Federal Communications Commission to end the current pricing system that subsidizes basic phone services at low prices even in hard-to-reach places. According to MFS, these subsidies have become an impediment to an open market. For example, regulators have blocked new competitors in California from offering intrastate long-distance service at a price much lower than Pacific Bell's, because Pacific Bell would have to replace artificially high prices for intercity connections by raising below-cost prices for basic services. MFS argues that the current system should be replaced with a system in which all companies in the market contribute to a pool used to underwrite low-income customers and people in hard-cost areas.

- A court declared valid a basic patent held by Spectrum Information Technologies Inc. covering key methods for sending computer data over cellular networks.

- The Business Software Alliance, which includes Microsoft, Lotus, and WordPerfect, endorsed the North American Free Trade Agreement and hailed its definition of software as "literary work" deserving the highest level of protection against copyright infringement.

- The United States government has written to protest a Japanese proposal that Japanese copyright law legalize "reverse engineering" (decompilation) of computer software.

- The National Writers Union will file suit in federal court against the country's largest newspapers and information services to determine whether writers should get paid when their stories are read or reproduced electronically.

- A former Anaheim, California, police employee pleaded guilty to disclosing to anti-abortion activists confidential state driving record information on four individuals. Three of the four individuals were employees of a family planning clinic, targeted for picketing by anti-abortion groups. The former police employee, Lisa Lorraine Villarreal, was sentenced to three years probation and two-hundred hours community service.

- The *Los Angeles Times* recalled a well-regarded journalist, Michael Hiltzik, from its Moscow bureau after he was caught reading other correspondents' electronic mail in a sting operation set up by the paper. Mr. Hiltzik was reassigned to a position in Los Angeles as a disciplinary action.

- According to the Secret Service, fifteen salespeople at a car dealership in New Jersey stole at least $285,000 after illegally gaining access to credit reports of individuals across the country and ordering credit cards, loans, and cash advances. At least forty-four victims have been identified, though the Secret Service states there may be hundreds more.

- The U.S. Patent & Trademark Office will reexamine a patent issued to Compton's New Media Inc. on a multimedia information retrieval system that would give Compton's rights to virtually all forms of interactive multimedia communication.

- The National Writers Union filed a copyright lawsuit against the *New York Times, Newsday, Time* magazine, Mead Data Central Corp. and University Microfilms International, claiming that they place writers' works on electronic databases and CD-ROMs without consent or payment of royalties.

- Two men were found guilty of using a fake automated teller machine at a Connecticut mall to take personal identification codes from dozens of customers and make counterfeit bank teller cards to obtain $107,460 from their accounts. Each defendant was sentenced to two and one-half years in federal prison and both were ordered to pay a total of $464,000 in restitution to victims of this scheme and of other crimes outside Connecticut.

■ Medphone Corp. settled its libel suit over downbeat postings about the company made by Peter DeNigris on a bulletin board run by the Prodigy computer service. Medphone had sued for $40 million, but each side agreed to exchange $1 and settle the dispute.

■ The Digital Privacy and Security Group, which includes some of the nation's largest computer makers and software publishers, announced that it may drop its opposition to the White House's Clipper proposal (a scheme that uses a special computer chip to encode digital information transmissions while guaranteeing the government the right to access the data) if the Clinton administration drops strict export regulations on sophisticated commercial cryptography technology and makes voluntary domestic adoption of the Clipper chip.

■ Berkeley Systems Inc. and Delrina Corp. settled a copyright and trademark infringement suit over a version of Delrina's "Opus 'n Bill" screen-saver program that parodied the "flying toaster" icon used in Berkeley's "After Dark" screen-saver.

■ The federal Government sued Suburban Cable TV Company and its parent, Lenfest Communications, alleging that the companies failed to pay royalty fees based on the total amount of income collected from viewers to whom they retransmit television programs. In the government's first lawsuit in a cable television royalty case, the companies are accused of mail fraud and making false statements to federal authorities.

1994

■ A California judge barred a former employee of a software manufacturer in Santa Cruz, California, from using the company's e-mail system to contact the company and its employees. The court's order does allow the former employee, a programmer, to contact company employees by ordinary mail.

■ A group of thirty-eight of the nation's leading computer scientists, computer-security specialists, and privacy experts sent a letter to President Clinton urging that the Clipper plan be stopped. The Clipper plan is a Clinton Administration attempt to establish a standard for encrypting electronic communication that allows a back-door means for law-enforcement eavesdropping. Computer hardware, software, and telecommunications companies as well as a major bank have announced that they intend to adopt an industry coding standard commercialized by RSA Data Security Inc., rather than support the Clipper plan. Apple Computer, Inc., I.B.M., Hewlett Packard Co., Sun Microsystems, Digital Equipment, and Unisys have all licensed RSA software.

■ Electronic Arts Productions Inc. and the American Federation of Television and Radio Artists announced the first contract for performers who talk and act in video and computer games. The contract sets a minimum salary of $485 for day performers.

■ Vice President Gore outlined a policy for the telecommunications industry that includes a new regulatory regime, universal service, and open access. Under the new regime, companies providing interactive services would be freed from previous regulatory burdens in exchange for giving information and entertainment providers the ability to offer their services over network distribution systems at fair, competitive prices.

■ Cable television companies drafted a plan creating a rating system for violence in broadcasts. The companies also plan to introduce a device to automatically block violent programs.

■ The Computer Emergency Response Team warned that unknown intruders planted software on computers throughout the Internet to steal passwords and electronic addresses. One major Internet service provider, Panix, reported that about three-hundred computers were compromised as a result of a security breach in its computer. Security experts said that all Internet users should immediately change their passwords and make a habit of doing so frequently. There has been speculation that the break-ins are connected to a handful of students known as the "Posse."

■ A couple in Milpitas, California, were arrested and charged with operating an alleged obscene computer bulletin board. They will be prosecuted in Tennessee, from where a computer hacker broke into the couple's sexually explicit bulletin board and then complained to Memphis authorities.

■ The Clinton Administration announced that it will proceed with its voluntary "Clipper Chip" program, which concerns a coding technology for computer and telephone equipment. Law enforcement officials will have access to electronic "keys"—held jointly by the Treasury Department and the National Institute of Standards & Technology—to unscramble the encrypted data. The announcement resulted in a storm of criticism from computer industry associations, lawmakers, and privacy advocates.

■ The Clinton administration is pressing for legislation to compel telephone and cable television companies to install software allowing law enforcement officials to eavesdrop on phone calls and computer transmissions. Industry executives believe that the initiative will cost as much as $300 million, to be paid with higher rates from consumers. Civil rights groups argue that the legislation is unnecessary and threatens privacy—allowing access to the "kind of movies we watch, what kind of commerce we engage in, what kind of political parties we want to communicate with. . . ." The legislation would allow the attorney general to seek fines of $10,000 per day for firms that do not provide access and in some cases, to shut them down.

- The Justice Department is investigating whether computer network companies linking automated teller machines have pressured banks to buy other services as a condition of joining the networks.

- The Clinton administration announced a proposal to rewrite the 1979 Export Administration Act. The Commerce Department also announced that it is relaxing restrictions on the sale abroad of high-speed mainframe computers, revising its definition of a supercomputer to one that can perform 1,500 million theoretical operations per second.

- The U.S. Supreme Court ruled in a case concerning 2 Live Crew and the Roy Orbison classic "Oh, Pretty Woman" that parodies are generally exempt from copyright suits under the doctrine of fair use, and overturned a lower court blanket conclusion that every commercial use of copyrighted material is an unfair exploitation of the copyrighted work.

- The director of the FBI warns that unless a new telecommunications bill proposed by the Clinton administration is passed, law enforcement will be crippled in pursuing wiretaps. The proposed legislation would require telephone companies to install software in new digital switching systems at a cost of between $300 and $500 million.

- The Clinton administration is ending virtually all export controls on the sale of civilian telecommunications equipment and computers (up to 1,000 millions of theoretical operations per second) to civilian companies in former communist countries, except those the State Department lists as supporting or abetting terrorism (e.g., Cuba, North Korea, Iran, Iraq, Syria, and Libya). Export restrictions on encryption products are continued.

- The National Archives released rules requiring the preservation of the most important e-mail messages sent throughout the government.

- An MIT science major, David LaMacchia, was indicted for allegedly transforming two MIT computers into electronic bulletin boards, called Cynosure I and Cynosure II, on which Internet users could place copies of commercial programs, allowing others to receive over $1 million of pirated software. The indictment does not say who made the software available. Under a law passed in 1992, it is a felony to make ten or more copies of a copyrighted program or to copy and distribute programs worth $2,500 or more.

- Suarez Corporation Industries, a direct-mail company, filed a defamation suit against Brock Meeks for criticizing a Suarez foray into online commerce in his electronic newsletter, named Cyberwire Dispatch.

■ RSA-129, a 129-digit number suggested seventeen years ago by inventors of a coding system said to be provably secure, was cracked by an international effort involving more than six-hundred Internet volunteers. At the time, it was thought it would take forty quadrillion years to factor it with the methods of the time and that no one would be able to break the code until well into the next century.

■ A warning to parents to beware with whom their children chat on computer bulletin boards was issued by Santa Clara County, California, sheriff's detectives. A computer engineer named Donald Matthew Deatherage, of Cupertino, California, known by the computer tag "Headshaver," was arrested by deputies for molesting a fourteen-year old boy he met through an online service. Investigators would like to know of any other area boys who may have exchanged messages with Deatherage. Area police note a small but increasing number of cases in which pedophiles make contact with children through computer services.

■ An informal study of top Silicon Valley companies shows that a majority retain the right to review employee e-mail.

■ Random House plans to offer its authors a flat five percent royalty on electronic versions of their works and will retain all future electronic publishing rights.

■ A man has been charged with violating Michigan's anti-stalking laws for continuing to send e-mail after a woman and police told him to stop. If convicted of the misdemeanor offense, the alleged stalker may be jailed for one year or fined $1,000.

■ A former San Francisco, California, policeman pleaded no contest to a misdemeanor charge of illegally using a police computer in surveillance of political activists over a seven-year period. The defendant was sentenced to forty-five days in jail, fined $2,500 and placed on three years' probation.

■ The federal government adopted the digital signature standard, first proposed by the National Institute of Standards. The standard has been the subject of much criticism, including that the underlying mathematical algorithm is not public, there was not sufficient time for public analysis, and the algorithm chosen may infringe patents held by RSA Data Security and others. One critic notes that the government's algorithm has a hidden flaw that allows information unknown to the signer to be hidden in the digital signature number. The unknown information might range from credit ratings to political affiliations.

■ A Seattle man, 51, has been arraigned in New York on a misdemeanor charge of endangering the welfare of a fourteen-year-old girl in a case involving the exchange of sexually explicit electronic mail. Alan Paul Barlow is accused of contacting the girl at her residence in the New York area, by computer and phone. Barlow flew from Seattle to meet the girl, and the police were alerted when the girl's mother found her and a ten-year-old brother in Barlow's company at a shopping mall.

■ Kevin Lee Poulsen, 28, pleaded guilty to seven federal charges, including conspiracy and computer and mail fraud, and faces a trial in federal court on fourteen other counts ranging from espionage to breaking into private and government computers and eavesdropping on telephone calls, including those of a former girlfriend. On the charges to which he pleaded guilty, Poulsen faces up to forty years in prison and a $1.75 million fine. He could receive up to sixty-seven years in jail on remaining charges.

■ The U.S. Supreme Court, by a one-vote majority, upheld a broad federal regulation of cable television, but ordered a lower court to reexamine a law requiring cable television systems to carry all of the broadcast television stations in their market area. The Court held that the rationale for limited First Amendment protection for television broadcasters does not apply to the cable industry, but did not find that cable operators enjoy the same First Amendment protections as newspapers.

■ The Federal Communications Commission will reserve more than onethousand new radio licenses for small businesses, women, and minority groups to operate "personal communication services," which includes pocketsized telephones, hand-held computers, advanced pagers, and facsimile machines.

■ Jefferson Airplane filed a copyright infringement lawsuit against Berkeley Systems, alleging that Berkeley's on-screen flying toaster infringes the toaster on the cover of the group's 1973 album "Thirty Seconds Over Winterland." Last year, Berkeley Systems sued a rival firm for using a similar toaster in its screen saver.

■ Novell Inc. will ask the federal government to overturn a software patent awarded in 1987 to Roger E. Billings, of Blue Springs, Missouri, which purports to cover technology that is basic to using a central file server to store data and make it available to a network of other computers. Novell said that it found at least thirteen examples of software technology that predate the patent. In 1992, Billings and his company, the International Academy of Science, sued Novell and Bank of America for $672 million, alleging violation of the patent. Bank of America settled with Billings for $125,000. The case is set for trial in September.

■ Compton's New Media requested that the Patent and Trademark Office reconsider awarding it a multimedia patent on a commonly-employed method of retrieving graphic, video, and text information.

■ The Software Publishers Association said that it will work with four other industry groups to develop ratings criteria and symbols for a voluntary system to label the sex and violence content of new computer games. The group will try to coordinate its ratings with those of video game makers.

■ A Milpitas, California, couple were convicted in a Tennessee federal court for the transmission of "obscene" pictures over a bulletin board system operated in the San Francisco area. The determination of whether the pictures are obscene was made by Memphis standards, as it was the locale where the material was "received." The couple face up to five years in prison and fines of $250,000 on each of eleven criminal counts of transmitting obscenity over interstate phone lines.

■ Lawrence Livermore Laboratory, one of the nation's three nuclear-weapons labs, confirmed that hackers obtained access to one of its computers and were using it to store and distribute hard-core pornography. The lab believes that at least one of its employees was involved.

■ The Defense Information Systems Agency reported that hackers have gained unauthorized access to hundreds of sensitive, but not classified, government and military networks connected to the Internet. Some intruders have been able to take control of several military computer systems, allowing them to steal, alter, or erase files, or shut the systems down. The Defense Department reports that the hackers have adversely affected Defense Department military readiness.

■ The Internal Revenue Service investigated 1,300 IRS employees for using IRS computers to snoop on taxpayers, including review of the financial status of friends, neighbors, enemies, potential in-laws, stockbrokers, celebrities, and former spouses. A few cases involved tampering with data and kickbacks to employees. In one third of the cases, employees were punished.

■ The Clinton administration said that it was willing to explore alternatives to the Clipper encryption system for anything beyond basic telephone calls. The administration is not, however, willing to compromise on the key-escrow feature of Clipper, which allows law enforcement agencies access to the content of a message encrypted by the Clipper system.

■ Kevin Mitnick, a convicted hacker, is suspected of stealing software and data from leading cellular phone manufacturers. Mitnick is currently being hunted for violating a federal probation requirement of not entering computers illegally or associating with other persons convicted of similar crimes.

■ Microsoft Corp. entered into a consent decree with the Justice Department in which it agreed to abandon a number of practices the government said had smothered competition. Among other things, Microsoft agreed to abandon immediately its practice of licensing MS-DOS and Windows on a "per processor" basis, under which computer manufacturers were provided steep discounts for agreeing to pay a royalty based on every computer shipped. Microsoft also agreed to abandon long-term contracts that obliged manufacturers to commit themselves to particular volumes of software for several years and also to abandon its policy of demanding extremely strict nondisclosure agreements from independent developers of applications programs, banning the developers from working on software for competing operating systems for up to three years.

- The Commerce Department released a draft proposal for changes to copyright law to protect copyright owners from challenges posed by development of the nation's information infrastructure and the Internet in particular.

- The Justice Department approved AT&T's takeover of McCaw Cellular Communications, which will allow the nation's biggest long-distance carrier to also become the largest operator of wireless communications. AT&T agreed to give cellular customers access to the long-distance carrier of their choice and also to insulate its cellular operations from its equipment subsidiary, which makes cellular switches and transmission systems. AT&T still needs to obtain Federal Communications Committee approval and a waiver of the antitrust decree that broke up the old Bell system.

- Two industry groups, the Recreational Software Advisory Council (backed by computer game publishers) and the Interactive Digital Software Association (formed by video game companies), unveiled separate proposed rating systems to appear on computer and video games.

- The Federal Communications Commission approved Bell Atlantic's application to offer interactive television service to 38,000 homes in New Jersey. This is the first time a telephone company has received approval to offer commercial cable television.

- Legislation compelling telephone and cable television companies to modify their networks to make it easier for law enforcement agencies to conduct wiretaps and trace messages will be introduced in Congress. The bill promises $500 million to help communications companies pay for the development and installation of necessary software. The legislation is sought by the Federal Bureau of Investigation and backed by the Clinton administration. As drafted, the legislation will not require computer network operators to provide special access for law enforcement agencies, but they could seek a warrant to examine billing records and other auditing information to determine who had been communicating with whom.

■ A New York state judge dismissed 113 lawsuits over injuries allegedly caused by computer keyboard use, filed against IBM and at least twelve other computer keyboard makers. The judge ruled that the state's statute of limitations had expired three years after a carpal-tunnel sufferer first developed the condition, not three years after the sufferer realized the condition could be linked to keyboard use.

■ Bob Dylan filed a trademark infringement lawsuit against Apple Computer, Inc. for using the name Dylan (short for Dynamic Language) for a computer programming language.

■ The Patent & Trademark Office tentatively approved Microsoft Corp.'s application for trademark protection for the word "Windows."

■ Suarez Corp. and writer Brock Meeks, author of the Cyberwire Dispatch "newswire," have settled a defamation suit over a harshly critical article about Suarez that Meeks had published on the Internet. Under the settlement, Meeks agreed to pay Suarez's $64 court-filing fee, to fax questions to the company if he writes any articles about it in the next eighteen months, and to pay a $10,000 fine if he violates the settlement terms. Meeks had run up a $25,000 bill for legal costs defending himself.

■ Federal judge Harold H. Greene (who oversees the antitrust consent decree that broke up the old Bell System) ruled that AT&T may purchase McCaw Cellular Communications Inc., the nation's biggest cellular telephone company. The Federal Communications Commission still needs to approve the transfer of McCaw's radio licenses.

■ The Business Software Alliance, backed by Microsoft Corp. and other software producers, is pushing for legislation that would prevent the Federal Communications Commission from setting standards for the computer operating system interfaces to be used in set-top boxes that are expected to be used by consumers for access to networks being developed by phone and cable companies. Opponents say that the half-dozen critical interfaces should be standardized and available equally to all competitors.

■ A California school, Santa Rosa Junior College, paid three students $15,000 each in settlement of charges stemming from its men-only and women-only computer conferences. Last June, the Department of Education's Office for Civil Rights advised the school that it had found a probable violation of federal law prohibiting sex discrimination in schools. Two female plaintiffs allegedly were the subject of anatomically explicit and derogatory remarks in the men-only conference. The third plaintiff, a male, saw the computer messages and broke the system's confidentiality rule to tell the women. He claimed that the school had retaliated against him. The creation of the segregated conferences was found by the Office of Civil Rights to be discriminatory in itself, and the remarks were said to be a form of hostile environment that had created a hostile environment for one of the women. The Office of Civil Rights has proposed a ban on computer bulletin board comments that harass, denigrate, or show hostility toward a person or group based on sex, race, or color, including slurs, negative stereotypes, jokes, or pranks.

■ A closely-guarded trade secret of RSA Data Security Inc., known as RC4, was sent from a computer in the Netherlands running an anonymous remailer program to a computer mailing list of computer researchers who oppose stringent government control on data encryption. RC4 is the de facto coding standard for many popular software programs and is the only software-based formula that the National Security Agency will permit to be easily exported.

■ The operator of a computer bulletin board known as Davy Jones Locker, Richard Kenadek, of Millbury, Massachusetts, was arrested on charges of illegally distributing copyrighted software to paying subscribers. Kenadek faces up to six years in prison and fines of $270,000.

■ Five men from Louisiana and one from New York were charged with using computers to gain access to credit-reporting service computers and steal credit card numbers. The numbers were allegedly used to buy $210,000 in coins and high-tech hardware. They were charged with conspiracy, computer fraud, access device fraud, and wire fraud. One of the men faces up to fifty years in prison and $2.25 million in fines. The others faces lesser sentences and fines.

■ A federal court stopped a promotion on America Online after the Federal Trade Commission filed a complaint for false advertising, relating to the promotion of a credit-repair program. The FTC charged that the promotion claimed to provide legal ways to repair credit, while suggesting illegal steps. The advertiser, Brian Corazine (doing business as Chase Consulting), agreed to refrain from further advertising and to inform potential clients that many of the activities suggested in the $99 program could be illegal.

■ The Ninth Circuit Court of Appeals rejected Apple Computer's appeal in its $5.5 billion copyright suit against Microsoft Corp. and Hewlett-Packard Co. The Ninth Circuit sent the case back to the lower court with instructions for the judge to reconsider rejection of Microsoft's and H-P's requests for attorneys' fees.

■ Apple Computer, Inc. confirmed that it will license its Macintosh System 7.5 operating system to other personal computer makers.

■ Despite assurances that China's security agents are not censoring or monitoring pager messages, an elite task force of one-hundred was sent by Beijing police in response to a beeper message that read, "Please send twenty guys with knives and guns to Dabeiyao." It was sent by a person testing his new beeper by sending a message to himself.

■ An employee of MCI Communications, Ivy James Lay, was charged with stealing 60,000 calling card numbers from MCI and other long-distance companies, used to make $50 million worth of long-distance calls. Lay, also known as "Knightshadow," allegedly devised software to trap calling card numbers from local and long-distance companies coming across MCI telephone switching equipment. Customers who suspect that their calling card numbers were illegally used should contact the customer service departments of their long-distance carriers immediately.

■ The leader of an international ring of computer hackers—Max Louran, of Majorca, Spain—pleaded guilty in a U.S. district court to stealing thousands of telephone calling card numbers used to make $140 million in unauthorized long-distance calls. Louran pleaded guilty to conspiracy and wire fraud charges.

■ Clinton Watson, of San Jose, California, was arrested and charged with making illegal cellular phones used to defraud local cellular phone companies of about $500,000 in three months. Watson allegedly created more than 1,000 clone phones and sold them for $1,000 to $2,000 each. Watson is also charged with writing a computer program to alter cellular phones so they could be reprogrammed repeatedly. He allegedly sold the program for $60,000–$100,000 in Singapore and the Philippines. Two other men were arrested with Watson, including his son.

■ An arbitration panel in New York ruled that the Princeton Review has no right to establish an Internet address (kaplan.com) using the name of its chief rival, Stanley H. Kaplan Educational Centers Ltd. The parties agreed to arbitration after suit was filed in U.S. District Court in Manhattan.

■ Congressman Edward Markey warned that America Online's practice of selling lists of its subscribers to other companies could pose a new threat to privacy. In response, the computer communication and information service said that it would suspend its practice until all the issues are satisfactorily resolved and would remove names at customers' request.

■ The Federal Communications Commission ordered Trans Union Corporation, one of the three largest credit checking companies in the United States, to stop renting marketing lists based on credit checks it is authorized to carry out. According to the FCC, Trans Union's actions were restricted by the Fair Credit Reporting Act.

■ The State Department denied a request by a California engineer to export a computer disk holding samples of some powerful and widely-used software encoding formulas. The engineer, Philip R. Karn, Jr., of San Diego, filed the request as a challenge to the International Traffic in Arms Regulations. The disk is a companion to a popular textbook on coding techniques by Bruce Shneier, titled "Applied Cryptography." Included on the disk is source code, including instructions for the Data Encryption Standard and Pretty Good Privacy (widely known as D.E.S. and PGP, respectively). Karn argued that the restrictions were meaningless because the same information can be obtained in standard cryptographic textbooks that can freely be exported and the same software is already freely available around the world.

■ FBI director Louis Freeh reportedly indicated that the FBI will seek congressional help if the public's use of cryptography foils its ability to implement authorized wiretaps. The FBI disputes that Freeh spoke about Congress or any attempt to ban forms of cryptography. Freeh's reported comments come within a few weeks of passage of the Digital Telephony bill, which compels telephone companies to install new switching gear that will allow law enforcement officials to conduct court-authorized wiretaps on calls routed through them. The government will pay $500 million for the installation of appropriate switches.

■ The Federal Communications Commission appeared to rule that the cost of telephone companies' building video networks should be borne by video, not phone, customers. The FCC also ruled that a single programmer cannot control "all or substantially all" of the channels on the new systems.

■ Thirteen parties lost rights to deliver wireless services when they failed to pay for licenses won at government auction in July. The parties will have to pay a penalty.

■ A U.S. District Court dismissed a copyright suit by Jefferson Airplane against Berkeley Systems Inc. over the winged toaster in the "After Dark" computer screen saver program. The court ruled that Jefferson Airplane failed in 1973 to obtain a separate copyright registration for the cover art of its album "Thirty Seconds Over Winterland," which shows a flock of winged toasters.

■ The U.S. Patent & Trademark Office rejected forty-six patent claims filed by Compton's New Media in June 1994. In August 1993, a patent was issued that Compton's says gave it exclusive rights to a method of allowing multimedia software users to search in and retrieve graphics, sound, and video within the same program. The August 1993 patent was reexamined and rescinded earlier this year. Compton's filed an appeal in June 1994 with some new and different claims.

■ The Federal Communications Commission issued regulations allowing five rivals (Motorola Inc., TRW Inc., Loral Corp., Ellipsat, and Constellation Communications) to share a scarce number of available radio frequencies. The rivals all hope to provide a global wireless network to allow people to make and receive calls on pocket-sized telephones from almost anywhere in the world.

■ Stratton Oakmont, Inc., an investment banking firm, sued Prodigy Services Co. and a subscriber, David Lusby, over alleged defamation of Stratton Oakmont, its president, and a firm the company took public, posted by Lusby on Prodigy's Money Talk bulletin board. The suit requests $100 million in money damages and another $100 million in punitive damages.

■ Microsoft Corp. and Intuit Inc. confirmed that they received a second request for information from the Justice Department on their proposed merger. A Silicon Valley law firm, Wilson, Sonsini, Goodrich, & Rosati, filed a brief with the Justice Department on behalf of clients that declined to be named, arguing that Microsoft's acquisition of Intuit is anticompetitive in the present market for personal finance software and that its future implications are even more troubling.

■ Robert and Carleen Thomas, who operated a computer bulletin board in Milpitas, California, were sentenced to two and one-half and three years in prison, respectively, for transmitting pornographic images over interstate telephone lines. The Thomases were prosecuted and convicted in federal court in Tennessee after a Memphis postal inspector logged into the Milpitas (a town close to San Francisco) bulletin board under a false name and downloaded the images, later found to be obscene under Memphis community standards. The Thomases will appeal their conviction, focusing on the definition of obscenity under local community standards. This case also raises serious issues related to the conduct of the federal government in prosecuting this case in Tennessee, as far away as possible from the residence of the defendants and in a jurisdiction with possibly the highest likelihood of conviction.

■ A U.S. district court dismissed wire fraud charges against David LaMacchia, a student at MIT. LaMacchia ran a computer bulletin board service that allegedly was used for the copying of copyrighted commercial software. In April, LaMacchia was indicted on one count of conspiracy to commit wire fraud. Judge Richard Stearns ruled, however, that LaMacchia could not be prosecuted for criminal copyright infringement under the wire fraud statute. Stearns noted that permitting the case to proceed would allow prosecution of home computer users for copying a single program for their own personal use.

■ The Ninth Circuit ruled that privacy rights were not violated in the search of a rented locker that revealed a classified 1987 Air Force order listing targets to be attacked in wartime. The ruling comes in the first espionage case against an alleged computer hacker, Kevin Lee Poulsen. He is charged with illegal possession of government secrets and other counts, including eavesdropping on private telephone calls and tapping into Pacific Bell computers and an unclassified military network. Poulson's trial had been delayed pending prosecutors' appeal of a ruling finding the locker search illegal.

■ The Simon Wiesenthal Center in Los Angeles wrote to Prodigy Services Company protesting the "continued use of Prodigy by bigots to promote their agenda of hate." The center called on online services to keep out hate groups and for the government to play a similar role on the Internet.

■ A former employee of Prodigy Services Company, David Lusby, of Key West, Florida, will be dropped from a defamation suit brought by Stratton Oakmont, Inc., over a series of messages posted in Prodigy's Money Talk online forum about the company and its president. Lawyers from Prodigy and Stratton agree that an anonymous hacker used Lusby's account without authorization, after Lusby left his employment with Prodigy. Prodigy remains a defendant in the case.

■ A U.S. district court dismissed Carl Sagan's claims against Apple Computer's use of his name. Apple used Sagan's name as the internal code name of a computer that became the Macintosh 7100. After Sagan complained to Apple, the internal name was changed to "BHA," which Sagan's lawyers allege stands for "butt-head astronomer." Sagan sued Apple for defamation, copyright violation, unfair competition, and right to privacy. Sagan's defamation claim was dismissed earlier.

■ The University of Illinois reached an out-of-court settlement with Netscape Communications Corp., formerly known as Mosaic Communications. The dispute arose after most of the team that developed Mosaic (the Internet browsing software) at Illinois' National Center for Supercomputer Applications joined the Mountain View, California, company to commercialize the product. Marc Andreessen, the lead developer, is quoted by the *San Jose Mercury News* saying, "You go to school, you do research, you leave and they try to cripple your business—is this the way you want to be treated?"

■ MCI Communications Corp. filed a complaint with the California Public Utilities Commission against Pacific Bell, alleging that Pac Bell is denying access to local toll call business by refusing to program five-digit access codes into its Centrex system (remote switchboards). Without this programming, consumers must dial an extra set of five digits to reach a different local toll call carrier. A Pac Bell spokesman commented that Pac Bell is not allowed to provide long-distance calls. When Pac Bell can do so, he said, it would make sense to have the same kind of access for both kinds of calls.

■ Microsoft Corp. filed copyright infringement lawsuits against two Los Angeles companies allegedly discovered illegally distributing Microsoft software. Microsoft states that the suits were filed as a result of its efforts to clean swap meets and trade shows of illegal hard disk loading and sale of counterfeit Microsoft products. At the Pomona Computer Trade Fair, other companies illegally selling Microsoft software immediately agreed to stop and settled without litigation. The suits were filed against the two companies that did not—Evertek Computers (also known as Pony Technologies) and ATC, or A-Tech, Computers.

1995

■ The Computer Emergency Response Team (CERT) at Carnegie-Mellon University, in Pittsburgh, Pennsylvania, warned of a new method of attacking computers of Internet users, called Internet protocol spoofing. The CERT team recommends four types of routers that are equipped to guard against this type of intrusion, in which an intruder enters a computer network and masquerades as a friendly machine. The advisory was issued after an attack in December 1994 on the San Diego Supercomputer Center.

■ Computer hackers broke into the Stanford Linear Accelerator Project computer system, accessing a single computer to change files that would give them future entry into the network and its e-mail system. Stanford University officials were forced temporarily to cut off outside access to the lab.

■ A federal district court in Washington issued an injunction against Stratton Oakmont, requiring it to comply with an out-of-court settlement it reached with the S.E.C. last year. The settled suit alleged that Stratton used abusive sales practices. A hearing on a permanent injunction against the firm has been scheduled. Stratton Oakmont is the firm that filed a libel suit against Prodigy, after a posting on the computer network accused the firm of violating securities laws.

■ On December 29, 1994, CompuServe Information Service posted an electronic demand for royalty payments from companies that make graphic software for viewing pictures in the Graphic Interchange Format (GIF). The companies had until January 10, 1995, to pay CompuServe a royalty on the programs they sell. The fee demanded by CompuServe is 1.5% of the price of any program plus a one-time fee of $1. GIF was developed by CompuServe in 1987 and is the most common way to store, view, and transmit photographs and other graphic images. (GIF is the standard format for images posted on the World Wide Web.) GIF became a standard because CompuServe encouraged its adoption by not charging a licensing fee. But GIF is based on a software algorithm patented by Unisys in 1985. Unisys notified CompuServe about infringement two years ago and the companies reached a licensing agreement in June 1994. Unisys is demanding royalty payments from dozens of companies other than CompuServe.

- Declining to be identified for fear of reprisal, several software companies asked U.S. district court judge Stanley Sporkin not to approve the July 1994 consent decree between Microsoft and the Justice Department. The brief alleges that while Microsoft engaged in illegal activities between 1988 and 1994, the decree does not deprive Microsoft of the consequences of those actions—its near-monopoly position in PC operating systems and growing strength in the applications market. The companies also complain that there is now less competition and higher prices in the operating system market, contrary to predictions of the Justice Department after the decree was announced. Microsoft and the Justice Department attacked the "last-minute" opposition to the proposed antitrust settlement.

- A former McDonald's supervisor, Michael Huffcut, is suing McDonald's, a franchise owner, and an employee for $2 million and punitive damages, alleging that the employee copied voice-mail messages between Huffcut and a McDonald's manager with whom he was having an affair and transmitted the messages to the franchise owner. The owner played the tape to Huffcut's wife and then fired him.

- A suburban Philadelphia plumber, Michael Lasch, was charged with ordering call-forwarding service for competitors' telephones, allowing him to siphon off customer calls. Bail for Lasch was set at $50,000.

- A case believed to be the first involving repetitive stress injuries and IBM and Apple Computer is on trial in Minnesota, where the companies are charged with knowingly making a dangerous product—their computer keyboards.

- The 9th Circuit U.S. Court of Appeals removed an obstacle to Pacific Telesis Group offering video programming. Pacific Telesis had raised a First Amendment challenge to 47 U.S.C. section 533(b), the telephone company-cable television cross-ownership prohibition. In a separate decision involving US West, the 9th Circuit held that section 533(b) violates the First Amendment. In a separate case, U.S. district court judge Gladys Kessler, in Washington, also declared the law unconstitutional.

- Apple Computer, Inc. asked the U.S. Supreme Court to review its unsuccessful "look and feel" suit against Microsoft Corp. and Hewlett-Packard Co.

- The Internal Revenue Service is reconsidering plans to greatly enlarge a computer database of personal information on Americans, so that it can match and compare tax returns with consumer information.

- Under the General Agreement on Tariffs and Trade passed by Congress in December 1994, patent applications filed June 8, 1995, or thereafter will be valid for twenty years from the date the application is filed. Applications filed prior to June 8 will be valid for seventeen years from the date of issue or twenty years from the date of first filing, whichever is longer. Design patents will remain valid for fourteen years from the date of issue.

- The French government–owned company Cie. des Machines Bull settled its lawsuit against Texas Instruments over a computer chip Bull alleged it had invented and patented. Documents filed in court reveal a French espionage scheme in which an alleged spy passed Texas Instruments secrets to French agents for nearly thirteen years.

- A student at the University of Michigan, Abraham Jacob Alkhabaz (writing under the name "Jake Baker"), has been jailed without bail for posting a sexually violent work of fiction in the Internet newsgroup, alt.sex.stories. The story uses the name of a female student who had been in one of his classes last semester. Alkhabaz was arrested by the FBI and charged with transporting threatening material across state lines. Three weeks after he used the school's computer to post the story, Alkhabaz was suspended by the University of Michigan.

- Kevin D. Mitnick, one of the most wanted computer criminals, was arrested in Raleigh, North Carolina, by a team of FBI agents. Mitnick, 31, is a convicted felon who has been sought since September 1992. Mitnick is charged with breaking into the Internet computer of a highly-regarded computer security expert (who then assisted in tracking down Mitnick) and several other computer systems, including the WELL and Netcom Inc., stealing credit card numbers, cellular phone codes, security tools, and other proprietary information from high-technology companies.

- A sixteen-year-old San Francisco high school junior pleaded not guilty to eight felony computer hacking counts based on alleged used of a false password, trying to download student files, and changing records to show that he made a "C" in biology instead of a "D." Last year, the student received a certificate of merit for helping teachers with computer problems.

- The New York Public Affairs Commission stated that through phone company error, for a period of months as many as 30,000 Nynex customers did not receive the privacy they were promised, when their phone numbers were revealed to persons with Caller ID.

- A federal judge in San Jose refused a request by the Church of Scientology that would have required Netcom On-line Communication Service to install software to monitor the activities and Internet postings of a critic of the church, Dennis Erlich, who allegedly posted church publications and documents online. In its lawsuit, the church alleges that Erlich has copied copyrighted material and disclosed trade secrets

- Thieves in Oregon used a stolen bank card 724 times over a fifty-four-hour period to withdraw $346,770 from forty-eight cash machines. Daily A.T.M. cash limits were not working over the weekend the card was used because the Oregon Telco Credit Union was changing its computer software. The stolen card was taken from a purse in a locked car. The PIN number for the card was written on a piece of paper in the purse. Three persons face charges of unauthorized use of an access device. Convictions could bring each up to sixty-three years in prison.

- A New Jersey teenager agreed to pay $25,000 to Microsoft Corp. and Novell Inc. in a court-approved settlement of a civil lawsuit over operation of a computer bulletin board, named the Deadbeat Bulletin Board, that illegally distributed free copies of their copyrighted computer software.

- AT&T Corp. and VLSI Technology agreed to develop security chips to protect a broad array of devices with triple the data encryption standard formula that the National Security Agency opposes. VLSI is the designated contractor to make the government's Clipper chips.

- Equifax Credit Reporting Services Inc. agreed to settle charges by the Federal Communications Commission that it violated the Fair Credit Reporting Act by failing to protect the accuracy and privacy of consumer credit reports. Equifax agreed to reinvestigate within thirty days information in a consumer's credit report disputed by the consumer and upon receipt of documentation from a consumer confirming his or her version of a dispute, to accept the consumer's version.

- A researcher at Stockholm University's Institute of Computer and System Science reports counting 5,561 messages or postings about child pornography in four electronic bulletin boards listed in USENET during a seven-day period between late December 1994 and early January 1995. Eighty-five percent of the messages were fantasy stories or tips on transmitting pictures. The postings included eight hundred graphic pictures of adolescents engaged in sexual acts.

- A Florida middle school teacher, Richard Lee Russell, was arrested and charged with exchanging child pornography in interstate commerce after meeting other computer users interested in child pornography through America Online. Another Florida teacher was similarly charged. The U.S. Customs Office says it expects more arrests to follow.

- U.S. district court judge Stanley Sporkin rejected the Justice Department's agreement with Microsoft Corp. that would have settled allegations that Microsoft unfairly competed with its rivals. The Justice Department appealed, claiming that the judge was wrong and had overstepped his authority.

■ The Federal Communications Commission approved wireless licenses for Iridium, Goldstar, and TRW, each of which plans to launch "low earth orbit" satellite systems.

■ The Computer Emergency Response Team, based at Carnegie Mellon University, warned of a vulnerability in twenty commonly used e-mail programs running on Unix systems connected to the Internet that may be exploited by hackers to read, overwrite, or destroy files.

■ Representatives of a computer dealer buying group, ASCII, will meet with the Justice Department over concerns that computer hardware and software companies will use Microsoft's online service (to be launched with Windows '95) to bypass them and go directly to customers.

■ The U.S. Supreme Court denied Apple Computer's appeal, ending the copyright infringement suit the company had brought against Microsoft Corp. and Hewlett-Packard over the "look and feel" of the Macintosh user interface.

■ The thirteen-year-old daughter of a Florida hospital clerk was arrested on charges that she called people treated at an emergency room and falsely told them they had tested positive for H.I.V., the virus that causes AIDS. One teenage patient tried to kill herself after receiving a call. The defendant had visited her mother at work and used a computer to print out a list of patients and telephone numbers. She was charged with assault, aggravated assault, and making threats, but she may be charged instead with making harassing telephone calls and disseminating false information about someone having a sexually transmitted disease. The defendant claims that the calls were a prank.

■ The Senate Commerce Committee approved a proposal attached to the nation's communications laws that would level fines as high as $50,000 and jail terms of up to two years on anyone who transmits material that is "obscene, lewd, lascivious, filthy, or indecent." Drafted by Senator Jim Exon (Dem. Nebraska), the bill as adopted by Senate committee exempts companies that merely provide transmission services, navigational tools for the Internet, or "intermediate storage" for customers moving materials from one location to another.

■ A panel of the U.S. Court of Appeals for the First Circuit reversed Judge Keeton's decision that Borland's Quattro Pro violated the copyright on

Lotus 1-2-3 by adopting 1-2-3's menu and command structure. Lotus Development Corp. will ask the U.S. Supreme Court to review the decision.

■ U.S. district court judge Manuel Real rejected a plea agreement worked out with a thirty-year-old hacker, Kevin Lee Poulsen, after he pleaded guilty to seven counts of conspiracy, fraud, and intercepting wire communications. According to Judge Real, federal guidelines do not allow for a long enough sentence to punish Poulsen. Sentencing has been delayed until April 10. Poulsen was originally arrested on eighteen counts of telecommunications and computer fraud. Poulsen faces separate espionage charges related to his hacking.

■ Kevin D. Mitnick, a recently captured fugitive computer hacker, was indicted on twenty-three counts of fraud involving computer-access devices. Mitnick allegedly possessed illegal equipment that allowed him to make a cellular telephone work as someone else's phone. Mitnick also commandeered a cellular-compatible modem to gain access to computer systems, where he allegedly stole information worth more than $1 million, including 20,000 credit card numbers. Mitnick apparently did not use the card numbers for financial gain.

■ Four students, at State University of New York at Stony Brook, Queens College and Queensborough Community College in New York, have been charged with grand larceny, forgery, and scheming to defraud over use of credit card numbers stolen with the aid of a specialized computer program. The four allegedly went on a one-year, $100,000 shopping spree.

■ The Securities and Exchange Commission (SEC) sued Pleasure Time, Inc., which does business as Telephone Information Systems, and Group Dynamics Downline over pitches on computer networks (including America Online) for shares in an "American Indian Lottery" that were allegedly unregistered securities amounting to little more than a high-tech pyramid scheme. According to the SEC's Chicago office, this is the first case the SEC has brought in which most of the offer and sale of securities occurred in cyberspace. A federal district judge in Ohio issued a temporary restraining order over the defendants, freezing their assets in Florida, Indiana, and Ohio. According to the SEC, over $3 million flowed in from over 20,000 investors.

■ The district attorney for Merced County, California, filed a civil suit against leading computer companies for false advertising and unfair business practices over the sale of computer monitors that are on average seventeen per cent short of the advertised length. The companies sued are Acer, Apple Computer, Inc., AST Research Inc., Daewoo, Dell Computer Corp., Goldstar, IBM, Leading Edge, NEC Technologies, Packard Bell, and Tandy Corp.

- The U.S. Supreme Court overturned a ruling by the Arizona Supreme Court that the Fourth Amendment requires exclusion of evidence seized as a result of computer errors leading police to make an invalid search or arrest.[515]

- In a setback for Viacom Inc., the Senate voted to repeal the minority communications tax break that allows a company to avoid capital gains if it sells a broadcasting or cable system to a company controlled by members of a racial or ethnic minority. The House had approved a similar measure, and House and Senate members will work on a compromise bill. Last year, Viacom agreed to sell its cable television system for $2.3 billion to an investor group led by Frank Washington, a black entrepreneur in California, with backing from Telecommunications Inc. Viacom would reportedly receive a $400 to $600 million tax break under the program. The deal is contingent, however, on Viacom's obtaining tax treatment available under existing law.

- In January 1995, the Federal Communications Commission (FCC) ruled that telephone companies providing ISDN (Integrated Services Digital Network) service must price each channel in an ISDN bundle as a separate phone line and charge accordingly. The FCC is currently examining ISDN and similar technology.

- A Minnesota jury concluded that neither IBM nor Apple Computer Inc. are responsible for injuries a former secretary claimed were caused by the design of computer keyboards. According to IBM's lead counsel, the jury rejected arguments including those that keyboard design was defective, that IBM had a duty to warn users, and even that plaintiff had injuries associated with keyboard work. Apple Computer had already settled with the plaintiff, after learning its lawyers had failed to turn over important documents during discovery.

- Intel filed a settlement proposal under which it would settle the class action breach of warranty and false advertising suit over the flaws in the Pentium processor for up to $6 million.

- Federal district court judge Harold Greene ruled that Bell Atlantic Corp. may compete with cable operators and broadcasters by transmitting programming anywhere in the country. The ruling, which finds that rules that prohibit the regional Bell companies from providing long-distance communications service do not apply to Bell Atlantic's request to transmit television programming, is expected to be extended to all seven regional Bell companies. Pacific Telesis also received from Judge Greene a more limited waiver to transmit programming.

---

[515] *Arizona v. Evans*, 115 s.ct. 1185, 131 L. Ed.2d 34 (1995).

■ A federal court in Delaware found that Motorola did not infringe any of four wireless phone patents owned by Interdigital Communications Corp. in a trial concerning time-division multiple access (TDMA), a wireless technology that allows voice and data to be transmitted in digital form. The jury also found invalid twenty-four claims at issue in the suit, saying that the claims would be obvious to "one of ordinary skill in the art."

■ Telephone Electronics Corp., of Jackson, Miss., agreed to withdraw a lawsuit alleging that Federal Communications Commission (FCC) special wireless telephone license preferences for small businesses, minorities, and women are arbitrary and unconstitutional. In return, the FCC will allow a waiver for Telephone Electronics, allowing it to qualify for the small-business bidding discount of ten percent for a limited number of licenses in eight markets in which it now operates rural telephone companies.

■ A Nebraska man, Thomas D. Wallace, filed a $40 million suit in federal district court in Los Angeles after finding the word "nigger" in Compton's Interactive Encyclopedia, a CD-ROM product. Wallace claims that he found the slur when he inadvertently typed "nigger" when looking for references to the Niger River. Wallace sued Compton's New Media, its owner (the Tribune Company of Chicago), as well as the store that sold him the software (Best Buy), claiming emotional distress, deceptive trade practices, and libel.

■ Microsoft urged a federal appeals court to overturn Judge Sporkin's decision not to approve the proposed consent decree between the Justice Department and Microsoft. Microsoft also asked the appeals court to disqualify Judge Sporkin, alleging that he relied too much on a popular book about Microsoft (*Hard Drive*) that he had read. The Justice Department has argued to the appeals court that the judge overstepped his authority in refusing to approve the consent decree.

■ In March 1995, the state of Utah adopted the world's first comprehensive Digital Signature Law (1995 UT S.B. 82).

■ Macromedia, Inc., a developer of computer software products, filed suit against individual America Online subscribers, alleging that these subscribers (using sixty-seven pseudonyms) infringed Macromedia copyrights by copying and distributing its works through use of America Online's e-mail system. America Online is not a named defendant.[516]

■ The state of New York says that ninety-four pay phones it owns were switched to a different long-distance carrier without permission. Acting on

---

[516] *Macromedia, Inc. v. VRHacker, et al.*, Case No. C95-1261 (N.D. Cal. filed April 13, 1995)

New York's complaint, the Federal Communications Commission proposed a $1.41 million fine against Oncor Communications Inc. for repeatedly switching the pay phones to its long-distance service without consent, an illegal practice commonly known as "slamming."

■ Kevin Lee Poulsen, 29, was sentenced to fifty-one months in federal prison and three years supervised probation upon release, and ordered to pay $58,000 in restitution. Poulsen, a computer hacker, seized incoming phone lines of radio stations during call-in contests to win prizes and cash. Poulsen, who pleaded guilty to seven felony counts, has confessed also to using computer skills to penetrate the FBI, locating and identifying undercover businesses and wiretaps. Poulsen faces additional charges of stealing classified Air Force documents listing the names and locations of structures that would be attacked in the event of war.

■ A thirteen-year-old Florida girl was sentenced to five years probation and therapy after she pleaded guilty to taking confidential information from a computer at a medical center where her mother works and calling seven emergency room patients falsely to inform them that they had tested positive for HIV, the virus that causes AIDS.

■ U.S. Customs agents arrested Fan Zhang, a native of China, who was allegedly carrying 29,000 counterfeit holograms to be used to authenticate fake packages of MS-DOS 6.2 software. Zhang allegedly purchased the holograms in Shanghai for $3,000 and planned to sell them in Los Angeles for $10,000. He faces charges of smuggling and trafficking in counterfeit goods.

■ Two members of the House of Representatives, Tony Hall (D-Ohio) and Chris Smith (R-New Jersey), introduced proposed legislation to ban explicit sex and "indecent" programming from basic cable packages.

■ Federal judge Harold H. Greene ruled that the seven regional Bell companies may offer long-distance cellular and other wireless service, on condition they demonstrate measurable competition in their own markets. Judge Greene did not accept the Bell companies' argument for a larger local calling area for cellular service.

■ Three regional Bell companies (BellSouth, Bell Atlantic, and SBC Communications) sued the Federal Communications Commission (FCC), alleging that new FCC standards they must meet to deliver video service infringe their right to free expression. The Bell companies are joined in the suit by the U.S. Telephone Association and two other telephone industry groups. Telephone companies, like cable television companies, must obtain a municipal franchise to deliver video services. In March, the FCC announced that phone companies must also obtain a construction permit, granted by the FCC on a project-to-project basis in a process that could take months.

- According to a proposed ruling by an administrative judge for the California Public Utilities Commission, Pacific Bell is attempting to maintain a monopoly in the local toll-call market. This market was opened to competition in January 1995. MCI complains that Pacific Bell is holding business customers hostage by refusing to program five-digit access codes into Centrex switching systems Pacific Bell maintains for thousands of business clients. Pacific Bell, for its part, says it will eliminate the cumbersome access-code procedure when it is allowed to compete in the long-distance market.

- A federal jury found that keyboards made by IBM and Altex Inc. were not responsible for hand-nerve damage suffered by a reporter for the *Philadelphia Inquirer*. According to the jury, neither production defects nor design flaws in the keyboards caused carpal tunnel syndrome in the reporter's wrists.

- The Tokyo High Court, in *Japan Auto Products, Inc. v. BBS Inc.*, ruled that two companies could legitimately import patented products made in Germany and sell them at a higher price in Japan without violating the patent holder's rights. This ruling departs from long-standing practice in the United States and Japan, which prevented competitors from buying patented products sold cheaply in one country and then selling them in a country where a similar patent was issued but where the product fetches a higher price.

- The Antitrust Division of the U.S. Department of Justice sued to block Microsoft Corp.'s acquisition of Intuit Inc., maker of the popular Quicken personal finance program. The Antitrust Division argues that the purchase would cause higher prices and less innovation in personal finance software.

- Compaq Computer Corp. filed suit against Packard Bell Electronics Inc., alleging that Packard Bell sells products that it represents as new but that actually contain used components.

- Paul K. Kim, a graduating senior in a suburb outside Seattle, Washington, was severely sanctioned by his principal for publishing a lampoon of his school (Newport High School) on the Internet, including links to Internet sites with sexually-explicit material. The principal withdrew support for Kim as a National Merit Scholarship finalist and faxed letters to seven universities to which he had applied, informing them that the school was withdrawing its support for Kim as a National Merit Scholar and any recommendations the school may have given him.

- A New York judge cleared the way for a libel suit by Stratton Oakmont, Inc., an investment bank, and its president against Prodigy Services Company, ruling that the computer online network may be viewed as a publisher of information posted on its "Money Talk" bulletin board.

■ The Better Business Bureau filed suit against Mark Sloo, dba Clark Publishing, for acquiring registration of "bbb.org" and "bbb.com" allegedly to elicit money from the Bureau (which has used the BBB acronym for years) when it decides to use the Internet.

■ A New York court held that the Delphi computer online service is to be treated as a news disseminator in a suit brought by Howard Stern, dismissing allegations that Delphi's use of his name and photograph violated the New York Civil Rights Law.[517]

■ The Commerce Department approved the export of Cybercash Inc. encryption technology, which only encrypts a small section of a transaction message. Tight restrictions on encryption for "bulk" messaging remain.

■ An anti-terrorism law proposed in the wake of the bombing of the Federal Building in Oklahoma City would permit the government to obtain a wiretap to investigate any suspected federal felony and would lower legal barriers to the use of eavesdropping evidence in court. The law would also require telephone companies to help government wiretappers gain access to digital telecommunication lines under court orders.

■ Microsoft Windows 95 reportedly includes a Registration Wizard routine that interrogates each system on a network to determine what products are loaded (including products by competitors), creates a complete listing, and reports this listing back to Microsoft when a customer signs up for Microsoft Network Services. The routine can be disabled.[518]

■ The Federal Communications Commission established national rules for "Caller ID" under which callers may block their numbers from being seen by dialing *67 before each call or by special request to the phone company. Phone numbers of those who have unlisted numbers will be displayed if they do not take either step. In California, where the service is not offered, Pacific Bell will be required to send callers' numbers out of state by December 1, 1995.

■ A misdemeanor complaint was filed against a Los Angeles man, David Luera, on charges of possessing child pornography that prosecutors allege he obtained from the Internet. Luera faces one year in jail and a fine of up to $1,000. The Los Angeles Police Department's Sexually Exploited Child Unit began to investigate Luera after he placed an ad in *Loving Alternatives*

---

[517] *Stern v. Delphi Internet Servs. Corp.*, 626 N.Y.S.2d 694, (Sup. Ct. 1995).
[518] The Registration Wizard apparently creates a file on the user's disk and then asks for permission to transmit the file.

magazine, allegedly seeking to have an "open relationship" with couples interested in family nudity.

- IBM won a repetitive stress injury case brought by a former supermarket clerk in New York who claimed that she had been injured by using keyboards developed by IBM and NCR Corp.

- The Federal Communications Commission will allow the market to set prices on cellular phone service beginning in August 1995.

- The Federal Communications Commission will not enforce a ruling by its Common Carrier Bureau that would have required telephone companies to raise the price of ISDN (Integrated Services Digital Network) service. The Bureau had said that customers would have to pay a "subscriber line charge" according to the capacity of their ISDN connection, measured in equivalents to ordinary telephone lines.

- The California Public Utilities Commission (PUC) ruled that Pacific Bell violated state law by restricting use of its Centrex system. The PUC ordered the company to allow businesses to make local toll calls on competitors' lines without dialing five-digit prefixes. At the beginning of this year, the PUC had opened the market for local toll calls—those more than eleven miles from within one of the state's eleven local call regions.

- Microsoft announced that it is abandoning plans to acquire Intuit Inc. The announcement came a day after the Justice Department accused lawyers for Microsoft and Intuit of acting in bad faith, and requested delay of the trial scheduled to begin on June 26.

- The California State Senate passed a bill that specifically includes computer data and related information (including programming information) within the scope of civil discovery.

- A federal judge in Detroit, Avern Cohen, dismissed charges against Jake Baker, 21, who had been arrested and jailed for twenty-nine days earlier this year on charges of transmitting threats over a fictional rape and murder story that Baker had written and posted to an Internet area reserved for sex stories.

- The U.S. Senate approved a sweeping telecommunications reform bill. Included in the bill is the Exon amendment, a measure that imposes heavy fines and prison terms on people who distribute "indecent" material over the Internet. Although the measure includes protections for online services that merely act as a conduit for individuals that use their networks to disseminate sexually-explicit material, the commercial online industry fears that it might still be held liable for message content where their moderators monitor online discussion groups. Another part of the bill would require television manufacturers to install a computer chip that allows parents to prevent children from watching violent programs. Other provisions permit local phone companies to provide long-distance service, permit both types of phone companies to offer computer-based and video programming as well as, in certain cases, to own a cable company and a phone company in the same area, and to free cable companies from most regulation by the Federal Communications Commission.

■ Three software companies, Microsoft Corp., Netscape Communications Corp., and Progressive Networks Inc., agreed to form the Information Highway Parental Empowerment Group to develop technology to allow computers to identify and block certain information and images on the Internet.

■ A three-judge federal appeals court panel reinstated a July 1994 antitrust settlement between the Justice Department and Microsoft Corp., ruling that Judge Stanley Sporkin overstepped his authority in rejecting it. The panel disqualified Judge Sporkin and ordered the case reassigned to a different judge, to be picked at random. In its decision, the appeals court objected to Judge Sporkin's reliance on the book *Hard Drive*, by James Wallace and Jim Erickson, for examples of what were said to be Microsoft's unfair business practices, and to the admission of briefs filed by a Silicon Valley lawyer, Gary Reback, on behalf of three anonymous clients.

■ The Federal Communications Commission issued rules curbing the unauthorized switching of long-distance phone service, a practice known as "slamming." The rules forbid, among other things, promotional campaigns—such as prize giveaways or sweepstakes—to entice consumers to switch long-distance carriers. Consumers who receive higher bills as a result of being slammed may only have to pay the charges they would have owed to their original carrier.

■ The California Public Utilities Commission appealed to the U.S. Court of Appeals, challenging the Federal Communications Commission's plans to establish a national "caller ID" system by December 1, 1995.

■ Describing itself as a beleaguered victim of a "campaign of harassment" and "abusive behavior" by the Justice Department, Microsoft Corp. filed a petition in federal court asking that a civil investigative demand be set aside. The Justice Department is investigating whether Microsoft's plan to bundle its upgraded operating system, Windows 95, with access software for its online service will give it an unfair advantage in the online business. The European Community will conduct a similar investigation. The three leading commercial online services, America Online, CompuServe, and Prodigy, have also received civil investigative demands for information from the Justice Department.

- A coalition backed by Pacific Bell asked the California Public Utilities Commission to delay the start of competition in the local phone market until protections for "universal service" are in place. Pacific Bell also requested changes in rules governing the way long-distance and cable companies enter the market. All California markets are to be open by January 1997, and the PUC has proposed interim rules that would open the market one year earlier.

- Network Solutions Inc., the company that assigns Internet addresses, will suspend the use of a domain name if the first person to register the name does not relinquish it to a company that owns the trademark.

- Fry's Electronics, Inc., a California company, filed suit against Frenchy Frys and Network Solutions, Inc., (the company that assigns Internet domain addresses), among others, over use of the Internet domain name "FRYS.COM." In addition to unfair competition and trademark infringement, Fry's Electronics included a claim under the Racketeer Influenced and Corrupt Organizations Act of 1970 (RICO).[519]

- Two California lawyers and a law professor filed a class action suit against America Online, Inc., claiming breach of contract, fraud, and unfair trade practices over the alleged inflation of time charges. The complaint[520] alleges that America Online rounds up fractions of minutes to full minutes and fractions of forty-six seconds or more are rounded up with an additional minute tacked on.

- Computer hacker Kevin Mitnick agreed to the transfer of his case from North Carolina to Los Angeles, where he faces charges including probation violation. Mitnick, charged with twenty-three counts of computer fraud, also agreed to plead guilty to one count of illegally using fifteen stolen phone numbers to dial into computer databases, for which he faces eight months in jail.

- The European Council of Ministers formally adopted a Directive on the Protection of Personal Data. The directive includes an obligation to collect data only for specified, explicit, and legitimate purposes, and to be held only if it is relevant, accurate, and up-to-date. Data subjects are granted im-

---

[519] *Fry's Electronics, Inc. v. Octave Systems, Frenchy Frys, Network Solutions, Inc., et al.*, No. C95-2525-CAL (N.D. Cal. filed July 13, 1995).
[520] *Hagen v. America Online, Inc.*, No. 971047 (S.F. Sup. Ct. filed July 14, 1995).

portant rights, including the right of access to data, to know where it originated, and to rectify inaccurate data. Sensitive personal data can only be processed with an individual's consent, except in important public interest cases where safeguards have to be established. Where data is transferred to non-EU countries, the directive prevents EU rules from being circumvented.

- A computer programmer in East Germany posted confidential information about Intel's Pentium processor on the Internet.

- Congressmen Christopher Cox (R-Calif.) and Ron Wyden (D-Ore.) introduced a bill named the "Internet Freedom and Family Empowerment Act," which would bar the government from regulating content on the Internet or commercial online services and allow service providers to filter out some objectionable material without being held liable for what they do not block.

- The Federal Communications Commission approved Pacific Telesis's Video Dialtone service, offering consumers services such as movies on demand, home shopping, video games, and high-speed Internet access.

- Packard Bell Electronics Inc. settled a class-action lawsuit claiming that the company put used or returned parts in computers it sold as new without informing buyers. Packard Bell could pay out more than $2 million in customer refunds and PC repairs.

- The Federal Trade Commission requested information from Compaq Computer Corp. and Packard Bell Electronic Inc. on their policies for returned equipment and use of used parts in new computers.

- The U.S. District Court of Appeals for the District of Columbia upheld regulations that prohibit radio and television stations from carrying sexually-oriented "indecent" programming between 6 a.m. and 10 p.m. The court found that the government had a "compelling interest" in shielding children from indecent materials.

- The Federal Communications Commission struck down the twenty-five-year-old prime-time access rule, which prevented broadcast networks from supplying programs for one hour in the evening (7 to 8 p.m. in the East).

- President Clinton endorsed congressional proposals to require television makers to install computer chips that can screen out programs coded as violent.

- Federal Communications Commission officials will solicit public comments about how airwaves should be used in the digital age. The FCC will determine, among other things, when broadcasters must give up analog and shift over to digital transmissions, as well as how, or whether, broadcasters will be granted a second slice of airspace. Proposals under consideration may eliminate high-definition television (HDTV) in favor of a wide range of wireless communication services.

- The U.S. Court of Appeals for the District of Columbia ordered the Federal Communications Commission to delay an auction for licenses for personal communications services, blocking the FCC from reserving a block of licenses for small businesses. The order comes in response to a complaint from Omnipoint Corp., which argues that the FCC made it too easy for small companies to serve as fronts for large companies.

- The Justice Department withdrew a disputed subpoena requesting a broad array of information from Microsoft Corp., saying it has enough information to determine whether to proceed with an antitrust action against the company over packaging of access software for the Microsoft Network with its Windows 95 operating system. The three leading online services, CompuServe, America Online, and Prodigy, have received requests from the Justice Department for information on how much they pay computer manufacturers to install their software on new computers.

- The FBI is launching "cyber-swat" teams in San Francisco, Washington D.C., and New York to investigate hacking, industrial espionage, pirating, and other computer crimes. Says Tom Fuentes, head of the operation, "The security of the country is at stake."

- A southern California retired police detective, Robert Muldrew, and two private investigators, Steven Kudler and David Westland, were charged with unauthorized access to police and other computers, conspiracy, and fraudulent telecommunications access, as well as selling confidential information.

- Seven subscribers to a Cincinnati electronic bulletin board system filed a class action lawsuit over a June raid on the offices of the Cincinnati Computer Connection BBS. The Hamilton County Computer Crimes Task Force seized the entire computer system, including all the private electronic mail of the subscribers, in the course of seeking forty-five computer image files. The lawsuit claims violation of the First Amendment, the Fourth Amendment, the federal Electronic Communications Privacy Act of 1986, and Ohio common law privacy rights.

- The publisher of Multimedia Wire (MMWIRE) sued Walt Disney Co. for copyright infringement. The suit claims that Disney "systematically" produced multiple copies of MMWIRE's copyrighted newsletter (an electronic daily delivered overnight by fax and electronic mail to executives at entertainment, media, technology, and telecommunications companies) and distributed copies through Disney's offices in Los Angeles, and elsewhere in the U.S. and Canada.

■ Carnegie Mellon University ordered an investigation into whether a researcher, Martin Rimm, committed scientific misconduct in his nationally publicized study of dissemination of pornography on the Internet and private computer bulletin board services. The study reached the cover of *Time* magazine, but has come under harsh attack.

■ Damien Doligez, with the National Institute for Research in Computer Science and Control in France, networked 120 computers, including two supercomputers, to read a supposedly secure message sent using the export version of Netscape Communications Corp.'s Navigator software. Experts say the problem is a predictable consequence of U.S. export laws, which prohibit U.S. companies from exporting powerful encryption software. The international version of the Netscape Navigator uses a 40-bit key in compliance with U.S. export restrictions, while the U.S. version uses a 128-bit key. Netscape previously said it would take a top-of-the-line desktop computer six months nonstop to crack a message encrypted with its 40-bit key.

■ A twenty-four-year-old mathematics graduate, Vladimir Levin, allegedly used a computer in his office in St. Petersburg, Russia, to hack into Citibank New York and remove $2.8 million. U.S. authorities are seeking his extradition from Britain. Authorities also arrested two people in the United States, one in Israel, and two in the Netherlands.

■ The Securities and Exchange Commission filed a civil complaint in Rhode Island against a nineteen-year-old San Jose man, Daniel Odulo, charging him with posting a false and misleading securities solicitation on the Internet. Odulo had sought to sell $1,000 bonds that would pay twenty percent, saying they had a "very low risk," so he could fund a $500,000 venture to raise cultured eels. Odula gave the impression that his company was an ongoing business, when it is in fact a proposed venture, and included endorsements from fictitious financial advisers.

■ Capital Cities/ABC Inc. reportedly dismissed the manager of online services at ABC News, Mitch Davis, for transmitting a sexually-explicit photograph over the company's computer network. ABC has reportedly referred the matter to the FBI.

■ U.S. Marshals seized the computer of a former employee of the Church of Scientology, Arnaldo P. Lerma, who allegedly posted the 134-page text of a Scientology document setting out its secret scriptures. Lerma was told that the computer would be returned after Scientology documents had been deleted.

- Network Solutions, Inc., the company that assigns Internet domain names, announced a new policy requiring companies that register a domain name to indemnify Network Solutions in any legal action and cover its legal fees, and also requiring a company disputing an Internet address to prove that it holds a trademark certificate for the name from the U.S. Patent and Trademark Office.

- Interactive Gift Express Inc. announced that it filed a patent infringement suit against eighteen computer and publishing companies for alleged infringement of a patent granted in 1985 and licensed by Interactive in 1994, allegedly covering a system and method "whereby digital information is sold and downloaded from a catalogue that comes from a host computer to a point-of-sale terminal," such as a home computer. The companies named in the suit include Adobe Systems, Inc., Broderbund Software Inc., Compu-Serve, Intuit Inc., McGraw-Hill Cos. Inc., Waldenbooks, and Ziff Communications Co.

- Three writers' groups, the Authors Guild, the American Society of Journalists and Authors, and the National Writers Union, criticized a new policy by the *New York Times* requiring outside writers to relinquish all rights, including electronic rights, to materials published in the *Times*. The policy does not cover writers for the newspaper's Op-Ed page or the *New York Times Magazine*.

- The Federal Trade Commission issued new national standards for telephone sales, effective January 1, 1996, requiring telemarketers to say at the outset that it is a sales call and explain the product or service offered. Total cost must be disclosed prior to asking for payment. The FTC also imposed stiff fines on "credit card laundering," in which money is collected through a credit card even if companies like Mastercard and Visa have refused to authorize the transfer. This is done by a company not authorized to receive money electronically persuading an authorized company to collect the money for it by running the credit card through the legitimate company's card-swipe machine.

- In the midst of trial, a San Francisco court dismissed a repetitive stress injury case brought by a San Francisco graphic designer against Apple Computer, Inc. The plaintiff, Carolyn Brust, claimed that injury in her right hand was caused by her Apple mouse and keyboard. The dismissal came after Judge James Warren disallowed testimony by an occupational health professor, because it did not meet the California legal standard for admissibility.

- The Justice Department extended its investigation of Microsoft Corp. into the bundling of Internet browsing software. The Justice Department also announced that it would not take antitrust action against Microsoft Corp. before the August 24, 1995, introduction of the Microsoft Network, but that its investigation will continue.

■ The Computer & Communications Industry Association asked U.S. district court judge Thomas Penfield Jackson to broaden the government's antitrust settlement with Microsoft Corp. to extend to Windows NT the same restrictions the settlement places on licensing and marketing practices involving DOS and Windows operating system software.

■ The Securities and Exchange Commission will maintain free Internet access to its library of corporate records. Although private companies have offered to take over the Edgar online service that allows the reading of corporate filings made with the agency, SEC chairman Arthur Levitt Jr. said that taxpayers and shareholders have already paid to compile this information and should not have to pay again, "[a]nd a library that charges people by the page, or by the minute, is no longer a library." The cost for the SEC to take on Edgar would be "quite modest," said Levitt.

■ The House of Representatives approved a telecommunications bill that vastly reduces regulation on everything from cable television to local and long-distance phone service. The bill would eliminate limits on cable rates, allow long-distance carriers, cable companies and others to compete with local phone companies, allow Bell companies to offer long-distance service if there are local competitors offering business and residential service, and require new television sets to contain a feature (the V-chip) that would allow parents to block violent materials, among other things.

■ The Justice Department searched 125 homes across the country, including New York, Newark, Dallas, and Miami, and announced a dozen arrests in a two-year investigation of use of America Online (AOL) for distribution of child pornography and to lure minors into sex. More arrests are expected. One person arrested, Craig Zucker, ran a day-care center in his home in Chicago, Illinois, and is charged with distributing by computer three pictures of underage girls engaged in sexually explicit acts. The investigation began in 1993, after the abduction of ten-year-old George Stanley Burdynski from his neighborhood in Brentwood, Maryland. The boy has not been found. AOL notified the FBI after users reported that photos of nude children were circulating, and announced that it would not tolerate use of its network for illegal activities. Violation of federal law on child pornography, including creating, possessing, and disseminating child pornography, may result in ten years' imprisonment and a $10,000 fine.

■ The Secret Service created a computer bulletin board system, called "Celco 51," using it to buy hundreds of stolen cellular phone codes. Traffic on the board led to raids in several states, the arrest of six persons, seizure of more than twenty computer systems as well as equipment used to make cellular phones operate with stolen codes. The suspects allegedly broke into the computer system of McCaw Cellular (now named AT&T Wireless).

■ The Russian who allegedly masterminded a break-in of Citicorp's computers, making unauthorized transfers of $40 million and withdrawals of $400,000, was ordered to stand trial in the U.S. Vladimir Levin, arrested at Heathrow Airport in England, will face charges of theft, computer misuse, forgery, and false accounting.

■ Two Berkeley, California, men were indicted by a federal grand jury in Sacramento, California, on charges of conspiracy, fraud, and destruction of computer data related to the theft of credit card numbers from Tower Records/Video stores throughout the country. Terry Patrick Ewing, 21, and Michael Yu Kim, 20, who face more than twenty years in prison and a $250,000 fine, allegedly used computers over the course of four months to tap into a central computer owned by M.T.S., Inc., the parent company of Tower Records/Video stores, gathering two thousand credit card numbers and account information, and also to delete files in an attempt to cover their tracks. They allegedly ran up $20,000 in unauthorized charges.

■ A San Jose, California, man was found guilty on three counts of phone fraud for making, using, and cloning cellular phones. Clinton Watson, 45, allegedly was involved in or connected to the sale of more than one thousand cloned phones or programming chips, and had six hundred unauthorized phone numbers in his possession.

■ Federal district court judge John Kane ordered the Church of Scientology to return computers and files seized by federal marshals and the church from two men in Boulder, Colorado, (Lawrence Wollersheim and Robert Penny) who used a computer bulletin board named Factnet to disseminate information critical of the church.

■ America Online asked its subscribers to change their passwords on a regular basis to counter problems caused by hackers and persons posing as AOL staff. Hackers have reportedly tampered with AOL's business and customer information files.

■ The Clinton administration announced proposals to relax restrictions on export of cryptographic software, allowing export of encryption algorithms using 64-bit keys in place of the 40-bit keys currently permitted, but only if individual keys are given to "escrow agents" who could make them available to law enforcement agents under standard legal procedures.

■ FBI director Louis J. Freeh said that the FBI might consider other approaches if consensus is impossible on the administration's proposal for voluntary compliance with a "key escrow" plan for public use of strong cryptography.

- Two first-year graduate students at the University of California at Berkeley discovered a serious security flaw in the Netscape Navigator (the Internet browser software) that could allow a person with a computer to break Netscape's public key encryption system in less than a minute. The company said it would release a new version without the flaw the following week.

- Microsoft Corp. and Visa International announced a standard for online payments and financial transactions, called "Secure Transaction Technology," intended to guarantee security and privacy of payment and purchases made over computer networks. The announcement was met with criticism that the proposal is an attempt to make the online world beholden to Microsoft and Visa. Mastercard has been developing a separate system, named "Secure Courier," with Netscape Communications Corp.

- A Caribbean resort owner and a scuba instructor, Arnold Bowker and John Joslin, filed suit in Cook County, Illinois, requesting that a circuit court order disclosure of the name of an America Online subscriber that allegedly defamed them on an AOL bulletin board. Posting under a pseudonym (Jenny TRR), the subscriber explained that she had a bad experience at the resort while learning to dive with an instructor who used drugs—writing, in part, that "diving with a stoned instructor was a little scary." Bowker, owner of a dive shop at the Carib Inn in Bonaire, Netherlands Antilles, heard of the allegations from a visitor, and investigated. Believing the allegations to be untrue, Bowker posted a rebuttal on the same bulletin board and asked the subscriber to recant.

- MCI Communications Corp. and AT&T Corp. asked the Federal Communications Commission to block French and German telephone companies from collectively buying twenty percent of Sprint Corp. MCI and AT&T want France and Germany to open their telecommunications markets to U.S. companies.

- A presidential study group headed by Bruce Lehman, U.S. commissioner of patents and trademark, issued a report titled "Intellectual Property and the National Information Infrastructure," recommending changes to bring copyright law into line with current technology.

- Network Solutions, Inc. announced that Internet users will have to pay $50 per year to maintain domain names they have registered. Network Solutions will send out three electronic reminders, sixty, thirty and fifteen days before the due date.

- The Federal Communications Commission accelerated repeal of regulations blocking television networks from entering the syndication market that were scheduled to be lifted in November 1995.

- A federal court in New York barred Time Warner from scrambling sexually explicit programs broadcast over its cable system. At issue is the 1992 Federal Cable Act, which allows cable operators to voluntarily ban sex programs on leased-access stations, and also provides that if such programs are not banned, operators must scramble the signal. In July, a U.S. court of appeals in Washington placed a stay on the latter part of the law, pending review by the U.S. Supreme Court. The New York ruling said that the law was likely to be held unconstitutional, as amounting to government censorship, and pointed out the potential stigmatization of subscribers who ask for the pornographic shows.

- A court of appeals gave the Federal Communications Commission permission to proceed with an auction of radio frequencies for personal communication services previously enjoined because of plans to give women and minorities preferences by reducing the cost of their bids. The issue had been resolved by extending preferences to all small business, but was again delayed by claims that the new rules made it too easy for large corporations to gain de facto control of bidders.

- Infinity Broadcasting Corp., the employer of radio disk jockey Howard Stern, agreed to pay the government $1.7 million to settle accusations of indecent radio broadcasts, ending a dispute with the Federal Communications Commission dating back to 1992.

- The U.S. Supreme Court will decide whether Lotus Development Corp. has a valid copyright in the series of commands used to operate the Lotus 1-2-3 spreadsheet program. The case involves claims brought by Lotus against Borland International, which designed its own spreadsheet program, Quattro Pro, so that users could operate it as if they were using 1-2-3.

- A member of the Federal Communications Commission, James H. Quello, accused the commission's chairman (Reed Hundt) and a senior White House official (Greg Simon) of pressuring Westinghouse Broadcasting to offer more educational programming as a condition for approval of its plan to acquire CBS Inc.

- The Patent and Trademark Office will make abstracts of its patent database freely available on the Internet, beginning November 9, 1995.

- Stratton Oakmont, Inc. agreed to drop its $200 million libel suit against Prodigy Services Corp., in return for Prodigy saying it was sorry.

Prodigy will pay nothing to Stratton Oakmont or its president, Daniel Porush, who contended that they had been libeled in messages posted on Prodigy's "Money Talk" electronic bulletin board. Prodigy says it is sorry they were hurt, but does not say it was responsible.

- Packard Bell Electronics Inc. countersued Compaq Computer Corp. for unfair competition and defamation. The lawsuit was begun over claims by Compaq that Packard Bell uses recycled parts in new computers, falsely advertising its machines as new.

- Apple Computer, Inc. agreed to pay the legal fees of Microsoft Corp. and Hewlett-Packard Co. in settlement of claims over Apple's ill-fated suit against the companies. The settlement is believed to have cost Apple millions of dollars.

- U.S. district court judge Ronald Whyte issued a ruling in the copyright infringement case brought against Netcom On-Line Communications and others over Internet posting of Scientology works, finding that Netcom may be liable for contributory infringement if it can be proven that Netcom knew of the copyright violations and neglected to prevent recurrence and remove the offending works.

- The FBI proposed a national wiretap system providing the capacity to monitor simultaneously as many as one out of every hundred phone lines in some high-crime areas. At minimum, the FBI would be able to monitor 74,250 phone lines at once, which is ten times the number of surveillance orders in 1993.

- Virgin Atlantic Airways was fined by the U.S. Department of Transportation for publishing misleading advertising on the Internet. Virgin published details of its transatlantic air fares on its Web page, but failed to update them. In particular, Virgin advertised a round-trip air fare of $499 between Newark, New Jersey, and London, England, for passengers booking twenty-one days in advance. But a consumer calling Virgin was told that the fare was no longer available because the season had changed from off-peak to peak. Virgin Atlantic agreed to pay a $14,000 fine.

- Cornell University officials are investigating four freshmen for sexual harassment and misuse of computer resources in connection with an e-mail message joking about rape and listing "75 reasons why women should not have freedom of speech." The message was apparently sent to twenty of the students' friends and then forwarded to countless Internet e-mail addresses.

- Frank Music Corp., The Harry Fox Agency, Inc., and CompuServe Inc. agreed to settle a class action lawsuit for copyright infringement, *Frank*

Music Corp. v. CompuServe, Inc., Civ. No. 93-Civ-8153-JFK (S.D.N.Y.). The suit alleged copyright infringement of the song "Unchained Melody" and more than nine hundred other songs, based upon the uploading and downloading of sound recordings by CompuServe subscribers, and the alleged facilitation of this copying by CompuServe. CompuServe does not admit liability, but will make payments to be divided among the music publishers involved. CompuServe will work with the Harry Fox Agency on a licensing arrangement allowing CompuServe to obtain licenses permitting the uploading and downloading of the publishers' songs on the CompuServe system.

- America Online alerted its subscribers to a destructive computer virus, known as "AOLGold" or "install.exe," that arrives attached to e-mail. The virus is activated once downloaded, and proceeds to restart the computer and rename the program that controls the computer's monitor. When the computer is next restarted, the virus begins deleting files in alphabetical and numerical order. The virus in not specific to America Online, and has been spotted on the Internet.

- Randall Schwartz, a former Intel systems administrator, was convicted under Oregon law on three felony counts of altering a computer system without authorization and gaining access to a system with the intention of committing theft. Originally hired as a contract programmer and systems administrator, Schwartz conducted routine security checks using a program called "Crack," which guesses user passwords. After being hired by another Intel division, Schwartz performed a security check on his old division, despite reprimands by Intel for two previous incursions into computers at Intel and other companies. During that check, Schwartz used Crack to determine the password of a user, gained access to a core cluster of Intel computers, moved a password file from a computer to a quicker one, where he used Crack to break forty-eight of six hundred passwords. Intel conceded that there was no evidence that Schwartz took passwords out of the system, but maintained that merely moving the passwords constituted theft. Schwartz was sentenced to five years probation, a deferred ninety-day jail term, 480 hours of community service, and $170,000 in legal fees. He also faces a $72,000 damages claim.

- Autodesk's anti-piracy squad and Los Angeles, California, district attorney agents raided the residence of "Captain Blood," who was arrested on software piracy charges. Captain Blood, whose real name is Thomas Nick Alefantes, had been sought for five years by Autodesk, the nation's fourth largest PC software maker. The raid uncovered over $1 million worth of software, including copies of Autodesk's AutoCAD program—which investigators said were being sold for as little as $79. Alefantes, held on $1 million bail, is charged with two counts of counterfeiting a registered trademark and computer fraud.

■ Justin Tanner Petersen, 35, also known as "Agent Steal," was sentenced to forty-one months in federal prison for taking part in a scheme to rig radio station contests and illegally possessing forty passwords to various financial accounts. He was also placed on three years' supervised probation, ordered to use computers for employment only, and to pay more than $40,000 restitution. Petersen's lawyer plans to appeal the sentence, on grounds that it was unfairly enhanced by two special circumstances: that Petersen used "special skills" in committing his crimes and fled while on bail, and that he helped the federal government pursue cases against other hackers. Petersen admits that before he became a fugitive, he had conspired to transfer $150,000 from Heller Financial in Glendale, California, to the Union Bank account of an unidentified person. He also admits that to cover the crime and divert attention from the transfer, he phoned two phony bomb threats to Heller to force its evacuation.

■ Kevin L. Poulsen, 30, a computer hacker serving a four-year prison term for rigging Los Angeles radio station contests, pleaded guilty to unauthorized intrusion into the files of Pacific Bell. Poulsen admitted burglarizing phone company offices and obtaining manuals and access codes to obtain free phone service and bogus credit cards. He also admitted obtaining a list of FBI wiretaps from phone company computers. Federal prosecutors dropped espionage charges against Poulsen, saying that a military document found in his possession was obsolete and also acknowledging that he had lawful access to the document and that he did not share the information.

■ LambGroup, Inc., a Miami, Florida, company providing local tourist information on the World Wide Web, sued a competitor for plagiarism of data. The company based its claim on British common law, rather than copyright law.

■ CompuServe Inc., in what it describes as a temporary move, blocked subscribers in the U.S. and around the world from access to more than two hundred sexually explicit computer discussion groups and picture databases after a federal prosecutor in Munich, Germany, said that the material violated German pornography laws. Most of the banned groups are within the alt.sex Usenet hierarchy. Critics note that some of the banned groups are devoted to topics like homosexuality that are not necessarily pornographic or a threat to children.

■ A coalition of commercial online services and some civil liberties groups agreed to accept a compromise on the provisions of federal legislation that seeks to keep sexual material off the Internet. The compromise, drafted by Rep. Rick White (R.-Wash.), would impose fines and prison sentences on those who transmit pornography, but would change the prohibition from making indecent material available to children to a prohibition on material "considered harmful" to children—said to apply only to graphic or explicit sexual matter that has no redeeming literary or social value. It also adds protection to online services and information providers who make a good-faith effort to keep sexual material away from children.

■ House and Senate negotiators reconciled measures that would make it a federal crime to transmit sexually explicit and other "indecent" materials over the Internet and online services to minors under eighteen years of age. The restrictions would include "any comment, request, suggestion, proposal, image, or other communications, that, in context, depicts or describes, in terms patently offensive as measured by contemporary community standards, sexual or excretory activities or organs."

■ In the first case involving a court-approved wiretap of the Internet, three people were charged with engaging in an international conspiracy to sell illegal electronic equipment. Federal officials obtained permission from CompuServe to obtain access to the e-mail account of the leader of the alleged conspiracy, and then posed as buyers of illegal equipment for over six months of communications with him over the Internet. The investigation began following a complaint by AT&T that cellular telephones programmed with stolen numbers were advertised for sale on a World Wide Web site. The three defendants, Bernard Bowitz, Rachel Bowitz, and Gregory Brooks, were charged with conspiracy, fraud, and international sales of illegal merchandise.

■ A federal district court panel upheld government must-carry rules requiring cable-television channels to carry local broadcast channels. The rules require all but the smallest cable operators to set aside up to a third of their channel capacity for local broadcasters.

■ Judge Stuart L. Ain declined to reverse his ruling in the case brought by Stratton Oakmont, Inc. against Prodigy Services Company, in which he held that Prodigy could be held liable for comments posted on its computer bulletin boards by subscribers because it acted as a publisher, not merely as a passive carrier. That case, originally asking for $200 million, was settled in return for Prodigy saying it was sorry that an unidentified subscriber had posted messages accusing Stratton Oakmont of fraud.

■ The Computer Emergency Response Team (CERT) issued an alert about several hundred attacks, many successful, on computer networks over the last few weeks. CERT says that the attacks are coming at sites that haven't patched specific vulnerabilities, some dating to 1992. Internet sites are apparently coming online with novice system administrators who do not know that their systems are vulnerable and that patches are available.

■ Software piracy charges have been filed against Howard Dennis Barnes, who is suspected of copying and selling hundreds of copies of Autodesk's $4,000 AutoCAD program for as little as $60. He faces up to ten years' imprisonment and $2 million in fines. Another AutoCAD software pirate, Thomas Nick Alefantes (also known as "Captain Blood") recently pleaded guilty to charges of possession of more than $1 million of pirated software and awaits sentencing.

■ House and Senate conferees agreed to require television manufacturers to include in new televisions the so-called V-chip, a computer chip that would allow parents to block out violent programming.

■ The Justice Department is looking into whether Microsoft's Windows 95 disables a computer's ability to use other products to connect with the Internet via phone lines. The Justice Department has subpoenaed records from CompuServe and Netscape Communications Corp., both of which have reported problems.

■ The Federal Communications Commission lifted obstacles blocking Sprint Corp. from selling a twenty percent stake to two foreign telephone companies, Deutsche Telekom and France Telecom. The F.C.C. attached conditions that prevent the two foreign companies from using monopoly powers in their home countries to put companies in the U.S. at a disadvantage or to increase international telephone call rates for U.S. customers.

Early 1996

■ The U.S. Supreme Court refused to hear a challenge to a federal law banning indecent radio and television programming during the day and prime-time evening hours, leaving intact a federal appeals court ruling upholding the Public Telecommunications Act of 1992. The Clinton administration had urged the Court to defer action until the Court decides a case that it agreed to review over curbs on access to indecent programming on certain cable television channels.

■ The Los Angeles–based Simon Wiesenthal Center sent letters to hundreds of Internet providers, asking them to refuse to carry messages that "promote racism, anti-Semitism, mayhem, and violence." According to the center's associate dean, Rabbi Abraham Cooper, Internet providers have a First Amendment right and moral obligation not to provide a platform for destructive propaganda.

■ CompuServe says that it is powerless to block access to neo-Nazi material on the World Wide Web, as German authorities have requested. A state prosecutor in Mannheim, Germany, said that he was not sure whether CompuServe could be held legally responsible for Internet content. In December 1995, CompuServe blocked access to two hundred Internet newsgroups, following the "advice" of a Munich prosecutor who said that they violated Germany's pornography laws.

■ Deutsche Telekom's T-Online Service, with more than one million German customers, voluntarily blocked access to a World Wide Web site belonging to Ernst Zuendel, a neo-Nazi in Toronto, Canada, after a state prosecutor in Mannheim, Germany, warned the company that they were investigating whether the service was "helping to incite racial hatred." Zuendel seeks to rewrite the history of World War II, denying that the Holocaust took place. Access was also cut to 1,500 other sites, ranging from financial services to "Santa Claus Online."

■ China announced that it will closely regulate international wire agencies that supply economic news to the country. The official New China News Agency will "supervise" Reuters and Dow Jones for content as well as the subscriptions they sell. Chinese officials recently lectured China's Internet providers on the dangers of pornography on the Internet.

■ Pacific Bell, a unit of Pacific Telesis Group, and U.S. West are asking for rate increases that would more than double the price of consumer ISDN (Integrated Services Digital Network), arguing that costs of providing service and use are far higher than anticipated. Critics believe that the telephone industry is price gouging, as a number of studies show that ISDN costs less than $10 per month more than analog telephone service.

■ The Justice Department will not prosecute Phil Zimmerman, the software designer who wrote a free, popular public-key encryption program named PGP (for Pretty Good Privacy). In the spring of 1991, the program was placed on the Internet, where it could be copied internationally in violation of U.S. export laws. Zimmerman maintains that he did not put the program on the Internet.

■ The Commerce Department will recommend easing export controls on encryption software. A study by the Commerce Department and National Security Agency found that U.S. companies are being hurt by export restrictions.

■ An equally divided U.S. Supreme Court affirmed the decision of the U.S. Court of Appeals for the First Circuit in favor of Borland International, Inc., in the lawsuit brought against Borland by Lotus Development Corp.

■ Four lawsuits, three in California and one in Illinois, were filed against Intel over an error in a software program used to measure chip speed that caused the company to overstate performance of the Pentium processor by about ten percent. The suits allege false advertising and unfair competition.

■ The U.S. Court of Appeals for the Sixth Circuit upheld the Tennessee convictions of a Milpitas, California, couple (Robert and Carleen Thomas) for violating federal obscenity laws in connection with their operation of an electronic bulletin board.

■ A federal judge ruled that a Virginia man, Arnaldo P. Lerma, violated Church of Scientology copyrights by posting on the Internet confidential church documents, called "Operating Thetan scriptures," despite having obtained them from public court records. Lerma posted the documents without comment, criticism, or other changes that would constitute a fair use. Previously, the judge ruled that the *Washington Post* had fairly reprinted portions of the documents in news accounts of the lawsuit and seizure of Lerma's computer equipment.

■ The U.S. Congress approved the final version of a sweeping bill that rewrites the nation's communications laws. The new telecommunications bill replaces the antitrust decree that broke up the Bell system in 1984, freeing the "Baby Bells" to offer long-distance service, while opening local phone service to new competitors. It lets cable television and telephone companies enter each other's markets, deregulates price controls on phone, cable television, and other services, and relaxes broadcast ownership restrictions, among other things. The bill also makes it a crime to transmit indecent sexual material over computer networks, and requires television manufacturers to include V-chips to allow parents to block undesirable programming. The bill is criticized by consumer advocates and civil liberties groups. Rep. Patricia Schroeder (D-Colo.) complains that late additions to the bill could make it a crime even to transmit the word "abortion" on the Internet.

■ President Clinton signed into law the Telecommunications Act of 1996. In response, the American Civil Liberties Union and nineteen other groups filed suit in federal court in Philadelphia to block one of its provisions, the Communications Decency Act of 1996. They say that the Decency Act's provision banning "indecent speech" amounts to censorship, which will restrict even the availability of abortion information. In Brooklyn, abortion rights groups went to court to block an amendment added by Rep. Henry J. Hyde of Illinois that extends to computer networks the Comstock Act of 1873, which prohibits dissemination of abortion information. The Justice Department says that the provision is clearly unconstitutional and would never be enforced. Parts of the Internet went into "virtual mourning," changing the background color of their World Wide Web pages to black for forty-eight hours.

■ China issued regulations on Internet use, requiring networks offering Internet service to be closely supervised by the Ministry of Post and Telecommunications or one of three other government agencies. The regulations require organizations applying for an Internet node to have perfect safety and security control measures, and that no organization or individual may engage in activities at the expense of state security. Obscene and pornographic materials are banned.

- German prosecutors warned three online services, America Online, CompuServe, and T-Online (a division of the German phone company), that they may be charged with inciting racial hatred by allowing Internet access to material posted on a California computer by Ernst Zuendel, a German neo-Nazi living in Toronto. German law prohibits the publication or distribution of Nazi literature or literature denying that the Holocaust occurred. T-Online responded by blocking access to the site.

- CompuServe Inc. will restore worldwide access to most of the two hundred Internet-based newsgroups recently blocked under pressure from German prosecutors. Instead, CompuServe will provide subscribers with software to allow them to block material they find offensive.

- The four broadcast television networks, ABC, NBC, CBS, and Fox, are seeking to establish their own rating system. The system would eventually allow consumers to block certain programs by using an electronic device known as the V-chip, which will be required in new televisions by the new Telecommunications Act.

- Canada's two biggest cable systems, Shaw Communications and Rogers Cablesystem, will launch a third round of testing V-chips installed in cable boxes. The test will include 200–250 families and last at least a month.

- Federal district judge Ronald L. Buckwalter, in Philadelphia, Pennsylvania, blocked enforcement of the "indecency" provisions of the Communications Decency Act, ruling that the term is unconstitutionally vague and not defined in the new law. A three-judge panel will review the law's constitutionality.

- More than twenty corporate and trade organizations—including America Online, CompuServe, Prodigy, the Microsoft Network, the American Library Association, and the Society of Professional Journalists—filed suit in Philadelphia seeking to overturn the Communications Decency Act, arguing that the Internet is more like a newspaper than television and deserves the same First Amendment protection. The suit will be consolidated with an earlier suit filed by the American Civil Liberties Union and other civil rights groups.

- An unauthorized and unknown person persuaded Network Solutions, Inc.—the gatekeeper for Internet addresses—to change the Internet address for computer security expert Tsutomu Shimomura's Web site from takedown.com to takendown.com. The result was that anyone who wanted to access Shimomura's home page was sent to a different site. This is not an isolated event, and there have been calls for increased use of digital signatures and stricter authentication before Internet addresses can be changed.

- Visa International and MasterCard International will announce industry-standard technology to protect the security of electronic payments. The standard, called Secure Electronic Transactions, has been agreed to by Netscape Communications Corp. and Microsoft Corp. GTE, IBM, Terisa Systems, and Verisign also helped develop the standard. It is based on the Data Encryption Standard and will allow consumers to send credit card numbers in scrambled form.

- The National Consumers League launched Internet Fraud Watch (www.fraud.org), a coordinated effort with law enforcement agencies to combat Internet fraud. It is funded by MasterCard.

- AT&T Worldnet said that it will assume costs that its customers—who sign up using the AT&T Universal Card—might incur because of credit card fraud over purchase of merchandise or services over the Internet.

- Ram Avrahami sued *U.S. News & World Report* for selling his name and address to another company without his consent. The suit is based on a Virginia law prohibiting unauthorized use of a person's name for commercial purposes without permission.

- A feature of World Wide Web browsers named "cookies"—found in Netscape's Navigator for example—allows Web sites to store information about a person's visit using a file (called "cookies.txt" or "MagicCookies") on the visitor's own hard drive. Cookies can store information about specific pages a person views and for how long, among other things.

- Police wired a sixteen-block area of downtown Baltimore with enough video cameras to monitor every street, sidewalk, and alley twenty-four hours a day. In late December 1995, police in Redwood City, California, installed throughout a section of the system a listening system that will detect and locate gunfire within ten yards of where shots were fired.

- The Ninth U.S. Circuit Court of Appeals ruled that California must allow Caller ID, which displays the phone number of a phone caller, to start on June 1, 1996, without the privacy measures ordered by the California Public Utilities Commission—including not allowing display of the number of a person with an unlisted number without his or her consent.

- Three thirteen-year-old boys in Syracuse, New York, are charged with plotting to set off a homemade fertilizer bomb in their junior high school, having obtained the plans for the bomb from the Internet.

■ A Florida salesman, Kenneth T. Kaltman, 50, was arrested and held on $510,000 bail for illegally tapping into his former employer and competitor's voice-mail system to steal clients. He was charged in state court with harassment, larceny, and twenty-nine counts of computer crime.

■ The entertainment industry demands that Congress pass the proposed NII Copyright Protection Act (HR 2441), which would formally extend copyright law to digital copies and transmission of intellectual property. It would also make illegal the sale of hardware or software that might be used to circumvent anti-copying techniques used to protect intellectual property in digital form, among other things. Opponents contend that the proposed law puts too much power in the hands of copyright owners. It is also opposed by providers of online services, home electronics companies, consumer groups, library associations, and related organizations.

■ Sprint Corp., Deutsche Telekom, and France Telecom completed a $3.7 billion deal to form a new global telecommunications alliance, called Global One.

■ Harper's magazine will be the first publication to share profits from electronic publishing with authors. It will evenly split all CD-ROM and on-line royalties with authors, and retroactively pay writers for electronic distribution of articles since January 1994.

■ The Securities and Exchange Commission will issue an "interpretative release" covering electronic mail and electronic communications between brokerage firms, investment advisers, and others with their customers. The Securities Industry Association urges the SEC to avoid a one-size-fits-all rule requiring burdensome recordkeeping for all electronic mail and computer communications between broker and customer, regardless of content. The association says that the focus should be on the purpose and nature of the message, not the manner of sending it.

■ A 1994 patent held by Prodigy Services Co., describing sending chunks of computer code in small packages for use in a remote computer, may be broad enough to cover Sun Microsystem's Java computer language.

■ The U.S. Department of Justice is looking at Microsoft's efforts to market World Wide Web software. It asked a small software company, The Internet Factory, for documents showing how Microsoft hurts its business. In December 1995, Microsoft said that it would give away software to enable companies to create their own Web pages and handle online transactions.

■ Local Bell companies complain that a loophole in the nation's telephone accounting rules will compel them to provide free local connections to AT&T's long-distance network, which will provide low-cost residential access to the Internet.

■ The Japanese government plans to modify its copyright law to honor music copyrights dating back fifty years. Presently, Japanese law only covers music copyrights dating back to 1971.

15

Glossary

ARPA—Advanced Research Project Agency. The Internet began in 1969 as an experimental ARPA project. It was first called the "ARPANET," then the "DARPA Internet," and finally, the "Internet."

Baud—the number of "state" changes per second when transmitting data. Baud is not the same as bits per second (BPS), which is the speed at which bits travel.

BBS—computer bulletin board service.

Domain name—the elements in an electronic mail address directly following the symbol "@," which identifies a computer or group of computers, separated by periods. The rightmost domain (e.g., com, edu, gov, mil, org, net) is known as the top-level domain.

DNS—Domain Name System. Translates computer names into numeric IP addresses.

FTP—File Transfer Protocol. An application protocol used for sending or receiving files. FTP requires specification of the remote computer. To access some ftp sites, an account, login, and password are required. "Anonymous FTP" allows users without an account, login, and password to access certain files on a machine. In many cases, the user is given the login "anonymous" and the user inputs his or her e-mail address as the password string. Typically, anonymous users can only retrieve copies of files, but cannot place files on the remote computer.

GIF—Graphical Interchange Format.

Gopher—a menu-driven lookup tool, allowing users to browse and retrieve resources across the Internet. When a resource is located, gopher chooses the appropriate utility (e.g., ftp, telnet) to work with it.

HTML—Hypertext Markup Language.

HTTP—Hypertext Transfer Protocol. Used to transfer documents between Web servers and Web clients.

IP Address—numeric identification of an Internet location, e.g., 192.100.81.101.

IRC—Internet Relay Chat. Allows people across the Internet to chat in real time.

ISP—an Internet service provider

ISDN—Integrated Services Digital Network. A set of digital transmission protocols for carrying both voice and data. ISDN systems may run as fast as 1.544 Mbps. Compare Asynchronous Transfer Mode (ATM), which can run at 45 Mbps and may be able to run at 2.5 Gbps.

Listserv—an automatic electronic mailing list service that allows efficient communication on discrete areas of interest.

MIME—Multipurpose Internet Mail Extensions. Allow Internet transmissions to include formatted documents, fax, sound, and video.

Mosaic-type browser—a graphical interface to the World Wide Web (e.g., Netscape Navigator), using hypertext markup language for formatting and linking files and documents across the Internet.

Newsgroups—the Internet equivalent of a bulletin board system.

Packet—block of data, including addressing information, among other things.

PPP—Point-to-Point Protocol. For exchanging Internet packets with computers connected to the Internet using a dial-up phone line; more advanced than SLIP.

SLIP—Serial Line Internet Protocol. For exchanging Internet packets with computers connected to the Internet using a dial-up phone line.

TCP/IP—Transmission Control Protocol/Internet Protocol. TCP breaks up data into pieces and numbers it so that it can be reassembled. IP controls addressing and reassembling data that has been transmitted in pieces.

Telnet—a way to access and control remote computers on the Internet. Once connected, your keyboard appears to be directly connected to the remote computer. An account, login, and password are typically required to use the remote computer.

URL—Universal Resource Locator. The address of a data set within the Internet.

USENET newsgroups—see Newsgroups.

VRML—Virtual Reality Modeling Language.

WAIS—Wide-Area Information Servers. A distributed text-searching mechanism based on groups of words.

X.25—a packet switching standard. Information is divided into small packets, each of which contains an address and sequencing codes. At the receiving end, the packets arrive and are assembled into proper sequence.

X.500—an electronic mail address standard.

16

Recommended Reading

J. Bamford, *The Puzzle Palace* (New York: Penguin Books, 1982)

J. Brunner, *The Shockwave Rider* (New York: Ballentine Books, 1976)

W. Gibson, *Neuromancer* (New York: Ace Books, 1984)

K. Hafner and J. Markoff, *Cyberpunk* (New York: Simon & Schuster, 1991)

L. Levy, *Emergence of a Free Press* (New York: Oxford University Press, 1985)

S. Levy, *Hackers* (New York: Dell Publishing Co., Inc., 1984)

R. McChesney, *Telecommunications, Mass Media, & Democracy* (New York: Oxford University Press, 1994)

G. Orwell, *1984* (New York: Signet Classic, 1949)

I. Pool, *Technologies of Freedom* (Cambridge, MA: Belknap Press, 1983)

L. Patterson and S. Lindberg, *The Nature of Copyright* (Athens, GA: University of Georgia Press, 1991)

H. Rheingold, *Virtual Reality* (New York: Touchstone, 1991)

T. Shimomura, *Takedown* (New York: Hyperion, 1996)

M. Slatalla and J. Quittner, *Masters of Deception* (New York: Harper Collins Publishing, 1995)

B. Sterling, *The Hacker Crackdown* (New York: Bantam Books, 1992)

N. Stephenson, *Snow Crash* (New York: Bantam Books, 1993)

J. Wallace and J. Erickson, *Hard Drive* (New York: Harper Business, 1992)

C. Stoll, *The Cuckoo's Egg* (New York: Doubleday, 1989)

P. Wright, *Spy Catcher* (New York: Viking Penguin Inc., 1987)

Cases

Index